*Rulers and Realms
in Medieval Iberia,
711–1492*

Rulers and Realms in Medieval Iberia, 711–1492

TIMOTHY M. FLOOD

McFarland & Company, Inc., Publishers
Jefferson, North Carolina

ISBN (print) 978-1-4766-7471-1
ISBN (ebook) 978-1-4766-3372-5

Library of Congress cataloguing data are available

British Library cataloguing data are available

© 2019 Timothy M. Flood. All rights reserved

No part of this book may be reproduced or transmitted in any form or by any means, electronic or mechanical, including photocopying or recording, or by any information storage and retrieval system, without permission in writing from the publisher.

Front cover photograph of fortified Islamic palace, Zaragoza, Spain © 2019 iStock/Leamus

Printed in the United States of America

McFarland & Company, Inc., Publishers
Box 611, Jefferson, North Carolina 28640
www.mcfarlandpub.com

For my wife Carol

Table of Contents

Preface   1

1. On the Eve of Conquest: Before 711
The Visigoths in Iberia   3
The Arab Conquest of North Africa   10
Count Julian and Musa ibn Nusayr   11

2. The Muslim Invasion and the Period of Governors: 711–756
The Muslim Invasion of Iberia   13
The Arrival of Musa ibn Nusayr: 712–714   14
The Campaigns of Abd al-Aziz: 714–716   15
The Administration of al-Hurr: 716–718   16
Pelagius (Pelayo) and the Beginning of Christian Resistance   16
A Rapid Succession of Governors and Muslim Expansion North of the Pyrenees   17
Berber Uprising and Civil War   20
Expansion of Asturias During the Reign of Alfonso I (739–757)   21

3. Umayyad Emirs and the Emergence of the Christian North: 756–912
The Rise of Abd al-Rahman ibn Marwan   23
The Christian North During the Time of Abd al-Rahman I   25
The Asturian Kingdom and the Reigns of Hisham I (788–796) and al-Hakam I (796–822)   26
Carolingian Influence in the Pyrenees After 778   27
Carolingian Control Rebuffed in the Western Pyrenees   28
The Banu Qasi and Pamplona Versus Córdoba   29
Ramiro I (842–850) of Asturias   29
Mid–Ninth Century Changes in Leadership   30
Internal Unrest in al-Andalus Under Muhammad I (852–886)   32
The Short Unfortunate Reign of al-Mundhir (886–888)   33
The Reign of Abd Allah (888–912)   34
Emerging Independence in the Eastern Pyrenean Counties   35
Fortún Garcés (880?–905), the Last of His Dynasty in Navarre   36

4. The Age of Abd al-Rahman III: 912–961
Abd al-Rahman III Restores the Authority of Córdoba   38
The Sons of Alfonso III: 910–925   39

The Struggle for La Rioja	40
The Christian North in a State of Flux: 925–931	42
The Surging Influence of Castile	44
The Emir Abd al-Rahman III (912–961) Becomes Caliph	45
The Resumption of Conflicts During the Reign of Ramiro II (931–951)	47
Ordoño III (951–956), Sancho I (956...966), and Ordoño IV (958–959)	49

5. From Dominance to Decadence in al-Andalus: 961–1031

The Kingdoms of León and Navarre in Contest with al-Hakam II (961–976)	51
The Reign of Hisham II (976...1013) and the Usurpation of al-Mansur	53
The Christian North Oppressed by the Dictatorship of al-Mansur	56
Abd al-Malik al-Muzaffar (1002–1008) Maintains Muslim Dominance Over the North	60
The Short Dictatorship of Sanchuelo (1008–1009)	61
Sancho García Aligns with Caliph Sulayman Against Caliph Muhammad II: 1009	63
From Ali ibn Hammud (1016–1018) to Hisham III (1027–1031)	66
The Christian North Benefits from the Civil War in al-Andalus	69

6. The Vacillation of Power Between Christian and Muslim Realms: 1035–1109

The Disintegration of the Caliphate into *Taifa* States	73
The Four Sons of Sancho Garcés III—García, Ramiro, Gonzalo, and Fernando: 1035–1065	74
The Sons of Fernando I—Sancho, Alfonso, and García: 1065–1073	78
The Early Success of Alfonso VI: 1073–1085	80
Changes in Leadership in the Eastern Counties: 1035–1096	82
The Rise of the Almoravids	84
The Hegemony of Alfonso VI Is Challenged: 1086–1109	87

7. Christian Civil War and Waning Almoravid Power: 1109–1157

The Failed Marriage of Urraca and Alfonso I of Aragon and Civil War: 1109–1117	92
León-Castile During the Final Years of Urraca's Reign: 1117–1126	95
The Eastern Counties Under Ramon Berenguer III (1097–1131)	96
The Emergence of Portugal	98
Alfonso I of Aragon, the Battler, During the Truce with León-Castile: 1118–1126	99
Young Alfonso VII and the Elder Battler in Contest: 1126–1134	100
The Reign of Ramiro II and the Union of Aragon and Catalonia: 1134–1137	101
The Re-Alignment and Stabilization of Four Christian Realms: 1137–1143	103
The Rise of the Almohads	104
The Christian North Confronts a New Power in al-Andalus: 1143–1157	106

8. The Division of León-Castile and the Decline of the Almohads: 1157–1214

The Division of León-Castile and the Regency of Alfonso VIII: 1157–1169	109
Almohad Campaigns During the Early Reign of Alfonso VIII: 1169–1188	112
The Almohads Successfully Contest Christian Aggression: 1189–1195	115
A Defeated Alfonso VIII Triumphs at Las Navas de Tolosa: 1196–1212	118
The Death of Three Leaders and the End of an Era: 1213–1214	121

9. The Age of the Great Christian Conquests and the Era of Alfonso X: 1214–1284

The Unfortunate Reign of Enrique I and the Ascendance of Fernando III: 1214–1224	123
The Early Years of Jaume I of Aragon-Barcelona: 1213–1228	124
The Reign of Afonso II of Portugal: 1211–1223	125
The Almohad Empire in Disorder and the Renewal of Christian Offensives: 1224–1230	126
Relentless Strikes from a Reunited León-Castile: 1231–1235	130
Jaume I of Aragon Advances on Valencia: 1232–1238	131
Córdoba and Its Environs Fall to the Crown of Castile: 1235–1241	132
The Fall of Murcia, Jaén and the Vassalage of Granada: 1243–1246	134
The Deposition of Sancho II and Portugal's Advance on the Algarve: 1245–1249	136
The Conquest of Seville and the Last Days of Fernando III: 1246–1252	137
The Early Reign of Alfonso X: 1252–1275	139
The Final Years of Alfonso X: 1275–1284	143

10. A Rebellious Nobility During War, Plague and Famine: 1284–1369

The Reign of Sancho IV (1284–1295)	146
The Reigns of Pere III (1276–1285), Alfonso III (1285–1291), and Jaume II (1291–1327) of Aragon	150
The Reign of Fernando IV (1295–1312)	152
The Minority of Alfonso XI: 1312–1325	155
Leadership Changes in Portugal, Navarre, Aragon, and Granada in the 1320's	156
The Majority of Alfonso XI: 1325–1350	159
The Reign of Pedro I, *el Cruel* (1350–1369)	162

11. The Age of the Trastámaras: 1369–1479

The Reign of the First Trastámara, Enrique II (1369–1379)	167
Juan I (1379–1390) of Castile and the Failed Annexation of Portugal	170
The Reign of Enrique III (1390–1406) of Castile	172
The End of the Male Line in Aragon: 1387–1410	174
The Minority of Juan II of Castile and the Rise of Fernando de Antequera: 1406–1419	176
The Majority of Juan II of Castile: 1419–1454	179
The Reign of Enrique IV (1454–1474) of Castile	183
Civil War in Navarre and Aragon During the Reign of Joan II: 1441–1472	186
Portugal Under Duarte (1433–1438) and Afonso V (1438...1481)	188
Isabel and Fernando Struggle for Unity and Pacification: 1474–1479	190

12. The Catholic Monarchs and the Conquest of Granada: 1480–1492

A New Order in Iberia and an Escalation of War with Granada: 1480–1486	193
The Fall of Málaga, Eastern Andalucia, and Granada: 1487–1492	197

Appendix I: Lists
Visigothic Rulers   201
Umayyad Governors, Emirs, Caliphs 632–1031   201
Almoravid and Almohad Leaders   202
The Nasrids of Granada   203

Appendix II: Maps
Map 1: Roman Provinces   204
Map 2: Visigothic Settlement Between Bordeaux and Toulouse   205
Map 3: Visigothic Conquests Under Leovigild, Sisebut and Suintila   206
Map 4: The Muslim Conquest of North Africa   206
Map 5: Muslim Invasion Routes in Iberia: 711–714   207
Map 6: Iberia Circa 930   208
Map 7: The Early County of Castile   209
Map 8: Locations in La Rioja   210
Map 9: Christian Advances by 1076, 1086, 1157, 1230, and 1252   210

Appendix III: Genealogical Charts
Chart 1: The Kings of Asturias: 718–910   211
Chart 2: The Counts of Aragon: 809–922   211
Chart 3: The Kings of Pamplona: 824–905   212
Chart 4: The Counts of Ribagorça-Pallars   212
Chart 5: The Counts of the Eastern Pyrenees: 812–1038   213
Chart 6: The Banu Qasi   214
Chart 7: The Kings of Navarre: 905–1076   214
Chart 8: The Kings of León: 866–1037   215
Chart 9: The Counts of Castile: 931–1037   215
Chart 10: The Kings of León-Castile: 1037–1252   216
Chart 11: The Kings of Aragon: 1035–1162   216
Chart 12: The Counts of the Eastern Pyrenees: 1035–1162   217
Chart 13: The Kings of Navarre Restored: 1134–1305   218
Chart 14: The Count-Kings of Aragon-Barcelona: 1131–1387   219
Chart 15: The Kings of Portugal: 1139–1367   220
Chart 16: The Kings of León-Castile: 1252–1369   221
Chart 17: The Kings of León-Castile: 1350–1504   221
Chart 18: The French Rulers of Navarre: 1305–1518   222
Chart 19: The Kings of Portugal: 1357–1495   223
Chart 20: The Count-Kings of Aragon-Barcelona: 1387–1516   223

Works Consulted   225

Index   229

Preface

Rulers and Realms in Medieval Iberia, 711–1492 presents the rulers who exercised authority over the Iberian Peninsula from 711 to 1492 during a very complex and sometimes confusing period. The Muslim conquest of the Middle East and North Africa during the seventh century enabled their armies to cross the Strait of Gibraltar in 711 and overthrow the kingdom of the Visigoths that had been in power for more than two centuries. The invaders' military strength immediately dominated the entire peninsula, but their political administration was less complete. Opposition to Muslim authority appeared just seven years later when a small band of Christian rebels in the Picos de Europa of northern Iberia established their own ruling class.

A rapid succession of Muslim governors sent from North Africa failed to achieve administrative stability, and the overthrow of the Umayyad caliph in Damascus by the Abbasids in Bagdad in 750 spawned the appearance of an Umayyad branch in Iberia in 756. The Umayyad emirs and caliphs established a central Muslim authority from their capital in Córdoba and ruled al-Andalus for two hundred and seventy-five years. By 1031, however, competing forces within the caliphate had weakened it and led to its collapse into smaller city states, known as *taifa* kingdoms. The need for Muslim military power was subsequently filled by successive North African dynasties, the Almoravids and the Almohads, that were as foreign to the Muslims of Iberia as they were to the Christians. After their withdrawal to North Africa, the Nasrid dynasty of Granada rose to power in 1232 and ruled over a smaller al-Andalus until its final breath in 1492.

Meanwhile, during the nearly eight centuries of Muslim governors, emirs, and caliphs in the peninsula, the Christian realms expanded ever southward from their small hideaway in the northern mountains. The Christian rulers of Asturias expanded their realm from Galicia to Old Castile. The Christians of Pamplona established their own kingdoms in Navarre and Aragon, while the counts of southern France conquered land south of the Pyrenees to establish their own eastern counties, later to become Catalonia. The tranquility among the Christian realms was no more stable than in the Muslim dynasties. The Christian kings often divided their holdings among their sons, who fought among each other as much as they battled against the Muslims. A recalcitrant branch of the kingdom of León engendered the kingdom of Portugal. Nonetheless, the Christian monarchs' insatiable desire for expansion gained momentum during the twelfth century and afterwards, when the popes declared Crusades against the Muslims. The lust for expansionary power combined with Christian religious zeal sounded a death knell for Muslim rule in Iberia.

The lists and genealogical charts of this book record the tenure of the rulers, while the content narrates the major events of their ascension, deposition, or demise. I have included substantial references to indicate the sources of the content. The copious references may encourage the reader to delve further into the subject, and at the same time, they will serve as *points de repère* for the seasoned medievalist.

I am indebted to the numerous authors who have contributed to the history of this period. Their works have facilitated this publication. In fact, there has been a burgeoning of interest in the study of medieval Iberia in recent decades, and both the quantity and quality of volumes on the subject is remarkable.

I am particularly grateful to my wife, Carol, who made numerous suggestions on the draft, and finally, to the staff of the small village library of Bellaire, Michigan, who procured books on loan that would have otherwise been inaccessible to me.

CHAPTER 1

On the Eve of Conquest: Before 711

The Visigoths in Iberia

On the eve of the Islamic conquest of Iberia in 711, the Visigoths had been *de facto* rulers of the peninsula for more than two centuries. The story of their journey into Iberia begins in the northeast corner of the Roman Empire above the Danube and north of the Black Sea where Germanic peoples, then known simply as Goths, were set in motion by the incursion and expansion of the Huns. In 376, one tribe of Goths known to the Romans as the *Tervingi*, led by Fritigern and Alavivus, and another known as the *Greuthungi*, led by Alatheus and Saphrax, appeared on the northern banks of the Danube appealing to Constantinople for asylum from the Huns. The practice of the Roman Empire towards admitting immigrants was first to control them militarily and politically and then to divide them into small groups and disperse them over a wide area. The eastern Emperor Valens (364–78) was compelled to amend this practice, because he had enough troops in the area to control one but not two groups (Heather 131–2). Consequently, he decided to admit the *Tervingi* and alerted his imperial army to keep the *Greuthungi* north of the Danube.

Only the *Tervingi* were ferried across the Danube, but the decision to admit them resulted in a disastrous outcome for the Roman emperor. The immediate interplay between these Goths and Roman soldiers resulted in treachery and abuse. One account reveals that the Roman commander Lupicinus invited the Gothic leaders to a dinner in Marcianople and attempted to assassinate them. The Gothic leader Fritigern escaped, but history records nothing more of his co-leader Alavivus. Other reports relate that the Roman commanders exploited the Goths, who suffered from food shortages. Whichever account renders the events more accurately, the resulting breach led the *Tervingi* into a revolt that could not be easily contained due to the shortage of Roman troops. Meanwhile as the *Tervingi* moved southward from the Danube, they learned of a forced crossing by the *Greuthungi* and delayed their advance so that the *Greuthungi* could reunite with them. To contest this incursion, Emperor Valens himself led an army against the Goths but was defeated and killed at the battle of Adrianople in 378 (Heather 132–4).

It was not until early in the following year that the western Emperor Gratian appointed Theodosius (379–395) as eastern emperor in charge of managing the incursion of Goths, who in the meantime had moved from Thrace into Moesia in search of food supplies. It was during this time that the Bishop Ulfila converted this band of Goths to Arian Christianity (Thompson *The Visigoths* 94). The Goths continued warring and vandalizing for six years until 382 when the Roman state granted them land for farming and allowed them to maintain their own laws in exchange for their military service. It was in service to the eastern Emperor Theodosius that the Gothic armies were used in 387 against the usurper Maximus, who had murdered the western Emperor Gratian. Later in 392–393, the Goths were asked to battle against the western usurper Eugenius. Their military duty as mercenaries severely eroded their manpower. Nevertheless, the treaty with the Eastern Empire lasted until the death of Theodosius in 395 when the Goths, who were now under the command of Alaric (395–410), again rose in revolt. The turmoil and disunity between the Eastern and Western Roman Empires permitted the success of Gothic booty raids into Macedonia and Greece with only a temporary hiatus from vandalism in 397. At that time, Alaric was appointed as a general in the Eastern Empire and moved his troops unsuccessfully against the western General Stilicho in 401. His defeat drove the Goths to the Balkans where they were not allied with any part of the Empire.

In 405–406, a separate band of Goths under the leadership of Radagaisus invaded Italy from the north. To contest this incursion, General Stilicho, who held considerable influence over the western Emperor Honorius, assembled an army that was up to the task of defeating the insurgents. Radagaisus and his men were trapped in a northern pass where he was executed. His men were either killed, sold into slavery, or else drafted into Stilicho's army. The surviving draftees played a role a few years later when Alaric attacked Italy again. Stilicho's time as a major influence over Emperor Honorius was nearing its end. The historic crossing of the Rhine by the Vandals, Sueves, and Alans in December 406 caused a collapse of political unity in Western Empire. The generals of Great Britain and Gaul had broken with Honorius and were attempting to carve out their own smaller empires. Someone was to pay for this collapse, and it turned out to be Stilicho. In the summer of 408, Honorius had Stilicho and his son both arrested and killed. The combination of these events offered Alaric an opportunity once again to move into Italy. The Gothic forces of Alaric found themselves knocking on the door of the Western Roman Empire demanding recognition and tribute. As they waited impatiently in 409 and early 410, Alaric's band swelled in size from the soldiers of the army of Radagaisus, who were drafted by Stilicho, and from numerous Roman slaves, who deserted to join the Goths (Heather 145–8). Either Honorius did not believe that an attack on Rome would be successful or else it was not feasible for him to meet Alaric's terms. At any rate, no agreement was forthcoming. Alaric's patience had run its course, and he sacked Rome on August 24, 410.

Alaric died of natural causes soon after sacking Rome, and he was succeeded by Athaulf (410–415), who carried off the emperor's half-sister, Galla Placidia, and subsequently married her. Now in command of the Goths, Athaulf faced the continuing problem of how to maintain a very large band of men, women, and children. He decided to move his group into Gaul. Negotiations with Honorius were ongoing, and it appears that preparations were being made to employ the Goths against the Vandals and Sueves, who were ravaging the Romanized citizenry of Iberia. The Romans had effectively lost control of the Iberian Peninsula in autumn of 409 when groups of Alan, Sueves, and Vandals had crossed the Rhine into Gaul three years earlier and then crossed the Pyrenees unopposed. Before Athaulf could implement a campaign against them, he was assassinated by Sigeric, a rival Goth, in Barcelona in 415. In turn, Sigeric was assassinated shortly after. Leadership of the Goths then fell onto the shoulders of Wallia (415–419), who after returning Gallia Placidia to her brother's court, struck an agreement with the Empire in 416 to subdue the marauders on the peninsula (Orlandis 26; Wolfram 165–71). Wallia succeeded in this effort although no details of the conflicts were recorded. Honorius rewarded the Goths for their campaigns with a new treaty in 418, which gave them the Aquitaine region in southwest Gaul between Bordeaux and Toulouse. The Goths settled there and established Toulouse as their administrative capital in 419 (See Map 2). Aquitaine became the realm of their new leader, Theodoric I, (419–451), and history identifies this group as Visigoths to distinguish them from the Ostrogoths, who later ruled from Italy. The work to control the Sueves in Iberia was yet to be completed.

There is scant documentation of Visigothic campaigns in Iberia under their early kings, Wallia (415–419), Theodoric I (419–451), and Thorismund (451–453). While the Vandals moved on to North Africa in the following decades, the Sueves strengthened their positions in Iberia. They established Mérida as an administrative center in 439, and from there, they extended their influence over all of Iberia except for Tarraconensis, which remained nominally under Roman control (See Map 1). During this period, the Visigoths campaigned in Iberia on the orders of the Roman state. In 446 they fought under General Vitus against the Sueves in Carthaginiensis and in Baetica, but they made no territorial gains. Beginning with the rule of Theodoric II (453–466) and in cooperation with Rome, however, the Visigoths began to gain wealth and territory. Furthermore, they began to control their own fate as they contested the growing power of the Sueves. The Suavian King Rechiarius attacked Tarraconensis and posed a threat not only to the Roman Empire but also to the Visigoths just north of the Pyrenees. In response, Theodoric II initiated a campaign against King Rechiarius, his brother-in-law, with the cooperation and consent of the Rome. At a battle on the river Órbigo near Astorga, the Visigoths routed the Sueves. Theodoric pursued and executed Rechiarius, and the Visigoths became the controlling power in most of Iberia except for Tarraconensis, which remained for the moment under Roman rule. In return for supporting the Roman Empire, the Visigoths gained Narbonne in 462–463. King Euric (466–484), who murdered his brother Theodoric II, at last seized control of Tarraconensis and the prized Ebro Valley in 476 (Collins *Visigothic Spain* 31–3).

The Visigoths had been settled in their new homeland in the Garonne Valley between Bordeaux and Toulouse for decades when evidence indicates that there was a substantial migration across the Pyrenees into the Iberian Peninsula during the 490s (Collins *Visigothic Spain* 33). It has been suggested that the reasons for this movement two decades after King Euric had taken control of the Ebro Valley was that the Visigoths would be safer from the growing power of the Franks to the north. Moreover, the Ebro Valley offered a greater opportunity for land acquisition (Heather 201). Thus, Iberia was to play a greater role in the future the Visigoths.

By the beginning of the sixth century under the rule of King Alaric II (484–507), the Visigoths still controlled the Aquitaine and Provence in the south of Gaul. Moreover, they had annexed much of the Iberian Peninsula as a result of their campaigns of 456 as allies of the Romans and later in 476 under King Euric. But now the Salian Franks were menacing their northern borders. This Germanic tribe in northern Gaul had established a dynasty known as the Merovingians, and they had expanded their influence and control down to the Loire Valley. They had pushed the Alemani eastward from Gaul and had reduced the territory of the Burgundians down the Rhone Valley. Despite the diplomatic attempts of the Ostrogothic King Theodoric to restrain the expansionary designs of their leader, Clovis, hostilities between Franks and Visigoths broke out in 507. A battle was fought at Vouillé near Poitiers in which the Visigothic army was defeated, and King Alaric II (484–507) was killed. The Franks with the Burgundians as their allies overran the Gothic kingdom in the south of Gaul including the Visigothic capital at Toulouse. A complete annihilation of the Visigothic regime was prevented only by the intervention of the Ostrogoths who forced the armies of Clovis to withdraw.

Alaric's illegitimate son, Gesalic (507–511), was installed as king of the Visigoths, but his reign was shortened when he suffered a defeat by the Burgundians in 511 and was exiled to Africa. The accession of Alaric's son Amalaric (511–531) is generally dated from 511. However, since he had not attained the age of majority, he did not assume control until about 522. During the period of Amalaric's minority, the Ostrogothic King Theodoric ruled the Visigoths through appointed governors. The motive behind this minority accession of Amalaric was that his father, Alaric, was married to the daughter of Theodoric, making Amalaric Theodoric's grandson. The death of Amalaric in 531, attested only by conflicting reports, marks the end of the blood line of this Visigothic dynasty which lasted more than a century and reached back to Alaric I (Collins *Visigothic Spain* 41–2).

What little we know of the reigns of the next several kings can be characterized by treachery or conspiracy until the strong regal presence of Leovigild (569–586) ushered in a sense of stability and unity. Theudis (531–548) aka Theodoric III, who had served as governor during Amalaric's minority, was chosen as the new leader of the Visigoths and served until he was murdered in 548. Theudis was succeeded by Theudisclus (548–549), a commander in the army who subsequently was assassinated at a banquet in Seville and replaced by Agila I (549–554). It has been suggested that Athanagild (554–568) challenged the reign of Agila from its beginning, which prompted Agila to appeal to Constantinople for assistance. This appeal to external support resulted in a Byzantine enclave being established in the southeast of Iberia in 550–551 which proved to be fruitless for Agila, who died at the hands of his own men, allowing the accession of Athanagild (Collins *Visigothic Spain* 48). The latter died of natural causes in 568, the first to do so since Euric in 484. After a five-month hiatus, the Hispano-Visigothic magnates elected a new king Liuva I (568–573), who took the unprecedented measure to assure the continuation of his dynasty by granting half of the kingdom to his younger brother, Leovigild (569–586). Liuva ruled from Narbonne and Leovigild from Toledo. Upon Liuva's death in 573, both kingdoms were reunited under Leovigild in Toledo.

The reign of Leovigild is characterized by his strong leadership and his struggle to bring political unity to the peninsula. We are informed of this period through the chronicles of John of Biclaro (Wolf 60+), who tells us that Leovigild initiated his unifying campaigns by driving imperial forces from Málaga in 570. In the following years, he did the same for Medina-Sidonia and Córdoba that had both fallen out of Visigothic control during the time of Agila. Then in 574 he brought order and control to Cantabria in the north. In 578, he took a break from campaigning and devoted himself instead to the foundation of Reccopolis, a new city on a bend in the river Tagus near the village of Zorita de los Canes in the province of Guadalajara. He resumed his unifying efforts in 581 when he campaigned against the Basques. In the interim, he found that his son, Hermenegild, had revolted against his authority and had seized control of Seville. Leovigild put the city under siege in 583 and subjugated it the following year. Hermenegild managed to escape to Valencia only to be killed later in Tarragona by an assassin named Sisbert. In 576 Leovigild campaigned against Miro, the Suevic king of Galicia, and exacted a promise of tribute from him. Miro's son Eboric ascended the throne upon his father's death but was deposed in 584 by the Suevic noble Audeca. This disruption prompted Leovigild to intervene and banish Audeca into exile. However, a second revolt led by a noble named Malaric immediately followed. Leovigild returned to put down the insurrection, but this time his intervention effectively put an end to Suevic rule in Iberia. After decades of infighting and civil strife, Leovigild's greatest accomplishment was to unite many of the political factions within the Visigothic regime (Collins *Visigothic Spain* 61). Moreover, he rightly perceived that the religious split between Visigothic Arianism and Hispano-Roman Catholicism was an obstacle to increased unity. To convert Catholics into the Arian sect, he called the Arian synod of bishops in 580 for the purpose of amending Arian doctrine. The new doctrine announced that those coming from the Roman faith need not be baptized again but only need to take communion. Leovigild's attempt at religious unification had little effect, and he died in 586 without having fused the religious divide.

Leovigild's son, Reccared I (586–601), inherited a largely unified kingdom. The Visigothic realm controlled virtually all of Iberia and Gallia Narbonensis except for the coastal regions in the southeast from Cadiz to Denia, which were still controlled by the Byzantines. Additionally, a strip in the Basque country from Pamplona along the northern coast to Galicia remained out of the rule of the Visigoths. In the first year of his reign, Reccared converted to Catholicism and encouraged Arian bishops to do so as well. He assembled the Third Council of Toledo in 589 at which Catholicism was affirmed as the official religion of the Visigoths. By the time of his death in 601, Reccared had extinguished pockets of resistance to this mass conversion, thereby accomplishing religious unity where his father had failed.

Reccared's son, Liuva II (601–603), ascended the throne, ruled for only two years, and was deposed by Witteric (603–610) who killed him after cutting off his right hand. Witteric accomplished nothing during his tenure and was unceremoniously assassinated during a dinner (Wolf 105). The short reign of King Gundemar (610–612) was noted by Isidore of Seville only for having campaigned against the Basques and against the Byzantines, although he gained no territory before dying a natural death. Under Sisebut (612–621), who succeeded Gundemar, three accomplishments are recorded. He enacted a forced conversion of the Jews, brought the rebellious northern coast under his control, and he expelled the Byzantines from most of the southern coastal regions. Isidore of Seville records that Sisebut "left a small son Reccared, who was recognized as king [Recarred II (621)] for a few days after the death of his father until his own death intervened" (Wolf 106). The next king, Suinthila (621–631), subdued the Basques in the Ebro Valley and more importantly captured the remaining cities that were controlled by the Byzantines. He thereby brought all of Iberia along with Gallia Narbonensis under complete control of the Visigothic king (See Map 3). Nonetheless, the unification accomplished under Suinthila was apparently not enough to satiate all the nobles. A rebellion in the Ebro Valley under Sisenand (631–636) overthrew Suinthila's army at Zaragoza and elevated Sisenand as king for five years. Nothing is recorded of Sisenand's death, but we observe that as the Fifth Council of Toledo was convened in 636, Chintila (636–639) had ascended the throne. To assuage overthrow and confiscation of property, the tenets of the Fifth Council stressed the protection of the king and his family and of the court that surrounded him. These canons proved to be ineffective when Chintila died and was succeeded by his son Tulga (639–642). A gathering of nobles deposed Tulga, tonsuring him to render him ineligible for rule. The nobles subsequently installed Chindasuinth (642–653), who appointed his son, Reccesuinth (649–672), to serve as co-ruler.

Begun under Chindasuinth and continued under Reccesuinth, significant changes to the Visigothic legal codes were implemented. The Eighth Council of Toledo in 653, the Ninth Council in 655, and the Tenth Council of 656 delimited the confiscatory powers of the king and defined the notion of regal property, which belonged to the realm, as distinct from the king's personal property. These canons also limited the possibility of dynasty building by specifying that the election of a new monarch could transpire only in the *urbs regia*, that is the royal city where the previous king was holding court. Further the new king could be elected only by the bishops, the principal office holders, and commanders of the royal court, who numbered 18 in the year 653. Changes relating to property, known as the *Leges Visigothorum* or the *Forum Iudicum*, were also enacted into the civil code implemented in 654 (Collins *Visigothic Spain* 82+). After serving for 23 years, Reccesuinth died a natural death in 672 at his villa west of Salamanca without leaving an heir to his legacy.

The Chronicle of Alfonso III informs us that Wamba (672–680) was duly elected by those in attendance at Reccesuinth's death and was immediately taken to the regal city to be anointed at the church of St Mary (Wolf 161). Despite the authenticity of his accession, Wamba's immediate task in early 673 was to snuff out dissident revolts in the Ebro Valley and Narbonne. Little else is recorded of his administration. In October 680, Wamba fell mysteriously ill and was considered moribund. Consequently, he accepted the state of penitence, which could be done only once in a lifetime. Surprisingly he recovered, but because of his state, he abdicated and retired to a monastery where he lived for another seven years and three months (Wolf 163).

The bizarre deposition of Wamba led to the elevation of Ervig (680–687), who called the Twelfth Council of Toledo in January 681 shortly after his appointment. He is known for undertaking a complete review and revision of Reccesuinth's law code in which numerous laws were amended or clarified. Very importantly and possibly as a payback for his appointment, he made concessions to the nobility which lightened their penalties under the law and protected their privileges. More specifically during his tenure, he cancelled unpaid taxes on slaves, gave amnesty for nobly-born rebels, and enacted additional laws against the Jews, e.g., forced baptism. In imitation of Chintila's effort, he attempted to protect his family by having the bishops proclaim that no injustices should be inflicted on future kings and their families and that no one should deprive them of their property, tonsure the males, or banish the females to religious life (Thompson *The Goths in Spain* 238–9). Ervig died a natural death in Toledo, having ruled for six years.

Before he died, Ervig had named his son-in-law, Egica (687–702), who had married his daughter Cixilo, as his chosen successor. Shortly after Ervig's death in 687, Egica called the Fourteenth Council, whose primary business it appears was to repeal the provisions of the Thirteenth Council with respect to protecting the families of previous kings. This reversal of the Council's ruling permitted Egica to send Ervig's wife and family into monastic seclusion, arrogate their property, and repudiate his wife, Cixilo, allowing him to remarry (Collins *Visigothic Spain* 105–6). However, while they were married, Cixilo bore Egica a son named Witiza. Towards the end of his reign, Egica established a co-rule with his son Witiza, sending him to govern in Galicia and portending his inheritance as king. The reign of Witiza (698–710) as a co-ruler with his father, Egica, is traditionally dated from the 698. However, a more reasonable dating of the co-rule would begin on 694 based on number of coin types issued during the period of co-rule (Collins *Visigothic Spain* 108). The period of co-rule endured until the death of Egica in 702. In the interim, Witiza was anointed as king in 700 while his father was still alive. During his reign, Witiza chose to restore property that had been confiscated from certain nobles during his father's tenure. He also relinquished some inherited personal property to the public treasury, thus acknowledging the distinction between personal property and property that belonged to the fisc. Details of Witiza's death in 710 are unknown, but we find a new King Roderic (710–711) being installed in that year. *The Chronicle of 754* informs us that in 711 "Roderic rebelliously seized the kingdom of the Goths at the instigation of the senate [presumably the nobles]. He ruled for only one year" (Wolf 131).

A view of the Visigothic realm during its last century paints a picture of unity, organization, and stability. The entire peninsula had been brought under the central control of Toledo. Laws of civil code of conduct had been established, revised, and improved. Rules for the orderly succession of the monarch had been agreed upon by the nobles and bishops of the royal court. And yet upon closer examination, we find a thread of disunity which parallels this organizational structure. Primogeniture had never been a principle of Visigothic governance, and yet there is a continual effort of monarchs to pass the crown to their sons. Monarchs enacted laws to protect their families, and yet these very laws were being overturned on the ascendance of the next family. Very often we find that the new king's first obligation was to subdue or bring to submission outlying rebellious regions, often the Basques or the nobility in the Ebro Valley. Therefore, the Arab armies that invaded the peninsula in 711 found an incipient and fragile monarchy with a governance structure still in disarray and smarting from a recent change of rulers. The nobles of the Iberian Peninsula were not uniformly prepared for the challenge that they were about to face from North Africa.

The Arab Conquest of North Africa

After the death of the Prophet Muhammad in 632, the armies of Islam unleashed a rapid and ferocious conquest of the Middle East and North Africa. The first caliph, Abu Bakr (632–634), started by stabilizing regional dissent caused by the change in leadership in the Muslim community. He assigned to his fellow Quraysh tribesman, Khalid ibn al-Walid, the duty of suppressing opposition in the Yamama district of eastern Arabia. From there, Khalid continued northward into Syria, and by 640 under the rule of the second caliph, Umar (634–644), all of Syria, except for the coastal town of Caesarea, was under Muslim rule. Umar's forces had also taken control of irrigated lands in Iraq, from Tikrit in the north to the gulf in the south. He campaigned as far east as the Zagros Mountains. December 639 marked the beginning of the conquest of Egypt under the Quraysh general Amr ibn al-As. After the fall of Alexandria on November 8, 641, there was little resistance remaining. In a short span of two years, Egypt had fallen entirely under Arab rule (Kennedy *Arab Conquests* 148–60). After the surrender of Alexandria, Amr led his army westward to Barca in the Roman province of Cyrenaica. There Amr found that the land owners had been forewarned of his arrival and had already departed from the nearby port of Tocra, leaving only a populace of Luwata Berbers, who submitted and agreed to pay tribute. Amr spurred his men past the Gulf of Sirte and on to Tripoli, which was also pillaged. He pressed on to plunder Sabratha, that was caught unaware. Finally, the city of Leptis Magna, the modern location of Lebda, Libya, fell under Amr's forces. This great campaign of Amr had amassed a vast fortune in booty but had accomplished very little in establishing an administration. Amr's singular administrative accomplishment was at Barca, where he had appointed Uqba ibn Nafi as vice-governor to collect taxes for transmittal to the caliph.

The new caliph, Uthman (644–656), removed Amr from the governorship of Egypt in 645, which marked a short hiatus in operations, only to be revived in 647 with a fresh army and a new Egyptian governor, Abd Allah Saad ibn Abi Sarh. Abd Allah quickly moved his forces across the North African coast, advancing towards the Byzantine stronghold of Tripoli. The Byzantine General Gregory elected to leave the walls of Carthage and to engage Abd Allah's legions in open combat near the city of Sbeitla, Tunisia. The Byzantine forces were soundly defeated, and the surviving imperial army limped back to Carthage, leaving enormous amounts of booty in its wake. After this victory, the Arab forces appeared to disengage from further conquests of North Africa for the next twenty years. Under the remaining years of Caliph Uthman and under Caliph Ali ibn Abi Talib (656–661), westward expansion in North Africa was halted. Expansionary efforts would be renewed only with the ascent of the new caliph, Muawiya (661–680) (Kennedy *Arab Conquests* 200+).

In 670, Caliph Muawiya appointed Uqba ibn Nafi as governor of western North Africa. Uqba, the nephew of Amr, was the former vice-governor at Barca and now reported to the currently-installed governor of Egypt, Maslama ibn Mukhallad al-Ansari. The first objective of Uqba was to establish a base of military operations in North Africa by founding the city of Qayrawan, which he thought to be far enough inland to be out of the reach of Byzantine naval attacks. After suffering a short political setback, Uqba was again free to pursue the westward conquest of North Africa during the reign of Caliph Yazid I (680–683), Muawiya's son. Uqba was successful at amassing booty, reported largely in female slaves, but he was surprised and killed in the Atlas Mountains by hostile Berbers. He had accomplished little to further administrative and tax collecting operations. Apart from the fall of Carthage under General Hassan ibn al-Nuaman al Ghassani in 698, the Arab forces in North Africa were occupied with fighting battles with dissident Berber tribes. Little had been done during the reign of Caliph Abd al-Malik (685–705) to subdue the local populace. However, the arrival of governor Musa ibn Nusayr in 704 changed the course of Arab operations in western North Africa. Musa reasserted administrative control from the provincial capital at Qayrawan, but more importantly, he took control of Tangier. He established administrative control there and installed an army of thousands of converted Berber warriors under the command of his General Tarik ibn Ziyad (D. Lewis *God's Crucible* 101–4). The Muslim conquest and settlement of Tangier was probably complete around 708, which enabled the imminent crossing of the Strait of Gibraltar into Iberia.

Count Julian and Musa ibn Nusayr

Musa ibn Nusayr had finally subjected western North Africa to Arab administrative rule. He maintained the seat of governance at Qayrawan and had installed General Tarik ibn Ziyad as his administrative hand in Tangier. After the fall of Carthage in 698, all the remaining populace in this region would have fallen in line with Arab rule. It is likely then that the Byzantine port of Ceuta (Septem), where the legendary Count Julian held court, would have, no doubt, submitted to Muslim terms. This mysterious Count Julian appears in the legends and literature of both Arabs and Spaniards. As the story of latter day is told, Julian was out to seek revenge against King Roderic (710–711), the new king of the Visigoths. Following the common practice of lesser nobles, Julian had entrusted his daughter to the court school in Toledo when Roderic had become enraptured by the beauty of this maiden. The story reveals that he seduced and raped her. For this, Julian had sworn revenge.

Medieval literature is rife with historical inaccuracies. Contemporary storytellers embellished the deeds of their heroes and conjured plots involving jealousy, pride, or revenge, often as a didactic or hagiographic contrivance. Therefore, it is with reason that historians discount the romantic drama of the violation of Julian's daughter. Since Roderic had assumed his leadership in Toledo only in mid 710 shortly before the Arab invasion, the very narrow timeframe for the incident with Julian's daughter, by itself, casts doubt on its actual occurrence. There is, however, some scant evidence of an historical figure who had a role in assisting the initial invasion (Lévi-Provençal *Histoire* 1: 13–4). Moreover, it just makes sense that Musa had logistical assistance from local dissidents, collaborators, or mercenaries to facilitate the crossing and to maneuver through Iberian terrains. That assistance can likely be attached to the historically obscure figure of Julian.

The legends go on to say that Julian hastened to meet with Musa to instill visions of the great wealth in Iberia and to convince him that the peninsula could be conquered (Lévi-Provençal *Histoire* 1: 15). Consequently, Musa asked Julian to perform a reconnaissance mission to the peninsula. One story has Julian debarking from Ceuta and landing at Algeciras, and within a few days he returned with booty and captives. Encouraged by the vision of greater conquests, Musa obtained the permission of Caliph al-Walid I (705–715) to test the resistance of the Visigoths and to determine the political environment. In 710, Musa instructed his Berber officer, Tarif ibn Malluk, to undertake an expedition along the southern coast of Iberia. Arab sources (Lévi-Provençal *Histoire* 1: 15) and the *Chronicle of 754* (Wolf 131) both point to Arab incursions into the peninsula that occurred in the year or two before 711. These successful raids could only have encouraged the larger effort to follow.

CHAPTER 2

The Muslim Invasion and the Period of Governors: 711–756

The Muslim Invasion of Iberia

It was the year of the Hegira 92 AH as determined by the Muslim calendar. The Visigoths in the Iberian Peninsula calculated the year as Era DCCXLIX (749), while for Europeans who observed the Roman calendar, the year was AD 711.

General Tarik ibn Ziyad crossed the Strait from North Africa on the orders of Governor Musa ibn Nusayr and installed himself on the flank of the mountain which would ultimately take his name, *Djabal Tarik,* Tarik's Mountain, known to us as Gibraltar. The crossing probably took place during the months of April or May (Lévi-Provençal *Histoire* 1:18). Once all forces were assembled, Tarik initiated his campaign by securing the ancient city of Carteia at the head of the Bay of Gibraltar on the river Guadarranque and then established a base camp at the present-day site of Algeciras, which would serve as a fallback position.

As the Muslim forces arrived in the peninsula, King Roderic was directing a campaign in the far north against a Basque rebellion. Learning of the invasion, he hastened back to Córdoba to gather more men. Tarik, for his part, remained close to his base camp and requested more reinforcements from North Africa. He then moved slowly in a northwesterly direction towards the river Barbate. Roderic led his army from Córdoba southward and engaged the Muslim forces on July 19, 711 at the *transductinis promonturiis*, a location thought to be in the Medina-Sidonia region (Wolf 131; Collins *Conquest* 28). Reports of the battle are very sparse. Some reports have Visigothic dissidents fighting on the side of the Muslims (Lévi-Provençal *Histoire* 1: 19), while *The Chronicle of 754* (Wolf 131) implies that some of Roderic's forces were not faithful to him and ran from the battle. Whatever the case, the Visigoths were completely routed during this conflict commonly referred to as the battle of Guadalete, and Roderic lost not only his rule and his homeland, but also his life.

After this resounding victory, Tarik led his men up the valley of the Guadalquivir with Córdoba as his target. He met his first resistance at Ecija on the river Genil but took little time to overcome his weakened opponents. Tarik then decided to split his army, and he sent his officer, Mughith, onward to Córdoba, where the city was put under siege. Córdoba fell in October 711, and the life of the captured governor was spared so that he could be sent to the caliph in Damascus.

Meanwhile, with the remaining portion of his forces, Tarik pressed on to the Visigothic capital of Toledo. The city had been forewarned of the impending arrival of the Muslims, and much of the citizenry had taken flight, leaving vast amounts of booty in their wake. Even the Bishop Sindered had taken flight to Rome. The city surrendered to Muslim rule without resistance on November 11, 711 (Sánchez-Albornoz *Orígenes* 86). From Toledo, Tarik continued along the Roman road to Zaragoza, campaigning as far as Guadalajara before returning to Toledo for the winter (See Map 5).

The Arrival of Musa ibn Nusayr: 712–714

Musa disembarked from North Africa to land at Algeciras in June of 712. Unlike Tarik's army, which consisted mostly of Berber converts, Musa's troop was composed of nearly all Arabs. These were the new aristocracy of the Muslim community who had firsthand knowledge of the Prophet. They were clan leaders of the Arabian Peninsula who brought their own retinue of combatants to the front. Rather than proceeding directly to Toledo to rendezvous with Tarik, Musa sought to reassure the conquest and security of the southern flanks of the peninsula by removing the stronghold threats of Medina-Sidonia, Carmona and Alcalá de Guadaíra to the east of Seville before laying siege to that city itself, which in the end offered little resistance (Lévi-Provençal *Histoire* 1: 25). The Visigothic garrison of Seville had taken flight to the west. When Seville fell, Musa pressed on to Mérida where the remaining body of Roderic's supporters were gathered. Resistance to the Arab siege of that city was formidable and dragged on through the winter and spring, and it was not until June 30, 713 that the city surrendered. Following the capitulation, the Muslims seized the goods of the Church as well as the property of the slain and of those who fled. As a precautionary measure, Musa dispatched his son Abd al-Aziz to reinforce the rear guard at Seville to quell unrest there and to widen the sweep of conquest to include the areas around Niebla. At this point, Musa then turned his attention to his general, Tarik, whom he advised to meet him. Musa advanced towards Toledo and met Tarik half way at Talavera. All accounts of this meeting report Musa's indignation and ire surrounding Tariq's insubordination for not following the orders that were given him. Tarik's reprimand included a blow from Musa's riding crop.

The winter in Toledo provided Musa an opportunity to send a report of his accomplishments to the caliph in Damascus. In the spring of 714, he struck out in a northeasterly direction through Sigüenza and Calatayud to Zaragoza on the Ebro River, where he established a garrison and a mosque. That same year, he captured Lérida and followed the Roman road that led to Barcelona and Narbonne. His campaign was shortened when he received a message from Caliph al-Walid I ordering Tarik and him to Damascus. But before he would comply with this order, he and Tarik would set off on an additional mission to follow the Roman road up the Ebro towards Galicia. This final campaign of Musa and Tariq led to the submission of Fortún at Tudela and of the cities of Amaya (Burgos), Soria, León, Astorga, Oviedo, and Gijón, where many of the inhabitants had already fled to high ground and the safety of the Picos de Europa.

The submission of Fortún at Tudela in the Ebro Valley would have lasting consequences. This group would be known as the Banu Qasi, the sons of Cassius, who not only submitted willingly but also converted to Islam. The persona of Cassius has little historical support, but legend has him accompanying Musa back to Damascus after his conversion. Since Cassius and Fortún had names of Latin origin, it can be assumed that they were of Hispano-Roman nobility serving, possibly as malcontents, under the Visigothic regime. Fortún and his descendants would go on to serve the Arab administration and play a role in the politics of the upper Ebro Valley for nearly two centuries.

Entrusting his son Abd al-Aziz with the governorship of al-Andalus and leaving a faithful advisor in Abi Abda, Musa set off for Damascus with Tarik in the fall of 714, carrying a cargo of riches as a gift for the Caliph al-Walid I (705–715). Upon their arrival, the two warriors found that al-Walid had died and was succeeded by his brother Sulayman (715–717). Both Musa and Tarik were stripped of their spoils and died in obscurity (Lévi-Provençal *Histoire* 1: 27–9).

The Campaigns of Abd al-Aziz: 714–716

The governorship of Abd al-Aziz (714–716) brought additional major urban centers into submission. In the north, the fallen cities included Pamplona, Tarragona, Barcelona, Girona, and Narbonne. To the far west, the cities of Evora, Santarém and Coimbra surrendered to Arab control. Al-Aziz then focused on eastern Andalucia, where he seized Málaga and Elvira. In the province of Murcia, al-Aziz encountered Count Theodemir, a governor from the previous Visigothic regime, who remained in command of the region. A treaty negotiated between Count Theodemir and al-Aziz allowed the population to continue practicing their own religion and granted them freedom of autonomous rule in exchange for an annual tribute and a promise not to harbor the enemies of Islam. This treaty encompassed seven towns under Theodemir's control, Orihuela, Valentilla, Alicante, Mula, Bigastro, Ello, and Lorca. The original document has survived to the present day. A translation from the Arabic follows:

> In the name of God, the merciful and the compassionate. This is a document [granted] by 'Abd al-'Azīz ibn Mūsā ibn Nuṣair to Tudmīr, son of Ghabdūsh, establishing a treaty of peace and the promise and protection of God and his Prophet (may God bless him and grant him peace). We ['Abd al-Azīz] will not set special conditions for him or for any among his men, nor harass him, nor remove him from power. His followers will not be killed or taken prisoner, nor will they be separated from their women and children. They will not be coerced in matters of religion, their churches will not be burned, nor will sacred objects be taken from the realm, [so long as] he [Tudmīr] remains sincere and fulfills the [following] conditions that we have set for him. He has reached a settlement concerning seven towns: Orihuela, Valentilla, Alicante, Mula, Bigastro, Ello, and Lorca. He will not give shelter to fugitives, nor to our enemies, nor encourage any protected person to fear us, nor conceal news of our enemies. He and [each of] his men shall [also] pay one dinar every year, together with four measures of wheat, four measures of barley, four liquid measures of concentrated fruit juice, four liquid measures of vinegar, four of honey, and four of olive oil. Slaves must each pay half of this amount (Constable 37–8).

This document begs the question of how many more similar documents could have been produced during the initial conquest. If the treaty with the Banu Qasi, for instance, did produce a document, history did not reveal it to us.

Abd al-Aziz had established his residence in Seville during his short governorship and had taken as his wife the former widow of Roderic named Egilona, who had given him a son named Asim. The conduct of al-Aziz had caused him to fall out of favor with the Muslim faithful. One account relates that he had become too influenced by his new wife, while another account has him accused by the new caliph, Sulayman (715–717), of abuses of power. Either way, Abd al-Aziz was assassinated in March 716 (Lévi-Provençal *Histoire* 1: 33). The local Arab leadership selected Ayyub ibn Habib al-Lakhmi (716), the son of Musa's sister, as an interim governor of the peninsula. It took six months for the governor in Qayrawan, Muhammad ibn Yazid, to designate a replacement.

The Administration of al-Hurr: 716–718

Al-Hurr ibn Abd al-Rahman al-Thaqafi (716–718) arrived in al-Andalus from North Africa accompanied by hundreds of Arab nobles. According to the *Chronicle of 754*, al-Hurr accomplished four major administrative initiatives. First, he dispatched judges to all the large population centers to assure that Islamic law was being properly observed. He also established a system of taxation in *Hispania Ulterior*, the southern areas of Iberia. Then, by restoring the ownership of confiscated estates, an additional source of tax revenue would accrue. Finally, he imposed sanctions on the Berber population for concealing booty obtained during campaigns, for this was revenue that rightfully belonged to the caliph in Damascus (Wolf 136–7). The entire period from the initial invasion up to about the year 747 witnessed a swift turnover in governors of al-Andalus. There were no less than twenty governors from Musa (711–714) to Yusuf (747–756). At best, each lasted no more than three or four years until the reign of Yusuf, who managed to hang on for nearly a decade before being deposed. As al-Hurr's governance came to a close, the remnants of the Visigothic nobility, tucked away in the safety of the Picos de Europa Mountains, were preparing to take a stand.

Pelagius (Pelayo) and the Beginning of Christian Resistance

The first half-decade of the Arab conquest had been resoundingly successful. There were no military setbacks. Wherever a campaign met with resistance, submission soon followed. Wherever agreements could be reached without resistance, an orderly compliance prevailed. But not all the peninsula was satisfied with this state of affairs. Some of the dissidents who refused Muslim rule fled to the mountainous regions of the north, where the terrain was less conducive to Arab military success. While the new conquerors established northern garrisons in population centers serviced by Roman roads, such as Pamplona, León (Castra Legionis) and Gijón, the high valleys of Galicia, Asturias, and Cantabria were much less accessible. In these remote locations, the remnants of the Visigothic nobility and their followers could bide their time and plan their future.

Pelagius (Pelayo) had been gathering forces at a cave near Mount Auseva, later known as Covadonga. While later texts are not totally in agreement, he is thought to have been a Visigothic noble who perhaps transgressed against the Muslim administration, or perhaps he harbored a grudge against some Muslim infraction against himself or the nobility. On this issue, the Christian texts are inconclusive, and the Arab accounts are silent. What we do know is that the Arab Commander Alqama was dispatched with a substantial army to subdue this renegade leader refuged high in the northern mountains and bring him back for punishment. The date for the battle of Covadonga is generally accepted as 718 or possibly 719, that is around the time of the end of the rule of al-Hurr and the beginning of the reign of al-Samh (718–721). However, some believe the battle to have occurred in 722, which Arab sources place, possibly erroneously, during the rule of Governor Anbasa (721–725) (Collins *Conquest* 150). The *Chronicle of Alfonso III* reports that Pelayo had served as king for nineteen years and that he died a natural death at Cangas de Onis in Era 775, AD 737 (Wolf 169).

Certain accounts relate a verbal exchange at the mouth of the cave of Covadonga between Pelayo and a certain Bishop Oppa, who entreated him to surrender. We know for certain only that Pelayo and his followers were victorious in defending their positions. Their victorious defeat of Alqama's forces induced an immediate withdrawal of the Muslim troops, and the position of the upstart rebellion was secured. What prompted the campaign led by Alqama? Did the Arab leadership in Cordoba or Toledo feel threatened by reports of a military force gathering in the mountains? Were local Muslim garrisons being harassed by rebels? Was the local population unwilling to submit and pay taxes? Or as some reports have suggested, was there a grudge against Pelayo for escaping Toledo after a political disagreement? The lack of credible documentation obscures the reason for this campaign, but Alqama's failure did not appear to provoke additional attacks. In fact, no further assaults against Asturias are recorded during the reign of Pelayo, nor are any recorded by Pelayo against the Muslims. Rebel entrenchment at Covadonga would serve as a focal point for future Christian military success. Pelayo established himself as the first king of Asturias, and his reign would endure until 737 when his son, Fafila (737–739), assumed control. Of Fafila, we know only that he achieved the construction of a church, probably in Congas de Onís, dedicated to the Holy Cross. Pelayo's daughter, Ermensinda, would marry the third Asturian king, Alfonso I (739–757), the son of Peter the Duke of Cantabria (See Chart 1).

A Rapid Succession of Governors and Muslim Expansion North of the Pyrenees

Al-Samh's governorship over al-Andalus (718–721) is marked by a tightening of administrative rule and an expansion of conquest out of Iberia to the north of the Pyrenees. Upon his arrival into the peninsula, al-Samh immediately undertook two major initiatives. First, he ordered a census of the entire peninsula, both *Hispania Citerior* in the northeast and *Hispania Ulterior* in the south. A census would ensure greater reliability in tax assessment and collection. A portion of the plunder from the conquest was then divided among the conquerors, and the remaining portion, which included moveable and immovable goods, would be assigned to the public treasury. Secondly, with fiscal matters in place, al-Samh then commanded an army across the Pyrenees against Narbonne. This city had been conquered earlier by Abd al-Aziz, but the entire region had not submitted to his administration. In principle, the Aquitaine region from the western Pyrenees to the Loire River had been under Frankish Merovingian rule since the time of Clovis in the fifth century, but by the eighth century it was in the hands of the Frankish partisan, Duke Eudes (Odo). By contrast, the Narbonnaise region, north of the Pyrenees on its eastern flank, had remained under Visigothic control for three centuries. By 719, al-Samh had re-taken Narbonne without incident, and by 721, he had decided to lay siege to Toulouse that was controlled by Duke Eudes. This time, al-Samh's efforts were not rewarded. Duke Eudes had assembled a substantial force of his own and prevailed over the Muslim attacks. Al-Samh was killed, and the invaders were repelled. With the death of al-Samh, his second in command, Abd al-Rahman ibn Abd Allah al-Ghafiqi (721), assumed control of the governorship of al-Andalus until a replacement could be assigned by the governor in North Africa just one month later (Wolf 138–9). Nonetheless, this same Abd al-Rahman al-Ghafiqi would regain a leadership role a decade later. The absence of recorded military activity within the peninsula during the next twenty years indicates that the administration of al-Andalus had been stabilized. With Iberia pacified, the Muslim leadership began to direct their military attention across the Pyrenees.

Anbasa (721–725) was installed as governor in 721, and the *Chronicle of 754* reports that he doubled taxes on the Christians. This statement could mean simply that the Muslim administrative net was widened and control was extended to a greater number of locations (Collins *Conquest* 82). Anbasa then dispatched his deputies to advance extended forays into eastern Gaul. Muslim forces began consolidating their forward post at Narbonne. They immediately seized Carcassonne and met no resistance at Nîmes, where hostages were offered as a condition of surrender. The hostages were sent back to Barcelona before the campaign moved farther to the east. The Rhône Valley witnessed a rapid, ferocious pillaging campaign with no serious Christian opposition. The attackers swept past Lyon and continued north into Burgundy as far as Autun. The city was sacked in August 725 and was relieved of its wealth before the Muslim army returned to the peninsula (Lévi-Provençal *Histoire* 1: 59). Apparently disappointed by the performance of his commanders, Anbasa sought to take personal control of his forces in late 725 to inflict greater damage to Frankish positions. However, soon after he assumed control of his army, he died of natural causes. Aware of his imminent demise, Anbasa had the time to appoint his successor in the person of Udhrah ibn Abd Allah al-Fihri (725–726), but within a mere six months, Yahya ibn Salama al-Qalbi (727) was sent from Qayrawan as an official replacement.

The *Chronicle of 754* characterized Yahya as a cruel and terrible despot, who raged for almost three years. According to the *Chronicle,* there were continuing disputes and disagreements between Arabs and Berbers about land ownership and its restoration to Christians (Wolf 141). However, the reign of Yahya was much shorter than the three-year period stated in the *Chronicle,* for there were no less than four additional successors before Abd al-Rahman al-Ghafiqi was installed in 730. Governor Hujefa (728) took charge for six months, only to be succeeded by Uthman ibn Abi Nasah (728) for only four months, followed by al-Haythan ibn Ubayd al-Kilabi (729–730) and Muhammad ibn Abd Allah al-Ashjai (730) before Abd al-Rahman al-Ghafiqi (730–732) was finally assigned (Collins *Conquest* 85–6). This disorderly parade of successive governors can only be a reflection of the political unrest at Qayrawan in North Africa as well as in Damascus.

The governorship of Abd al-Rahman al-Ghafiqi (730–732) ushered in a renewed aggression toward the Aquitainians. Al-Ghafiqi was the first locally appointed governor in more than a decade. His appointment may have been prompted by the discontent of the Muslim population of al-Andalus, who were perhaps sensing a notion of their own sovereignty, since many of them had made the peninsula their home for two decades. Alternatively, his appointment could have been a response to the rapid turnover and the difficulties experienced by the preceding governors (Collins *Conquest* 86). At any rate, al-Ghafiqi's reinstatement brought a renewal of campaigns to the north of the Pyrenees, which may have been prompted by the memory of the death of his superior, al-Samh, who perished at the hands of Duke Eudes. During the summer of 732, al-Ghafiqi assembled an army at Pamplona and crossed the Pyrenees into Gascony before advancing northward across the Loire River. The Muslim army met little resistance until facing a much greater threat near Poitiers. The opposing army of the Merovingian *maréchal*, Charles Martel, inflicted a devastating defeat on the invading forces and mortally wounded Abd al-Rahman al-Ghafiqi. While details of the battle are absent, this defeat represents the first major blow to Muslim supremacy since their campaigns north of Gibraltar began. Following the battle, Charles Martel re-established Eudes in the Aquitaine as Duke of Toulouse. The contest of littoral regions on both sides of the Pyrenees would intensify into the next century.

The defeat of Abd al-Rahman al-Ghafiqi staged the arrival of Abd al-Malik ibn Qatan al-Fihri (732–734), whom the *Chronicle of 754* describes as a wealthy man. He was indeed a member of the influential Quraysh tribe of Arabia. The *Chronicle* portrays him as a man who defiled the beauty and good things of *Hispania* and with his greed led it into ruin (Wolf 146). Abd al-Malik was criticized by the caliph for not leading successful campaigns against the Franks, and so he launched an expedition against some minor unrest in the Pyrenees. He achieved nothing, while a portion of his army perished in the campaign. He withdrew to Córdoba and was soon replaced by Uqba ibn al-Hajjaji al-Saluli (734–740), who, according to the *Chronicle*, relieved the country of the destructive practices of his predecessor. Uqba threw Abd al-Malik into chains and deported the judges appointed by him. It was during the reign of Uqba that Arab forces stationed in Narbonne conducted four-year raids throughout the Rhône Valley, Provence, and Avignon. These raids provoked the intervention of Charles Martel who put Narbonne under siege in 737. When Uqba dispatched an army to repel the siege, Martel successfully routed the Muslim army but then chose to lift the siege, which left Narbonne in Muslim control (Lévi-Provençal *Histoire* 1: 63). Uqba died in 740 and was replaced by the very man whom he had replaced, Abd al-Malik (restored 740–741). The next few years witnessed a major Berber revolt in North Africa and its spillover effect into the peninsula.

Berber Uprising and Civil War

Governor Uqba (734–40) was at the command of his army in the Ebro Valley in 739 when news of a major Berber revolt in North Africa prompted him to retreat immediately to Córdoba. The threats from North Africa were so menacing that Uqba launched his own expedition across the Strait before returning to the peninsula where he died in 740.

Events in North Africa had a dramatic effect on the politics of the peninsula. Even though it was now decades since the Berbers of Iberia had left North Africa, they still maintained a close relationship with their North African brothers. The Berbers, although equal to the Arabs in the eyes of Islam, were treated as second class citizens by the Arab elite of the peninsula. For example, the Berbers were settled in regions that were less desirable to the Arabs, such as mountainous regions in the south and in the northern lands of Galicia.

During the second reign of Abd al-Malik (740–741), a major Berber revolt in North Africa was escalating. A large army of Syrians had been dispatched from Damascus in 741 under the leadership of Kultum (Collins *Conquest* 108). Kultum and his vice-commander, Balj ibn Bishr al-Qushayri, were charged with annihilating the Berber rebels at Tangier. Kultum underestimated his opponents, and his army suffered an embarrassing defeat. The forward guard led by Balj escaped to Ceuta where they remained trapped by Berber rebels. Meanwhile, Abd al-Malik faced serious threats of his own. The Arabs of the northern and western regions of the peninsula had fled to the south to escape the Berber menace in those areas. Toledo was also threatened. Trapped in Ceuta, Balj had petitioned Abd al-Malik several times for assistance and requested ships to bring his army to the safety of the peninsula. Abd al-Malik had turned a deaf ear to these requests until his own position in Córdoba was endangered by Berber threats. Reasoning that accommodating Balj was the only way to save his own situation, Adb al-Malik agreed to send ships to rescue Balj on the condition that he would leave the peninsula after assisting Abd al-Malik campaign against the peninsular Berbers.

The Berbers of the peninsula had divided their forces into three units. The first was to take Toledo. The second was to march on Córdoba and kill Abd al-Malik, while the third unit aimed at controlling the access to the Strait, which would permit them to cross over and join the Berber forces at Ceuta. All three units met with defeat. The unit which held Toledo under siege was defeated by an army led by Abd al-Malik's son. The Berber unit advancing on Córdoba was driven back, and the Syrian forces led by Balj crushed the Berber unit at Algeciras. At this point, Abd al-Malik asked Balj to honor his agreement and return to North Africa. Rather than honor this request, Balj instead marched on Córdoba and killed Abd al-Malik in 741. Balj (741–742) became the *de facto* ruler of al-Andalus until the following year when he was killed fighting against Abd al-Malik's son, Umayya, allied with North African troops led by Abd al-Rahman ibn Habib (Collins *Conquest* 110).

All this civil unrest was subdued with the arrival of the new governor Abu al-Kattar (743–745) sent by Damascus. The remaining Syrian forces of Balj did not oppose him because of his exalted status in the ruling aristocracy. Al-Kattar first freed the captives held from the previous victories of Balj. He then proclaimed an amnesty for the remaining forces that were loyal to Abd al-Malik, that had re-grouped in the north. And finally, al-Kattar needed to accommodate the Syrian forces that had accompanied Balj. He proposed giving them fiefs in various locations in exchange for their military support in time of need. This military conscription program was entirely acceptable to these warriors, since it was exactly the type of program that they were adapted to in Syria. These soldiers were placed on fiefs ranging across the southern peninsula from Algarve (today southern Portugal) in the west to the eastern province of Murcia (Lévi-Provençal *Histoire* 1: 49). Al-Kattar's actions achieved a short hiatus in the civil unrest, only to be broken by the conspiracy of al-Sumail ibn Hatim al-Kilabi, who over a period of time assembled a coalition of forces opposed to al-Kattar. Various versions relate how the plot unfolded, but in the end, al-Kattar was unseated and killed. In his place, a poorly identified co-conspirator, named in *The Chronicle of 754* as Thalaba (Wolf 153–6), by Lévi-Provençal as Thawaba ibn Salama (Lévi-Provençal *Histoire* 1: 50), and by Collins as Tawaba ibn Yazid (Collins *Conquest* 111), was elevated to the throne in 746. His reign lasted a little more than a year when he died of natural causes.

The control of al-Andalus then passed into the hands of Yusuf ibn Abd al-Rahman (747–756), who previously served as the local administrator in Narbonne in the 730s during the period of active raids into Gaul. Yusuf was politically aligned with al-Sumail and, no doubt, conspired with him in the downfall of al-Kattar. Yusuf rewarded al-Sumail's support with autonomous control of Toledo and then of Zaragoza (Lévi-Provençal *Histoire* 1: 50–2). Yusuf's reign would last nearly ten years, the longest of any of the governors of al-Andalus since the beginning of the invasion.

Expansion of Asturias During the Reign of Alfonso I (739–757)

The small, incipient kingdom of Asturias had been tucked away undisturbed and quiet in the Picos de Europa Mountains ever since the victory of Pelayo over Alqama in 718 (or 722 as some would have it). The civil unrest and chaos in Muslim al-Andalus beginning in 740 allowed the Asturians to profit from the Muslim's pre-occupation with civil war. In 739, Alfonso I (739–757), son of Peter, the Duke of Cantabria, and son-in-law of Pelayo, "was elected king by all the people, receiving the royal sceptre with divine grace" as reported by the *Chronicle of Alfonso* III (Wolf 170). The reign of Alfonso I coincides with the beginning of the Berber revolt.

At a time when this small kingdom seemed to be destined to occupy a meagre enclave in the mountains, Alfonso I witnessed the exodus of Arab garrison commanders in Galicia and in the Duero Valley due to Berber threats. Then in 741 the Berbers themselves exited these same regions to rally against Arab control in Córdoba. Routed by the Arabs in these civil conflicts, the Berbers who were not killed or captured fled back to the safety of the north. A second Berber migration occurred nine years later in 750 when a great famine and drought plagued the northwest of Spain, causing a mass exodus of Berbers, who simply gave up and went back to the Maghreb in North Africa (Lévi-Provençal *Histoire* 1: 69). Alfonso seized the moment of every Muslim distraction by assembling enough forces to invade the regions vacated by the Arabs and Berbers. He did not intend to occupy the areas, for he did not possess the military power to withstand a counter attack from the south. During the eighteen years of his reign, his campaigns accomplished two aims: increasing the population of his own realm, and depopulating the periphery around Asturias. The first goal was accomplished by emigrating the Christian populations of the Duero Valley and Galicia and repopulating them into the flanks of Asturias. His campaigns removed any remaining Muslim population that hadn't already fled upon his arrival. The immigrating Christians marched with all mobile possessions into western Asturias, Galicia's northern coast, or into Vardulia (i.e. Old Castile). Their migration created a large, depopulated buffer zone around the southern periphery of Asturias. By the end of his reign, Alfonso and his brother Fruela had depopulated most of the areas along the Duero. An army attempting to cross this zone would be disadvantaged by a lack of provisions. They would have to transport their own over a large distance.

The *Chronicle of Alfonso III* reports that: "He [Alfonso I] took: Lugo, Tuy, Oporto, Anegia, the metropolitan city of Braga, Viseo [sic], Chaves, Ledesma, Salamanca, Numancia, which is now called Zamora, Ávila, Astorga, León, Simancas, Saldana, Amaya, Segovia, Osma, Sepúlveda, Arganza, Clunia, Mave, Oca, Miranda, Revenga, Carbonarica, Abeica, Cenicero, and Alesanco, with their fortresses, villas and villages. Killing all the Arabs with the sword, he led the Christians back with him to his country" (Wolf 170). While the accuracy of the Chronicle's report may lack the precision of a more contemporary account with respect to the times and places that were actually overrun by Alfonso and his brother Fruela, the lasting effect of their actions is certain. Resistance had begun in earnest.

CHAPTER 3

Umayyad Emirs and the Emergence of the Christian North: 756–912

The Rise of Abd al-Rahman ibn Marwan

The year AD 750 witnessed a violent upheaval in the Islamic world. The Umayyad dynasty, which had risen to power under Muawiya I (661–680), was falling apart and was under attack from opposing Islamic forces. In the decades preceding this upheaval, the ruling class was considered largely incapable of governance and was accused of fiscal tyranny and worldly pleasures. They had lost touch with their subjects. While Caliph Marwan II (744–750) was basking in luxury in Damascus, opposing forces were gathering in the Iraqi village of Koufa. Abu al-Abbas Abd Allah, great grandson of Abd Allah ibn al-Abbas, a first cousin of the Prophet, had revealed himself as the long-awaited imam and in doing so inspired the Abbasid revolution. Abu al-Abbas gathered a large revolutionary force and marched from Mesopotamia to Syria to engage and defeat the reigning Caliph Marwan II. The Shiite armies of Abbas were not satisfied with slaying the caliph. They relentlessly pursued the relatives of Marwan II throughout Syria, Palestine, and Egypt and slew them wherever they found them. Marwan's grandson Abd al-Rahman was one of the very few relatives to escape the grasps of the Abbasid slaughter. With the assistance of agents loyal to the Umayyads and with a loyal assistant named Badr, Abd al-Rahman escaped to the security of western North Africa. There he would find support from Umayyad nobility and regional officials, and because his mother was Berber, that population would sense an affiliation with him as well (Lévi-Provençal *Histoire* 1: 95).

Abd al-Rahman spent four years in exile in North Africa, biding his time, strengthening his political position, and observing the political environment across the Strait of Gibraltar. Finally, in the summer of 754, he dispatched his trusted assistant Badr to the Iberian Peninsula to assess the possibility of his immigration. Badr initially sought an audience with the military leaders who had previously been installed by Umayyad caliphs from Damascus. These leaders were the ones who had been rescued from Ceuta and who later were given lands in Andalusia in exchange for becoming consigned mercenaries. After they listened to Badr, the leaders decided to recognize and honor the royal heritage of Abd al-Rahman. They then cleared a path for Abd al-Rahman's entrance into Iberia with al-Sumail, the governor of Zaragoza and close ally of Yusuf ibn Abd al-Rahman (747–756), the highest-ranking governor in the peninsula. With the fall of the Umayyad caliph in 750 and with the Islamic world now being ruled from Bagdad under the Abbasids, Yusuf as governor of Andalusia was now operating as a free agent with little attention or tribute paid to Bagdad.

In August of 755, Abd al-Rahman set sail for his future kingdom and landed at the port of Almuñécar on the coast of Andalusia. He wasted no time in obtaining the allegiance of the Syrian mercenaries and of the Yemenites who were politically opposed to Yusuf. Meanwhile, Yusuf had been on a mission to subdue revolts in the northeast and had returned to Córdoba. He attempted to ply the loyalty of Abd al-Rahman by offering his daughter's hand in marriage. Abd al-Rahman not only refused the offer, but he began a westerly march towards Seville, gaining the support of Yemenites and Syrians as he went. The campaign culminated in a battle outside of Córdoba where Yusuf was soundly defeated, and the town accepted Abd al-Rahman as their new prince. He had not yet reached his twenty-sixth birthday (Lévi-Provençal *Histoire* 1: 104).

Yusuf and al-Sumail had been beaten, but they remained in competition until 759–760. Thus, Abd al-Rahman cautiously guarded his position during the first years of his reign. Yusuf was later assassinated by a contingent of his own revolutionaries, and al-Sumail would be strangled in prison. Abd al-Rahman then set about establishing an army that he could rely on, so he selected them from his most loyal supporters. He opened the doors to immigration of the disenfranchised Umayyad tribesmen who had not been eliminated by the Abbasids. The Umayyad clan inherited their name from their early leader, Umayya, a cousin of the Prophet's grandfather. They constituted a major part of the prestigious Quraysh tribe. Abd al-Rahman and his Umayyad supporters would form a new aristocracy in Córdoba (Lévi-Provençal *Histoire* 1: 108).

One of the bloodiest and greatest threats to Abd al-Rahman arose in 763 when al-'Ala' ibn Mughith in the district of Beja aligned himself with the Abbasids and attempted to replace the Umayyad prince. Well-supplied with money, arms, and moral support from the Abbasid caliph and flying the black flag of the Abbasids, al-'Ala' lay siege to the town of Carmona where the prince had sought refuge. A sudden and bold counterattack by Abd al-Rahman and his faithful dealt a lethal blow to the rebel forces. All the rebel leaders were decapitated on the field of battle. Their heads were embalmed and sent to Qayrawan along with the black flag of the Abbasids as a message for the caliph.

While the Yemenites of Andalusia supported the rise to power of Abd al-Rahman, they presented a continual source of unrest during his administration. In 766 a group of dissidents in the region of Niebla attempted to take control of Seville, and a second attempt at overthrow took place in 774. Similarly, the Berbers around the region of Medellín and Mérida carried out troublesome and prolonged attacks that could not easily be suppressed, since the rebels would retreat to the safety of mountainous areas whenever threatened by Abd al-Rahman's generals. The Umayyad prince contested these affronts to his authority during the years of 768–776, and the last surviving son of Yusuf was not put down until 785, just three years before the death of Abd al-Rahman (Lévi-Provençal *Histoire* 1: 110). All this preoccupation with internal strife left Abd al-Rahman little time and resources to deal with the Christians in the north of the peninsula.

The Christian North During the Time of Abd al-Rahman I

About the time that the Umayyad dynasty in Damascus was falling apart, Christian factions were vying for supremacy just to the north of the Pyrenees. Pepin the Short had inherited the leadership of the Franks and had decided to extend his power into the Aquitaine region. A local Gothic count, Ansemund, went over to Pepin's cause, while another local Goth, Duke Waiofar, led the opposition to the Frankish alliance. Waiofar had attacked Muslim-held Narbonne in 751, but the city remained under Muslim rule, while the Christians struggled among themselves for regional control for nearly a decade. Several locations such as Nîmes, Maguelonne, Agde, and Béziers were delivered to Frankish control by Ansemund, but he was reportedly killed by his own men while attempting to take Narbonne. Regional control was finally settled in 759 when the local population of Narbonne massacred the Muslim garrison and handed over the keys of the city to Pepin's rule (Collins *Conquest* 173–4; A. Lewis 24–5). This event signaled the end to Muslim control north of the Pyrenees and enabled Christian influence to slip ever farther towards the Ebro Valley.

Frankish authority passed from the hands of the Merovingian dynasty to the Carolingians with the ascent of Charlemagne (768–814) in 768. Ten years after his ascendancy, the great and legendary Frankish king was lured into a campaign south of the Pyrenees. At that time, the governor of Zaragoza, Sulayman ibn Yaqzan, had been approached by agents of the caliph in Bagdad, hoping to arouse a conspiracy against Abd al-Rahman in Córdoba. Sulayman agreed to align with Bagdad to free himself from Abd al-Rahman's authority. However, the Umayyad prince was informed of this treachery and prepared to send an army against Sulayman. Realizing that the Abbasids could not provide much military support, Sulayman decided to appeal to Charlemagne. He promised to pledge allegiance to Charlemagne and to surrender the city of Zaragoza. Under the Frankish king, Sulayman expected to keep his position as governor, rid himself of the loose ties with Córdoba, and nullify the possibility of being removed from his position by Abd al-Rahman. Charlemagne decided to accept the offer, and in the spring of 778 his army crossed the western Pyrenees through the pass of Roncesvalles. His forces proceeded on to Pamplona and Huesca, where they were well received by the populace. But upon arriving at Zaragoza, he found that the gates of the city were not open to him. Sulayman had for some reason changed his mind and refused to admit the Franks into the city. Charlemagne at once made plans for a siege when news arrived that the Saxons were again in revolt. Since the stability of Saxony was of much greater importance, Charlemagne immediately lifted the siege and retraced his march back to Pamplona, where he ordered the destruction of the centuries-old, Roman-built walls. His order to destroy the city's walls possibly came out of frustration for his failure at Zaragoza, or perhaps he intended to eliminate obstacles to future Christian campaigns south of the Pyrenees. As Charlemagne's army advanced through the pass at Roncesvalles, its rear guard was attacked and destroyed by the Basques (Lévi-Provençal *Histoire* 1: 121–5; Collins *Caliphs* 206; O'Callaghan *A History* 101–2). The Frankish king's campaign was a complete failure, but it evolved into a longer-term strategy to strengthen the southern frontier against the Muslims. Upon his return to France, he appointed his son, Louis the Pious, as king of Aquitaine with the aim of securing a stronger foothold in the region. In 785, the people of Girona handed over the keys of the city to the Franks, while Abd al-Rahman watched powerlessly from Córdoba. This giant step south of the Pyrenees portended the later incursions into the Spanish March, a military buffer zone created by Charlemagne.

The Asturian kingdom experienced an era of relative peace during the reign of Abd al-Rahman. Alfonso I (739–757) and his successors seldom fought against the Muslims. *The Chronicle of Alfonso III* (Wolf 171) records a battle at Pontuvium in Galicia in which Fruela I (757–768) defeated a force sent from Córdoba. Its leader Omar was captured and subsequently decapitated by Fruela. It was not this event that earned Fruela his nickname as "the Cruel." He had reportedly murdered his own brother, Vimara, and was later murdered at Cangas de Onís by his own men. During the reigns of Aurelius (768–774), of Silo (774–783), who moved his capital from Cangas to Pravia, and of Mauregatus (783–788), no further hostilities with Córdoba are recorded.

The Asturian Kingdom and the Reigns of Hisham I (788–796) and al-Hakam I (796–822)

An inversely proportional relationship can be observed between the level of unrest in al-Andalus and the number of expeditions to ravage Christian territories in the north. Abd al-Rahman I was predominantly occupied with pacifying al-Andalus, which left him little time and resources for northern campaigns. On the other hand, his son and successor, Hisham I (788–796), enjoyed a period of peace in al-Andalus, which enabled him to launch expeditions into Asturias on an annual basis. Vermudo (788–791), who had succeeded Mauregato as king of Asturias, was so overwhelmed by Hisham's incessant attacks that he abdicated in favor of his cousin Alfonso II, "the Chaste" (791–842), whose victory over the Muslims at Lutos (Lodos) in 795 restored Asturian confidence and put a stop to the raids. Hisham died the following year (O'Callaghan *A History* 103). The long reign of Alfonso II paralleled and even outlasted the reign of Hisham's successor, al-Hakam I (796–822), whose reign in al-Andalus was challenged from the onset. Al-Hakam's uncles opposed his accession but failed in an attempted overthrow. During the second year of his reign, a revolt broke out in Toledo led by Ubayd Allah ibn Hamir. Al-Hakam instructed the commander of the Berber garrison at Talavera to put down this threat, and through various ruses the Berber commander, Amrus, gained entrance to the city to implement a gruesome plan. As the revolutionaries arrived for a dinner, Amrus directed them through a designated door, where his men beheaded them one-by-one and threw them into a ditch that had been prepared for that purpose. This horrific incident was remembered as "The Day of the Ditch" (Lévi-Provençal *Histoire* 1: 157; Collins *Caliphs* 32–3). In 805 when al-Hakam uncovered a plot against him in Córdoba, he had seventy-two conspirators publicly crucified in an obvious attempt to send a message to the populace. Provoked by conspiracies and rebellions throughout his reign, al-Hakam's ferocious responses earned a reputation for tyranny.

While al-Hakam was dealing with internal conflict in al-Andalus, Aflonso II (791–842) in Asturias attempted to re-create a civil and ecclesiastical order after the fashion of the Visigothic monarchy. He moved his capital from Pravia to Oviedo and surrounded himself with a royal court. He re-shaped Oviedo into a royal city and as an episcopal center complete with palaces, baths, churches, and other public buildings. It was during the reign of Alfonso II that the supposed tomb of the Apostle Saint James the Great was discovered in Galicia. The story goes that a hermit saw some angels singing over the tomb and reported the sighting to the local bishop who, in turn, reported the event to the king. A church was erected on the site, which became known as *campus stellarum,* field of the stars, today known as Santiago de Compostela. This site became a source of psychological inspiration for the people of Galicia and very quickly became the destination of religious pilgrims. It evolved into an instrument of economic trade and social interaction between Spain and the rest of Europe. Spared of Muslim attacks, Alfonso II grew his realm and occasionally ventured into Muslim held territories. In 798 he overtook Lisbon only to lose it later (O'Callaghan *A History* 104–5).

Carolingian Influence in the Pyrenees After 778

The failure of Charlemagne at Zaragoza and Roncesvalles emphasized the need for a different strategy to protect and expand the southwest flanks of the Carolingian Empire. While Duke Lupo in Gascony had sworn allegiance to Charlemagne, he also demonstrated a penchant for independence, which prompted Charlemagne to appoint Seguin, from a rival family, as Count of Bordeaux. Later, he organized an additional Gascon county of Frezenac and entrusted it to Count Burgund, who was replaced upon his death (c. 801) by Count Liutard. The new counts along with Count William of Toulouse, serving as viceroy in southern France, provided a counterbalance to the power of Duke Lupo (A. Lewis 37–8).

Charlemagne's reorganization of leadership and alliances began to bear fruit just a few years later when in 781 Pallars and Ribagorça high on the southern banks of the Pyrenees came under the control of the Count of Toulouse. Then in 785 Girona and nearby Besalú accepted Frankish control and were followed by Urgell-Cerdanya. Feeling an erosion of power, the Muslims staged a counteroffensive which defeated Count William of Toulouse in a battle near Carcassonne in 793. The walls of Narbonne and Girona withstood the attacks, however, and the Muslim army withdrew to al-Andalus without establishing a permanent presence.

The campaign of Charlemagne south of the Pyrenees in 778 appeared to encourage some of the Christians under Arab control to migrate into Christian lands north of the Pyrenees. These people were granted waste lands called *aprisiones* for clearing and cultivation. *Aprisiones* served to populate unused parcels and provided an additional source of soldiers for the local counts. The concept of *aprisiones* was continued over the next century as the counts under Frankish rule spread their control southward.

In 799, Pamplona accepted Carolingian overlordship when Count Velasco defeated and killed its ruler, Mutarrif ibn Musa. At that time, Pamplona was garrisoned and/or ruled by clients of the Emir al-Hakam I (796–822). Arab history records the defeat of Mutarrif ibn Musa by Velasco the Basque in that year (Collins *Caliphs* 207). Mutarrif was quite possibly the great grandson of Cassius, the Lord of the Ebro Valley who submitted to Musa ibn Nusayr and converted to Islam. The line of the Banu Qasi, or sons of Cassius, included his son Fortún (Fortunatus), Musa ibn Fortún, and Mutarrif ibn Musa (See Chart 6). By 801 these preliminary forays south of the Pyrenees gave way to a major offensive. In that year, a large force of Franks, Burgundians, Aquitanians, and Provençals assailed and captured Barcelona and the nearby castle of Tarrassa. This victory led to the installment of Count Bera (801–820) who would take charge of Barcelona, Girona, and Besalú.

During the first decade of the ninth century, Aragon came under Carolingian overlordship with the installment of Count Aureolus (?–809), who was succeeded by Aznar Galíndez (809–820). Meanwhile, Count Velasco in Pamplona continued his allegiance to the Carolingian emperor. At the time of Charlemagne's death in 814, the *Marca Hispanica*, the Spanish March, had been established. Its boundaries extended along the Mediterranean south of Narbonne including Girona, Besalú, Urgell, Cerdanya, Barcelona and as far as the river Llobregat. The March extended westward along the southern slopes of the high Pyrenees including the valleys of Pallars, Ribagorça, the valley of the Aragon, and the area around Pamplona later to become Navarre.

Carolingian Control Rebuffed in the Western Pyrenees

Carolingian hegemony was not to endure intact. A Muslim expedition of 816 was sent by Emir al-Hakam I (796–822) against Velasco of Pamplona, and thirteen days of fighting resulted in Velasco's defeat (Collins *Caliphs* 207). History records nothing more of him. In Aragon, Aznar Galíndez (809–820) was overthrown by his son-in-law, García the Bad (820–833), who during a heated dispute with his wife and brother-in-law, Centullo, killed the latter and subsequently deposed his father-in-law. He reportedly replaced his wife by marrying the daughter of Iñigo Arista and thereby solidified relationships with the future kings of Pamplona. Aznar Galíndez went on to become Count of Urgell and Cerdanya until his death. Aznar's sons and grandsons eventually overthrew García the Bad and his son, Galindo Garcés (833–844), and the heirs of Aznar Galíndez later resumed control over Aragon until 922 (See Chart 2). The transfer of Count Aznar Galíndez to Urgell and Cerdanya also coincided with a change of leadership in Barcelona, Girona, and Besalú. Count Bera (801–820) was accused of disloyalty by a Goth named Sanila. Bera was challenged to a duel and then subsequently removed and replaced by Count Rampon in 820. While the history of this issue is clouded, some see this move as the effect of a family rivalry between the sons of Duke William and the family of Count Belló of Carcassonne, whose descendants will later play an important role in the governance of Catalonia (A. Lewis 44–5).

The Carolingians made a final attempt to control Pamplona in 824 when an army of Gascons, under the leadership of counts Eblo and Aznar, was dispatched to re-gain that city. The Carolingian counts were soundly defeated by the forces of Enneco (Iñigo Arista 824–851) and his allies, the Banu Qasi, led by Musa ibn Musa (See Chart 3). Count Eblo was sent as a hostage to the emir in Córdoba, but Aznar, because of his Basque heritage, was sent home. This event closed the brief chapter on the Carolingian control of this sector of the Spanish March. Pamplona, Aragon, and the Rioja were lost to the Arista family and their Banu Qasi allies, who ruled the Ebro valley from Tudela as clients of the Muslim emir (Lacarra *Historia* 33).

The Banu Qasi and Pamplona Versus Córdoba

The victory at Pamplona by Iñigo Arista (824–851) and the Banu Qasi ushered in a period of peace for more than a decade. Musa ibn Musa of the Banu Qasi and Iñigo of Pamplona maintained a close relationship and allegiance throughout their reigns, because they were half-brothers through their mother Onneca. She was first married to Musa's father Musa and then re-married to Iñigo's father Jimeno. Even with their close ties to Christian Pamplona, the Banu Qasi remained trusted clients of the emirs in Córdoba during the reigns of al-Hakam I (796–822) and Abd al-Rahman II (822–852). However, the installation of two new Muslim governors in Zaragoza and Tudela ended the friendly relationship between the Banu Qasi and the emir in 841. Both new governors were dedicated to raiding the properties of the Arista family, and they also harassed the Banu Qasi, who were forced to move to Arneda. Musa solicited the aid of Iñigo's son García Iñiguez (851–880?), and their combined forces produced successful skirmishes against Harit ibn Bazi, the governor of Zaragoza. They succeeded in capturing him near Calahorra. To punish and avenge this disloyalty, Abd al-Rahman II campaigned against Pamplona the following year. He inflicted serious property damage and carried off captives destined for slavery. Musa struck an ephemeral truce with the emir which carried certain conditions. Musa insisted on being named governor of Arnedo, and the emir demanded that Musa release Harit and other Muslim captives. Musa asked that the truce be granted to Iñigo Arista as well. However, Musa did not abide by the terms of the treaty, and in 843 the emir again sent a large force against Pamplona. The combined forces of Musa and the Arista family met with disaster as they engaged the emir's troops. Musa was unseated from his horse and fled on foot. Iñigo Arista and his son Galindo escaped with severe wounds, while other officers lost their heads. The warring continued almost annually, alternating between temporary truces and revenge against broken promises. In 850, Musa finally guaranteed a truce by sending his son, Ismail, to Córdoba as a hostage. Iñigo Arista died the following year (Lacarra *Historia* 35–7).

Ramiro I (842–850) of Asturias

About the time that conflicts erupted between Pamplona and the Banu Qasi against Córdoba, the reign of Alfonso II of Asturias had come to an end. *The Chronicle of Alfonso III* informs us that at the time of Alfonso's death, Ramiro I (842–850) "was away from the throne because he had travelled to the province of Vardulias (Castile) to take a wife" (Wolf 174). During his absence, Nepotian, the Count of the Palace, had taken control of the kingdom either by consent of the court or by force. In any case, when Ramiro heard what happened, he immediately went to Lugo in Galicia to assemble an army and then returned to meet and defeat Nepotian's forces at a bridge over the river Narcea. Nepotian fled but was pursued and captured by counts Scipio and Sonna who blinded him and returned him to Ramiro I, who in turn sent him to a monastery to live out his days. Later in Ramiro's tenure, he was faced with an insurrection headed by the count of the castle and another nobleman. Ramiro quelled the threat by blinding one conspirator named Aldroitus, and then had the other named Piniolus decapitated. Early in his reign, Ramiro was faced with a Viking attack at a place called *Farum Brecantium*, believed to be present-day A Coruña. He is credited with killing a part of their horde and burning their ships, before the remaining band set sail southward to Baetica, where they raided the Muslims at Seville. Ramiro is said to have defeated the Muslims twice in battle, and he added to the royal and ecclesiastical buildings in Oviedo before he died in 850 (Wolf 174–5). Meanwhile over in Aragon, Galindo Aznárez (844–887) had regained control from García the Bad's son, Galíndo Garcés (833–844) to reassert his family's authority in that valley.

Mid–Ninth Century Changes in Leadership

The decade of the 850s witnessed a change in political climate occasioned by changes in leadership and alliances. Ramiro I of Asturias died in 850 and was succeeded by Ordoño I (850–866). Iñigo Arista of Pamplona, who had been in poor health for several years, expired in 851. He had delegated his field command to his son García Iñiguez (851–880?) during his final years. Abd al-Rahman II died in 852 and was succeeded by his son Muhammad I (852–886). Meanwhile, Musa ibn Musa, from his fortified stronghold of Albelda, had mended his differences with Córdoba and became the unchallenged Muslim power in the Ebro valley. This decade would see the distancing of Pamplona from the Banu Qasi as García Iñiguez of Pamplona strengthened his bonds with Asturias.

During the first half of the ninth century, little is recorded of the relationships between the kingdom of Asturias and the allied partners of the kingdom of Pamplona and the Banu Qasi. When Ordoño I ascended to the Asturian crown in 850, his first campaign was to subdue an uprising by the Basques in the eastern provinces of Asturias. Musa ibn Musa, sensing an infringement to his border areas in the Ebro Valley, responded by sending an army against Ordoño I. Conflicting reports of this encounter only obscure its outcome, and nothing was accomplished by this confrontation. The struggle for rule over this border region would be settled only later in the decade. In the meantime, the Arista family of Christian Pamplona was cooling relationships with Musa and warming to the overtures of Asturias. Not only had Pamplona sent ambassadors to the court of Charles the Bald in 850 just before the death of Iñigo Arista, but we also learn of the marriage of a daughter of Ordoño named Leodegundia to a prince of Pamplona around that same year (Lacarra *Historia* 39).

In al-Andalus, the transition from Abd al-Rahman II to Muhammad I (852–886) was accepted peacefully and without resistance by the Umayyad family. The calm and cooperation in the Lower March permitted Muhammad I to augment the number of mercenaries in his army while reducing the tax burden of the people of Córdoba, thereby allowing resources to fully concentrate on summer raids to the north. However, Muhammad's ascendance was not so willingly accepted in the Middle March. A revolt against Muhammad in Toledo persisted for several years. The governor of the city was held as ransom in exchange for prisoners held in Córdoba. Then in 853, the Toledans launched an attack against Calatrava la Vieja, causing expeditions to be sent from Córdoba against

Toledo. The following year, the rebels in Toledo formed an alliance with Asturian forces, led by Count Gaton of Bierzo, including a contingent from Pamplona. The emir's army engaged the combined rebel forces and handily defeated them. Thousands of rebels were reportedly slain. Nonetheless, the resistance continued in 855, 857 and 858 with Emir Muhammad gaining the upper hand in battles, but failing to win submission. Only in 873 did the emir win a decisive victory over Toledo with an expedition that lay siege to the city and forced the citizenry to submit to his authority (Collins *Caliphs* 43).

The entry of the kingdoms of Asturias and Pamplona into Toledo's conflict with Muhammad in 854 spawned additional military actions in the north. Muhammad had named Musa ibn Musa as *walí* (governor) of Tudela, Zaragoza, and of all the Muslim Upper March. The emir expected loyalty from him in return. Muhammad demanded that Musa retaliate against the Christians for their complicity with Toledo. The following year, Musa campaigned in the countryside of Alava, destroying crops and devastating castles (Lacarra *Historia* 39). This action widened the distance between Pamplona and the Banu Qasi, and strengthened the ties between Pamplona and Asturias.

In 859 Viking invaders appeared at the steps of Pamplona. They looted the countryside and killed many who were not taken prisoner. Among those captured was King García Iñiguez himself, who was held until a substantial ransom assured his release. To add to the misfortune of García in the following year, Muhammad directed campaigns against Pamplona that not only devastated villages, crops, and castles, but also captured prisoners who were delivered to Córdoba. The captives included García's son Fortún (880?–905). The future king of Pamplona would remain there as a hostage for some twenty years (Collins *Caliphs* 44–5).

The Chronicle of Alfonso III (Wolf 176–7) informs us that King Ordoño I of Asturias moved an army against the fortress of Albelda, just south of present-day Logroño in the Rioja, and besieged it in 859. To counter this offensive, Musa's army set up camp on nearby Mount Laturce. Ordoño then decided to divide his army into two units, one to maintain the siege, and the other to engage the forces of Musa. The narrative reveals that Musa's soldiers sustained huge losses, including the death of his son-in-law García (Lacarra *Historia* 46). Having won the field battle, Ordoño then sent his troops against the city itself. After seven days, Albelda was overtaken and completely razed. Musa escaped the battle with serious wounds but went on to live another three years. Musa's son Lubb, governor of Toledo, apparently submitted himself to Asturias for the remainder of Ordoño's reign. Musa ibn Musa, one of the most celebrated and colorful figures of the ninth century, died in battle at Guadalajara in 862. With his death, the influence of the Banu Qasi began to wane for a brief period, only to be revived later by his sons and grandsons. *The Chronicle of Aflonso III* tells that Musa referred to himself as the third king of Spain.

Muhammad I directed attacks against Alava and Old Castile almost annually during the 860s, which caused the northern Christian realms to tighten their bonds with each other. In 863, Muhammad I sent a large army of some 20,000 cavalrymen to pillage the countryside of Alava, cutting down fruit trees and destroying crops just before the harvest. The summer raids of 865 saw the Muslim armies destroy walled villages in Castile, and they burned the castle of a Count Rodrigo. Ordoño's resistance failed to prevent the devastation. In 863, many of his counts fell on the field of battle, and in

865 he suffered a disastrous defeat on the banks of the Ebro (Lévi-Provençal *Histoire* 1: 317).

In 866, Alfonso III (866–910) was enthroned in Asturias, and García Iñiguez of Pamplona was quick to solidify his relationship with the new monarch by marrying his daughter, Jimena, to Alfonso. García also covered his easternmost flank by marrying another daughter, Onneca, to Aznar Galindez II (867–93), the new ruler of Aragon, thereby establishing royal blood lines from Pamplona into Asturias and Aragon.

Unrest in the Muslim Upper March continued throughout the reign of Muhammad I of Córdoba. The warlord Amrus ibn Umar overthrew the emir's local governor of Huesca, Musa ibn Galindo, and two years later in 872 the four sons of Musa—Lubb, Mutarrif, Fortun, and Ismail—captured Tudela, Zaragoza, Huesca, and Monzón. The emir could retaliate only by sending his son, al-Mundhir (886–888) to pillage and destroy the northern countrysides. Al-Mundhir failed to occupy any of the cities. In consecutive years, raids were directed at Alava and Castile (877), against Zaragoza, Tudela and Pamplona (878), against Zaragoza, Borja, Tarazona and Tudela (879) and finally again against Zaragoza (881) (Lacarra *Historia* 41). Attacks against the Christian North would decrease only as Muhammad I became more occupied with rebellions in the Lower March later in his reign.

Internal Unrest in al-Andalus Under Muhammad I (852–886)

The administrative legacy left to Muhammad I (852–886) by his father, Abd al-Rahman II (822–852), remained intact and efficient. The coffers in Córdoba were full, and the peace and prosperity of the Lower March permitted Muhammad's administration to maintain a wealthy state. Tax revenues were steady except for two periods of famine from 865 to 868 and from 873 to 874 when Muhammad I forgave the ten percent tax levy on crops (Lévi-Provençal *Histoire* 1: 285). However, internal tranquility was about to end. Not only was there growing religious unrest represented by Muslim ascetics such as Baki ibn Makhlad, who had imported heretical notions from his long stay in the Orient, but an element of the Mozarabic community, that is the Christians living under Muslim rule in the south, were preaching a principle of voluntary martyrdom as a protest to Islam. Moreover, elements in the larger population of Berbers and *muwallads*, the recently converted from Christianity, resented Umayyad supremacy. The hour was approaching for internal rebellion.

In 875, a rebel from Mérida named ibn Marwan al-Jilliqi "the Galician" had escaped from prison in Córdoba. He rallied his forces and took refuge in Badajoz. As his name implies, ibn Marwan was probably a descendant of a noble family dating from the Visigothic regime. Muhammad I sent his son, al-Mundhir, to Badajoz to dislodge ibn Marwan from his sanctuary, but the rebel and his partisans held their positions in the city. The initial failure to re-capture ibn Marwan had disastrous consequences two years later when a Muslim raid to the north in 877 was ambushed by the combined forces of ibn Marwan and Asturian troops. The surprise attack resulted in the loss of several hundred Muslim cavalrymen and the capture of one of Muhammad's ministers. Ibn Marwan promptly handed the minister over to Alfonso III to be held in Asturias for ransom. Later that year, ibn Marwan was successfully expelled from Badajoz and was forced to take refuge in Asturias. Muhammad I dispatched a large army to attack Asturias in 878, but Alfonso III successfully met this challenge at Polvovaria, and just a few days later, he completely routed the Muslims in the valley of Valdemora. Ibn Marwan regained Badajoz in 885 (O'Callaghan *A History* 113).

Another rebel, Umar ibn Hafsun, was the *enfant terrible* of al-Andalus in the final decades of the ninth century. Ibn Hafsun descended from a high-ranking *muwallad* family near Ronda and was described by contemporaries as having a hot temper. After killing one of his neighbors in a quarrel, his father, fearing the consequences, sent ibn Hafsun off to live in the countryside some distance to the east of Ronda on the banks of the Guadalhorce River. There he made the acquaintance of other misfits who began pillaging the locality. He was arrested by the district governor, who was not informed of the previous murder and only had him whipped. After a brief exile in Africa, Umar returned to his life of ambush and robbery, and with the help of his brother, based his operations at the fortified promontory of Bobastro near the town of Ardales, Málaga. From this fortification, he harassed and raided the surrounding villages without contest from the local governor. In 883, one of Muhammad's generals, Hashim ibn Abd al-Aziz, successfully cornered Umar at Bobastro and negotiated his surrender. Umar was taken to Córdoba where he was not only well-received, but he was conscripted into the emir's army and sent off to pillage Alava. Upon his return to Córdoba, Umar escaped with his men and resumed his thuggery from the fortress at Bobastro. In 886, the emir's son al-Mundhir led an expedition against Bobastro, but after a siege of two months, he received word that his father, Emir Muhammad I, had just died. Al-Mundhir lifted the siege and returned to Córdoba. Umar ibn Hafsun continued to be a thorn in the side of the Umayyad regime for two more decades (Lévi-Provençal *Histoire* 1: 300–6).

The reign of Muhammad I is characterized by near-annual raids to the north that produced little results, other than booty, but had a destabilizing effect on the peninsula. His authority in the Upper March, which had fallen to local warlords, was reduced, and in the Central March, Toledo had become virtually independent. Mérida would fall to the control of the rebel ibn Marwan, and local warlords continued to exercise power throughout the Lower March.

The Short Unfortunate Reign of al-Mundhir (886–888)

On August 9, 886, al-Mundhir was elevated to the position of emir. His immediate concern was to establish a following that was loyal to him, which did not include his father's vizier and favorite general, Hashim ibn Abd al-Aziz. Al-Mundhir had al-Aziz thrown into prison and then had him executed. His family was stripped of its land holdings. Meanwhile, ibn Hafsun was preaching revolution against the Umayyads, who, as he had it, were levying high taxes on the populace and treating them like slaves. In the summer following his ascension to the throne with a new court aligned in his favor, al-Mundhir dispatched three of his generals to Andalusia to bring ibn Hafsun to justice. These forces succeeded in driving off the garrisons that ibn Hafsun had established in villages around Lucena, but they accomplished nothing more before returning to Córdoba. In the spring of 888, al-Mundhir himself led a large army against the celebrated rebel and set up camp in front of the walls of Bobastro. The clever ibn Hafsun immediately engaged the emir in negotiations and agreed to conditional surrender. He asked only that he and his men be treated with respect and dignity. The emir was favorable to his offer, and was preparing to send a peace offering when ibn Hafsun slipped out of Bobastro at night and attacked the emir's convoy. Furious at this breach of oath, the emir redoubled the siege only to fall ill a few weeks later. Al-Mundhir sent for his brother, Abd Allah, who watched his brother die on June 29, 888. Abd Allah had the emir's body carried back to Córdoba on the back of a camel. The siege of Bobastro was again lifted (Lévi-Provençal *Histoire* 1: 306–10).

The Reign of Abd Allah (888–912)

Abd Allah ibn Muhammad (888–912) was born on January 11, 844 and was forty-four years old when he ascended as emir. His brother, al-Mundhir was born the same year, but of a different mother. Abd Allah's mother was a slave from whom he inherited reddish-blond hair and blue eyes. By contrast, his brother had dark, curly hair. Abd Allah had eleven sons, and one of his wives, Durr, had given birth to a son named Muhammad, who was the presumptive heir. According to Aragonese manuscripts, Muhammad's mother was Onneca (later written as Iñiga), the daughter of Fortún Garcés, who was married first to Abd Allah and to Asnar Sánchez of Navarre. Onneca must have accompanied Fortún Garcés during his long incarceration as a hostage in Córdoba from 860 until sometime before his ascendancy to the throne of Navarre around 880. Onneca was married to Abd Allah during this period and was known to the Arabs as Durr, the mother of Muhammad (Lacarra *Textos* 231; Cañada Juste "Doña Onneca" 485).

Abd Allah's administration was marked by family intrigues and dramas. He accused his son Muhammad of conspiracy to usurp the throne and had him incarcerated. The conspiracy could have been fabricated by Muhammad's younger brother, al-Mutarrif, just to get rid of the elder inheritor. Whatever the case, on the eve of Muhammad's release in January 28, 891, al-Mutarrif stabbed the elder brother to death in his prison cell. Some reports, however, indicate that it was the father, Abd Allah, who authorized the stabbing of his son Muhammad. Twenty-one days after this incident, a son of Muhammad is born, who is the future Abd al-Rahman III (912–961). This royal intrigue is not yet finished. In 895, Abd Allah accused his son al-Mutarrif of treason for inciting revolts around Seville. He then had al-Mutarrif beheaded and burried under myrtle in his garden. Further assassinations follow. In separate incidents in 987, Abd Allah suspected his two brothers, Hisham and al-Kasim, of plotting an overthrow and had them both killed (Lévi-Provençal *Histoire* 1: 335).

When Abd Allah ascended as emir, the treasuries of Córdoba were filled, but year after year the emir witnessed a diminution of regional payments. He was compelled to dispatch his generals to collect revenues and to keep rebellion at bay. At the same time, he refused to increase the taxes on those who were loyal just so annual expenses could be met. His coffers were stressed, but he was not greedy. He assumed a longer vision of stabilizing and maintaining al-Andalus for his successor.

Following the failure to defeat ibn Hafsun at Bobastro in 888, the drums of revolution were beating in nearly every corner of Andalusia. The atmosphere had become partisan, confusing, and embroiled. Muslim factions were divided between Arabs, Berbers, and *muwallids*, the recently converted from Christianity, and the latter two segments resented the superior status assumed by the Umayyad Arabs. The *mozarabes*, the Christians living under Muslim rule, were even lower in social status and were taxed at a higher rate. Small rebellions prevailed throughout Andalusia, but the smaller players were eventually subsumed by the more powerful revolutionaries. Three major areas were controlled independently of Córdoba. The Arab Sawwar rose to power in the region around Elvira following a conflict between *muwallids* and local Arabs; in Seville, Kuraib ibn Khaldun and Ibrahim ibn Hadjdjadj were independent usurpers; and ibn Hafsun remained in charge of the regions around Bobastro. The latter controlled the province of Jaén, the cities of Archidona, Baeza, Ubeda de Priego, Écija, and eventually he subsumed the territory of Sawwar around Elvira (Lévi-Provençal *Histoire* 1: 341, 371).

After years of embarrassing raids on his sovereign regions, Abd Allah decided that he had no choice but to engage ibn Hafsun head on. In the spring of 891, the emir assembled a large army and set out for Poley, where ibn Hafsun with an even larger force had installed himself in a fortified castle. The two armies faced each other in front of the castle when the emir's generals charged the wing of the opposing brigade and caused them to take flight. Ibn Hafsun took refuge in the castle with his remaining men, who, at this point with their convictions demoralized by defeat, exited from the back of the castle in the dead of night along with ibn Hafsun. They headed for the safety of other regional strongholds. Ibn Hafsun would continue to lead regional dissidents for years into the reign of Abd al-Rahman III, but he would no longer be a major influence in Andalusia, and his power would continually weaken during the remaining years of Abd Allah's tenure.

Emerging Independence in the Eastern Pyrenean Counties

During the last quarter of the ninth century, the eastern Pyrenean counties gained greater independence from their overlord, Count Bernard of Toulouse, after he was murdered by the agents of his rival, Bernard Plantevelue in 872 (A. Lewis 111). Bernard's overthrow permitted local counts in competing, influential families to establish themselves independently of Toulouse. Such was the case of Count Raymond (872–920) in Pallars-Ribagorça high on the southern slopes of the Pyrenees between Aragon in the west and the county of Urgell to the east. Raymond also ruled the Val d'Aran, on the northern slopes of the Pyrenees, which is part of present-day Catalonia. The valley of Ribagorça bordering Aragon to its west, and the parallel valley Pallars to the east, both opened onto the lower Ebro valley and were therefore vulnerable to occasional attacks from Muslim held Huesca. Ribagorça and Pallars were never controlled by Huesca, possibly because of the impoverished circumstances of the regions. It may not have been worth the trouble for the Muslims to control. At any rate after the demise of Count Bernard of Toulouse, Count Raymond became the *de facto* independent count of these valleys where his descendants would rule for more than a century. Count Raymond's sister, Dadildis, married García Jiménez and was the mother of Sancho Garcés I (905–925) and of Jimeno Garcés (925–931) of Navarre, while Raymond's son, Bernardo (920–955) married Toda Galíndez, daughter of Galindo Aznárez II (893–922) of Aragon (See Chart 4 and Chart 7). It is interesting to note that the Val d'Aran, a pleonasm meaning valley of the valley (*val* is from Latin *valles* and *Aran* = Basque *haran*, both meaning "valley"), is the only territory on the northern slopes of the Pyrenees which belongs to present-day Spain. The language spoken today in the Val d'Aran is not Catalan, but rather Occitan, a southern French dialect.

The counts of the far eastern regions were also released from their ties with Toulouse. From the time that the Carolingians had conquered Barcelona in 801, a Count Bera had been installed as its governor. Recall that in 820, Count Bera was accused of treason and defeated in a duel by a Goth named Sanila. Consequently, he was stripped of his title, and Barcelona was awarded to Count Rampon, whose reign did not endure. Count Belló, as head of one of the oldest of families in the region, had ruled from Carcassonne since the days of Charlemagne, and from 844 to 848 we see that Belló's son Sunifred I was recognized as Count of Barcelona (Collins *Caliphs* 228; A. Lewis 44). The influence and rule of the descendants of Count Belló would be extended throughout the counties of the eastern Pyrenees (See Chart 5). Belló's grandson, Count Guifred (or Guifré), "the Hairy" (870–898), ruled Urgell-Cerdanya, Barcelona, and Girona-Osona, indeed all the Catalan counties south of the Pyrenees, until he met his death on the field of battle against Lubb ibn Muhammad of Lérida, whom he attempted to prevent from erecting a new fortress there. Guifred worked tirelessly to re-populate his counties with disenfranchised Christians and supported the establishment of churches and abbeys in the region. Guifred is recognized as the father of Catalonia.

Fortún Garcés (880?–905), the Last of His Dynasty in Navarre

The death of King García Íñiguez (851–880?) of Navarre is poorly documented, but by around the year 880, we see that his son Fortún Garcés (880?–905) had been establish as monarch of that realm. Fortún had just returned from a nearly twenty-year stay in Córdoba as a hostage, which had not prepared him for the military duties required of the ruler of Pamplona. While Muhammad I of Córdoba and his sons were preoccupied with internal revolts in Andalusia, Muhammad ibn Lubb of the Banu Qasi was preparing to increase his power and extend his control over the Ebro Valley. In 882, Muhammad ibn Lubb succeeded in capturing his uncle Ismail as well as his cousins, Ismail and Lubb, the sons of Fortún ibn Musa, at the fortress of Viguera. He forced his relatives to surrender the towns of Tudela, Valtierra, Zaragoza and the castle of San Esteban (See Chart 6). Even though his power had been increased through this maneuver, Muhammad ibn Lubb could not reconcile with Emir Muhammad I, who wanted him to hand over Zaragoza. The idea then came to Muhammad to sell Zaragoza to the emir. With this transaction, Muhammad became the emir's loyal subject and while Zaragoza came under the rule of the emir's governor, Muhammad still controlled Tudela and was appointed governor of Arnedo and Tarazona by the emir. From these strongholds in the Ebro Valley, he attacked Pamplona and the region of Alava at will, embarrassing the powerless Fortún Garcés (Lacarra *Historia* 45–7).

The sons of Emir Muhammad I (852–886) of Córdoba, al-Mundhir (886–888) and Abd Allah (888–912), retained Muhammad ibn Lubb as governor in the Upper Ebro. Muhammad fortified old encampments, and he reconstructed the castles at Nájera and Viguera. His expedition of 886 ravaged the countryside of Alava and inflicted death on many Christians, while in 891, we hear of his attack on a castle named *Silbaniano* in the realm of the king of Pamplona. In the intervening years, the city of Zaragoza had fallen out of the hands of the emir's governor and into the hands of the warlord Muhammad al-Tujibi. Muhammad ibn Lubb died fighting al-Tujibi near Zaragoza in 898.

The death of Muhammad ibn Lubb did not bring peace to Navarre nor to the eastern regions of Asturias controlled by Alfonso III, who along with Fortún Garcés celebrated Muhammad's death. Lubb ibn Muhammad continued the pace of war where his father had stopped. He fortified his regional cities, provoked a conflict with al-Tawil, the new warlord of Huesca, from whom he accepted compensation in the form of surrendered land holdings and the hand of al-Tawil's daughter in marriage. Lubb sent his brother Mutarrif to be installed as governor of Toledo in 903 in exchange for future military support to that city. In 904, he pillaged the lands of Raymond of Pallars (872–920), stormed several castles, and either slaughtered or captured numerous Christians in that valley (Lacarra *Historia* 47–8). The futile reign of Fortún ushered in a new dynasty of the local, powerful Jimeno family in the person of Sancho Garcés I (905–925). History reveals nothing about the change in dynasty that swung in favor of the Jimeno family in 905, but it was probably years in the making. The ineffectiveness of Fortún was no doubt a contributing factor, but we can also point out that family marriages to the crown of Aragon and Ribagorça fortified the prestige and power of the Jimeno family. We recall that the mother of Sancho Garcés was the sister of Raymond of Ribagorça (872–920), and Sancho's sister, Sancha, was married to Galindo Aznárez II (893–922) of Aragon. Galindo would have supported the ascension of his brother-in-law Sancho. The Jimeno family line would govern Navarre for more than a century and would even spawn additional branches in Castile, e.g., Fernando I (1037–1065), and in Aragon, e.g., Ramiro I (1035–1063) (See Chart 7).

As the first decade of the tenth century drew to a close, the death of Alfonso III of Asturias in 910 left his kingdom to his three sons García (910–914), Ordoño II (914–924), and Fruela II (924–925). In the far eastern counties, the sons of Guifred, "the Hairy," controlled the Christian regions south of the Pyrenees, while the elderly Ramón continued to govern Ribagorça for another decade. Galindo Aznárez II (893–922) was in the middle of his tenure in Aragon, and a new, more vibrant leader in Sancho Garcés (905–925) was installed in Navarre. In Córdoba, Emir Abd Allah will pass away in 912, and his grandson Abd al-Rahman III will establish a new order for al-Andalus.

Chapter 4

The Age of Abd al-Rahman III: 912–961

Abd al-Rahman III Restores the Authority of Córdoba

Abd al-Rahman III (912–961) was born on January 7, 891, just three weeks after the tragic demise of his father, Muhammad, who was killed for treason by Abd al-Rahman's grandfather Abd Allah (888–912). Abd al-Rahman's mother was a slave of Frankish or perhaps Basque origin, and his paternal grandmother was the daughter of Fortún Garcés, the Princess Iñiga, who lived with her father in Córdoba during the years that he spent there as a hostage. Because of his lineage, Abd al-Rahman III had inherited blue eyes and reddish-blond hair, which he was said to have dyed black (Lévi-Provençal *Histoire* 2: 2). Grandfather Abd Allah had raised the young Abd al-Rahman with great care in preparation of his leadership role as emir. His ascendance to the throne occurred on October 16, 912 and was neither contested nor opposed by his uncles and great-uncles.

Abd al-Rahman inherited a realm which in the previous decades had been reduced to little more than Córdoba itself. Parts of al-Andalus had been fragmented by independent rebels, who collected taxes and tribute from the local residents, but who sent no revenue to Córdoba. Abd al-Rahman implemented a plan to restore the authority and dignity of Umayyad rule by reconquering those territories that had become independent and by snuffing out rebellion throughout Andalusia. Unlike his predecessors, who attempted unsuccessfully to engaged the major rebels head on, he would begin by re-establishing the loyalty of the small localities which had rallied around these rebels, so that taxes would be sent to Córdoba rather than to the rebel chiefs.

He began by restoring authority to the Sierra de Almadén and to Caracuel, fortresses held by the Berbers near Ciudad Real. A few weeks later in January 913, he retook the city of Écija, the center of resistance closest to Córdoba. The city walls were razed, and the bridge across the river Genil was destroyed, which cut off communication with the rebel Umar ibn Hafsun. Next, he organized a campaign against Andalusia proper in March of 913. He forced the submission of Jaén, Monteleón, and a fortress near the mountain of Somontín, and then finally a stronghold at Mentesa. He enlisted the troops from these areas, garrisoned them, and sent the women and children of the newly-enlisted to Córdoba as hostages to ensure their fidelity. He conquered Juviles and promised to release the Christian soldiers that ibn Hafsun had left there. However, upon submission, Abd al-Rahman changed his mind and had these soldiers beheaded. Before returning to Córdoba, Abd al-Rahman took possession of the anchorage of Salobreña on the southern coast. He followed up by capturing the two small fortresses of San Esteban and Peña Forata. This initial foray, called the Campaign of Monteleón, garnered nearly seventy strongholds and hundreds of strategic positions. His strategy separated these locations from the sphere of influence of ibn Hafsun and re-attached them to his own, without assailing the rebel's stronghold directly. The following May of 914, Abd al-Rahman employed the same tactics in the Serranías of Ronda and Málaga. He conquered the castle of Ojén (just north of Marbella), burned the supply boats of ibn Hafsun at Algeciras, and then overcame the environs of Morón and Carmona (Lévi-Provençal *Histoire* 2: 6+).

The rebel Ibrahim ibn Hajjaj had ruled Seville and its environs independently of Córdoba for over a decade. When Ibrahim died, he left the city of Carmona to his son Muhammad ibn Ibrahim, and he left Seville to his son Abd al-Rahman ibn Ibrahim. Because Seville was of greater value than Carmona, Muhammad was jealous of his brother Abd al-Rahman and had him poisoned. This assassination turned out to be a useless effort when Muhammad's cousin Ahmad was elevated to power in Seville. Consequently, when Abd al-Rahman III decided to force submission of the region around Seville, Muhammad was left estranged from his family and had no choice but to yield the city of Carmona. As the ruler of Seville, Ahmad also found himself in an isolated condition and solicited the support of ibn Hafsun, who immediately led his forces toward Seville against Abd al-Rahman III. In his first encounter with superior forces, ibn Hafsun retreated to Bobastro, leaving Ahmad to his own devices. In 913, realizing that his situation was hopeless, Ahmad sent word to Abd al-Rahman III that he was ready to surrender Seville. By 917, a famine devastated the entire Lower March, and ibn Hafsun was stripped of support and in ill health. Under these circumstances, Abd al-Rahman III no longer felt any need to wage war against him. Ibn Hafsun confined himself to the church at Bobastro and died in September 917 (Lévi-Provençal *Histoire* 2: 6+). The four sons of ibn Hafsun inherited fortified positions in Andalusia, but they would play only minor roles. They would not be eliminated from the scene entirely until a decade later. Within six years of his ascendance, the emir had restored his authority over the Lower March, and over the next decade, he would accomplish the same for the Middle March.

The Sons of Alfonso III: 910–925

The passing of Alfonso III (866–910) in December 910 followed the conspiracy of his three sons, García (910–914), Ordoño II (914–924), and Fruela II (924–925), who deposed him in his final days. The eldest son, García, was reportedly caught and incarcerated for a short time in 910 near Zamora, but the mounting political pressure applied collectively by the three sons and their allies caused the aging Alfonso to abdicate in favor of García. Alfonso III would pass away later in the year. It was during the short reign of García that he transitioned the seat of the kingdom of Asturias from Oviedo to León. Ordoño II was also recognized as *rex* "king" in 910 at least in certain parts of

Galicia, and Fruela assumed some subordinate rule in parts of Asturias. There are varying accounts of how García died in 914, but since he left no heirs, Ordoño II (914–924) succeeded him as king of León, apparently without controversy, and thereby re-united Galicia and León.

In August 913, Ordoño II led a successful attack on the city of Evora in which the Umayyad governor Marwan ibn Abd al-Malik was killed along with his garrisoned soldiers. The poorly-fortified location was easily pillaged, and Ordoño II's army carried off thousands of women and children as captives. After he inherited García's realm in 914, Ordoño II attacked the region around Mérida, confronting little resistance and equaling his success at Evora. Since Ordoño II knew that Abd al-Rahman III was fully engaged in restoring his authority throughout Andalusia, he expected little retaliation. In 916 however, Abd al-Rahman took the offensive by dispatching Ahmad ibn Muhammad ibn Abi Abda, one of his most trusted generals, to raid Leonese territories. This sortie was repeated the following summer with an attack on San Esteban de Gormaz, a stronghold in the Duero Valley where Ordoño II was expanding his control. The Muslim general at the head of a large army of North African mercenaries and volunteers bent on holy war lay siege to the fortress for several days. Just when it looked as if the fortress was going to fall, Ordoño II's troops arrived to rout the Muslims, who abandoned their leader and fled. Their general was left to perish with a few of his faithful men. This serious defeat left Abd al-Rahman resolved to settle the score with his northern adversary (Lévi-Provençal *Histoire* 2: 36–8).

The Struggle for La Rioja

When Sancho Garcés I (905–925) came to power in Navarre, the Banu Qasi, the sons of Cassius, then led by Lubb ibn Muhammad along with his ally and father-in-law, the war lord Muhammad al-Tawil, were establishing fortifications on the very doorstep of Pamplona. Lubb from his citadel in Tudela controlled the regions from Nájera to Monzón, and al-Tawil governed Huesca. In 907, Lubb had begun fortifications to encircle Pamplona from the south, and al-Tawil attempted to control the route to Pamplona through the Valdonsella and Sos. These advances provoked retaliatory skirmishes by Sancho. He set an ambush for Lubb in September 907 in which Lubb and many of his men were killed. The succession of Abd Allah ibn Muhammad, Lubb's brother, and the death of al-Tawil in 913 gave Sancho an opportunity to launch a series of attacks against the Banu Qasi at Estella on the frontier of the Ebro. He occupied San Esteban de Deyo (Morhandín), and then fortified Cárcar and Calahorra. At the same time, García I (910–914) of León overran Arnedo in the Rioja (Lacarra *Historia* 54). The Banu Qasi immediately regained Calahorra, while Yunus, a brother of Abdallah ibn Muhammad fortified Valtierra and Caparroso, and a third brother, Yusuf, destroyed Christian defenses at Arnedo, Alfaro, and Falces. In July 915, Sancho Garcés I surprised Abd Allah at Tudela and killed most of the defenders of the city. Abd Allah was forced to surrender and yield positions at Falces and Caparroso. As additional terms of surrender, he offered his daughter Urraca and his son Fortún as hostages. Abd Allah died two months later. Urraca would later marry Fruela II of Leon, and Fortún converted to Christianity. In

June 918, the combined forces of Sancho I (905–925) of Navarre and Ordoño II (914–924) of León advanced on Nájera, but were not able occupy that location. They pressed on towards Tudela and did capture Calahorra, Arnedo, and Viguera. Sancho I subsequently moved on to Valtierra, where he destroyed the mosque and the surrounding area but failed to take the castle (See Map 8).

In 920, Abd al-Rahman III (912–961) of Córdoba decided to lead an elite reserve army against the Christians. Feigning an attack against Navarre and the Upper Ebro Valley by way of Calatayud and Zaragoza, Abd al-Rahman III instead headed from Medinaceli to Osma on the Upper Duero where the Christian residents were taken by surprise and fled. After pillaging and setting fire to the settlement, he hastened to San Esteban de Gormaz on the Duero to avenge the defeat of his general three years earlier. The garrison of the fortress had fled in the face of a far superior army, leaving all the defenses and structures in the area to be sacked and destroyed. Having met little resistance and with minimal losses, Abd al-Rahman directed his forces northward to punish Sancho Garcés I (905–925) in Pamplona for warring against the Muslims of the Ebro Valley. Upon learning of the Abd al-Rahman III's intention, Sancho I left Arnedo and headed northward to join the forces of Ordoño II who was coming to his aid. In July of 920, the Muslim army met the combined forces of León and Pamplona between Muez and Salinas de Oro in the valley of Junquera (Valdejunquera), where the emir's troops awaited in a flat terrain that best suited their military tactics. They dealt an overwhelming blow to the Christians, killing many nobles. The bishops Dulcidio and Ermogio were taken as hostages. The Muslim army then took the castle of Viguera to the east and continued to pillage the countryside for three weeks before returning to Córdoba (Lévi-Provençal *Histoire* 2: 41–3; Martínez Díez *El Condado* 248–57).

In 921, Ordoño II conducted raids deep into the Ebro Valley without retaliation from Córdoba. He regained Nájera in La Rioja with the aid of Sancho Garcés I, who continued eastward to re-take the castle of Viguera. In 923, the Banu Qasi leader, Muhammad ibn Abd Allah, now governing Tudela for Abd al-Rahman III, mounted a counter offensive against Nájera and Viguera. Sancho I alerted Ordoño, who defended Nájera, while Sancho himself took the castle of Viguera that was occupied by Muhammad ibn Abd Allah. Muhammad died during this encounter, and the emir was prompted to send Abd al-Hamid ibn Basil as the new governor of Tudela (Lacarra *Historia* 56; Cañada Juste "Los Banu Qasi" 88). With these conquests, the entire province of La Rioja became annexed to the kingdom of Navarre. Sancho Garcés I had in succession removed Lubb ibn Muhammad in 907, Abd Allah ibn Muhammad in 915, and Muhammad ibn Abd Allah in 923. These maneuvers eliminated once and for all the influence of the Banu Qasi in the Upper Ebro Valley and marked the end of a Muslim dynasty that had persisted for more than two hundred years since the initial invasion.

In the spring of 924, Abd al-Rahman was planning an attack against Pamplona when he received word that Ordoño II had been overcome by an illness and had been replaced by his weak, leprous brother, Fruela II (924–925). Nevertheless, the emir did not postpone his plans. His campaign of Pamplona was initiated from Tudela on the Ebro and eradicated the strategic fortifications of Sancho Garcés I (905–925) along the valley, including Cárcar, Peralta, Falces, Tafalla, and Carcastillo. The Muslim army then advanced to the valley of the river Aragon. The army of Sancho Garcés I was waiting for their adversary near a pass named *Foz de Lumbier* across the river Irati. The ensuing battle put Sancho's army to flight, which left the route to Pamplona unprotected. Abd al-Rahman's army was free to pillage Pamplona at will. The villagers had fled to the countryside. The Muslims burned churches and monasteries from Pamplona back to Calahorra and Valtierra before returning to Tudela and then on to Córdoba. These forays were entirely punitive, and La Rioja remained under the control of Navarre (Lévi-Provençal *Histoire* 2: 44–7).

The kingdom of Navarre had strengthened its political influence through family alliances from León to Aragon to Huesca. Sancho Garcés I (905–925) was the son of Dadildis, the sister of Count Ramón of Ribagorça (872–920) and Sancho's sister Sancha had married Galindo Aznárez II (893–922) of Aragon. To complicate these relationships, Galindo's sister, Sancha Aznárez, was married to Muhammad al-Tawil and therefore was the mother of Fortún ibn Muhammad al-Tawil, who had been reigning in Huesca since 919. Galindo Aznarez II continued to rule Aragon amidst this tangled web of relationships until his death in 922 at which time Aragon was incorporated as a county into the kingdom of Navarre under Sancho Garcés I.

The Christian North in a State of Flux: 925–931

With the death of Ordoño II (914–924) in 924, the crown of León passed to his brother, Fruela II (924–925), the third son of Alfonso III, apparently without contest. Fruela had been reigning in a small area of Asturias north of the Cantabrian Mountains for fourteen years, ever since the three sons had deposed their father Alfonso III in 910. The sons had, no doubt, struck an agreement among themselves as to how the realm would be divided as well as the order of succession to the throne. Thus, Fruela II ascended without incident. Fruela II was accustomed to a pacific, pastoral life. During his short reign of fourteen months, he fought no battles against the Muslims, but he did dispatch counts from Álava and Castile to fight with Sancho Garcés I (905–925) of Navarre against Abd al-Rahman III in 924 (Martinez Díez *El Condado* 263).

However, the death of Fruela II in 925 spawned a power struggle for the crown between his own sons and the sons of his brother Ordoño. The two brothers King Ordoño II (914–924) and King Fruela II (924–925) each left three sons who were old enough to govern as king. In order of age, the sons of Ordoño II were named Sancho, Alfonso, and Ramiro; the sons of Fruela II were Alfonso, Ordoño and Ramiro. Fruela II's son Alfonso had designs on ascending to the throne of Asturias with the support of his two brothers. However, the three sons of Ordoño II garnered far greater support from within the realm as well as from neighboring realms. The eldest of Ordoño's sons, Sancho, had the backing of the nobility in Galicia above the Miño River because of his marriage to Gotona Núñez of a powerful northwest family. Ordoño's second son, Alfonso, had the support of Sancho Garcés I of Navarre because of his marriage to Sancho's daughter, Iñiga (Onneca). The third son Ramiro was favored by the aristocracy south of the Miño down to Coimbra, because he was married to Andosina Gutiérrez from a powerful family of that region.

Influence and power favored the sons of Ordoño II, but harmony did not resonate between them. As the eldest, Sancho intended to exercise his right of primogeniture to claim the throne of León, but the outside influence of his brother Alfonso's father-in-law succeeded in elevating Alfonso as king. Sancho was not to be denied. He successfully defeated his brother Alfonso in battle and drove him from León. Alfonso sought refuge in Astorga and aligned himself with his namesake cousin Alfonso, son of Fruela II. He continued the struggle for power until Sancho was deposed and removed from the regal city. Even though Alfonso IV Ordoñez (925–931) was installed as king in León, Sancho (925–929) successfully maintained control over Galicia and was recognized as king there. Similarly, the territory south of the Miño was ceded to the third brother Ramiro II (931–951). Meanwhile, Alfonso, the dispossessed son of Fruela II, installed himself in the region around Santillana. He exercised sovereign powers there and entitled himself as king. The triumph of Alfonso IV as king in León can be viewed as the decisive influence of his father-in-law, Sancho Garcés of Navarre (Martínez Díez *El Condado* 269). After the final installation of Alfonso IV in 925 and the agreement to permit his two brothers a certain degree of autonomy in their respective regions, peace prevailed for the next four years. The three brothers did not engage in battle; the Muslims of al-Andalus did not attack the Christians; and Alfonso IV did not wage any campaigns against the Muslims. In the summer of 929, King Sancho of Galicia died, and Alfonso IV assumed control of that regal domain as well.

In 931, Iñiga, the wife of Alfonso IV and daughter of Sancho Garcés I of Navarre, had died. Alfonso IV was grief stricken and decided to abdicate the throne in favor of his remaining brother Ramiro II. A rapid succession of events—the death of Iñiga, Alfonso's grief-stricken decision, an appeal to his brother, and the immediate arrival of Ramiro in León—all led to the hastened coronation of Ramiro II (931–951) on November 6, 931. The transition was seamless and without contest until the former King Alfonso IV regretted his decision. He left the monastery where he had sequestered himself after abdicating and travelled to Sahagún. Nothing became of this first flight except that it made the new king suspicious and mistrustful of his brother. Alfonso was then visited at the monastery by the enemies of Ramiro II, who encouraged the former king to re-consider and overthrow Ramiro II. The instigators were none other than the three sons of the former King Fuela II accompanied by several counts from Álava and Castile. This rebellious entourage hastened to León while Ramiro II was in Zamora, preparing an army to respond to an appeal from Toledo for military assistance. León was left undefended, and the former king and his instigators took control of the city without incident. Learning of this turn of events, Ramiro II returned from Zamora with a substantial army and pursued and captured Alfonso and the sons of Fruela II. Ramiro II had all four of them blinded and sent to a monastery on the river Torío near León in 932 (Martínez Díez *El Condado* 278).

While the drama for the succession of the crown of León was unfolding, the stage to the east of Asturias in Navarre and in the eastern counties of Catalonia would also witness a realignment of leadership throughout the decade of the 920s. In Navarre, the great leader and fighter, Sancho Garcés I, died on October 11, 925. Since Sancho's only son, García Sánchez (931–971) was just six years old at the time, Sancho's brother, Jimeno Garcés (925–931), was elevated to the throne in December 925 under the watchful eye of Sancho's widow, Toda, who would guard the inheritance of her son. When

Jimeno died of natural causes in May 931, Toda acted as regent for her son, García, until he reached the age of majority and was crowned in the summer of 934 (Ubieta Arteta "Los reyes pamploneses" 82). There can be little doubt that Toda continued to be the power behind the crown of Navarre throughout the reign of García.

Galindo Aznárez II (893–922) of Aragon had passed away in 922, and the county would be ruled by the crown of Navarre going forward. Farther to the east, the patriarchal Count Ramón I (872–920) of Ribagorça-Pallars had died in 920, and his domains were divided among his four sons (See Chart 4). Pallars was shared by Isarn and Llop, while Ribagorça was divided between Bernat-Unifred and Miró. In addition, Bernat, through his marriage with Tota, the daughter of Galindo Asnárez II, received control over Sobrarbe to the west of Ribagorça (Abadal *Els Comtats* 147).

After the death of Guifré, "the Hairy" (870–897), the patriarch of the far-eastern Pyrenean counties that were to become Catalonia, the counties of Barcelona, Girona, and Osona were inherited by his eldest son, Guifré II (897–911), known as Borrell. After Guifré II, the inheritance passed to the youngest son Sunyer (911–947). The county of Urgell was inherited by Sunifred II (897–950), and Miró II (897–927) became Count of Cerdanya. The county of Besalú continued to be ruled under the regency of Guifré I's brother, Radulf (878–920?) until his death when responsibility for the region was transferred to Miró II (897–927) of Cerdanya. When Miró died in 927, the counties of Cerdanya and Besalú passed to his son Sunifred II (927–965) (See Chart 5).

The Surging Influence of Castile

The region on the eastern end of the Asturian kingdom that was eventually to become the county and then the kingdom of Castile was known originally as Vardulias, a name derived from the pre–Roman tribe of the *varduli* that inhabited this area. In fact, *The Chronicle of Alfonso III* indicates that the name Vardulias was used in the days of Alfonso I, but by the time of Alfonso III, the region was referred to as Castile (Wolf 170). Castile derives its name from the Latin word *castrum* "fortification" used in the diminutive and in the plural, *castella*, which evolved into the Spanish *Castilla*. The area was referred to as the Castles, because during the repopulation process, numerous small fortifications were erected throughout the countryside to shelter against attacks. These small castles could not withstand a siege, but they offered protection against the frequent raids and plundering from the Ebro Valley and from Córdoba. The Arab texts refer to Castile as *al-Qila*, usually mentioned in conjunction with Álava. Both contiguous areas were frequently plundered together during the same Muslim campaign. The areas of Castile and Álava included the area from the Bay of Biscay in the north to the Duero River in the south by the time that Ramiro II (931–961) came to power in 931. At that time, the northern reach of Castile extended from west of present-day Santillana eastward into Álava and today's province of Vizcaya. The western boundary approximated the course of the river Pisuerga, and in the east, it was bounded by La Rioja. A repopulation effort, which was begun under Ordoño I (850–866) and continued under Alfonso III (866–910), was intended to expand the realm of Asturias and to protect its flanks (See Map 7).

The Asturian monarchs began to appoint counts for the areas of Castile and Álava during the second half of the ninth century and put them in charge of repopulation and defense of these regions. A dozen counts figure in to the early history of Castile, and although they usually have a location attached to their title, such as Castile or Álava or even a more specific locality such as Lantarón, the precise reach of their authority is difficult to pinpoint, and the duration of their tenure in various localities is poorly documented. The first count of Castile was Rodrigo (860–873) whose main charge from Ordoño I (850–866) was to repopulate Amaya. From 863 through 867, Rodrigo withstood a barrage of attacks from Córdoba, but thereafter, he enjoyed six years of peace, probably because of the famine during these years. When Rodrigo died, his son, Diego Rodríguez (873–885) assumed control and is credited with founding Ubierna and Burgos.

Chronologically, the counts mentiioned in the earliest documents regarding Castile and Álava are listed here along with the location attached to their authority. 1. Rodrigo (860–873) Castile; 2. Diego (873–885) Castile; 3. Vela Jiménez (882) Álava; 4. Gonzalo Téllez (897) Lantarón, Castile, Cerezo; 5. Munio Núñez (899) Castile; 6. Gonzalo Fernández (899) Burgos, Castile; 7. Munio Vélaz (919) Álava; 8. Fernando Díaz (923) Lantarón; 9. Nuño Fernández (926) Castile; 10. Fernando Ansúrez (929) Castile; 11. Álvaro Herramélliz (929) Lantarón, Álava; 12. Gutier Núñez (931) Burgos.

When Ramiro II (931–950) came to power in 931, he removed from office all the counts who exercised control over these areas including Fernando Ansúrez and Álvaro Herramélliz (See Chart 9). He appointed Fernán González as count of Castile and Álava, which consolidated the authority of the region under a single count and which thereby created a very large subordinate jurisdiction under the kingdom of León. The removal of Fernando Ansúrez and of Álvaro Herramélliz can probably be attributed to their political ties to the previous King Alfonso IV (Martinez Díez *El Condado* 444).

The Emir Abd al-Rahman III (912–961) Becomes Caliph

During the first decade of Abd al-Rahman III's reign, he successfully restored the authority of Córdoba across most of the Muslim Lower March. His organized and methodical campaigns against small localities broadened his sovereignty and enlarged his tax revenue. In 913, he gained submission of Seville and surrounding localities. Yet even with the death of the rebel ibn Hafsun in 917, there remained small pockets of independence in the Lower March that did not recognize Abd al-Rahman III's sovereignty and paid no tribute or taxes to Córdoba. In 919, he made a brief foray into the region around Antequera and vanquished the castles in that region. He then directed his attention to the four sons of ibn Hafsun, Djafar, Sulayman, Abd al-Rahman, and Hafs, who remained the only independent rebels in the Lower March. Only a short siege of Bobastro for one month would suffice to bring Djafar, the eldest son of ibn Hafsun, to accept a truce which included hostages and tribute. In 920 Djafar was assassinated at Bobastro, and the second son, Sulayman hastened to usurp the fortress and authority at Bobastro. Sulayman's resistance was formidable, and it took Abd al-Rahman III several years to neutralize his rebellious activites. It was not until 927 that Abd al-

Rahman III trapped Sulayman near Bobastro. The rebel was decapitated, and his mutilated body was sent to Córdoba where it was crucified at a city gate. The third son, Abd al-Rahman ibn Umar ibn Hafsun was living quietly at Ojén. He decided to ask for mercy and was led to Córdoba where he spent the rest of his days in peace. After the demise of Sulayman, the fourth son of ibn Hafsun, Hafs, claimed his inheritance and installed himself at Bobastro. In the summer of 927, Abd al-Rahman III lay siege to that fortress. After six months, Hafs realized that to continue resistance was useless. He surrendered peacefully on January 17, 928. Since no blood was shed during this encounter, Hafs was permitted to live out his days as a subject of the emir in Córdoba (Lévi-Provençal *Histoire* 2: 16+). After more than a decade had passed since the death of ibn Hafsun, the emir successfully eliminated the final remnants of rebellion and independence throughout the Lower March. It was time for the emir to enjoy his victories.

The moment was propitious for the Emir Abd al-Rahman III to exalt his victories and use them to elevate his status in the *umma*, the Muslim community. In 929, he chose to transform al-Andalus into a caliphate. He elevated his own status from emir to caliph, but in doing so, he represented the Umayyad dynasty as *al-Nasr li-Din Allah*, "Champion of the Religion of God," and successor of the Prophet's legacy as the deputy of God here on earth. This proclamation tendered a direct challenge to the waning Abbasid dynasty in Bagdad and to the more recent proclamations of the Shi'ite Fatimids of North Africa. The elevation of Abd al-Rahman III to caliph was commemorated by the construction of a new palace city, *Medinat al-Zahra*, to the northwest of Córdoba and by the minting of gold dinars which had not been produced since the fall of the Umayyad dynasty in Damascus in 750.

With the complete subjugation of the Lower March and the elevation of al-Andalus as a caliphate, Abd al-Rahman III then directed his attention to the Middle March, more specifically to Badajoz and to Toledo. Badajoz had been ruled as an independent state ever since ibn Marwan al-Jilliqi, "the Galician," rebelled in 875. His descendants were still in charge there. In 929, Abd al-Rahman put Badajoz under siege while he campaigned in the southwest against Beja (Lévi-Provençal *Histoire* 2: 25). In the Algarve district, a small independent ruler peacefully submitted to the caliph of Córdoba and agreed to pay an annual tribute. In the following year, Badajoz yielded to the authority of Córdoba, and the siege was lifted.

The final segment of the Middle March that remained outside of the caliph's command was the intractable city of Toledo. The citizens of Toledo guarded their independence with ferocity and had constructed large grain silos to withstand extended sieges. Nevertheless, Abd al-Rahmen III decided that it was time for Toledo to be added to his realm. He sent word to the administrator of Toledo, Thalaba ibn Muhammad ibn Abd al-Warith, that the city should peacefully submit to his authority. When a positive response was not returned, he led his army to the environs of Toledo in 930 and prepared for an extended siege. The standoff dragged on for two years until the populace became weary and surrendered to Abd al-Rahman III in the summer of 932 (Lévi-Provençal *Histoire* 2: 29). The conquest of the Middle March was now complete, and with the loyalty of the Muslim governor of the Upper March controlling the Ebro Valley from Zaragoza, all Muslim al-Andalus recognized the sovereignty of the caliph in Córdoba (See Map 6).

The Resumption of Conflicts During the Reign of Ramiro II (931–951)

During the reign of Alfonso IV (925–931), the Christians and Muslims had suspended military operations against each other, which permitted Abd al-Rahman III to extend his sphere of influence over al-Andalus and to elevate his stature from emir to caliph in 929. However, after Ramiro II ascended to the crown of León on November 6, 931, he resumed military activity. The new king had put the internal conflicts of his realm behind him and intended to weaken the Muslim positions that threatened the borders of his kingdom. In 933, Ramiro dispatched an assault on Madrid that inflicted serious damage and destroyed the city walls. In retaliation, Abd al-Rahman assembled his forces in 934 and personally led a campaign against Castile, passing through the usual path from Córdoba through Toledo, Guadalajara, Zaragoza and up the Ebro Valley. Before advancing on Navarre and Castile, Abd al-Rahman needed to assure the loyalty of the governor of Zaragoza, Muhammad ibn Hashim, who recently did not respond to the caliph's call to battle. The governor had been making his own deals with the Christians. Abd al-Rahman III conducted a minor campaign in the lower Ebro Valley to demonstrate his superior force to assure the loyalty and obedience of the Muslim vassals of the Upper March. Abd al-Rahman III advanced up the valley and camped at Calahorra with the intention of wreaking devastation on Navarre, Castile and Álava.

Observing the advance of the Muslim army, Queen Toda of Navarre needed to hatch a plan which would save her kingdom from the impending destruction that was soon to arrive in 934, the very year that her son García Sánchez I (931–971) would be released from her regency and rule in his own name (Ubieta Arteta "Los reyes pamploneses" 82). Toda had a message delivered to Abd al-Rahman III at his camp in Calahorra that promised her obedience to the caliph and pleaded for peace based on their common heritage. As his father's half-sister, Toda was indeed Abd al-Rahman's aunt.

In response to Toda's request, Abd al-Rahman III invited her to meet with him in Calahorra where Toda pledged her submission and the vassalage of Navarre. With this pact completed, Abd al-Rahman quickly crossed the lands of Navarre without leaving any destruction and directed his troops to Grañón in Castile where the devastation began. The path of Muslim pillage continued from there through Oña, Alcocero, Burgos, Palenzuela, Escuderos, and Lerma (Martínez Díez *El Condado* 320). Navarre had escaped damage, but the punitive punishment in Castile was appreciable.

The remaining fifteen years of Ramiro II's reign would experience broken truces with Córdoba and successive campaigns that were interrupted only briefly by more broken truces. In 935, the same year that the great Count of Castile, Fernán González, married Toda's daughter Sancha, Ramiro II dispatched an envoy to Córdoba to propose a truce, so that he could have an opportunity to repair the devastated areas of his county. In response, Abd al-Rahman III dispatched a team of negotiators to León, and a pact was reached. Nonetheless, Ramiro II broke the agreement the following year by aiding the Muslim rebel of Zaragoza, Muhammad ibn Hashim al Tujibi. Al-Tujibi's rebellion prompted Abd al-Rahman to wage an eight-month-long campaign in the Ebro Valley, Castile, and Navarre, which served three purposes. The first was to assure the complete

4. The Age of Abd al-Rahman III: 912–961

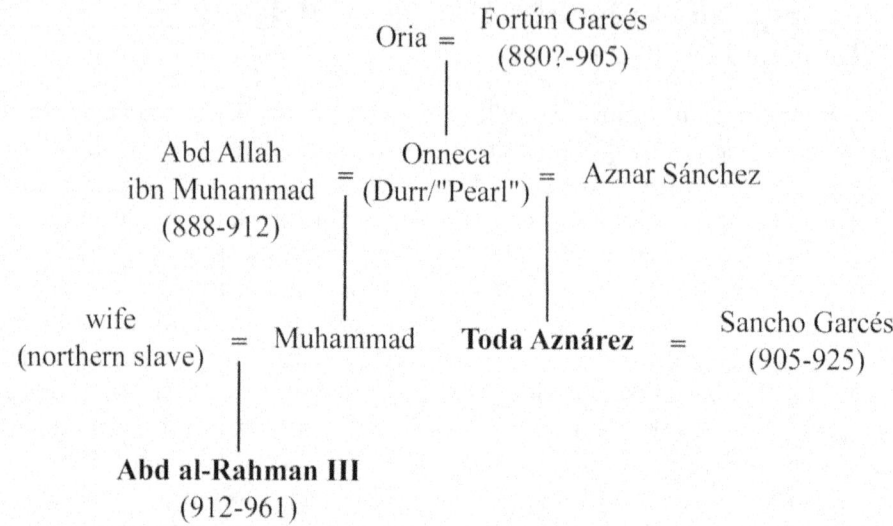

The Mutual Descendance of Abd al-Rahman III and Toda Aznárez.

submission of the rebel of Zaragoza. The second was to punish the people of Castile and more specifically Fernán González. The third was to pillage the lands of Navarre to punish Toda for having re-united her support with Ramiro II of León (Martínez Díez *El Condado* 339).

The caliph took a respite of one year to prepare for a lethal blow focused directly at Ramiro II. He alerted all corners of his realm that he was declaring a holy war against the Christians. He called this great excursion his "campaign of omnipotence." On June 1, 939, the caliph left Córdoba with the largest Muslim army ever assembled in Iberia. After camping beneath the walls of Toledo, Abd al-Rahman deviated from usual campaign paths through Guadalajara and Zaragoza and directed his army to the southern reaches of León, specifically towards Simancas where the river Pisuerga joins the river Duero. Simancas was the greatest Christian stronghold of the middle Duero and protected against attacks from the south. The Muslim army arrived at Simancas on August 6, 939 and faced a large force of Christians from León, Castile, and Navarre. The caliph had summoned Muhammad ibn Hashim al-Tujibi from Zaragoza, who had recently repledged his allegiance. The caliph decided to send him and his men as the first wave to attack the fortress. The Christian cavalry exited the fortress and engaged the Muslims beneath its walls. During the battle, Muhammad was unseated from his horse and was captured by the Christians.

Although not lethal, this turn of events dealt an immediate blow to the Muslim cause. Engagements continued beneath the walls of Simancas for three days when Abd al-Rahman realized that the formidable resistance that he was facing would be an obstacle in overcoming and occupying the castle. He decided to change his objective. He withdrew his army and moved it into other areas where he could inflict damage. In its retreat, the Muslim army swept up the course of the Duero, continuing a swath along the river Aza destroying everything in its path. The decision to follow this course back to Guadalajara resulted in the Muslim army unexpectedly being trapped by the terrain.

The army of Ramiro II had pursued the caliph, and when his army became hemmed in by the geography, Ramiro's men trapped and destroyed a major part of the Muslim forces. The flight of the remaining Muslim contingent was so spontaneous that the caliph abandoned many of his personal items including his cherished Koran. Abd al-Rahman III returned to Córdoba through Guadalajara and Toledo with all haste. This would be the last time that he would personally lead an army against the Christians (Martínez Díez *El Condado* 340+).

In 940, the year following the battle of Simancas, Ramiro II sent a proposal of truce to Córdoba, which the caliph was happy to entertain. Negotiations continued for a year until the terms that included the release of Muhammad al-Tujibi were finalized. The truce took longer to negotiate than it lasted, for in 942 Ramiro instructed Fernán González to lend armed support to García Sánchez (931–971) of Pamplona against the Muslims of the Ebro Valley. The caliph retaliated that same year with raids against Castile and Salmantica (Salamanca) and again in 944 with expeditions from Córdoba into Galicia that amassed booty and burned fortifications. At this juncture, the caliph felt that Toledo was too vulnerable to attacks. He decided to re-build Medinaceli and establish it as the capital of the Middle March. Meanwhile, Ramiro's attention turned to resolving internal power struggles, and the Muslims took advantage of his distraction to claim victories in 947 at Sepúlveda and in 948 in Galicia. Ramiro II launched his final campaign in 950 against the city of Talavera on the Tajo (Martínez Díez *El Condado* 369–96). He fell ill afterwards and died sometime during the first half of 951.

Ordoño III (951–956), Sancho I (956...966), and Ordoño IV (958–959)

When Ramiro II (931–961) died, the accession to the throne of León by his son Ordoño III (951–956) transitioned quickly and easily at first, but then led to a failed attempt at overthrow by Ordoño's half-brother Sancho I (956...966). Ordoño III was Ramiro II's first son with his wife, Andosinda Gutiérrez, and Sancho I was a son from Ramiro's second marriage to Urraca Sánchez, the daughter of Sancho Garcés I (905–925) and Toda of Navarre. García Sánchez (931–971) of Navarre and Count Fernán González of Castile combined their influence to attempt an overthrow of Ordoño II in favor of Sancho. They raised their collective forces against Ordoño III in 954, but their effort to elevate Sancho by force failed after Ordoño III learned of their intent and mustered his own defense of León. The forces of Navarre and Castile returned home to Pamplona and Burgos without lifting a sword. Nothing was accomplished. After the failed overthrow, no other attempt was made against Ordoño during the remainder of his short reign. Ordoño III withstood raids sent by Abd al-Rahman III nearly every year, specifically against some part of León in 951, 952, and 953. In 955, Ordoño III launched a successful counter-offensive against Lisbon. Perhaps that attack motivated Abd al-Rahman III to propose a truce, which both parties accepted in early 956. Ordoño had little time to enjoy his respite, for a few months after the truce was concluded, he died of natural causes in the fall of 956, leaving an infant son who was too young to govern (Martínez Díez *El Condado* 401–6).

Sancho I (956...966) was installed on the throne of León on November 13, 956 without contest. He garnered the support of his grandmother, Toda of Navarre, his uncle García Sánchez I (931–971) of Navarre, and of his brother-in-law, Count Fernán González of Castile. Although the transition was peaceful, the people of León and Galicia were not very accepting of Sancho I. They considered him to be more Navarrese than Leonese, and because of his extreme obesity, he was not capable of mounting a horse nor of leading an army. Shortly after the new year in 958, a unified group of palace soldiers conspired to remove Sancho from authority, and he was obliged to flee to the safety of his grandmother Toda and his uncle García Sánchez I of Navarre. The citizens welcomed Sancho's expulsion, and the powerful magnates of the realm elected Ordoño IV (958–959), the son of Alfonso IV (925–931), as their new king. Sancho I was sheltered away in Pamplona where his grandmother, Toda, was still the real power behind the crown of Navarre. She concluded that Sancho's greatest need was to be cured of his obesity, which impeded normal activity and prevented him from fulfilling his duties as a monarch. She realized that the Muslims of Córdoba were more advanced in medicine, and therefore she solicited the assistance of Abd al-Rahman III to cure her grandson of his obesity. Recognizing an opportunity to draw Navarre into his sphere of influence, the caliph sent his Jewish ambassador and physician, Abu Yusuf Hasday. This schooled diplomat offered a plan of action to enable Sancho to re-gain his Leonese throne. If Hasday's plan succeeded, Sancho, as restored king of León, agreed to relinquish several Christian strongholds along the frontier on the Duero. Further, the Jewish physician proposed that the aging Toda, Sancho I, and King García Sánchez I travel to Córdoba where they would receive a regal welcome. During their visit, Toda solicited a promise of peace between Navarre and Córdoba. Abd al-Rahman pledged armed assistance to return Sancho I to the throne. In 959, the caliph dispatched an expedition accompanied by Sancho which occupied the city of Zamora after a short siege. The Muslim army then advanced towards León, which caused Ordoño IV to vacate the capital for the safety of Asturias, allowing Sancho I to be re-installed (Martínez Díez *El Condado* 407–14). By April 959, Sancho I was back in power.

Following Sancho I's return, peace prevailed across the Christian north. Both Sancho I in León and García Sánchez I in Navarre had pledged submission to Abd al-Rahman III. The now powerless Ordoño IV was alive and well in Asturias, and Count Fernán González in Castile still recognized Ordoño's authority. In 961, however, the political landscape changed. Fernán González withdrew his support for his son-in-law Ordoño IV, no doubt under pressure from the unified front of Córdoba, León, and Pamplona (Martínez Díez *El Condado* 422). But the event that was to disrupt the status quo of the Iberian Peninsula was the death on October 15, 961 of the great Umayyad caliph, Abd al-Rahman III (912–961). The Muslim leader who had elevated his realm from emirate to caliphate during nearly a half-century of grandeur finally yielded to a year-long illness.

CHAPTER 5

From Dominance to Decadence in al-Andalus: 961–1031

The Kingdoms of León and Navarre in Contest with al-Hakam II (961–976)

The death of Abd al-Rahman III in October 961 brought the ascension of his designated successor and favorite son, al-Hakam II (961–976), as the second Umayyad caliph of Córdoba. Contemporary chroniclers are not very flattering of al-Hakam's appearance. Like many Umayyad princes, he favored some of the traits inherited from a maternal lineage tied to Navarrese or European slave origins. He had reddish-blond hair, large black eyes, an aquiline nose, short legs, a stocky body, and overly-long forearms. He projected the appearance of not being in very good health. When he assumed the control of al-Andalus, he had passed the age of forty and was known for his patronage of the arts. He had collected an immense library of scientific and literary works and is credited with the enlargement of the great mosque of Córdoba and with the restoration of the Roman bridge across the Guadalquivir. He carefully observed the rules and laws established by his father as he devoutly practiced his Muslim religion (Lévi-Provençal *Histoire* 2: 167–9).

The news of the caliphal change gave Sancho I (956–958; 959–966) of León the notion that he was released from his agreement with Abd al-Rahman III. Sancho had been re-installed to the throne of León with Abd al-Rahman's military support, and in exchange for this service, Sancho had agreed to surrender ten strongholds along the frontier. Perhaps Sancho I presumed that the new caliph al-Hakam was too much of a pacifist to enforce the agreement with León. At any rate, Sancho I did not delay in launching attacks against Muslim positions on the frontier. Al-Hakam proved Sancho's calculations to be misguided, for early in 962, the caliph transmitted orders to all his regional governors that they were to prepare for a holy war. From 962 through 966, he dispatched his General Ghalib into the fortified regions of León, Castile, and Navarre to inflict serious damage and pillage. Amid this changing political atmosphere, Ordoño IV (958–959), who had been exiled in Asturias since his dethronement by Sancho I, decided in 962 to seek asylum in Burgos with his father-in-law Count Fernán Gonzalez. However, Ordoño's arrival there only threatened relationships between Burgos, León, and Navarre, and a decision was reached that Ordoño IV should seek refuge with al-Hakam II in Córdoba. The caliph willingly accepted this proposal, thinking that Ordoño IV could be of some service in future negotiations. Ordoño IV would later die in obscurity in Córdoba. Meanwhile, al-Hakam II was obliged to re-direct his attention from the Christian north to the coastal regions of al-Andalus when news arrived in June of 966 that the Algarve and Lisbon were under attack from Viking pirates (Martínez Díez *El Condado* 423–34).

The reign of Sancho I reached an abrupt ending in 966. He was returning from a trip to settle unrest in the south of Galicia when he fell ill, apparently from a poisoned fruit given to him by Count Gonzalo Menéndez. He did not survive his attempted return to León and died on route towards the end of November 966. Sancho I left only one very young son, probably not more than five years old. The accession of that son, Ramiro III (966–985), was expedited on December 19, 966. This event marked the first time that the succession of the crown of León would fall to a person of minor age. Ramiro's early years were guided by the tutelage and regency of his aunt Elvira, who was Sancho I's sister and the daughter of Ramiro II (931–951). The passing of Sancho I in 966 precipitated a rapid dissolution of solidarity among leaders in the Christian north. The under-age monarch and female regent could not coalesce the northern leaders into a unified force. Consequently, a decade of peace would ensue when a constant parade of ambassadors was dispatched from the major rulers of the north, each pledging homage to Caliph al-Hakam II. They each bartered for the best truce available for their respective realms. The list of embassies counted by Muslim chroniclers were numerous. Count Borrell II (947–992) of Barcelona (See Chart 5), Sancho Garcés II (971–994) of Navarre, Elvira acting for Ramiro III (966–985), Count Fernán Laínez of Salamanca, Count García Fernández of Castile, Count Fernando Ansúrez of Monzón, and Count Gonzalo of Galicia all negotiated independently and in their own best interest (Lévi-Provençal *Histoire* 2: 181; Martínez Díez *El Condado* 464).

It was during this period of Muslim supremacy and Iberian peace during the last ten years of al-Hakam's reign that two major leaders of the Christian north had died and were succeeded by their sons. The great but aging Count Fernán González of Castile had died in 970 and was replaced by his son, García Fernández (970–995). Also, García Sánchez (931–971) of Navarre had died the following year and was succeeded by his son Sancho Garcés II, "Abarca," (971–994).

The impetuous, new Count of Castile, García Fernández (970–995), was the first to break the Iberian peace. While a delegation from Castile was sent to Córdoba to placate the caliph, García Fernández had attacked a Muslim position north of Medinaceli only three weeks earlier. After news of the attack reached the caliph, the Castilian delegation leaving Córdoba was captured and incarcerated. The Castilian count's return to hostility was no doubt precipitated by a turn in al-Hakam's health. In 974, the caliph suffered a stroke which left him paralyzed and debilitated for the remainder of his administration. Furthermore, General Ghalib, the chief enforcer of the Muslim frontier, had been sent to assist with rebellions in North Africa. It was at this point that García Fernández proceeded to convince his neighbors in León and Navarre to join forces to attack the Muslim fortress of Gormaz. García Fernández and the combined forces lay siege to the castle on the Duero in April 975. Ramiro III, accompanied by his aunt and regent Elvira, led the army from León, and Sancho Garcés II brought a contingent from Navarre. Their victory seemed imminent when General Ghalib, urgently called back from North Africa, arrived in support of the garrison at Gormaz and soundly routed the Christians (Lévi-Provençal *Histoire* 2: 183). The supremacy of Córdoba had been asserted and endured through the reign of al-Hakam II, who died the following year in 976.

The Reign of Hisham II (976...1013) and the Usurpation of al-Mansur

The death of al-Hakam II on October 1, 976 triggered a pivotal moment in the fate of the Umayyad dynasty that affected the future of al-Andalus and ultimately the future of the Iberian Peninsula. In the decades following the death of al-Hakam II, the decision to perpetuate his own blood line by passing the caliphate to his minor son would lead first to a diversion of his son's authority, then to a period of totalitarian dictatorship over the Muslim caliphate, and later to a civil war in al-Andalus.

Hisham II (976...1013) was not the caliph's first born, for in 962, the caliph's Basque wife Subh was at last to bear him a son named Abd al-Rahman who would to die in infancy just three years later. While Abd al-Rahman was still alive, the doting mother had the son endowed at birth with substantial wealth which needed an administrator. For this assignment, she turned to the caliph's *hajib* "prime minister" in charge of all civil administration, al-Mushafi, who found an appropriate candidate in the person of Abu Amir Muhammad ibn Abi Amir al-Mafiri, later known simply as al-Mansur, "The Victorious One," hispanicized as Almanzor. Al-Mansur was the descendent of a well-to-do Yemenese family of the region around Carteya. He had come to Córdoba to be educated in law and letters and subsequently served in functionary positions in the capital. Assigned as administrator of the estate of the caliph's son, al-Mansur gained open access and contact with Subh, and within a few months she recommended him for the important position as exchequer or treasurer for the city of Córdoba. In the initial years before the death of the caliph's first son, Abd al-Rahman, al-Mansur was successful in every administrative position entrusted to him, and he had forged a trusted relationship with both Subh and with al-Mushafi. When the first-born son died at an early age, al-Mansur was appointed as the administrator of the personal estate of the second son Hisham II, the sole surviving son of the caliph and his designated heir. Al-Mansur's influence was expanded into the military when he was appointed as governor general in charge of funding of the caliph's forces that were operating in the Magreb. Subsequently he became inspector general of all the caliph's mercenary forces in the capital. In a matter of months, al-Mansur had become very powerful and very connected at the highest levels of the Umayyad aristocracy (Martínez Díez *El Condado* 483–4).

The death of al-Hakam II in 976 ushered in a state of political crisis in al-Andalus. Al-Hakam had decreed that his only son, Hisham, even though only about eleven years old, should succeed him as caliph. The ascension of Hisham would protect the positions of some in power such as al-Mushafi and al-Mansur, and yet there were other forces who rejected the elevation of a young boy to this position. These latter supported the ascension of al-Hakam's brother al-Mughira as caliph, possibly to protect their own positions or simply to support a more elderly statesman. Al-Mushafi and al-Mansur, along with others in their camp, conspired to kill al-Mughira to eliminate the major obstacle to the accession of Hisham II. This deed was accomplished at the house of al-Mughira by al-Mansur himself, who apparently was the only one among the conspirators with enough *sang-froid* to complete the mission. With al-Mughira eliminated, Hisham became caliph and al-Mushafi continued as prime minister with al-Mansur as assistant prime minister and still in charge of the personal estate of Hisham II.

In 976, the Galician counts launched an attack deep into Muslim territories and advanced toward Córdoba before retreating. This assault unnerved the population of Córdoba and gave Abu Amir al-Mansur an opportunity to add military field experience to his résumé. With a well-equipped army, al-Mansur led a retaliatory raid against Los Baños de Ledesma in 977 that skirted main fortresses but devastated the outlying environs and returned fifty-three days later with some two thousand captives (Martínez Díez *El Condado* 485).

A second military excursion along with the great Muslim General Ghalib added to al-Mansur's military accomplishments, and he was designated as the person responsible for the public order and security of Córdoba. In a desperate attempt to maintain his eroding influence and power, the prime minister al-Mushafi proposed a marriage between General Ghalib's daughter Asma and his own son Othman. This maneuver was averted when al-Mansur persuaded the general to offer his daughter's hand to him. Stripped of power and support, al-Mushafi was superseded by al-Mansur as the prime minister, who in 978 became, with the support of the caliph's mother, the most powerful man in al-Andalus, except for the child Caliph Hisham II, who was already under the control of al-Mansur.

In 980, al-Mansur and his army had set out on a campaign towards Castile and met with General Ghalib at the castle of Atienza. The rendezvous resulted in a heated argument which became known as the "Campaign of Betrayal." Varying versions of the argument between the general and al-Mansur are narrated by Arab historians, but overall, we learn that General Ghalib berated Abu Amir al-Mansur for his treatment of the caliph, who was kept isolated in his own palace under strict watch. The caliph was separated from any ministers or functionaries and stripped of any decision making. The words became heated, and Ghalib drew his knife and wounded al-Mansur, who nevertheless succeeded in re-joining his troops. Al-Mansur led his army to Medinaceli, the headquarters of Ghalib. He looted Ghalib's personal wealth, that was stored at the fortress, and divided it among his own troops (Martínez Díez *El Condado* 493).

The disagreement was resolved unhappily for General Ghalib in the following year 981 when he engaged al-Mansur on the field of battle at Torrevicente to the north of Atienza. Al-Mansur had assembled all available forces, which included Berber contingents and Muslim warriors from the Ebro Valley. General Ghalib had convinced Count García Fernández of Castile and Navarrese militias of Sancho Garcés II (971–994) to join his side in overthrow of al-Mansur. In the heat of the battle of Torrevicente, Ghalib was unseated from his mount and lay dying on the ground. Al-Mansur would not believe reports that Ghalib had died until a hand with his ring and subsequently his head were delivered to him. The Christian forces fled to Castile and beyond, while the remaining

Muslim troops under General Ghalib surrendered to al-Mansur. It was from this battle forward that Abu Amir Muhammad ibn Abi Amir assumed the title of al-Mansur, "The Victorious One." No serious challenge remained to oppose the military power that al-Mansur exercised over Iberia.

By 989, al-Mansur had directed thirty-one successful military campaigns against the Christians, and no one in Iberia ventured to contest his military strength. However, a threat to his autocracy arrived in that year from an unlikely source. Al-Mansur's eldest son, Abd Allah, had become jealous of his younger brother, Abd al-Malik, and believed that his father was giving preferential treatment to him. At age twenty-one, Abd Allah was living in Zaragoza at the residence of the governor of the Upper March, Abd al-Rahman ibn Mutarrif, who fearful of being replaced, was desirous of seeing the demise of al-Mansur. Abd al-Rahman sensed the rancor of Abd Allah and fanned the flames of hatred towards al-Mansur. Enlisting the support of Abd al-Aziz al-Marwani, the governor of Toledo, the three plotted to attack al-Mansur at the first opportunity. However, al-Mansur's information network stretched throughout the caliphate, and news of the plot was relayed to him. Al-Mansur had the governor of Toledo placed under house arrest while he set out to campaign against Castile. The Muslim contingent from the Upper March, led by Abd al-Rahman ibn Mutarrif, was to join him in Guadalajara where al-Mansur staged his own intrigue. Al-Mansur had conscripted a number of the frontier warriors to accuse Abd al-Rahman ibn Mutarrif of misappropriating their pay. Al-Mansur used this pretext to have Abd al-Rahman arrested and sent back to Córdoba where he was later executed. Al-Mansur then summoned his son and attempted to ply him with kindness, but his compassion failed to mollify his son's rancor. While the Muslim army was preparing for battle against the Christians, Abd Allah fled the camp with several of his servants and found refuge in Castile with Count García Fernández. García initially refused al-Mansur's request of rendition but soon relented when al-Mansur seized a large part of Castile by force and took the castle at Osma where he garrisoned Muslim troops. García Fernández was compelled to deliver Abd Allah to a small detachment sent by al-Mansur, and on route to al-Andalus, Abd Allah was executed. His head was delivered to his father, and his remains were buried at the site (Martínez Díez *El Condado* 517–20). Al-Mansur remained in power.

An additional but futile attempt to dislodge the dictator al-Mansur and to establish Hisham II into his rightful position of power as caliph was devised by the caliph's Basque mother Subh in 996. Once a close ally, supporter, and rumored former mistress of al-Mansur, the dowager Subh had become his bitter enemy for having usurped the rightful caliph's power. After all, Hisham II had been installed twenty years earlier and had passed his thirtieth birthday, but he was still relegated to the position of figurehead and puppet. To build a war chest to fund a viable overthrow of al-Mansur, Subh and her co-conspirators were smuggling quantities of gold from the royal treasury out of the alcazar. Once again, al-Mansur's enforcers discovered the plot, and the royal treasury was confiscated. Subh would die before the end of the century, and Hisham II, although nominally the caliph and still alive, would continue to be isolated from the public (Lévi-Provençal *Histoire* 2: 230).

The powerful dictator al-Mansur launched his final holy war in May 1002, targeting San Millán de la Cogolla just to the south of Nájera in La Rioja. San Millán was the most venerated saint of La Rioja. He was the patron saint of Castile, and the site served as a pilgrimage location for the realm of Navarre and for the adjacent county of Castile. The selection of this military objective would cause the destruction of a large part of Castile as the Muslim army journeyed to their target. Moreover, the destruction of the monastery itself would inflict a moral humiliation on Count Sancho García of Castile and García Sánchez II of Navarre. When al-Mansur left Córdoba in May of 1002, he had passed his sixtieth year and had been tortured for years by bouts of severe arthritic gout. He was not deterred by his debilitated condition and spent nearly three months pillaging Castile and La Rioja. At the end of the campaign, he was bound to a litter, too weak to mount a horse and died on August 9, 1002. He was buried in the courtyard of the alcazar at Medinaceli (Martínez Díez *El Condado* 577). Between 977 and 1002, the great Muslim dictator waged fifty-six campaigns of holy war against the Christians, who had become defensive and helpless under his oppression. His two remaining sons survived to perpetuate his legacy for seven more years.

The Christian North Oppressed by the Dictatorship of al-Mansur

In 976 when al-Hakam II (961–976) died and the eleven-year-old Hisham II (976... 1013) was installed as caliph in Córdoba, the Christian north was ruled from León by the fifteen-year-old Ramiro III (966–985), who had ascended to the throne at age five. In Navarre, Sancho Garcés II (971–995) had been king for five years, and Borrell II (947–992) ruled the northeastern region as Count of Barcelona and Urgell. Count García Fernández (970–995) of Castile served the crown of León in principle, but in practice he governed his county in a broadly independent fashion.

To test the resolve and authority of the new child Caliph Hisham II, the Galician counts staged raids into Muslim territories when the caliph ascended in 976. In retaliation for these raids, al-Mansur launched punitive missions at Los Baños de Ledesma and Cuéllar designed to devastate the countryside and take captives. The following year, al-Mansur struck against Pamplona and Barcelona, followed later in 978 by yet another raid against Ledesma (Salamanca). In May 979, the raid of al-Mansur penetrated to the north of Ledesma into the region around Zamora (Martínez Díez *El Condado* 492). The years of 980 and 981 brought a short period of relief to the crown of León as General Ghalib and al-Mansur were settling internal conflicts with each other. After the battle of Torrevicente in 981 (discussed in the previous section), al-Mansur directed yet two more campaigns against the reign of León, the first against Zamora and the second against Trancoso and Viseu (Martínez Díez *El Condado* 501).

The battle of the Three Nations in 982 re-directed al-Mansur's military attention away from the crown of León and more specifically towards Castile, Pamplona, and Girona. It was during this campaign that Sancho Garcés II (971–994) of Navarre, nicknamed "Abarca," gave his daughter Abda as a wife of al-Mansur. This marriage produced Abd al-Rahman ibn Abi Amir, known as Sanchuelo or "Little Sancho," who would briefly rise as dictator of al-Andalus in 1008.

Al-Mansur's annual raids since 977 into the unprotected Galician and Portuguese territories weakened the resolve of the counts of these regions. Neither they nor King Ramiro III (966–985) could negotiate a truce with al-Mansur. The ineffectiveness of their King Ramiro motivated these counts to believe that a change in leadership would herald a new relationship with al-Mansur. Even as Muslim raiders were sacking the castle at Toro and devastating the environs of León, the Galician and Portuguese counts were crowning Vermudo II (982–999) as their new monarch in Santiago de Compostella on October 15, 982 (Martínez Díez *El Condado* 505). Vermudo II was the son of Ordoño III (951–956) and grandson of Ramiro II (931–951). While Ramiro III was also the grandson of Ramiro II, his father was Sancho I (956–958; 959–966), whom the western counts never appreciated. In fact, the Galician Count Gonzalo Menéndez had poisoned Sancho I in 966. This new coronation resulted in a divided kingdom. The Galician magnates were faithful to Vermudo II, and the counts of León and Castile sided with Ramiro III. The following year in 983, Ramiro attempted to get rid of Vermudo by attacking his army near Lugo. The outcome of this conflict was not decisive, and Ramiro returned to León with nothing accomplished. The kingdom remained divided, and the divided monarchy led to separate strategies with respect to al-Mansur. Vermudo II and the Galician magnates opted for submission to the authority of al-Mansur, while Ramiro III decided to resist the Muslim threat.

Scarcely had Ramiro returned from his encounter with Vermudo when the combined armies of Ramiro III, Count García Fernández of Castile, and Sancho Garcés II of Pamplona endured a devastating defeat at the hands of al-Mansur in a battle at Simancas. The greater Muslim army set the Christians into flight, destroyed the city walls, and either killed or captured the population that failed to escape. The Muslim army moved on to Roa to inflict the same outcome. Al-Mansur attacked Salamanca in September of 983 and Segovia in November. He specifically targeted the territories of the Count of Monzón. The Muslim devastation continued at Zamora in the spring of 984 and again at Sepúlveda in June before al-Mansur move on to raid Barcelona. By 985 following the slaughter at Sepúlveda, Ramiro III judged that he could not defend his realm from the wrath of al-Mansur and decided to recognize the dictator's authority. Now both kings north of the Duero were paying tribute, and Galicia and León were, for the first time in years, free from attacks from Córdoba. Al-Mansur then turned his attention to Barcelona, which was completely sacked and devastated. Most of the population was either killed or taken captive for the slave market (Martínez Díez *El Condado* 510).

On June 26, 985, Ramiro III died of natural causes at Destriana just to the south of Astorga. Vermudo II assumed the crown of León without dispute, and his rule was acknowledged by the magnates from Galicia to Castile. As Vermudo II examined the agreement that Ramiro III had concluded with al-Mansur, he had misgivings about the excessive terms, especially the amount of tribute to be paid. Vermudo refused to fulfill the agreement. The rejection of the terms of the submission provoked an immediate response from al-Mansur. In June of 986, he launched his "Campaign of the Cities," which devastated Salamanca, Albade, Tormes, Zamora, and even León itself, which caused the Leonese king to flee to Galicia for a short period. But al-Mansur was not finished that year (986). He departed on a second sortie into the regions around Coimbra and launched yet another in 987 against Coimbra itself. His intention was not to populate the conquered territory with Muslim occupants, but rather to destroy the habitat and annihilate the population, causing the remaining survivors to move back to the north. The devastation of 987 left Coimbra and the surrounding area deserted for seven years afterwards until it was rebuilt and settled by Muslims. The attacks along the Duero continued in 988, and in 989 al-Mansur struck again at Portillo and Toro, causing Vermudo II and Queen Velasquita along with their entourage to seek refuge again for a short time in Galicia to escape the menace.

At that moment, al-Mansur's attention was diverted away from the crown of León by the betrayal of his son Abd Allah ibn al-Mansur who was being harbored in Castile by García Fernández (discussed in the previous section). Consequently, al-Mansur waged punitive campaigns against Osma and Alcubilla in 990, which caused the rendition of Abd Allah and brought years of peace to Castile in 991 and 992. Yet after campaigning against Castile, there was still time remaining at the end of the year to conquer Montemor o Belho between Coimbra and the sea in December of 990.

The ephemeral peace in Castile allowed al-Mansur to wage consecutive attacks of 991 and 992 against Sancho Garcés II, "Abarca," of Pamplona, which prompted a trip to Córdoba by Sancho to ingratiate himself with al-Mansur. The trip gave Sancho the opportunity to visit with his daughter, Abda, whom he had given in marriage to al-Mansur some fifteen years earlier, and to meet his grandson, Abd al-Rahman ibn al-Mansur, given the nickname *Sanchuelo* or "Little Sancho" by his grandfather when they first met.

Vermudo II of León repudiated his first wife, Velasquita, in the fall of 991 and married Elvira García, the daughter of Count García Fernández, in an attempt to bring León and Castile politically closer. But the ephemeral peace in Castile dissolved in 993 and 994 when al-Mansur and García Fernández engaged in combat along the Duero at San Esteban de Gormaz and Clunia. When finished with Castile in the spring of 994, al-Mansur had enough time later in the year to attack Astorga and León (Martínez Díez *El Condado* 531–3).

At this juncture, the Christian North lost two of its leaders. In late 994, Sancho Garcés II (971–994) of Navarre died of natural causes and was succeeded by his son García Sánchez (995–1004) nicknamed "the Trembler." On May 18, 995, Count García Fernández of Castile lay wounded on the field of battle between Langa and Alcozar. He was taken prisoner by the Muslims and died on July 29, 995, two months later. García was the only son of Count Fernán González (931–970) and produced only one son himself, Sancho García (995–1017), who succeeded him as the uncontested Count of Castile (See Chart 9). No additional Muslim attacks were directed against Sancho and Castile until the year 1000.

Later in 995, al-Mansur resumed his attacks against the crown of León and continued for two more years. He destroyed the regions between Zamora and Castile namely the region controlled by the counts of the Banu Gómez family. That same year, he directed his troops against Aguiar to the southeast of Oporto, killing or capturing thousands. The following year, he attacked Astorga, and Vermudo II was obliged to promise a tribute to stop the bleeding. But in 997, Vermudo broke his promise, possibly thinking that, because al-Mansur was sending troops to North Africa, there would be no retaliation. Vermudo was mistaken. His broken promise brought al-Mansur's most memorable defeat of the Christians with the destruction of Santiago de Compostela. This campaign not only wrought havoc on the most far reaches of northeast Galicia, pillaging farms and villages, burning crops, and carrying off captives, but this attack represented a serious affront to western Christianity itself. Al-Mansur left Córdoba at the head of his army on July 3, 997 by way of Coria and Viseu. He was joined by the forces of several local counts who were obligated to provide military assistance because of previous peace agreements. He advanced to Oporto to collect additional foot soldiers and provisions supplied by a Muslim fleet. With this large contingent, he continued across the Duero and Miño rivers in the direction of Vigo, pillaging as he went. On August 10, the Muslim army arrived at Compostela, only to find the city entirely evacuated except for a solitary monk, who remained to protect the tomb of the saint. The monk was not harmed, and the tomb was respected. The church, however, was razed. The bells and the doors of the shrine were transported back to Córdoba to be used for additions to the main mosque. The shrine established by Alfonso I (739–757), enlarged into a basilica by Alfonso III (886–910) and visited by thousands of pilgrims from all over western Europe, was reduced to just the tomb of Saint James (Lévi-Provençal *Histoire* 2: 246–250).

The year 998 marked the only year in more than twenty that al-Mansur did not send an expedition against the Christian North, but the following year he resumed attacks against the count of Pallars and against the king of Pamplona. In September of 999, Vermudo II died at Villabuena del Bierzo while returning from Galicia. He was succeeded by his young son just five years old, Alfonso V (999–1028), who was to be educated under the tutelage of the queen mother, Elvira García, the sister of Count Sancho García of Castile.

On June 21 of the year 1000, al-Mansur left Córdoba, directing his army towards Castile with the idea of inflicting his usual damage. We are not informed of the reasons for this break in the truce with the Count of Castile, but apparently, the Christians were well informed of al-Mansur's intended route. The allied Christians from Astorga to Pamplona, led by Count Sancho García, had camped in wait on a high promontory identified as Cervera situated to the south of Burgos about half way between Aranda de Duero and the Sierras de Demanda. The united forces of the Christians surprised the Muslim army and inflicted a reported 700 casualties during an initial encounter. However, the ensuing battle of Cervera resulted in a rout of the Christian troops but perhaps prevented the complete sacking of Castile and even Burgos itself. Muslim chroniclers allude to al-Mansur's debilitated condition which at the time caused him to be transferred to a litter. Al-Mansur's army carried the day, but he was not satisfied with their performance, and he berated them for cowardice upon his return to Córdoba (Martínez Díez *El Condado* 563–72).

The last campaign of al-Mansur against the Christians, the fifty-sixth in his long list of strikes, left Córdoba on May 21, 1002, destined for San Millán de la Cogolla in La Rioja just a few miles south of Nájera, where the Muslims succeeded in sacking and burning the monastery there. San Millán was the most venerated saint of La Rioja as well as the patron saint of Castile. The location attracted numerous pilgrims from throughout northern Iberia. Al-Mansur's raid was successful, but the incessant campaigns of holy war against the Christians had taken a toll on his body. He was now more than sixty years old, and his health had been deteriorating for years. At the end of the campaign, he had to be transported to Medinaceli on a litter and died on August 9, 1002. He was buried in the courtyard of the fort at Medinaceli. The Christian North, experiencing yet another leadership deficit with the ascension of the under-aged King Alfonso V (999–1028), continued to experience the same hostilities from al-Mansur's son, Abd al-Malik al-Muzaffar from 1002 to 1008.

Abd al-Malik al-Muzaffar (1002–1008) Maintains Muslim Dominance Over the North

Abd al-Malik al-Muzaffar was returning from the campaign with his father, al-Mansur, against San Millan when the aging dictator died at Medinaceli in 1002. During his final days, the moribund father took the opportunity to instruct his son on how to proceed after his death. At twenty-eight years old, Abd al-Malik had gained experience as a general in North Africa and had served in several posts in the administration of the government of al-Andalus. He was a seasoned veteran of his father's politics.

Leaving his brother Abd al-Rahman in Medinaceli to tend to the funeral arrangements of their father, Abd al-Malik immediately directed al-Mansur's powerful army to Córdoba where he would have Caliph Hisham II confirm his appointment as *hajib* "prime minister." Hisham II hastened to sign a decree which conferred all al-Mansur's powers to Abd al-Malik. The decree was promptly read at the main mosque of Córdoba, and the transfer of power was swift and complete. Abd al-Malik would maintain the same iron-fisted grip on the governance of al-Andalus and the same domination of the Christian North as did his father.

The news of the death of al-Mansur in the Christian North provoked divergent reactions among the northern leaders. On one hand, only Count Ramón Borrell (992–1017) of Barcelona, Girona, and Osona broke the truce with Córdoba when he launched a victorious surprise attack on Muslim positions just to the north of Lérida in February 1003. On the other hand, Count Sancho García (995–1017) of Castile recognized that the military power of Córdoba had not been diminished. He preferred to negotiate a truce with the Muslim General Wadih in Medinaceli. Count Menendo González, the Gallego-Portuguese count acting as tutor of the young Leonese King Alfonso V (999–1028), was menaced by the reinforcements sent from Córdoba into the region around Coimbra. Consequently, he followed the path of Count Sancho García and agreed to a continued truce. The agreement furthermore obliged these counties to lend military support to Córdoba whenever asked. In response to Count Ramón Borrell's attack, Abd al-Malik immediately mobilized his regular and voluntary troops from Córdoba and notified his general in the Middle March to convene in Medinaceli at the end of June 1003. The army included Christian contingents sent by Sancho García and Menendo González as required by their recent truces. Abd al-Malik attacked and destroyed the castle at Monmagastre between the rivers Segre and Noguera just to the north of Artesa de Segre. From there, the campaign advanced towards Barcelona, where the countryside was destroyed during the month of August, and its inhabitants were either captured or killed. The serious punishment endured by Count Borrell prompted him to send ambassadors to Córdoba to negotiate a peace agreement that would at least give him time to repair the effects of this disaster. Moreover, he might salvage the release of some of the captives transported to Córdoba (Martínez Díez *El Condado* 587–92). He would need considerable time to recover from the devastation.

Count Menendo González had been acting as co-regent for the young King Alfonso V (999–1028), along with the king's mother Elvira García, ever since the death of the young king's father. However, Count Sancho García of Castile, Elvira García's brother, believed that after five years it was time for the regency of the Leonese crown to be transferred to his control. Since Count González was unwilling to relinquish his regency, the exchange between the two counts became adversarial. To avoid all out military combat, both parties agreed to have Córdoba mediate the dispute. The Christian judge, Asbag ibn Abd Allah ibn Nabil, that Abd al-Malik sent to decide the case, found in favor of Count González. Disgusted with the ruling, Sancho García broke the truce with Córdoba, which provoked Abd al-Malik to raid Sancho's domains. Abd al-Malik's campaign of 1004 against Castile was enough to persuade Sancho to return his county to a state of submission to Córdoba.

The counts of Saldaña, the Banu Gómez, had also broken with Córdoba. These counts were nominally under the control of Menendo González, since he was the acting regent for Alfonso V and therefore represented the crown of León. Abd al-Malik viewed the infraction by the counts of Saldaña as a violation of the truce by León, and he was provoked to attack the Christian regions of Zamora and its environs in the spring of 1005. The broken truce with León gave Abd al-Malik an excuse to expand his raids into other parts of the Christian North in 1006. Advancing from Zaragoza in that year, Abd al-Malik raided the valleys of Sobrarbe and Ribagorza, which were then under the reign of a very young Sancho Garcés III (1004–1035) of Navarre. Sancho was probably about fourteen years old at the time and still under the regency of his Leonese mother Jimena and his Castilian grandmother, Urraca Fernández (See Chart 7).

Count Sancho García of Castile had escaped the devastation of Abd al-Malik in 1005 and 1006 but was to feel the full force of his power in 1007 when Muslim armies overran the fortress of Clunia. Abd al-Malik's expedition defeated the combined forces of Castile, León, and Pamplona. After this campaign, the dictator assumed the epithet of al-Muzaffar, "The Victorious" (Martínez Díez *El Condado* 594–8).

The final campaign in the spring of 1008 against Sancho García was abruptly terminated when al-Muzaffar fell violently ill on route to Medinaceli. He returned to Córdoba to regain his health. Barely recovered by October 19, 1008, he belligerently attempted to lead his army against the Christians by horseback but was soon transferred to a litter. Al-Muzaffar succumbed to his illness on October 20, 2008, at the age of thirty-six, and his body was returned to the palace of al-Zahira outside of Córdoba. The nominal but powerless Caliph Hisham II was still alive and sequestered in the alcazar of Córdoba.

The Short Dictatorship of Sanchuelo (1008–1009)

Abd al-Rahman ibn Abi Amir, Sanchuelo, "Little Sancho," assumed power in October 1008 at the age of twenty-five from his older brother, Abd al-Malik al-Muzaffar. The body of his deceased brother, Abd al-Malik, had been transported to the al-Zahira palace, and Sanchuelo spent the following night there in anticipation of assuming his brother's position of power. With all the necessary dignitaries in attendance, Sanchuelo laid out the plan of his succession and took possession of all his brother's duties and powers without resistance. The absolute power in Córdoba continued in the hands of the al-Mansur family (Martínez Díez *El Condado* 604).

Sanchuelo was just as ambitious as his father and his brother, but his life was not as disciplined. He was given to excesses such as wine and festivity. Upon his ascendance, he had Hisham II bestow on him the honorific title of al-Mamun, "the faithful one by the grace of God." To bolster his vanity further, he had Hisham II decree that upon the latter's death, he would become the new caliph. This act of arrogance shocked and repulsed the population of Córdoba, for they believed that the legitimate path to the title of caliph derived from its Umayyad heritage. Certainly, Sanchuelo did not inherit this lineage. The numerous living descendants of the Umayyad family were vexed, and the horror of this development percolated through the Arab aristocracy.

The death of Abd al-Malik restored the resolve of the Christians and spawned a disdain for the new *hajib* "prime minister" of Córdoba. To respond to the new challenge presented from the Christians, Sanchuelo immediately assembled his standing army and left Córdoba in January 1009 in the harshest cold and rain of winter, which merited the name of "The Campaign of the Mud." The army's absence left Córdoba unprotected from the dissident population that was still enraged by the notion of Sanchuelo rising to the position of caliph. Allowing sufficient time for Sanchuelo to distance the army from Córdoba, the revolutionaries began their attack on February 15, 1009. They assaulted the royal palace and deposed the titular Caliph Hisham II. They replaced him with the great grandson of Abd al-Rahman III, Muhammad ibn Hisham ibn Abd al-Jabbar ibn Abd al-Rahman III. The life of Hisham II was spared once he officially agreed to abdicate. The following day the palace of Sanchuelo, al-Zahira, was overrun. The palace guards surrendered without resistance, and everything of value in the palace was stripped. The columns and stones were razed and salvaged for future construction. The site was left bare. At the mosque on February 25, the new caliph, Muhammad II ibn Hisham, presided over Friday prayers and took the honorific title of al-Mahdi, the spiritual and temporal leader who will restore religion and justice. From the pulpit, he declared a holy war against Abd al-Rahman, Sanchuelo. The revolutionary triumph of the Umayyads of Córdoba over the Amirids, that is al-Mansur, Abd al-Malik, and Sanchuelo, was fully complete, and yet Sanchuelo was still in charge of a formidable army. The news of the uprising reached Sanchuelo at Toledo, but instead of marching immediately back to Córdoba, he proceeded on to Calatrava, where he took several days to rest and to demand an oath of loyalty from all his troops, who instantly began to desert. On the return to Córdoba, the Berber regulars had dropped out and had already reached the city where they were well received. On February 28, two days from the city, Sanchuelo was accompanied only by his closest companions (Martínez Díez *El Condado* 606–8).

The new caliph, Muhammad II, understood Sanchuelo's debilitated position and sent a chancellor accompanied by two hundred horsemen to meet and apprehend the new dictator and would-be caliph. Riding back to Córdoba with hands restrained,

Sanchuelo asked for a moment of repose with his hands free. While in the act of freeing him, the chancellor drew his weapon and beheaded Sanchuelo (Martínez Díez *El Condado* 608). Thus ended the more than thirty-year Amirid usurpation of the Umayyad caliphate by al-Mansur, al-Muzaffar, and Sanchuelo. What's more, this event marked the beginning of the end of the Umayyad dynasty which would stumble and finally fall in a little more than twenty years hence in 1031.

Sancho García Aligns with Caliph Sulayman Against Caliph Muhammad II: 1009

In February 1009, the people of Córdoba rose up against Abd al-Rahman, "Sanchuelo," and proclaimed as caliph Muhammad II ibn Hisham ibn Abd al-Jabbar ibn Abd al-Rahman III, the great grandson of the first caliph, who took the honorific title of al-Mahdi. However, neither the Slavic servants and administrators in Córdoba nor the Berber military were satisfied with this development. Even the Umayyad aristocracy was divided on the selection of the new caliph. The unrest gave rise to a new pretender, a grandson of Abd al-Rahman III, Hisham ibn Sulayman ibn Abd al-Rahman III, who with the support of the Berber military, proclaimed himself caliph.

Nevertheless, Muhammad II had enough support and power to have the usurper Hisham beheaded on June 23, 1009. Further, he declared a bounty on the heads of all the Berber military. Those who succeeded in escaping fled northward to connect with a nephew of the recently-beheaded, self-proclaimed Caliph Hisham. The nephew, named Sulayman ibn al-Hakam ibn Sulayman ibn Abd al-Rahman, claimed the inheritance of his slain uncle and was recognized as the new caliph by the Berbers (Martínez Díez *El Condado* 611–2). Al-Andalus was now in full civil war. Muhammad II al-Mahdi ruled in Córdoba, and Sulayman, in exile, claimed to be caliph and was supported by the Berber soldiers. Sulayman and the Berbers proceeded to Medinaceli where the Slavic General Wadih defended the Muslim Middle March with his standing garrison of combatants. Sulayman attempted to persuade Wadih of the legitimacy of his cause, but the general held firm in his allegiance to Caliph Muhammad II in Córdoba.

Looking for support elsewhere, Sulayman and the Berbers sent ambassadors to Count Sancho García of Castile, only to find that ambassadors from Muhammad II al-Mahdi and Wadih were already negotiating with Sancho for his support. Each side offered Sancho the rendition of strategic positions along the frontier in exchange for Sancho's armed assistance. The count of Castile had a decision to make. Which army would have a better chance of victory and which would ultimately deliver the promised fortresses along the Duero? Would Sulayman and the Berbers be victorious? Or would the experienced General Wadih carry the day for Muhammad II? In the final analysis, Sancho decided to align himself with the Berbers and proceeded to supply them with food and other provisions. The Berbers now had the Christians of Castile in their camp and assumed that Wadih would now come over to their side. On the contrary, the general not only declined to unite with them, but he attacked the joint Berber and Castilian forces near Alcalá de Henares with the full force of the Middle March. Nonetheless, the Berbers and the Castilians proved to be more powerful, and Wadih was compelled to retreat to the safety of Córdoba where he intended to reinforce the army of Muhammad II al-Mahdi (Martínez Díez *El Condado* 613).

As al-Mahdi was reinforcing the defenses of Córdoba, news reached the city on November 3 that the Berbers and Castilians were only one day's journey away. The army of Córdoba had superior numbers but inferior military experience. Their military force consisted of ill-equipped townsmen, workers, and minstrels. This ragtag bunch left their fortified positions to engage the attackers on November 5, 1009. The experienced Berber fighters spent little effort in quickly slaughtering many of their opponents who did not first turn and flee. At the sight of this incompetence, General Wadih gathered his remaining forces and retreated to his seat of power in Medinaceli.

The citizenry of Córdoba went out to greet the victors and to welcome their new Caliph Sulayman, while Muhammad II al-Madhi fled to the safety of the caliphal alcazar palace. He later escaped to the safety of Toledo. The formerly deposed Hisham II escaped death again by renouncing his authority, this time in favor of Sulayman, who was proclaimed caliph in the great mosque on November 8, 1009.

Sancho García asked Sulayman to uphold his part of the bargain and surrender the agreed upon fortresses along the frontier, but the new caliph indicated that this was impossible, because these strongholds were in the Middle March that was still controlled by General Wadih. He added that he would do so when conditions changed. Sancho García and his men left Córdoba on November 14, enriched only by the booty obtained from the battle nine days earlier (Martínez Díez *El Condado* 614).

The provinces of al-Andalus generally did not accept the ascension of Sulayman as caliph, and the population of Córdoba was dead set against the Berbers. In the meantime, Muhammad II al-Mahdi found refuge and acceptance in Toledo, and all the Middle March including General Wadih, who regained Medinaceli, accepted him as the rightful caliph. General Wadih devised a plan to regain Córdoba with the help of the Christians. He began bargaining with the counts of Catalonia, Count Ramón Borrell II (992–1017) of Barcelona and his brother, Count Ermengol I (992–1010) of Urgell. He offered them considerable pay along with all the booty they could collect if they would join forces with the troops of the Middle March against Sulayman and the Berbers. With the bargain sealed, the army of Muhammad II al-Mahdi and Wadih, accompanied by the Catalan contingent, set out from Toledo on route to Córdoba, while the Berber army of Sulayman did not delay in advancing toward them from the capital. In May 1010, the two armies engaged to the north of Córdoba just southwest of Ovejo. The Berbers seemed to be carrying the day and inflicted severe casualties on the Catalan fighters. Count Ermengol of Urgell was among the fallen. Suddenly the rear guard of the Berbers broke in retreat, causing the Berber forces to scatter and take flight. The following day Muhammad II al-Mahdi and General Wadih entered triumphantly into Córdoba where al-Madhi was re-established as caliph. But the fight with the Berbers was not finished. The mixed army of Muslims and Catalans left Córdoba in pursuit of the Berbers who were headed in the direction of Algeciras, from where they would have access to North Africa if need be. Al-Mahdi's army engaged the Berbers near Ronda on June 21, 1010, and were completely routed by them. Remnants of al-Mahdi's army limped back to Córdoba. When the Christians were asked to return to re-engage the Berbers, they refused and opted to return to their own lands. Under these conditions, al-Mahdi decided to prepare the capital for a siege (Lévi-Provençal *Histoire* 2: 311–4).

General Wadih began to have second thoughts about his support for Muhammad II. He had waged war directly in concert with the caliph, and he came to see the faults and lack of character in him. The general began a plot to replace him. On July 23, 1010, Muhammad II was assassinated by some of his own slave officers, and Hisham II was restored as caliph of al-Andalus. However, the return of Caliph Hisham II from 1010 to 1013 did not have the effect that Wadih had expected. The Berbers and Sulayman refused to recognize the authority of Hisham II, and the Muslim populace viewed the restored caliph as just a puppet in the hands of the new prime minister General Wadih.

On November 4, 1010, the Berbers seized the caliphal palace of al-Zahra just outside of Córdoba and used it as a base camp to lay siege to the capital. While waiting for the citizens of Córdoba to surrender to starvation, some of the Berber forces were dispatched to other regions such as Jaén, Elvira, Málaga, and Algeciras to force them to submit to the sovereignty of Sulayman. The siege was in full force when an envoy of ambassadors from Sancho García of Castile presented themselves before the Berber camp requesting the rendition of several fortresses as had been agreed in exchange for their previous military assistance against Muhammad II. The Berbers directed the delegation to Hisham II and to his new prime minister, since the Middle March still recognized the authority of General Wadih. Castile promised not to assail Muslim position along the frontier and received in exchange the fortifications at San Esteban, Clunia, Osma and Gormaz (Lévi-Provençal *Histoire* 2: 316).

The Berbers were disposed to negotiation with Córdoba, but the Cordobans were more inclined to resistance and combat until they realized that they would have to fund an armed conflict. The treasury of Córdoba was empty and there were mouths to feed. Wadih was compelled to sell part of the remaining library of al-Hakam II to keep his administration solvent. Winter passed with the capital under siege, and the spring brought devastating floods from the Guadalquivir followed by a summer of plague that decimated a portion of the population. General Wadih was considering flight from the city back to the North when his intentions were discovered by the commander of the local police who, with several functionaries, confronted him and finished by beheading him on October 16, 1011. The city's first intentions of stubborn resistance were followed by failed negotiations. Córdoba finally offered to surrender with a plea for mercy on May 9, 1013. The offer was accepted with stiff penalties attached. Two days later Sulayman once again entered Córdoba as caliph. The city was to pay dearly. The citizens at all levels were treated badly. Many were beaten or killed including many intellectuals such as the celebrated biographer Ibn al-Faradi (Lévi-Provençal *Histoire* 2: 317–20).

Varying accounts obscure the fate of Hisham II. He was obliged to abdicate a second time in favor of Sulayman and was severely rebuked for his previous behavior. One account reveals that Sulayman simply had him killed. Another informs us that he slipped away and ended his days in obscurity. Whichever account is accurate, his abdication this time as he neared his fiftieth birthday terminated his role in the history of al-Andalus. His reputation will be remembered as dull and unfulfilled (Lévi-Provençal *Histoire* 2: 320).

Sulayman was indebted to the Berbers who re-established his reign in 1013, and he set about to reinforce Berber loyalty by granting their leaders fiefdoms throughout the Lower March wherever his authority was recognized. Similarly, he confirmed Mundhir ibn Yahya as the governor of the Upper March. Across the Strait of Gibraltar in North Africa, the authority of Córdoba had been reduced to the coastal regions from Ceuta to Tangiers to Arcila. The governorships of these regions were divided between two Berber generals, Ali ibn Hammud and his older brother al-Kasim. Following his appointment as governor, Ali ibn Hammud began circulating the rumor that Hisham II had designated him to be caliph upon the latter's death. Under the pretext of liberating Hisham II, whom no one believed to be still alive, Ali undertook measures to overthrow Sulayman. The Berber leaders who had installed Sulayman were now more interested in overseeing their fiefdoms than in rallying to his defense. Deprived of the Berber military, Ali defeated Sulayman's militia and captured him on July 1, 1016. The victorious Ali demanded to see Hisham II dead or alive. A cadaver was unearthed, identified, and then reburied in an act to establish the usurpation of the throne of the caliph. Sulayman was convicted of murder and killed along with his brother and father to assure that there would be no claim of inheritance. Ali ibn Hammud had the necessary legal proclamations drawn, and he adopted the same honorific title as Abd al-Rahman III, al-Nasir, as he was elevated to the position of caliph. This event marked the first time since the rise of Abd al-Rahman I in 756 that the throne of Córdoba was not filled by an Umayyad descendant. The reaction of the capital was subdued and stoic. The previous three-year reign of Sulayman resulted in a political fragmentation of al-Andalus which would never re-gain the unified political power and glory that it knew under Abd al-Rahman III (Lévi-Provençal *Histoire* 2: 320–5).

From Ali ibn Hammud (1016–1018) to Hisham III (1027–1031)

During the first few months of his administration, Ali ibn Hammud (1016–1018) attempted to ingratiate himself with the populace of Córdoba by curtailing the severe abuses of the Berber militia stationed in the city. The slightest infraction of the militia, which previously passed with impunity, was now dealt with extreme punishment. Nevertheless, the city's population was not endeared to Ali and criticized his every move. He then decided to depart from his initial policy, and the Berber militia returned to their abuses of arrests, confiscation of property, and seizure of arms. In March 1018, Ali ibn Hammud was attacked in his own palace by three household slaves and left for dead in a pool of blood.

About the same time that Ali ibn Hammud was to meet his demise, two conspirators, Khairan, a slave soldier from Almería and a Tujibid Arab named Mundhir ibn Yahya from Zaragoza were plotting to unseat Ali from his position of power in Córdoba. The two conspirators had found a great grandson of Abd al-Rahman III, named Abd al-Rahman ibn Muhammad ibn Abd al-Malik, who had left the capital and was living quietly in Valencia. The conspirators had convinced him to claim the caliphate of Córdoba as his rightful inheritance and had assembled a small army of faithful to support their cause. Their plot was short circuited by the assassination of Ali ibn Hammud in

March 1018. But not to be deterred, a month later they proclaimed Abd al-Rahman IV as caliph on April 29, 1018. The pretenders decided to defer their attack on Córdoba and first lay siege to Granada where the Berber General Zawi ibn Ziri had taken control. A furious counter attack from Granada sent all three leaders, the slave soldier Khairan, Mundhir the Tujibid, and Abd al-Rahman IV, into flight in different directions. Abd al-Rahman IV was caught at the river Guadix and assassinated on the spot. This Umayyad prince, whose name figures into the roles of the caliphs of Córdoba, never actually regained that city to rule over it. The plot to establish Abd al-Rahman IV died with him at the Guadix River.

Meanwhile, the Berber partisans of assassinated Ali ibn Hammud travelled to the residence of the deceased's brother, al-Kasim, in Seville to notify him of his brother's demise. Six days later, al-Kasim arrived in Córdoba to claim his inheritance and declare himself caliph with the honorific title of Mamun (Lévi-Provençal *Histoire* 2: 327–8). Al-Kasim (1018–1021) ruled for three years with a measure of moderation. His political skill earned a degree of popularity. He abolished the requirement that well-to-do citizens were required to pay the costs of maintaining a soldier. Then, to insulate himself against the Berber militia, he recruited a corps of Sudanese mercenaries for his own personal guard. It was inevitable that such a liberal regime would be vulnerable. Al-Kasim had two disgruntled nephews who were envious that he succeeded their father instead of one of them. Some of the disgruntled Berbers of Córdoba approached Yahya, al-Kasim's nephew in Málaga, and offered him their support in overthrowing al-Kasim. With his Berber partisans, Yahya marched on Córdoba. His uncle al-Kasim had no taste for battle and abandoned the city on August 5, 1021, for a refuge in Seville. Eight days later, Yahya (1021–1023) was installed in the alcazar palace and was proclaimed caliph by the Berbers. However, it took only a year and a half for Yahya's arrogance and vanity to alienate his partisans. Feeling threaten by them, Yahya slipped away to the safety of Málaga, and al-Kasim (1023 restored) had no difficulty returning to the capital to seize power once more on February 6, 1023. However, the citizens of Córdoba had had enough and mounted a full insurrection the following August. Al-Kasim's efforts to mollify the rioting were futile, and his flight to Seville was not welcomed this time. He was compelled to seek refuge in Jerez where his nephew, Yahya discovered him, took him to Málaga for incarceration, and finally had him assassinated (Lévi-Provençal *Histoire* 2: 331–3).

With the departure of al-Kasim, the people of Córdoba were resolved to select an Umayyad prince as their new caliph. To this end, the populace held a large convocation in the main mosque on December 2, 1023, with the intention of selecting one of three descendants of Abd al-Rahman III. The ostentatious entrance of Abd al-Rahman ibn Hisham ibn Abd al-Jabbar dressed in full warrior regalia won the hearts of the anxious crowd, and they immediately proclaimed a new caliph Abd al-Rahman V (1023–1024) with the honorific title of al-Mustazhir. However, his reign failed to re-establish the glory days of his ancestors. He was a very young man who surrounded himself with competent functionaries. However, since the Treasury was empty, he had no money for their salaries, and he resorted to bilking the lower and middle classes for revenue. Because he had no soldiers, he hired a Berber squadron. His actions unleashed a riotous attack on the alcazar palace where the mob apprehended a hiding Abd al-Rahman V.

The throng of rioters also found another Umayyad prince in the palace who was equally fearful of losing his life. On January 17, 1024, the very day of the riot, the crowd proclaimed Muhammad III ibn Abd al-Rahman ibn Ubaid Allah (1024–1025) as their new caliph with the honorific title of al-Mustakfi, without even asking whether he wanted the honor. Muhammad's first official act was to lead his predecessor Abd al-Rahman V to his execution. The reign of Abd al-Rahman V had endured only forty-seven days. Muhammad III (1024–1025) was in his fifties. He was weak, lazy, and surrounded himself with low-quality people. He managed to muddle along as the people of Córdoba ridiculed him. When a rumor circulated that Yahya ibn Ali ibn Hammud was planning to depose him, he decided to sneak out of Córdoba disguised as a singer on May 26, 1025. A few weeks later, he was killed in Uclés (Cuenca) by one the courtiers who accompanied him on his flight (Lévi-Provençal *Histoire* 2: 333–5).

By 1025, the city of Córdoba was no longer a prize. The Treasury was empty, and the city had no functioning governance, no military or police to enforce order, and its regional influence over any territory outside its city walls had been lost. There was little reason for anyone to claim its leadership. Yahya ibn Ali ibn Hammud after leaving as the caliph of Cordoba (1021–1023) had claimed authority of regions of the Lower March from Jerez to Málaga and was therefore not eager to re-gain the caliphate of that city. In fact, it was more than six months after the departure of Muhammad III that he decided to show up in Córdoba on November 9, 1025. His sojourn was short, and he was satisfied to leave a governor in charge by the name of Abu Jafar Ahmad ibn Musa with a few hundred Berber soldiers to support his authority. Yahya returned to Málaga in March of the following year (Lévi-Provençal *Histoire* 2: 337).

The Slavic slaves Khairan of Almeria and Mujahid of Denia, who in principle were the independent rulers of these regions, were not satisfied that Córdoba had been once again taken over by the house of Hammud. They assembled a small army and removed the installation left by Yahya on June 19, 1026. But neither of them had the intention of exerting their own authority thereby leaving the city in anarchy when they returned to their own realms.

With Córdoba relegated to a leaderless condition, the upper class of the city finally felt some responsibility to deal with its problems. They were looking for an Umayyad surrogate who could be accepted by the citizens without revolt. More importantly, they needed an Umayyad leader who could be recognized as the rightful heir to the august city and serve as a national champion against the Berbers, who they thought were the source of disunity since the fall of the Amirids. It was in June 1027 that Hisham III ibn Muhammad ibn Abd al-Malik, the older brother of Abd al-Rahman IV, was proclaimed caliph with the honorific title of al-Mu'tadd. However, Hisham III did not immediately leave his residence in Alpuente. On the contrary, he remained there for two years until a smooth acceptance by the city reassured him of his safety. He finally arrived at the capital on December 18, 1029, to reside at his ancestral alcazar palace. Hisham III quickly proved himself to be only a mediocre administrator. He selected Hakam ibn Sa'id as his prime minister, who favored indulging the excesses of his master rather than managing the state. Sa'id's failure to manage the state gave rise to another pretender, another Umayyad named Umayya ibn Abd al-Rahman ibn Hisham ibn Sulayman, who gained some local support with a promise to dethrone the caliph and get rid of the prime minister. Umayya recruited some disgruntled local militia men who ambushed and killed the prime minister Hakam ibn Sa'id on November 30, 1031. This murder unleashed an uprising of the people against the incompetence of the caliph. The rhetorical pleas of the city's aristocracy thwarted an attack on the alcazar itself, but in the end the nobility decided that Hisham III al-Mu'tadd would have to leave the city. Hisham III, the last in a long line of Umayyad princes, died in obscurity in the Upper March five years later (Lévi-Provençal *Histoire* 2: 337–41).

At last the city no longer had illusions about the rightful place of the Umayyad lineage in the governance of Córdoba and al-Andalus. The notion of the temporal and religious right of leadership of the Umayyad family in al-Andalus had been laid to rest by its citizens.

The Christian North Benefits from the Civil War in al-Andalus

The death of the dictator Abd al-Malik al-Muzaffar of Córdoba and the ascendance of his younger brother Abd al-Rahman Sanchuelo in 1008 led to a civil war in al-Andalus from which the Christian North benefited in various ways. The North gained relief from the incessant attacks on their territories that brought economic devastation and a depletion of their human capital. They were also relieved of paying *parias* or tribute to Córdoba. This change in condition brought renewed hope to their plight and ushered in a re-alignment in leadership and governance over the next quarter century from 1009 through the 1030's.

In Navarre, a young Sancho Garcés III (1004–1035) had probably undergone a short period of regency but by 1009 was reigning on his own behalf. Over the next two and one-half decades he would become the dominant figure among northern royalty and would deserve the sobriquet of *el Mayor*, "the Great." He began to figure in the politics of the entire North.

To the east of Navarre, the Countess Toda had inherited the counties of Sobrarbe and Ribagorça after her brother Count Isarn died fighting the Muslims at Monzón in 1003. The countess suffered a terrible setback in 1006 during the campaign of Abd al-Malik al-Muzaffar, the son of al-Mansur, when he assailed Roda, captured its bishop, and garrisoned the southern part of Ribagorça. Around 1010 the beleaguered and aging Toda, unable to mount a defense and administration of her own, decided to marry the neighboring Count Sunyers of Pallars, to assist in the defense of Ribagorça and to expel the Muslim garrisons in the south of her county. Count Sunyers with three adult sons of his own saw an opportunity to repudiate Countess Toda and to confiscate parts of her county. He aligned these lands under his own authority. In response to the actions of her faithless husband, Toda sought outside assistance in defending her county. She appealed to her nephew, Count Sancho García (995–1017) of Castile, the son of her sister Ava of Ribagorça and Count García Fernández (970–95). Sancho García dispatched an army along with two figures who would change the balance of power in defense of Toda. The first, Guillermo Isárnez, was the illegitimate son of the fallen Count Isarn of Ribagorça. He had been trained as a military leader under Count Sancho

García. Sancho also sent his sister, Countess Mayor, who as the daughter of Ava of Ribagorça, was Toda's niece. Countess Mayor would receive the legitimate inheritance of Ribagorça through the abdication of her aunt Toda. She would then marry Count Ramón of Pallars, the son of Sunyers and thereby re-unite the confiscated portions of Ribagorça under the new alliance. The militarily-trained Guillermo Isárnez, with the Castilian military forces under his control, defeated the Muslim garrisons in the south of the county and re-gained control over the entire county, which brought several years of peace. In 1016, however, Guillermo Isárnez was killed by a revolutionary contingent from the Val d'Arán, who claimed the legitimacy of their ancestry and the illegitimacy of Guillermo's. The death of Guillermo resulted in a short period of instability until after the untimely death of Sancho García of Castile in 1017. Sancho's death provoked the intervention of Sancho Garcés III of Navarre, whose wife, also named Mayor, was the niece of Doña Mayor the new countess of Ribagorça. Through this heritage, Sancho Garcés III asserted his sovereignty, and by 1025 all Sobrarbe and Ribagorça fell under the reign of the king of Navarre (Lacarra *Historia* 98–9; Martínez Díez *El Condado* 621–3). The destiny of Ribagorça would henceforth be tied to the history of Navarre and after Sancho's death in 1035 to the history of Aragon. Conversely, Pallars and the Val d'Arán would align with their eastern neighbor, the county of Urgell, and ultimately would become part of Catalonia (See Chart 4).

In the eastern Pyrenees, Ramon Borrell (992–1017) controlled the counties of Barcelona, Girona and Osona, while his brother, Count Ermengol I (992–1010) reigned in Urgell. Ermengol died in 1010 fighting beside General Wadih against Sulayman and the Berbers, and he was succeeded by his son Ermengol II (1010–1038). In 1016, Sancho García of Castile met with Ramon Borrell in Zaragoza, invited by al-Mundir the Muslim *taifa* king of that city, to arrange a future marriage between Sancho's daughter Sancha and Ramon's son Berenguer Ramon. Ramon Borrell died on February 25, 1017, and Berenguer Ramon I (1017–35), who succeeded him, accepted Sancho Garcés III of Navarre as his overlord. Sancha and Berenguer appear as a married couple by 1021, and she bore two sons, the future Ramon Berenguer I (1035–1076) and Prince Sancho, before she died around 1026 or 1027 (Martínez Díez *El Condado* 646–7; Bonnassie 554; See Chart 5).

In 1009, Count Sancho García (995–1017) of Castile was in his prime and by 1011 had recovered numerous castles and fortresses along and beyond the Duero as payment for assisting Sulayman and the Berbers defeat the General Wadih in the Muslim civil war. After Sancho García recouped the territories lost to al-Andalus during the previous three decades, he no longer intervened in the Muslim conflict. In 1016, Sancho García of Castile and Sancho Garcés III of Navarre agreed to define the boundaries between their respective realms to avoid potential disputes. When Sancho García (995–1017) died prematurely on February 5, 1017, the title of Count of Castile fell to his only son, García Sánchez (1017–1029) who was born in November 1009 and thus was only a little more than seven years old (See Chart 9). García's aunt Urraca, the abbess of Covarrubias, served as his regent, but Sancho Garcés III assumed the role of protector of Castile during this period, since he was married to García's sister Mayor (Collins *Caliphs* 254). Little else can be stated with certainty about the administration of Castile during the minority of García Sánchez (Martinez Díez *El Condado* 660–72). With Sancho, "the

Great," in Pamplona as a protector of the county of Castile and with his sister Urraca, the stepmother of Vermudo III in León, a marriage was proposed between García Sánchez (1017–1029), Count of Castile, and Sancha, the sister of Vermudo III and daughter of King Alfonso V (999–1028) of León. When the young García arrived in León to celebrate his betrothal, he was assassinated in 1028 or 1029 by two disgruntled exiles from Castile, Rodrigo and Íñigo Vela (Martinez Díez *El Condado* 672–80). With the assassination of the Count of Castile, Sancho Garcés III of Navarre peacefully took control of the administration of Castile, Álava, and Monzón (de Campos), since his wife, Mayor, was the sister of the assassinated count and second in line to inherit Castile. Further, the lands around Monzón to the west of the river Pisuerga had been under the rule of the counts of Castile for nearly fifty years (Martínez Díez *El Condado* 690). But rather than give himself the title of Count of Castile, Sancho had conferred this title on his youngest son Fernando (the future Fernando I of León-Castile), who was only about fifteen years old in July of 1029. We can assume that Count Fernando's early role was only titular and that any real governance occurred only with the supervision of his father.

In León, the leadership remained in a debilitated and controversial state. Born in 994, Alfonso V (999–1028) assumed the crown of León in 999 under the regency of his mother Elvira García, the sister of Sancho García (995–1017) of Castile. Menendo González the powerful Galician magnate who had served Alfonso's regency in concert with Elvira was mysteriously assassinated on October 6, 1008. Alfonso V would not be acting on his own until about 1013. About this same time, he married Elvira Menéndez, the daughter of the late Count Menendo González, which produced the future King Vermudo III (1028–1037) and a daughter Sancha who would later marry Count Fernando Sánchez of Castile, the future King Fernando I of León and Castile. Elvira Menéndez died in 1022, and the following year, Alfonso V married Urraca, the sister of King Sancho Garcés III (1004–1035) of Navarre (See Chart 8).

While the county of Castile regained many strongholds along the Duero in 1011 as payment for assisting Sulayman and the Berber Muslims defeat General Wadih in 1009, the territories lost in the southern parts of Galicia were not rendered under this agreement. Therefore, Alfonso V of León was pressed to recoup the lost lands as best he could. During his siege of Muslim-occupied Viseu, Alfonso V met an untimely death on August 7, 1028, from a well-placed arrow shot. This event plunged the crown of León into a state of disorder with the young inheritor of the crown, Vermudo III (1028–1037), just eleven years old and under the tutorage of his stepmother Urraca during his minority. The death of Alfonso and the premature reign of Vermudo III gave rise to minor rebellions and usurpations in the regions around Órbigo, Astorga, and Lugo which prompted the subsequent intervention of the queen dowager's brother Sancho Garcés III of Navarre. By March 1030, Sancho extended his sphere of control westward across the borders of Castile and Monzón into lands of the river Cea. The documents of the day testify that Sancho expanded his influence into León itself by 1032 where he played a stabilizing role in the reign of Vermudo III. During the period from 1030 to 1035, however, no military conflicts are recorded. Sancho remained in León long enough to see the marriage of Vermudo III to his daughter Jimena. Vermudo was eighteen years old in 1035, and Jimena was in her twenties. Less documented is the marriage of Fernando Sánchez, the future Fernando I, with Vermudo III's sister Sancha in 1032 or else 1035–6 (Martínez Díez *El Condado* 705). With the political condition of the kingdom of León stabilized, Sancho Garcés III, *el Mayor*, returned to Navarre early in 1035 where he died of natural causes on October 18, 1035. His realm would be divided among his three legitimate sons and one illegitimate son according to his wishes.

CHAPTER 6

The Vacillation of Power Between Christian and Muslim Realms: 1035–1109

The Disintegration of the Caliphate into *Taifa* States

The last caliph Hisham III (1027–1031) left Córdoba in 1031 at a time when the city no longer exercised authority over any part of al-Andalus, had no territorial pretensions, and was not even capable of stable self-governance. Following the death of Abd al-Rahman ibn Abi Amir, Sanchuelo, the ensuing civil war for control of the caliphate lead to its very disintegration. During the twenty-two years from Sanchuelo's death in 1009 to Hisham III's departure in 1031, more than thirty regional rulers had established control throughout the decimated caliphate. Historians have dubbed these rulers as party kings or *taifa* rulers from the Arabic word for party or group. The *taifa* kingdoms started to detach themselves from Córdoba as soon as the civil strife began, and by 1031 all areas of al-Andalus were under the control of a *taifa* king, who no longer recognized the authority of Córdoba.

In many cases, it was the local governor who declared independence from Córdoba and assumed control over the locality. Such was the case in the Upper March which for many decades was ruled from Zaragoza by the Banu Tujibi. This Muslim dynasty was first given the governance of Zaragoza in 886 after they had successfully ruled in Calatayud from 872. Al-Mundir I ibn Yahya al-Tujibi officially broke away from Córdoba in 1018 and ruled an independent Zaragoza until 1039 when he was deposed by a rival family, the Banu Hud, under the leadership of Sulayman ibn Hud al-Mustain I. The situation at Toledo was similar in that the local governor, Abu Bakr ibn Ya'ish ibn Muhammad, continued to rule independently after the fragmentation of the caliphate. In other cases, a council composed of the local aristocracy assumed administration. In Córdoba after 1031, for example, a council of aristocratic leaders assumed authority in place of a single *hajib* or leader. Subsequently control fell to the prestigious, powerful Banu Jahwar family, until Córdoba was eventually subsumed into the *taifa* of Seville in 1070. Seville was also governed by a council until submitting to the reign of the Banu Abbad, the most prestigious dynasty of the period. This dynasty succeeded in engulfing smaller *taifa* states such as Ronda (1059), Carmona (1067), Arcos (1068) and subsequently controlled Huelva, Niebla, Silves, Santa María del Algarve, Mértola, and even later Denia (Palenzuela 280). Their celebrated rulers were Abbad al-Mutadid (1042–1069) and his son Muhammad al-Mutamid (1069–1091).

Notably in the southern regions of al-Andalus, the recently arrived Berber warriors established their own *taifas*. They took early control of Arcos, Carmona, Granada, Morón, Ronda, Málaga and Algeciras. The principal Berber chieftain, Zawi ibn Ziri, the Berber general who sided with Caliph Sulayman ibn al-Hakam (1009–1010), seized control of the region around Elvira early during the civil wars and then founded Granada which was deemed to be a more defensible location than Elvira (Menéndez Pidal *La España* 74; Wasserstein 105). The brothers Ali and al-Qasim ibn Hammud of the Banu Hammud family became the *taifa* rulers of the coastal regions of Málaga and Algeciras and even seized control of Córdoba for a few years during the final years of the caliphate. In Badajoz, a former Slavic slave, Sabur, gained authority over that city until being displaced in 1022 by a family of Berber origin headed by Abd Allah ibn al-Aftas.

Members of the Saqaliba, or Slavic servant class, were successful in establishing their own *taifas*. Within weeks of the beginning of the civil strife in 1009, the Slavs, who had been trained as administrators in key governmental positions, withdrew from Córdoba and moved to the east coast carving out positions of authority for themselves. In due course, they became independent rulers over their petty kingdoms, notably in Tortosa, Valencia, Játiva, Denia, Orihuela, and Almería. One of the Saqaliba generals, Mujahid, began usurping territory in the east of the peninsula around Tortosa in 1010. By 1013, he controlled much of the eastern lands south of the Ebro down to and including Denia. The Saqaliba Khayran vied for control of Almería and then gained control of Murcia. Mujahid's dynasty survived until about 1075, and Khayran's lasted only until 1038. The *taifa* kingdom in Valencia was created under the authority of Abd al-Aziz ibn Abd al-Rahman, one of the two sons of Sanchuelo (Collins *Caliphs* 201).

In 1031, the fragmentation of the caliphate had reached its peak, and thereafter the more powerful realms began engulfing the smaller, weaker ones. A continual power struggle between them brought turmoil and mistrust and allowed the crown of León to impose its will on them. In the decades before the civil war, Córdoba exacted tribute from the northern Christians, but now the roles were reversed. The weakened condition of the *taifa* states that had been reduced to numerous small entities permitted the Christian monarchs to levy *parias* or tribute on them. Al-Andalus remained under the fragmented control of the *taifa* rulers until the arrival of the Almoravid Muslims in 1086 who later brought virtually all the *taifa* kingdoms under their own authority.

The Four Sons of Sancho Garcés III—García, Ramiro, Gonzalo, and Fernando: 1035–1065

Sancho Garcés III (1004–1035) returned from León to his own realm of Navarre early in 1035 and unexpectedly died there on October 28, 1035. The royal territories of his kingdom were divided among his four sons as specified in his will.

At the time of Sancho's death, his eldest legal son and primogenital heir, García Sánchez III (1035–1054), was on a pilgrimage to Rome. García inherited the territorial

The Four Sons of Sancho Garcés III—García, Ramiro, Gonzalo, and Fernando

seat of the realm, and it was Sancho's intention that the inheritors of the other pieces of the kingdom of Navarre would recognize García's authority. The area willed to García included not only Navarre proper around Pamplona but also the areas of Álava, Viscaya and half of the province of Santander and *castella vetula*, Old Castile, the northern part of the province of Burgos just to the north of the city. King Sancho Garcés III had retained these domains under his control when his brother-in-law, Count García Sánchez of Castile (1017–1029), was assassinated. Sancho considered these territories to be the legal inheritance of his wife Mayor (Muniadonna).

The eldest son Ramiro, born before the marriage of Sancho and Mayor, could not be endowed as Sancho's main benefactor due to his illegitimate status. Nevertheless, he inherited the valley of Aragon with the title of *regulus* that can be understood as viceroy or *reyezuelo* in Spanish. Ramiro I (1035–1063) of Aragon used the title of king, but under the terms of his inheritance he was to recognize the sovereignty of García as king of Navarre and to forego any expansion of his own authority. Ramiro's share was apparently granted during the lifetime of his father Sancho. Sancho's son Gonzalo (1035–1045) inherited the regions of Sobrarbe and Ribagorça also during the lifetime of Sancho, although no documents of that time have survived. This sub-kingdom was also to remain subject to the sovereignty of the realm of Navarre. Sancho's son Count Fernando Sánchez, the future Fernando I of León, continued as count of Castile, the position that he had assumed in June 1029 after the assassination of his uncle Count García Sánchez (1017–1029). As count of Castile, Fernando Sánchez reported to the king of León. However, the area of that county under Fernando's control was considerably reduced, because a large northern section had been subsumed by Sancho Garcés after the assassination of Count García Sánchez and remained under the control of kingdom Navarre (Martínez Díez *El Condado* 707+). The partitioning of Castile would be contested but not resolved until few decades later (See Chart 7).

In 1037 King Vermudo III of León campaigned against Fernando Sánchez and García Sánchez at the battle of Tamarón about fifteen kilometers to the west of Burgos. The motivation for Vermudo's aggression has been seen by some historians as an attempt to recover the lands lost to Sancho Garcés III around the river Cea (Palenzuela 258). Historian Gonzalo Martínez Díez, however, believes that this territory just to the east of León was yielded to Vermudo at the time that Sancho retired from León and when an agreement was reached for Vermudo to marry Sancho's daughter Jimena. According to Martínez Díez, the real quarrel was not between León and Castile but rather between the two monarchs Vermudo III of León and García Sánchez III of Navarre over Álava and northern Castile which were formerly part of kingdom of León and which had been willed to García Sánchez of Navarre. The brothers Fernando and García engaged and killed Vermudo III during this encounter which has been traditionally dated as September 4, 1037, but more recently placed at August 30, 1037 (Martínez Díez *El Condado* 724–9). At any rate, the death of Vermudo paved the way for Fernando to ascend to the crown of León, since his wife Sancha, the daughter of Alfonso V of León and sister of Vermudo III, was in line to inherit that kingdom. In the early months of 1038, Fernando traveled in Galicia with the objective of garnering recognition from the magnates of these far-western realms. On June 22, 1038, the Count of Castile, Fernando Sánchez, the son of Sancho Garcés III, "the Great," King of Navarrre, and grandson of Count Sancho García of Castile, was crowned king of León at the church of Santa Maria and became Fernando I (1037–1065) of León. Fernando would no longer use the title of Count of Castile, which ended the line of counts of Castile that had descended from Count Fernán González (931–970) (See Chart 9). The contest over Álava and northern Castile however, would be resolved only in later decades.

During the reign of García Sánchez III (1035–1054), the seat of the realm of Navarre was transferred from Pamplona to Nájera in the upper Ebro Valley upstream from Zaragoza. In 1045, García took advantage of the weakness in the kingdom of Zaragoza during the final days of al-Mustain, the *taifa* ruler of Zaragoza, by seizing the stronghold of Calahorra about 80 miles northwest of Zaragoza. Al-Mustain died the following year and divided his kingdom among his sons. Al-Muqtadir (1046–1082) inherited Zaragoza, but the other sons, Yusuf in Lérida, Lubb in Huesca, Mundir in Tudela, and Muhammad in Calatayud, were all given shares. By 1050, al-Muqtadir had overcome all his brothers except Yusuf, who continued to govern Lérida until 1081.

In 1054 García Sánchez III of Navarre and Fernando I of León found themselves at odds over the inheritance of the regions of Álava, Vizcaya and Guipúzcoa. García had alienated the local nobility of these regions by favoring the nobility of Pamplona with respect to land holdings. Additionally, the religious dioceses had been moved from Old Castile to Nájera. Moreover, the areas in the northern reaches of Castile had originally and rightfully belonged to the kingdom of León and therefore to Fernando I. A decisive battle ensued on September 1, 1054, at Atapuerca, some 20 kilometers to the northwest of Burgos where García Sánchez III would lose his life. Immediately following the battle, García's son was recognized by Fernando I as King Sancho Garcés IV (1054–1076) of Navarre. In the years that followed the battle of Atapuerca, Fernando I recovered a major part of the county of Castile that was inherited by his brother García (Martínez Díez *El Condado* 737). Over the next ten years, the domain of León-Castile was advanced to La Rioja northeast of Burgos. The remaining portion of the disputed territory in Old Castile would be settled later. The reaction of Ramiro I of Aragon was to agree to a mutual non-aggression pact with Sancho IV. In return for his future support and friendship, Sancho IV yielded to his uncle Ramiro the castle at Sigüenza (Reilly *The Contest* 36).

Just a few years after his coronation, Fernando I began a prolonged effort from 1040 to 1060 to colonize and re-populate the localities along the Duero River. The *taifa* states were weakened and no longer in a condition to contest this movement. Towns such as Zamora, Toro, Portillo, Peñafiel, Gumiel de Izán, and Arando de Duero all benefited from growing populations during this period (Palenzuela 260). With domestic matters under control, Fernando I turned his attention to expanding his influence over the Muslim *taifas* when perhaps as early as 1055 he attacked the territories around Badajoz. The following year, Fernando's armies took the town of Lamego south of the Duero which brought the entire stretch of the Duero basin under his control. On July 25, 1058, Fernando campaigned even farther to the south and succeeded where Alfonso V had failed in 1028 by taking Viseu, some 70 kilometers to the northeast of Coimbra. Fernando was now in control of the middle stretch of the Mondego River basin. In 1062, he launched raids against Badajoz, Toledo and Zaragoza. These cities became his vassals and began to pay tribute. In 1063, Fernando sent troops to raid the territories around Seville. The *taifa* ruler of Seville al-Mutadid (1042–1069) also began to pay tribute rather than suffer attacks. During this campaign, the relics of Santa Justa were demanded as payment of tribute, but since they were not located, the remains of Saint Isidore were rendered instead and transported back to the royal church in León (Palenzuela 260).

Fernando's half-brother Ramiro I of Aragon had expansionary designs of his own, but his inheritance of 1035 was bordered on all sides by other kingdoms. He had fewer options than Fernando. Ramiro was bordered to the west by the kingdom of Navarre, to the south by the *taifa* state of Zaragoza, to the east by his brother Gonzalo in Sobrarbe and Ribagorça, and beyond Ribagorça by Pallars and Urgell. Nevertheless, Ramiro did not delay in seizing the locations of Loarre and Samitier in Sobrarbe that rightfully belonged to his brother Gonzalo. On June 26, 1045, Gonzalo died under unknown circumstances, and Ramiro gained control of Sobrarbe and Ribagorça with the consent of the local magnates (Martínez Díez *El Condado* 713).

In 1063, Ramiro attempted to expand his territory southward against al-Muqtadir of Zaragoza by taking the city of Graus. Al-Muqtadir called on Fernando I to bring military assistance as expected of the annual tributes that he was paying the king of León. Fernando I dispatched his son, the future Sancho II, who had been living in Castile since about 1060. With the aid of Sancho and the Castilians under the leadership of Rodrigo Díaz de Vivar, *el Cid*, the Muslims of Zaragoza defeated and killed Ramiro I at Graus on May 8, 1063. Ramiro's marriage to Ermesinda, the daughter of the Count of Foix-Bigorre, produced his first-born son Sancho (1063–1074) in 1043, who inherited Aragon. Ramiro also left four younger children, García, Sancha, Teresa and Urraca (See Chart 11).

Fernando I had been successful from 1055 to 1058 in extending his control as far south as Viseu in the middle Mondego River basin, but seizure of the lower Mondego basin proved to be much more difficult. A six-month siege of Coimbra, following a grueling battle, resulted in success when that hilltop fortress finally fell on July 25, 1064. Coimbra is the southernmost city that Fernando would conquer. In that same year, an international force consisting of French, Norman, and Italian combatants along with Aragonese and a contingent from Urgell led by Count Ermengol III (1038–1065) assembled near Graus to attack the Muslim *taifas* of the Ebro Valley. They targeted and lay siege to the city of Barbastro which surrendered in August 1064. Most of the Muslim population of the city was either massacred or enslaved. The city was put under the sovereignty of King Sancho Ramírez of Aragón, the son of Ramiro. Count Ermengol III was left in charge of the garrison for the city's defense. However, al-Muqtadir of Zaragoza coveted control of Barbastro. The city was formerly ruled by al-Muqtadir's brother Yusuf, the *taifa* king of Lérida, who left the location undefended and vulnerable to the Christian attack of 1064. In April of the following year, al-Muqtadir attacked Barbastro with an additional force of 500 horsemen sent by al-Mutadid of Seville. Count Ermengol III and the entire garrison of French and Spanish defenders were slaughtered. By attacking the Christians and by aligning himself with Seville, al-Muqtadir had broken his pact with León-Castile. Fernando I immediately campaigned against al-Muqtadir to asssure that the payment of tributes would continue. He then continued his offensive southward toward Valencia. The final campaign of Fernando I in 1065 in the east of the peninsula and more specifically against Valencia was cut short when he fell ill and decided to return to León (Menéndez Pidal *La España* 147–52). Fernando I died in León on December 27, 1065.

The Sons of Fernando I—Sancho, Alfonso, and García: 1065–1073

Two years before his death, Fernando I (1035–1065) had established his last will and testament that provided an inheritance for all three of his sons. The eldest son Sancho II (1065–1072) received the kingdom of Castile. The second son Alfonso VI (1065–1109), considered to be Fernando's favorite, inherited the seat of León and the territories as far east as the Pisuerga River and as far as the Bierzo in the west. The youngest son García II (1065–1072) became ruler of Galicia with a kingdom that bordered the ocean from the Bay of Biscay down to the Mondego River in present-day Portugal.

It is notable that Sancho as the eldest did not inherit the kingdom of León. Moreover, his kingdom of Castile was constrained from expansion by León to the west, Navarre and Aragon to the east, and by the Muslims to the south. In 1066, the year after his inheritance, Sancho II of Castile decided to attack the castle of Pazuengos in La Rioja ruled by Sancho IV of Navarre. This act of aggression prompted Sancho IV to solicit the assistance of their mutual cousin Sancho Ramirez, the monarch of Aragon. The combined superior forces of Navarre and Aragon put the Castilians to flight back across the Ebro River near Viana. Sancho II of Castile, Sancho IV of Navarre, and Sancho Ramirez of Aragon were all the grandsons of Sancho Garcés III, *el Mayor*. The tradition of the time called for naming the eldest son after his grandfather, and therefore all three monarchs were named Sancho. The conflict between these three grandsons, which dates from the late summer of 1067, has been dubbed as "The War of the Three Sanchos," but the late documentation of this event has cast some doubt on its very occurrence (Palenzuela 269).

Sancha, the wife of Fernando I, died on November 7, 1067. She may have been a calming force in keeping potential hostilities among her three sons at bay. Early in the following year, Alfonso VI attended the general court of Sancho II which re-established the bishopric of Oca (Villafranca de Montes de Oca) on March 18, 1068. At this meeting, the two brothers still appear to be on friendly terms. However, on July 19 of the same year, the brothers Sancho and Alfonso skirmished on the border between their respective realms near the banks of the Pisuerga River. This encounter, known as the battle of Llantada, ended harmlessly with the flight of Alfonso back to León. Some historians propose that the intent of Llantada was to establish a winner take all contest in which the victor would claim the realm of the loser (Palenzuela 270). Poorly documented, this aspect of the skirmish may be more legend than history.

In 1068, Alfonso led a campaign to the *taifa* of Badajoz with the purpose of assuring continued payment of *parias*. These payments rightfully belonged to Garcia of Galicia, who turned out to be a weak, inept ruler, disfavored by the clergy, nobility and commoners alike. The administration of Galicia needed a change. A meeting was convened on March 26, 1071, at the court of Sancho II in Burgos attended by Sancho's Queen Alberta and all of Sancho's siblings except García II of Galicia (See Chart 10). The obvious objective of this conclave, witnessed by the clergy and prelates of Castile, was to decide on how to deal with the incompetence of King García II. In the final analysis, Alfonso agreed to allow Sancho to cross the kingdom of León into Galicia to wrest control of Garcia's kingdom. In return for safe passage through the kingdom of León, Alfonso would receive half of the spoils of Galicia. Sancho's advancing army caught up with García at Santarém where he was taken prisoner and transported back to Burgos for incarceration. Shortly afterwards, he escaped and sought refuge in the *taifa* of Seville, which owed him tribute by virtue of the inheritance from his father Fernando I. Sancho was now in charge of Galicia which was to be shared with Alfonso.

Sancho's realms of Castile and Galicia were separated by the kingdom of León and created an untenable situation. In January of 1072, Alfonso VI and Sancho II engaged at the battle of Golpejera near the shores of the Carrión River not far from the village of Carrión de los Condes. Later narratives of the battle recount the bitterness of the fighting, the great loss of life, and the valor and triumph of Sancho's *alférez* "military leader," Rodrigo Díaz de Vivar, *el Cid*. Sancho's resounding victory resulted in his seizure of the kingdom of León, and on January 12, 1072, he had himself crowned in the capital (Palenzuela 270–2).

Alfonso VI had been captured during the battle of Golpejera and was sent to Burgos for imprisonment while Sancho II decided his brother's fate. Sancho could have Alfonso blinded, thus rendering him incapable of governance, but he soon opted to have Alfonso exiled, a decision which may have been influenced by Alfonso's loyal sister Urraca and possibly by the intervention of some of the clergy who also favored Alfonso (Palenzuela 272). The former Leonese king was subsequently permitted to seek refuge and exile in Toledo at the court of the *taifa* King al-Mamun (1037–1074), who was paying tribute to Alfonso VI and to his father Fernando I before him.

In the meantime, Princess Urraca was domiciled at the castle of Zamora, a palace conferred to her by her brother Alfonso VI during his reign. The castle at Zamora was strategically placed on the Duero River and had been instrumental in Fernando I's colonizing efforts. It offered convenient access between León in the north and the Muslim territories to the south. A congregation of dissident nobility, who were favorable to Urraca and Alfonso and opposed to Sancho, had assembled at Zamora. They constituted a menace to Sancho's authority. Consequently, Sancho decided to put the castle at Zamora under siege with Rodrigo Díaz de Vivar, *el Cid*, as his *alférez* in charge of operations. After a few months, the siege was on the verge of bringing the castle to submission when a lone deserter headed for Sancho's camp and miraculously proceeded to gain his audience. The intruder succeeded in assassinating Sancho with a lance blow to the breast. Even more incredibly, the assassin escaped to the walls of Zamora castle without being apprehended. The death of Sancho II on October 7, 1072, at the age of thirty-four and without any descendants opened the door to Alfonso's re-emergence. Alfonso VI immediately left Toledo for Zamora and was recognized by the nobles and prelates of León, Asturias, and Galicia as their king.

The fate of García II was not as fortunate. He was duped into believing that he could re-gain his former kingdom of Galicia, but when he presented himself in León on February 13, 1073, he was promptly taken prisoner and sent to a castle in Asturias for incarceration where he died in chains in March of 1090. Alfonso VI had prevailed over his two brothers Sancho II of Castile and García II of Galicia and thus had reunited the realm of their father Fernando I, *el Magno*, in the royal city of León (Palenzuela 272–275).

The Early Success of Alfonso VI: 1073–1085

From the death of Fernando I in 1065 until 1073, Alfonso VI was pressed to establish the supremacy of crown of León over the three realms left in his father Fernando's will. The assassination of Sancho II of Castile in 1072 and the imprisonment of García II of Galicia in 1073 enabled Alfonso VI, with the recognition of the nobility and the clergy throughout his provinces, to unify once again the realm of his father from Galicia to Castile.

Alfonso began in 1074 to extend his authority by claiming tribute payments from Toledo and Zaragoza. This same year, he successfully campaigned against the *taifa* king of Granada Abd Allah and received *parias* from him as well. It is interesting to note that the *taifa* king of Toledo, al-Mamun, was not only paying tribute to Alfonso, but he had sent troops to assist Alfonso against Granada. Conversely, the *taifa* king of Seville, al-Mutamid, had in vain sent troops to Granada to assist Abd Allah. In addition to campaigning in al-Andalus, Alfonso found time in 1074 to marry the first of his four legitimate wives and two illegitimate partners. Queen Agnes (Inés), the daughter of Duke William VIII of Aquitaine, brought prestige to his kingdom but bore him no children (See Chart 10). In June of 1075, Alfonso's ally in Toledo, al-Mamun, was assassinated, leaving his weak son al-Qadir to rule over that city, which prompted other *taifa* rulers to take advantage of this opportunity. Al-Mutamid of Seville immediately claimed authority over Córdoba, a city that al-Mamun had conquered only the year before. Furthermore, Abu Bakr, the *taifa* king of Valencia, used the occasion to declare his independence from Toledo (Reilly *The Contest* 76).

Alfonso VI was preparing for a campaign into al-Andalus when news reached him in Castile that his cousin Sancho IV of Navarre had been assassinated. On June 4, 1076, Sancho IV was pushed into the ravine at Peñalén by a conspiring brother and sister, who were dissatisfied with Sancho's deviation from legal uses and customs. Alfonso left immediately for the Navarrese seat at Nájera where an agreement was reached to divide Sancho's kingdom between Alfonso VI and his cousin Sancho Ramirez I of Aragon (See Chart 11). Sancho would receive the lands around Pamplona as far to the southwest as Estella. Alfonso would command La Rioja and the Ebro Valley down to Calahorra. But more significantly, he claimed the Basque provinces of Álava, Viscaya, and Guipúzcoa, which constituted part of *castella vetula*, Old Castile, that was consolidated under Count Fernán González (931–970) during the reign of Ramiro II (931–951) and was more recently claimed by Sancho Garcés III (1004–1035) of Navarre when his brother-in-law Count García Sánchez (1017–1029) of Castile was assassinated in 1029.

The division of Navarre marks the demise of the Jiménez dynasty which dated from Sancho Garcés I (905–925). Moreover, Navarre itself is eliminated as a sovereign kingdom until its re-incarnation a half-century later (See Chart 7). Of the fratricidal siblings, the brother Ramón fled to the protection of al-Muqtadir in Zaragoza, while the sister Ermesinda and two other younger children, Urraca and Ramiro, fell under the custody of Alfonso VI. The assassinated Sancho Garcés IV (1054–1076) of Navarre is remembered in Spanish history simply as *el de Peñalén* (Reilly *The Contest* 77; Martínez Díez *El Condado* 733).

By 1078, Alfonso VI continued his expansionary efforts in Sepúlveda to the south of the Duero and began a major repopulation of the territories toward Toledo. This repopulation effort was a work in progress which probably carried on for several years and eventually settled the locations of Ávila, Salamanca, Segovia, Cuéllar, Coca, Arévalo, Olmedo, Medina del Campo, and Iscar. While repopulation was of strategic importance, Alfonso VI was distracted by military exigencies in the interim. By April 1079, Alfonso's armies were sent to the *taifa* of Toledo to assist its tribute-paying ruler, al-Qadir, who had undergone a revolt and had fled to the safety of Cuenca. Al-Qadir had lost control of Toledo and had previously been dethroned from Córdoba and Valencia. In his absence, the *taifa* ruler of Badajoz, al-Mutawakkil, was recognized by the population of Toledo as their sovereign. Alfonso's rescue forces overcame Coria to the west of Toledo, which opened access to Badajoz and mounted a direct threat to al-Mutawakkil. At the same time, Alfonso sent Rodrigo Díaz de Vivar, *el Cid*, to negotiate an alliance with al-Mutamid of Seville to join against al-Mutawakkil. The possibility of this combined attack was more than al-Mutawakkil had bargained for, and he withdrew from Toledo. The revolt was subdued, and al-Qadir was re-established. Al-Qadir would pay dearly for Alfonso's rescue. The Pact of Cuenca with al-Qadir allowed Alfonso to establish two garrisons within the realm of Toledo that were paid for by its citizens. A garrison to the west of Toledo protected against an attack from Badajoz while a second garrison to the east prevented incursions from Zaragoza and Valencia. Both stations protected the repopulation strategy south of the Duero (Reilly *The Contest* 79–81).

In 1080 or 1081, a band of Muslims from the *taifa* realm of Toledo launched a raid into Castile north of the Duero River around Gormaz, carrying off a large amount of booty. In immediate retaliation, the Castilian noble Rodrigo Díaz de Vivar, *el Cid*, waged a counter-attack deep into the sovereign lands of al-Qadir. Since Toledo was paying a heavy price for protection, Alfonso had no choice but to respond to this attack. In short order, *el Cid* was ostracized and sent into exile to the east of Castile. He first attempted to seek employment with Ramón Berenguer in Barcelona, but subsequently found employment in the service of al-Muqtadir (1046–1082) in Zaragoza, the builder of the *Aljafería* palace. When al-Muqtadir died in 1082, *el Cid* continued in the service of al-Muqtadir's son al-Mutamin (1082–1085) until 1085, becoming rich in the process (Fletcher *The Quest* 131–7).

In 1084, Alfonso attacked and pillaged the territories of al-Mutamid around Seville with impunity. His great army besieged the walls of Seville itself in a display of overwhelming force. Then for his encore, he rode to Tarifa on the southernmost coast where he drove his horse through the surf in a symbolic gesture to assure all al-Andalus that he was the most powerful monarch in all of *Hispania*. With a weakened Zaragoza, Toledo paying for his protection, and with Badajoz, Granada, and Seville unable to match his military superiority, Alfonso at last acted to bring Toledo under his complete control. In the fall of 1084, Alfonso set up camp to the south of Toledo and began a formal siege of the city, which lasted through the winter and prevented the ingress of supplies. On May 25, 1085, Alfonso made his triumphant arrival into Toledo (Reilly *The Contest* 84). The *urbs regia*, the royal city of the Visigothic kings, was now returned to the control of the crown of León-Castile.

After Toledo was conquered and under his control, the Leonese monarch generously found another city for al-Qadir. Valencia had recently been a part of the *taifa* kingdom of al-Qadir's father al-Mamun, but the city declared its independence from Toledo after al-Mamun's death in 1075. Abu Bakr had declared Valencia's independence, but he had died in 1085, leaving no apparent successor. In early March of 1086, Alfonso VI dispatched his troops under the capable leadership of commander Álvar Fáñez to lay siege to Valencia. Under pressure from such an impressive military force, the city acquiesced, and al-Qadir was established as its *taifa* king. At the same time, Alfonso himself was laying seige to Zaragoza to assure the continued payment of *parias* from al-Mustain following the death of his father al-Mutamin in 1085. The military power of Alfonso VI could not be challenged by any petty king of the peninsula, but a new threat from North Africa was poised to enter the combat. On July 30, 1086, while Alfonso VI was still at Zaragoza, the Almoravids landed at Algeciras (Reilly *The Contest* 87–8).

Changes in Leadership in the Eastern Counties: 1035–1096

Count Berenguer Ramon I of Barcelona died in 1035, leaving the administration of the counties under his control in dire straits. He was still a minor when he assumed control of the counties of Barcelona, Girona, and Ausona from his father Ramon Borrell in 1017. He reached the age of majority and ruled on his own in 1023, but his decision making continued to be influenced by his mother Ermessenda or by his wife Sancha, the daughter of Sancho García (995–1017) of Castile. He became the vassal of Sancho Garcés III, *el Mayor*, and his sobriquet of *Curvus* (*el Corbat*) "the bent one" has been interpreted as referring perhaps to his lazy submission to others rather than to a physical attribute (Bonnassie 555). During his weak reign, the control and unity of the eastern counties slipped away from Barcelona and into the hands of lesser magnates who seized the opportunity to exercise leadership when none was forthcoming from the count.

The death of Count Berenguer Ramon I did very little to ameliorate the county's prestige, and his will and testament only complicated the problems of succession and leadership. The eldest son Ramon Berenguer I (1035–1076) received the counties of Barcelona and Girona, and the second son Sancho Berenguer inherited the territory to the west of the Llobregat River, while the third son, Gillem Berenguer, was endowed with the county of Ausona under the guardianship of his mother Guisla, the second wife of Berenguer Ramon I (See Chart 12). However, the two younger sons were later to recognize the eldest as their overlord. The entire matter was further complicated by the fact that Ramon Berenguer I would not reach the age of majority until 1041. Furthermore, the dowager Countess Ermessenda, the grandmother of Ramon, Sancho, and Guillem, jointly controlled the governance of the three. This arrangement was all very confusing and perpetuated the lack of public authority which began under Berenguer

Ramon I and persisted until Ramon Berenguer I could later control his own destiny as an adult (Bonnassie 555).

During the decade of the 1050's, Count Ramon Berenguer I balanced his domestic affairs with his public duties. On the domestic side, his first wife Isabel died in 1050, and in the following year he married his second wife Blanca only to repudiate her in 1052 under pressure from the court judges for not adhering to custom. He subsequently married his third wife Almodis. This marriage provoked a feud between Almodis and his grandmother, the Countess Ermessenda, that resulted in a scandal and a break with his grandmother. Ultimately on July 4, 1057, the elderly countess capitulated to the wishes of Ramon and sold all her holdings in Girona and Ausona to Ramon and his wife. Ermessenda died the following year on March 1, 1058, leaving Ramon free to concentrate on public matters. His administrative rule had increased when his brother Sancho ceded him the rights to the territories across the Llobregat River in 1049. His other brother Guillem did the same for the county of Ausona in 1058, the same year that their grandmother Ermessinda died. In 1052, Ramon had begun a judicial process against Mir Geribert, the rebellious magnate of Panedès across the Llobregat, who was ruling independently of Barcelona. Finally, with domestic conflicts settled, Ramon decided to take military action and invaded Panedès in 1059 with an army that he had raised for defense against the Muslims. Mir chose to seek asylum in Tortosa rather than fight, and the territory southwest of the Llogregat River was returned to the authority of Barcelona (Bonnassie 640–4). After the downfall of Mir Geribert, the supremacy of the Count of Barcelona among the eastern counties was well established by 1060. Furthermore, Count Ramon Berenguer I was installed at the top of a new feudal structure that had been spawned by the revolution of the barons of the eastern counties during the preceding decades (Bonnassie 686).

During the years from 1063 through 1067, Ramon Berenguer I strengthened his control over the Panedès territory with the purchase of more than a dozen castles and fortresses from local magnates. In 1066, he employed another tactic to reacquire other castles that may have been usurped during the time of his father. At a council of magnates, he demanded that they produce the papers to show that his father had abdicated the property to them, or else they would have to submit to a judiciary duel. Not wanting to face a duel whose outcome was determined by God, the offenders rendered the property and submitted to the authority of the Count of Barcelona. He then followed this effort by calling for a formal recognition of his authority over all the counties where he exercised control, including Barcelona, Ausona, Manresa, Girona, and southern Ribagorça. Even the northern counties of Besalú and Cerdanya fell into line after the overthrow of the rebellious Mir Geribert (Bonnassie 692–9).

The hereditary rights to the county of Barcelona belonged to Ramon Berenguer's first born son Pere (Pedro) Ramon with his first wife Isabel. However, the Countess Almodis had purchased the hereditary rights of the county of Carcasonne-Rasés with the intention of bequeathing them to her twin sons by Ramon named Ramon Berenger II and Berenger Ramon II. This action led to increased tensions and a feud between the countess and Pere, which ended in her assassination in October 1071 (Palenzuela 264). Consequently, Pere was exiled and died in obscurity.

The long reign of Ramon permitted the consolidation of all the counties under his direction. Indeed, by the time of his death in 1076, all the aristocracy of the eastern counties had become the vassals of the count of Barcelona (Bonnassie 701). Pere was no longer in the picture, and the twin sons Ramon Berenguer II (1076–1082) and Berenguer Ramon II (1076–1096), born to Ramon Berenguer I and Countess Almodis, inherited everything and ruled jointly. (As an aside, Ramon Berenguer II was nicknamed *el Cap d'Estopes* "the tow head" for the color of his hair and for its unruliness. It is interesting to muse that Ramon was the grandson, six generations later, of Guifré, "the Hairy," and that both were labeled by the Catalans with reference to their hair, cf. Sobrequés i Vidal 118.) Shortly after the twins came to power, they devised a plan in conjunction with Count Ermengol IV (1065–92) of Urgell to extend their power and authority by exacting *parias* from the *taifa* rulers of the east coast. The combined forces of Barcelona and Urgell presented a formidable threat, but their expansionary efforts were unsuccessful. Their campaign against Murcia in 1077 could not overcome the more powerful al-Mamun of Toledo who also controlled and defended Murcia. The Catalans retreated without success. Again in 1081, another campaign against Denia was planned, but when the twins learned of the death of al-Muqtadir of Zaragoza, they envisioned easier prey in the sons of al-Muqtadir who inherited Zaragoza, Lerida and Tortosa. The offensive against Denia was postponed in favor of planning a strategy against al-Muqtadir's sons. The joint rule of the twins did not seem to be progressing successfully when in 1082 the body of Count Ramon Berenguer II was found murdered. Berenguer Ramon II was never proved to be responsible, but he would be suspected of murdering his brother for the rest of his days. He was permitted to continue as count of Barcelona on the condition that he surrender the title of count to his nephew Ramon Berenguer III (1096–1131), the son of the deceased twin, at the time that the nephew became of age (Bisson 26). Subsequent campaigns of Berenguer Ramon II in 1083 against Zaragoza in concert with Sancho Ramírez of Aragon, in 1086 against al-Qadir of Valencia, and again in 1089 against Valencia were all thwarted. Rodrigo Díaz de Vivar, *el Cid*, was in the employ of al-Mutamin in 1083, but by 1094, *el Cid* was acting on his own as an independent combatant. He took control of Valencia for himself. In 1096, Berenguer Ramon II was forced into a judicial duel to prove his innocence (Reilly *The Contest* 120). Losing this contest, he was forced to abdicate and sent into exile. His nephew Ramon Berenguer III became the new count of Barcelona. Fully in control by 1097, he successfully ruled well into the twelfth century.

The Rise of the Almoravids

The Sanhaja people were a confederation of about seventy Berber tribes living in the western Sahara Desert in what is today southern Morocco and northern Mauritania. They were a nomadic people following a cyclical migration to graze their herds of sheep, goats, and camels. Their tents, blankets, and clothes were made from the hair and skin of their herds, and their diet consisted of the milk and meat of their animals, unless supplemented with food traded by a passing caravan. The Sanhaja clothed themselves in dyed, indigo blue wool. They wrapped their heads in a turban and in a strict tribal custom wore a veil across their faces which left only their eyes exposed. These nomads differed from the Masmuda and Zanata Berbers of the Atlas Mountains and northern Morocco respectively, who had evolved into a settled, city existence. The Sanhaja developed and controlled the trade route across their domain from the ancient city of Sijilmasa on the north edge of the Sahara Desert south of Fez to Awdaghust, an oasis village in today's Mauritania. They not only drove their own trade caravans, they charged tolls for safe passage of others and raided those who did not pay (Kennedy *Muslim Spain* 154–6; Fletcher *Moorish Spain* 106–7).

The Sanhaja converted to Islam probably in the ninth century, but they were lax and uneducated in its practice. Around 1035 a chieftain of the Guddala tribe of Sanhaja, Yahya ibn Ibrahim, decided to undertake a pilgrimage to Mecca in fulfillment of one of the five pillars of Islam. On his return trip, he stopped at Qayrawan in Tunisia to hear the sermons of the Islamic scholar of the Malikite school, Abu Imran al-Fasi. As a center of Sunni Islam, this school based its doctrines on the Koran and on the *hadith*, the collection of sayings of the Prophet and on the *sunna*, the accounts of his daily practice. Sunni beliefs differ from those of the Shiite Muslims, who include the traditions of Ali, the son-in-law of the Prophet, whom they recognize as the first successor to Muhammad and the true *imam*.

Through contact with Abu Imran, ibn Ibrahim became increasingly enlightened to the fact that his own tribesmen were not moved to the strict piety of the Malikite school, nor were they learned in Islamic law. From this enlightenment, Yahya ibn Ibrahim requested Abu Imram to dispatch a teacher to accompany him back to his tribe to lead them on a righteous path. In response to this request, Abu Imran directed ibn Ibrahim to one of his former students who had founded his own school near Tangier, called *Dar al-Murabitin*, "the house of those who were bound together in the cause of God." Ibn Zalwi, the founder of this school, sent one of his students Abd Allah ibn Yasin to instruct the tribes of ibn Ibrahim in the ways of strict Malikite law, including holy war and the illegality of non-Koranic taxes (Messier 3+).

Ibn Yasin accompanied Yahya ibn Ibrahim to his own tribe, the Bani Guddala, and became their *imam*, instructing them in his strict interpretation of the laws of Islam. Finding that the Bani Guddala were ignorant of these laws, he imposed a strict religious enforcement and was intolerant of anyone who did not observe the prescribed practices. He meted out floggings of specified lashes for adulterers, drunkards, slanderers or for anyone who failed to attend Friday prayers. The Bani Guddala remained faithful to the teachings of ibn Yasin until the death of Yahya ibn Ibrahim, who was not only their chief but the great chief of the Sanhaja confederation as well. When the tribal elders of the Sanhaja confederation selected Yahya ibn Umar, the chief of another tribe, the Bani Lamtuna, as their new great chief, ibn Yasin followed the succession of power and placed his religious mission in the hands of ibn Umar, who gratefully accepted him as their *imam*. The loss of ibn Yasin to another tribe spawned jealousy in the Bani Guddala which in turn led to a conspiracy against him. The conspirators led an enraged mob to loot the house of ibn Yasin, causing him to flee to the safety of his teacher, al-Zalwi, the master of the *Dar al-Murabitin*. Al-Zalwi sent a messenger back to the Bani Guddala admonishing them severely, and informing them that anyone who rejected ibn Yasin would be banned from the Islamic community of believers. Al-Zalwi then sent ibn Yasin back to the Sanhaja to complete his mission.

When ibn Yasin returned to the desert, he established a *ribat* "a fortified monastery" in a remote location and resumed his teaching of the Malikite school. His followers at the *ribat* were called *al-Murabitun*, that is the people of the *ribat*, which became the Spanish deformation *almorávides*, the Almoravids. Ibn Yasin then led the Almoravids in a lesser holy war against any tribe of the Sanhaja who refused to follow the true faith as he taught it (Messier 10–2).

In 1054, the Almoravids embarked on a campaign to control the entire trade route of the western Sahara from Sijilmasa in the north to Awdaghust in the south seizing the gold trade from the south and using it to finance their campaigns. During one of their campaigns, their commander Yahya ibn Umar was killed, and ibn Yasin replaced him with Yahya's brother Abu Bakr ibn Umar. In just two years by 1056, the entire western trade route had fallen under the control of the Almoravids, and Amir Abu Bakr appointed a new commander, his cousin Yusuf ibn Tashfin, to garrison the post at Sijilmasa.

In bloody battle against the Barghwata tribe of Berbers, ibn Yasin was mortally wounded and died on July 8, 1059. A new *imam*, Sulayman ibn Abdu, was named, but the real power and leadership of the Almoravids lay in the hands of Abu Bakr, who used the city of Aghmat as his seat of power to control all northwest Africa. He dispatched Yusuf ibn Tashfin to extend their campaign into the northern Maghreb while he strengthened his control in the southern Maghreb and the western Sahara.

In September of 1068 Abu Bakr married Zaynab, a beautiful, educated, and wealthy widow of the former ruler of Aghmat. That same year, he decided to move his garrison from Aghmat further west and founded the city of Marrakech which offered a more defensible location. By early 1071, however, he decided to leave Marrakech, the city that he had founded, and resume his life in the desert to maintain control and authority there. He named his cousin ibn Tashfin as commander over all the forces in the Maghreb. He also realized that his wife Zaynab could not endure nomadic life in the desert. He therefore divorced her and asked her to marry ibn Tashfin after the mandatory waiting period as prescribed by Islamic law. Ibn Tashfin's marriage to Zaynab occurred in May 1071 (Messier 41–3).

Beginning around 1072, ibn Tashfin attacked small cities and fortresses to the south of Tangier in preparation for a successful campaign against that important city. By 1077, ibn Tashfin was ready to dispatch his general Salih ibn Imran against al-Barghwati, the ruler of Tangier. In that year on the banks of the Nina River, the ninety-year-old warrior, al-Barghwati, lost his life, and the Almoravids won the city of Tangier. After taking time to complete administrative control of his newly acquired territories, Yusuf ibn Tashfin marched on Tlemcen, the most eastern outpost that he would control, massacring the Maghrawa tribesmen that fought against him (Messier 64).

Ceuta was the only remaining stronghold in the Maghreb that ibn Tashfin had not conquered. As early as 1074, the *taifa* ruler of Seville, al-Mutamid ibn Abbad, had appealed to ibn Tashfin for assistance in defeating the Christians who were oppressing the Muslims of al-Andalus, but at that time, ibn Tashfin still had unfinished business in North Africa. Now it was al-Mutamid's turn to assist ibn Tashfin's campaign against Ceuta (Reilly *Alfonso* 166). Ibn Tashfin directed his son Tamim to lay siege to Ceuta from the west while al-Mutamid dispatched a naval force to blockade the city's waterfront from the east.

In August of 1084, Ceuta was forced to surrender, and the Almoravid conquest of the western Sahara and the Maghreb was complete. Yusuf ibn Tashfin could now look across the Strait of Gibraltar and consider what the Malikite believers, the *al-Murabitun*, could accomplish against the infidels of Iberia.

The Hegemony of Alfonso VI Is Challenged: 1086–1109

Yusuf ibn Tashfin landed at Algeciras with an army of faithful Almoravids on July 30, 1086. The *taifa* rulers of al-Andalus embraced their arrival with caution and suspicion. On one hand, they needed the Almoravids to free themselves from the grasp of Alfonso VI, who extorted *parias* from them and funded his armies to exact continued payments. They were powerless against him. On the other hand, they risked being overrun by a different power. The Almoravids were religious zealots who viewed the payment of *parias* to the Christians as forbidden by Islamic law. Further, they forbade the practices of drinking wine, astrology, and music. These desert nomads from North Africa were culturally far different from the educated, highly cultured Muslims of al-Andalus. The sentiment of the *taifa* rulers can be judged from al-Mutamid when he asserted that: "I'd rather be a camel driver in Morocco than a swineherd in Castile" (Fletcher *Moorish Spain* 108–11). In the end, the petty monarchs of al-Andalus traded one oppression for another.

Yusuf secured Algeciras as a base of retreat before advancing to Seville where he would be welcomed by al-Mutamid. The other petty kings were less responsive. The *taifa* rulers of the Ebro Valley did not answer the call against the Christians, and al-Qadir of Valencia remained loyal to the Christian monarch who had installed him as ruler of that city only in March of 1086. The *taifa* of Almería abstained, and Abd Allah of Granada joined the allied Muslims only when they had reached Jerez de los Caballeros between Seville and Badajoz. The allied Muslim army advanced from Seville in the direction of Badajoz, perhaps to assure the commitment of that city's leader, al-Mutawakkil, to support this campaign. They arrived there by October 1086 and waited for the Christian attack (Reilly *Alfonso* 186).

Alfonso VI was laying siege to Zaragoza to assure the continuation of their *parias* to him when the Almoravids landed at Algeciras. He immediately broke camp and sent word to his commanders in the eastern regions to meet him on the way to Toledo from where the combined army would proceed to Coria to rendezvous with western reinforcements. From there, Alfonso struck the Muslim army at Sagrajas, just to the northeast of Badajoz. This engagement, known also as the battle of Zalaca, took place on October 23, 1086. With limited accounts of this conflict, it appears that Alfonso's army enjoyed some initial success until the Muslims broke through to the Christian camp. The Almoravids then inflicted severe casualties and drove the Christians into a running retreat. Alfonso fled to the safety of Coria with his remaining troops and then regrouped at Toledo to prepare for a siege only to find that Yusuf ibn Tashfin had opted to return to North Africa by way of Seville (Reilly *The Contest* 88–9).

The Almoravids did not return to the peninsula in 1087 which afforded Alfonso VI the opportunity to turn his attention to domestic affairs. Alfonso's first marriage to

Agnes (Inés), the daughter of Duke William VIII of Aquitaine, produced no offspring and was dissolved in 1077. In 1079, he married Constance, the sister of Duke Eudes I of Burgundy, who bore one daughter, Urraca, around the end of 1080. Constance would remain queen until her death in 1093, but Alfonso had also taken a mistress in 1081 or 1082 as well. Mistress Jimena Múñoz was the daughter of a magnate of western Asturias and of the northern Bierzo who bore two daughters, Teresa (of Portugal) and Elvira (of Toulouse), but no sons. In 1087, Count Eudes of Burgundy visited his sister, Queen Constance, at the court in León, and brought with him his son Raymond and a cousin Henry of Burgundy. Alfonso's only legitimate heiress Urraca, a child of possibly seven years at the time, was betrothed to Raymond of Burgundy, making the Burgundian an apparent inheritor of the crown. Count Henry of Burgundy was later married to Alfonso's illegitimate daughter Teresa, and the second illegitimate daughter, Elvira, was married to Count Raymond IV of Toulouse (See Chart 10). While these betrothals were being arranged, a minor uprising was taking place in Galicia which was immediately suppressed, but which perhaps prompted Alfonso to visit that area the following year in 1088 to install his new son-in-law, Raymond, as viceroy over the entire province (Reilly *The Contest* 90–1).

Alfonso VI had been defeated at the battle of Zalaca, but he resumed the offensive by attacking and seizing control of the fortress Aledo (southwest of Murcia), which severed the lines of attack from Granada and Seville up the eastern seaboard. Yusuf ibn Tashfin returned to Algeciras in the late spring of 1088 and demanded the assistance of al-Mutamid of Seville and of Abd Allah of Granada in an attack on Aledo. After four months of a futile siege, ibn Tashfin returned to Africa, disgusted with his Muslim allies (Kennedy *Muslim Spain* 163–4). In 1090, ibn Tashfin made his third appearance in Iberia. After attempting an unsuccessful siege of Toledo, he led his army to Granada to unseat Abd Allah, whom the Almoravid clerics had declared impious, debauched, and deserving to be deposed. Indeed, all the *taifa* rulers were declared to be unfit, and the Almoravids began their overthrow of al-Andalus, petty kingdom by petty kingdom. Yusuf removed Abd Allah's brother Tamim from Málaga, and before returning to Africa, he left his cousin Sir ibn Abu Bakr in charge of a substantial army and gave him instructions to bring the remaining *taifas* under Almoravid control. Yusuf's commander seized Tarifa that same year and took Córdoba, Carmona, and even Seville by September 1091. The lesser *taifas* of Jaén, Murcia, and Denia submitted without a struggle. Of the southern rulers, only al-Mutawakkil of Badajoz remained independent and so began bargaining with Alfonso VI for protection from the onslaught. Al-Mutawakkil ceded the towns of Lisbon, Santarém, and Sintra, which Alfonso immediately assigned to his new son-in-law Count Raymond, who as viceroy now ruled from northern Galicia down to the mouth of the Tajo. The bargain between al-Mutawakkil and Alfonso soon went for naught; during the winter of 1092–1093, the populace of Badajoz rose up against al-Mutawakkil and turned the city over to Sir ibn Abu Bakr without any resistance. The following November 1094, the Almoravids attacked Count Raymond's position at Lisbon and defeated him, resetting the Christian boundary back to the Mondego River (Reilly *The Contest* 91–2; Kennedy *Muslim Spain* 163–4). The fate of the deposed petty kings was tenuous. Abd Allah of Granada and al-Mutamid of Seville were sent into exile in North Africa where Abd Allah would write his memoirs. Al-Mutawakkil and his sons were less fortunate. They were captured during the rendition of Badajoz and later slain on the road to Seville.

On the eastern front, Rodrigo Díaz de Vivar, *el Cid*, lay siege to and captured the city of Valencia with a band of well-trained, independent mercenaries in 1094. When the Almoravids arrived to retake the city later that year, Rodrigo dispatched a small force to distract their assailants from one direction, while a larger force bore down on them from another direction. This maneuver put the Almoravid army to flight, which was the first indication that Christian combatants could overcome their North African opponents in open-field combat (Fletcher *El Cid* 173). The Almoravids did not resume any campaigns against the Christians in 1095 and 1096.

Meanwhile the intrigue at the royal court of Alfonso carried on. Queen Constance of Burgundy died in 1093, and Alfonso took another Italian wife named Berta the following year. But more significantly, Alfonso had also taken a Muslim concubine named Zaida (later known as Elizabeth) in 1092 or 1093. This relationship produced the king's only son Sancho and potential heir to the throne in late 1093. The birth of Alfonso's son Sancho presented a threat to the ascendance of the king's son-in-law Raymond of Burgundy and gave rise to a conspiracy between Raymond and his cousin Henry. They agreed that upon the king's death, Henry would support Raymond's ascendance to the crown in exchange for Henry's rule of either Toledo or Galicia. Learning of this compact, Alfonso toured Galicia through the summer months of 1095 with his new wife Berta and mollified the threat to his authority by marrying his illegitimate daughter Teresa to Henry of Burgundy and by giving them control of the lands south of Galicia, that is south of the river Minho down to the Mondego River (Reilly *Alfonso* 254). This maneuver not only transferred some of Raymond's territory to Henry but also placed Henry himself in a position for ascendancy to the crown.

Over in Aragon, Sancho Ramírez (1063–1094), son of the first king of Aragon Ramiro I (1035–1063), died in 1094 and was succeeded by his son Pedro I (1094–1104) in June of that year (See Chart 11). From the early days of this kingdom, the crown of Aragon had expansionary designs on Huesca but was constrained by the powerful Muslim leaders of Zaragoza. The territorial expansion of Pedro I was now further hindered by the sovereignty of Alfonso VI over al-Mustain of Zaragoza, who was the last *taifa* ruler rendering payments to Alfonso in exchange for protection. Pedro hatched a plan to assuage these encumbrances and to muster assistance to conquer Huesca. In 1068, Pedro I's father, Sancho Ramírez, had travelled to Rome and had surrendered the kingdom of Aragon to the pope, receiving it back as a papal fief. Now in 1095, Pedro I renewed his recognition of papal sovereignty and received permission to attack Huesca as a papal vassal with the assistance of Christian allies from north of the Pyrenees. Pedro I began his assaults around Huesca before initiating a siege of that city in 1096. Huesca appealed to Zaragoza for assistance, and in November of that year, al-Mustain responded with a relief force that included Count García Ordóñez of Nájera and Count Gonzalo Núñez of Lara sent by Alfonso VI. On November 18, 1096, however, the combined Muslim and Christian forces from Zaragoza were defeated at Alcoraz just west of Huesca by Pedro I and his allies from north of the Pyrenees. Huesca immediately became the new seat of the crown of Aragon, but Pedro was not yet finished with his conquests. He continued his eastward push and on October 18, 1100, the Muslim fortress of Barbastro at the confluence of the rivers Cea and Vero surrendered to him. This acquisition threatened the security of the entire valley north of the Ebro and even Zaragoza itself (Reilly *The Kingdom of León-Castilla* 301–2). Pedro I maintained control of his conquests until his death in 1104, at which time his half-brother Alfonso I (1104–1134), known as the Battler, assumed the crown and carried on with the expansion of Aragon.

The Christian and Almoravid conflicts resumed in 1097 when Yusuf ibn Tashfin returned and attempted to retake Toledo. Alfonso VI had established lines of defense on the southern flanks of that city. The Christian losses were severe, but the Almoravids failed to overrun Toledo. The following year, Alfonso began his own offensive to claim the Muslim positions at Atienza, Medinaceli, and Sigüenza. This campaign intended to control the old Roman road from Toledo to Zaragoza. However again in 1099, an Almoravid army commanded by Yusuf's grandson, Yahya ibn Tashfin, successfully broke through the Christian lines south of Toledo and lay siege to that city in 1100. Once again the city held. This time the city's defenders were commanded by Count Henry of Burgundy. While Toledo was under siege, Alfonso journeyed to Valencia to assess the situation of that city. In July of 1099, Rodrigo Díaz had died of natural causes, which left his wife Jimena with the difficult task of managing the city's defenses. In 1102, Alfonso determined that he could not defend Valencia and oversaw the evacuation of the city. The Christian population was resettled into areas north of the Tajo, notably into Ávila and Salamanca. By June 1102 only two months later, Mazdali, the Almoravid emir of Denia, occupied Valencia. In July 1104, the Muslim position at Medinaceli that guarded the route to the Jalón River valley and to Zaragoza fell to the Christians after a long siege. The Christian offensive continued from there into the south of Toledo and by 1106 the campaigns extended from Seville to Málaga. Again, some of the Mozarabic Christian population was encouraged to migrate north into the areas controlled by Alfonso VI. On September 2, 1106, Yusuf ibn Tashfin died, leaving his son Ali ibn Yusuf, his designated heir, as leader of the Almoravid movement (Reilly *The Contest* 93–5).

The issue of succession of the aging King Alfonso VI was not entirely settled. In March of 1105, the king's daughter Urraca gave birth to a son Alfonso Raimúndez, which brought into question the succession of the king's favorite and only son, the illegitimate Sancho Alfónsez, born to his concubine Zaida. (NOTE: Zaida was in later years baptized with the Christian name of Elizabeth, which raises the question among historians as to whether Alfonso had a fourth marriage to another Elizabeth (Beatrice) or whether the contemporary documents are actually referring to Zaida (Elizabeth/Isabel). Two daughters, Sancha and Elvira, are recorded for Elizabeth, and our genealogical chart arguably places the daughters with Zaida, although a fourth wife of Alfonso (Beatrice) is also shown on our chart.) The king reinforced his favoritism to Sancho when in March 1106 he had his fourth marriage to Beatrice (Elizabeth) annulled in order to marry Sancho's mother Zaida (Reilly *The Contest* 96). He then had Sancho, who was about thirteen years old at the time, declared heir to the throne at a council in León. However, he also made provisions for Urraca and his grandson Alfonso Raimúndez (the later Alfonso VII) by arranging for Urraca to hold Galicia which would pass to her son Alfonso upon her death or remarriage. Later that same year, Count Raymond died unexpectedly which removed his threat to Sancho's ascendancy. Yet just as the question of ascendancy seemed to be settled, another misfortune befell the Leonese monarchy in 1108. A major Almoravid army commanded by Tamin ibn Yusuf, the brother of the new emir Ali ibn Yusuf, assembled a campaign against Toledo which first struck against the Christian outpost at Uclés. A Christian relief force was dispatched to support the outlying fortresses. The relief force was destroyed, and the fallen included not only several important counts, but the counteroffensive also took the life of the heir to the crown of León-Castile, Sancho Alfónsez (Lomax 72; Kennedy *Muslim Spain* 173).

With the unfortunate demise of Alfonso's son and heir, the king made a precipitated decision to marry his daughter Urraca to Alfonso I (1104–1134) of Aragon, the Battler. This move rejected the notion that Urraca could rule in her own name or as regent for her minor, three-year-old son Alfonso Raimúndez. Moreover, these nuptials united the two major Christian powers in Iberia, although perhaps it raised dissent among some of the magnates of León-Castile. However, the seventy-two-year-old monarch was not to witness his daughter's marriage, for after being carried to Toledo on a litter so that he could inspect the defenses of the city, he died there on July 1, 1109. The long and successful reign of Alfonso VI was left in the hands of Urraca and her son Alfonso Raimúndez to create the future of León-Castile.

CHAPTER 7

Christian Civil War and Waning Almoravid Power: 1109–1157

The Failed Marriage of Urraca and Alfonso I of Aragon and Civil War: 1109–1117

In front of the prelates and magnates of León-Castile assembled in Toledo just a month before his death on July 1, 1109, Alfonso VI had proclaimed his daughter Urraca as heir to his crown with the stipulation that she marry Alfonso I of Aragon, "the Battler." The intent of this proviso was to deliver a male ruler capable of defending the realm. Indeed, the choice of heirs was limited. In 1108, Alfonso VI declared his successor to be his son Sancho Alfónsez, born to his concubine and later wife Zaida/Isabel. Within months of this declaration, however, Sancho was killed at Uclés at age fourteen fighting against the Almoravids. Urraca's husband, Raymond of Burgundy, had died of natural causes in 1107, and their son Alfonso Raimúndez, born in 1105, was too young to lead. The king's illegitimate daughter Teresa and her husband Henry of Burgundy had their own pretensions of ascension, which were now rejected in favor of Alfonso of Aragon. The first-born son of Henry and Teresa, Alfonso Enríquez, was born in the same year as Alfonso VI's death and therefore was not a consideration (See Chart 10).

After the death of his half-brother Pedro I (1094–1104), Alfonso I (1104–1134) the Battler ascended to the crown of Aragon in 1104 and very quickly began the annexation of adjacent locations into his realm. In 1105, he took Ejea and Tauste, and two years later in 1107 he overcame Muslim positions at Tamarite de Litera and San Esteban de Litera (Ubieto Arteta *Historia* 141–3). The achievements of the Aragonese king qualified him as an appropriate match for Urraca in the eyes of Alfonso VI. Alfonso I of Aragon and Urraca were married at Monzón just to the north of Palencia in the fall of 1109. The terms of the marriage decidedly favored León-Castile and indicated that Alfonso was willing to make concessions to assume control of that realm. Under the terms of the agreement, the first party to desert the other would forfeit the loyalty of their supporters. Further, Alfonso agreed that he would not be deterred from the marriage by the argument of blood relationship—they were both the great-grandchildren of Sancho Garcés III (1004–1025) of Navarre—nor by the threat of excommunication because of consanguinity. If Alfonso predeceased Urraca, she and a future son, if any, would jointly inherit his territories. Otherwise, she would inherit them if there were no son. Conversely, if she died first, Alfonso and a future son would inherit jointly. In the absence of a son, he would have only the usufruct of her kingdom during his lifetime. Upon his death, León-Castile would be inherited by Alfonso Raimúndez (Reilly *Urraca* 64). It is curious that Alfonso of Aragon agreed to the terms of the marriage, since he would have been acutely aware of his personal situation. Specifically, he was passed thirty years old, unmarried, and was known not to have had any concubines. Countless historians have speculated as to the possible reasons for his celibacy. Homosexuality, misogyny, impotence, as well as a commitment to religious zeal have been suggested as possible reasons. Nonetheless, Alfonso I of Aragon acquiesced to the terms of the marriage contract that favored León-Castile.

The death of the seventy-two-year-old King Alfonso VI left the monarchy in complete disarray, and the appearance of Alfonso the Battler of Aragon only added to the power struggle. Urraca's deceased husband had served as a viceroy who exercised authority over the powerful counts of Galicia, and these magnates now favored the rightful claim of Urraca's son Alfonso Raimúndez. The young heir born in 1105 had some very powerful guardians and protectors in Count Pedro Froílaz of the Trastámara family and the very influentially connected Bishop Diego Gelmírez of Santiago de Compostela. Further, Urraca's illegitimate sister Teresa and her husband Henry of Burgundy had designs of aggrandizing their own power base by either replacing Urraca as monarch or else ruling over the *terra portucalense* (Portugal) independently of León-Castile. The authority of Alfonso the Battler only served to thwart the intentions of the other power brokers, and the fidelity of all these parties was capricious. Their allegiance to Urraca and to each other could change instantaneously to serve their own self interests. Urraca played one interest against the other throughout her entire reign as did the other power brokers.

While the Battler was occupied with wedding matters in the west, al-Mustain, the *taifa* ruler of Zaragoza, took advantage of his absence by launching an offensive against positions in Aragon. Alfonso hastened eastward to initiate a counteroffensive, and he defeated and killed al-Mustain at Valtierra north of Tudela on January 24, 1110 (Reilly *Urraca* 60). Al-Mustain's son Abd al-Malik was unable to establish himself with the population of Zaragoza, and the following May, Almoravid troops under ibn al-Hajj arrived to take control of the city. The arrival of the Almoravids in Zaragoza marked the dissolution of the last *taifa* state in Muslim Iberia. Returning to León-Castile, the Battler was compelled to subdue insurrection in Galicia, and while he was absent from Urraca, a papal condemnation of the marriage on the basis on consanguinity arrived in León. Consequently, Urraca agreed to separate. During the final six months of 1110, she received the support of the magnates of León, Castile, La Rioja, and of the trans-Duero region in addition to garnering some support in Galicia as well. By April 1111, Alfonso of Aragon had seized control of Toledo and had stationed a garrison there. In disregard for Alfonso's authority, the partisans of the Infante Alfonso Raimúndez, Urraca's son, had him anointed and crowned in Santiago de Compostela on September 19, 1111. Meanwhile, Queen Urraca had taken Count Gómez González de Lara as her lover, which galvanized her support in Castile.

The competing tensions for control of the realm culminated in civil war at the Battle of Candespino about 16 miles to the northeast of Sepúlveda. On October 26, 1111, the combined forces of Alfonso I the Battler and Henry of Portugal soundly defeated Urraca's troops, and Count Gómez was killed in the fray. With capricious expediency, Count Henry was enticed to ally with Urraca against the Battler, who fled to the safety of the castle Peñafiel on the Duero. The conflict continued in the spring of 1112. Count Henry again agreed to align himself with Urraca and joined her forces at Astorga. Alfonso I assailed them there and lay siege to the city, but the Roman walls of the former mining location withstood the Battler's attacks. However, Count Henry was mortally wounded in the encounter and died on May 12, 1112. His wife Teresa, Urraca's half-sister, was left to govern the *terra portucalense* on her own until the child Alfonso Enríquez, the future Alfonso I of Portugal, became of age. The following year, Urraca's forces re-took a few positions that were garrisoned by Alfonso of Aragon including Carrión de los Condes and Burgos, and later in the year they fended off Muslim attacks near Soria. But her campaign stalled in 1114 with no further success. That same year witnessed the death of Commander Álvar Fáñez, her father's faithful military leader who defended Toledo. He was killed at Segovia during a revolt against Urraca's authority. The only good news was that the Christian forces stationed in Toledo had resumed an offensive against Almoravid positions. Consecutively they raided Córdoba, killing the Muslim governor Emir Mazdali. In June of 1114, they claimed a victory over his son ibn Mazdali. The Christians then won a battle against a new Almoravid governor the following November. However, the civil war between Urraca and Alfonso of Aragon was deadlocked; the relative positions of León-Castile and Aragon had not gained an advantage between 1113 and 1116 (Reilly *The Contest* 132–7).

In 1116, Urraca initiated a reconciliation with the supporters of her son Alfonso Raimúndez, namely with Count Pedro Froílaz and Bishop Gelmírez. In October of 1116, she held court at Sahagún and ceded immediate control of the trans-Duero regions to her son Alfonso. She acknowledged that he would inherit the rest of her kingdom upon her death. Moreover, the guardianship of her son would be supervised by Archbishop Bernard of Toledo, the faithful ally of Urraca and of her father Alfonso VI before her. The young Alfonso VII would not only be entrusted to faithful hands, but more importantly for Urraca, control of the boy-king would be severed from the ambitions of his former advisors. Further, the authority of her son Alfonso over Toledo would impede the expansionary designs of Alfonso the Battler of Aragon. Alfonso Raimúndez was formally received into the *urbs regia* of Toledo in November 1117.

That same year, a papal legate was dispatched to the peninsula by Pope Paschal II (1099–1118) which brought about a truce between León-Castile and Aragon. Cardinal Boso, with the assistance and consultation of local bishops representing the interests of both realms, arbitrated a three-year truce which would be renewed for the remainder of Urraca's lifetime. Under this agreement, Alfonso I continued to hold La Rioja and the territory north and east of Burgos as well as a strip along the pilgrimage route through Castrojeriz to Carrión de los Condes up to about 50 miles to the east of León. Urraca retained Burgos, Asturias under the protection of her ally Count Rodrigo González, and the regions to the south of the Duero, guarded by Rodrigo's brother, Count Pedro González of Lara. Count Pedro also garrisoned the fortress at Peñafiel and was reported to be Urraca's lover. With this agreement, the open hostilities of civil war between León-Castile and Aragon came to an end in 1117 (Reilly *The Contest* 140–1).

León-Castile During the Final Years of Urraca's Reign: 1117–1126

In 1117, Urraca finalized a three-year truce with her former husband Alfonso I of Aragon and travelled to Santiago de Compostella to discuss matters of her authority there. The ambitious Bishop Gelmírez had consistently undermined her authority. Nevertheless, he was a substantial power in that region, sharing at times a close relationship with Pedro Froílaz of the powerful Trastámara family of Galicia. However, the bishop was having his own difficulties with the burghers of Santiago, who had substituted their own secular governance for his ecclesiastical authority. When Urraca and the bishop convened in Santiago, the burghers assumed that they were plotting to overthrow their local authority. Suddenly, inflamed rhetoric turned to violence when a mob attacked the episcopal palace where the two were meeting. Bishop Gelmírez and Urraca fled to a bell tower under construction, but the mob set fire to it. The bishop was able to escape in the confusion, but the bishop's brother and his majordomo were killed in the melee while Urraca was seized, stripped of her clothing, and subjected to a hail of refuse and stones. A few leaders with cooler heads rescued her and escorted her out of the city under the promise that she would not exact retribution for this incident. Once outside the city, Urraca reconnected with her forces under the command of her son and Pedro Froílaz. The queen immediately put the town under siege, and it didn't take long for the citizens to realize that their resistance was futile. They threw themselves at the mercy of the queen. The government of the city was restored to the bishop, which was certainly not ideal for Urraca, but alternatively, the burghers could not be left in charge. About one hundred of the instigators were stripped of their property and exiled from the city (O'Callaghan *A History* 217). Needless to say, this episode was an unanticipated, embarrassing, and dangerous moment for the queen of León-Castile.

In 1119, a new influence was added to the political mix. Pope Gelasius II (1118–1119) had died, and a new pontif, Pope Calixtus II (1119–1124) was elected. The new pope was Guy of Burgundy, who was not only a good friend of Bishop Gelmírez, but perhaps more importantly, he was the uncle of Alfonso Raimúndez.

Urraca was gaining nominal support from some of the counts south of the Miño River, and in 1120 she attempted a hazardous campaign into Teresa's domains of the *terra portucalense*. But before doing that, she marched into Galicia, along with a force led by her son Alfonso Raimúndez, and advanced to Santiago de Compostela. There Urraca requested the assistance of the Bishop Diego Gelmírez and his militia to campaign against Teresa across the Miño River. Considering the relationship between the new pontiff and Alfonso Raimúndez, the bishop was constrained to refuse. Advancing across the Miño from Galicia, Urraca's coalition met with unexpected resistance. To strengthen her alliances, Teresa had taken the son of Pedro Foílaz, Fernando Pérez, as a lover. Teresa, Pedro, and the magnates loyal to her took refuge in the castle of Lanhoso. The campaign against Teresa was unsuccessful in dislodging her from the castle, but

Urraca did succeed in wresting support from some of the dissidents of Teresa's domain, who were not satisfied with her relationship with Fernando Pérez. On the return to Santiago, Urraca plotted an ill-advised scheme to divest Bishop Gelmírez of some of his power. She took the bishop as a prisoner. Back at Santiago, she informed the church officials that she was revoking the secular authority of the See of Santiago and that she was taking control of the castles of the bishopric. With this announcement, she used the bishop as a hostage to assure compliance of her demands. An uncontrollable riot broke out in the city, and Urraca was compelled to release the bishop after only a week in captivity. The bishop at once began negotiating with Pedro Froílaz in the north, with Teresa to the south, and with Alfonso Raimúndez to establish alliances against Urraca. At the same time, Urraca attempted to detach her son from the conspiracy and disuade him from joining the bishop's allliance. Under pressure from the pope, Urraca rescinded her order, and secular authority was formally restored to the bishop the following year (Reilly *The Contest* 149–51).

In a turnabout of aggression, Teresa invaded the south of Galicia in early 1122, which threatened the division of governance between Galicia and the *terra portucalense* that had existed since Alfonso VI assigned authority for them respectively to Raymond and Henry of Burgundy in 1095. Civil war was avoided with an agreement that provided joint rule over the valley of the Miño from Ourense down to Tuy. This concession would lead to the permanent authority of Teresa and subsequently of her son Alfonso Enríquez, the future Alfonso I of Portugal.

The following year, a third three-year truce was renewed between León-Castile and Aragon. Agreements with both her former husband Alfonso the Battler and with her half-sister Teresa permitted Urraca to campaign against the Muslims south of the Upper Duero. By January 1124, the important fortress of Sigüenza, along with Atienza and Medinaceli, were retaken from the Almoravids. These latter positions controlled the Roman road from Córdoba to Zaragoza and interdicted the paths of campaigns from Aragon in the north or from the Almoravids in the south. This area was important to both Urraca and to Alfonso Raimúndez, because it protected the trans-Duero region on the eastern flanks of Toledo. On April 2, 1125, the aging Archbishop Bernard, advisor of Alfonso VI and now tutor and advisor of Alfonso Raimúndez VII died, leaving the twenty-year-old monarch to govern on his own. He was limited only by the constraints of his mother Urraca who was still queen. However, the following year on March 8, 1126, in Saldaña the Queen died in her mid-forties. The twenty-one-year-old Alfonso Raimúndez became King Alfonso VII, the undisputed monarch of León-Castile.

The Eastern Counties Under Ramon Berenguer III (1097–1131)

The young Ramon Berenguer III took sole control as count of Barcelona in 1097 at the age of fifteen. His uncle Berenguer Ramon II, the twin brother of Ramon's father, Ramon Berenguer II, was suspected of fratricide, but was permitted to continue his authority until Ramon Berenguer III became of age. Sometime in 1096, Berenguer Ramon II was sent into exile, resulting in the full recognition of Ramon Berenguer III as count of Barcelona and its related territories. Opinions vary regarding the exact chronology of the transfer of authority. Ramon Berenguer III may have exercised limited governance before 1097, and the exact date of Berenguer Ramon's disappearance is obscure. But by 1097, the young count was certainly in full control (Sobriqués i Vidal 161).

As early as 1104, Ramon Berenguer III can be seen participating in a military campaign against the Muslims of the Ebro Valley. He assisted his cousin Ermengol VI (1102–1154) in the siege and capture of Muslim-held Balaguer that year, but his realm suffered a serious defeat in 1107 at the hands of the Almoravids, who devastated the Penedès and carried off a large amount of booty including thousands of captives. Fortunately for Ramon, his forces fended off further intrusions toward Barcelona itself, and he successfully defended against a siege of the city (Sobriqués i Vidal 167–8).

Ramon Berenguer III continued the mission of his grandfather Ramon Berenguer I to unify the eastern counties and bring them under the singular authority of Barcelona. Early in his reign, Ramon married María, the daughter of Rodrigo de Vivar, *el Cid*. Maria died around 1105, leaving the widower Ramon with two daughters, one also named María and the younger Ximena. In 1107, Ramon married the eldest daughter María to the aging Count Bernat III of Besalú. The young María was only seven years old at the time in contrast to the count who was more than fifty years old. The wedding agreement stipulated that if the marriage did not produce a male heir, the count's domains would pass to his cousin Ramon. The demise of Bernat III occurred just four years later in 1111, and his domains were united to the realm of Ramon Berenguer III (Sobriqués i Vidal 169–70).

The year after his first wife María died, Ramon took a second wife, Almodis, of uncertain heritage, who once again left him a widower in just a few years. Around 1110, Viscount Gilbert of the Massif Central in France and count of Provence, died leaving a wife Gerberga and two young daughters, Dolça and Estevaneta. The widow Gerberga was left in an isolated and defenseless situation, and so began looking for means to protect and govern the vast domains of her deceased husband. An agreement was reached on February 1, 1112, whereby Gerberga transferred all the domains held by Gilbert to her daughter Dolça, who married Ramon Berenguer III two days later. After the marriage, Gerberga confirmed that the holdings of her late husband were transferred jointly to Ramon and Dolça with inheritance rights granted to any future children. When Gerberga died just a year later, Dolça granted all her inherited rights to her new husband Ramon (Sobriqués i Vidal 172). The authority of the count of Barcelona and now count of Provence doubled in size and prestige. Moreover, the increased lines of communication between Catalonia and Provence produced a burgeoning of culture and commerce.

Ramon's acquisition through inheritance continued when Count Bernat Guillem of Cerdanya died in the beginning of 1117. Bernat had no heirs, and Ramon was his closest relative. Bernat and Ramon were indeed cousins as were most of the counts of the eastern counties who descended from Guifré the Hairy. All the domains of Bernat then passed into the hands of the count of Barcelona. The alliances of marriage continued immediately after Ramon's acquisition of Cerdanya. He arranged the marriage of his second daughter, Ximena, to Roger of Foix, who became Roger III after the death of his father Roger II. Ramon's influence was now extended ever farther westward on the northern side of the Pyrenees (Sobriqués I Vidal 186–8). Ramon effected a final marriage of convenience by arranging the union of his daughter Berenguela/Berenguera to Alfonso VII of León-Castile in 1128 (See Chart 12).

During his reign, Ramon Berenguer III expanded his rule from Barcelona and immediate regions to include nearly all the counties of present-day Old Catalonia. He gained vast holdings northward into Provence, southward to Taragona and eastward into the Balearic Islands. The eastern counties were dotted with numerous castles with a castle governor or castellan in charge. The region came to be perceived as a land of *castlans* "castellans," and consequently in the twelfth century became known as Catalonia. Ramon Berenguer III died on July 19, 1131, at the age of forty-eight and was buried at Santa Maria de Ripoll as he wished.

The last will and testament of Ramon Berenguer III specified that all his holdings in Iberia as well as the contiguous domains of Carcasonne and Razès were bequeathed to his eldest son Ramon Berenguer IV (1131–1162), just seventeen years old at the time. The sovereign domains held in southern France, effectively those inherited through Ramon Berenguer III's wife Dolça, were left to Ramon's younger son Berenguer Ramon (1131–1144) (Sobriqués i Vidal 200).

The Emergence of Portugal

The seed for the germination of an independent Portugal was sown in 1095 when Alfonso VI entrusted his son-in-law Henry of Burgundy, the husband of his illegitimate daughter Teresa, with the governance of the territory south of the Miño River. The motivation for this measure was no doubt prompted by the rumored ambitions of his other son-in-law, Raymond of Burgundy, the husband of his daughter Urraca. Presumably, Raymond was colluding with Henry to inherit Alfonso's kingdom for himself. By splitting Galicia into north-south territories, Alfonso VI thereby separated the potential allegiance of the two counts. The division at the Miño was simply a convenient construct that had no logical division of people on the opposite sides of that river. To be sure, the magnates of the two respective territories were desirous of maintaining and aggrandizing local power, but otherwise neither ethnic nor linguistic differences separated them.

From the time of Urraca's inheritance of León-Castile in 1109, Henry and Teresa distanced themselves from her and attempted to gain the loyalty of the local counts under their authority. The death of Henry in 1112 left Teresa to her own resources where she remained in the shadow of her half-sister. However, we are informed that by 1118, Teresa had ceased using the title of infanta and began using the title of queen, which begs the question of how and when she was crowned and exactly what comprised her realm. The region under Teresa's control was called the *terra portucalensis,* and at that time it was not recognized as a kingdom. The Roman name for the port at the mouth of the Duero was *portus cale,* "the Cale port" where present-day Oporto sits, and the region around the port was referred to as the *terra portucalensis.*

Teresa maintained her power by aligning with her lover Fernando Pérez of the

Galician house of Trastámara. By 1128, the magnates of the new Portugal rejected the leadership of the self-styled queen and her Galician lover Fernando in favor her son Alfonso Enríquez. Teresa's relationship with Fernando threatened the power structure of the counts south of the Miño River and pushed them into an alliance with her son. The young Alfonso Enríquez rebelled against his mother and her consort and defeated them at the battle of Mamed near Guimarães (about 15 miles southeast of Braga) on June 24, 1128, which drove them to Galicia in exile (Reilly *Alfonso VII* 25). Alfonso Enríquez did not maintain the low profile that his mother had assumed since the death of Urraca in 1126. Alfonso's influence over the local magnates increased with the years, and minor revolts against his rule were easily rebuffed. In November 1130, Teresa died, leaving no serious challenges to his authority.

Following his rise to sole authority, Alfonso Enríquez continued to use the title of *infans* rather than king. However, by 1135 as his influence and power grew, he changed his title to *portucalensis princeps*. Later that same year, he began construction of the great fortification of Leiria that protected Christian-held Coimbra from Lisbon and Santarém that were controlled by the Almoravids. From 1137 to 1141, Alfonso of Portugal and Alfonso VII of León-Castile became involved in border skirmishes that eventually were mollified by the archbishop of Braga who arranged for a settlement. The castles held by Alfonso Enríquez in Galicia were to be returned to the crown of León-Castile; conversely the castles held by Alfonso VII in Portugal were to be returned to Alfonso Enríquez, who by 1140 was using the title of king (Reilly *The Contest* 202–3). The grandson of Alfonso VI, son of Alfonso's illegitimate daughter Teresa, now prevailed as Alfonso I of Portugal.

Alfonso I of Aragon, the Battler, During the Truce with León-Castile: 1118–1126

In 1117, Alfonso of Aragon agreed to a three-year truce with Urraca, which ended the open hostilities between the Battler and León-Castile. The settlement awarded to Alfonso additional territories to the west of Aragon including La Rioja, and a strip of terrain through León-Castile along the *Camino de Santiago* pilgrimage route up to about fifty miles east of city of León. Just as importantly, the truce enabled Alfonso of Aragon to resume his campaigns against the Almoravids.

In 1110, Alfonso had defeated and killed al-Mustain, the *taifa* ruler of Zaragoza, and when al-Mustain's son Abd al-Malik was unable to win the favor of the city's population, an Almoravid garrison was welcomed to protect and rule over the city. Zaragoza was the jewel of the Ebro Valley and had been in Muslim hands from the beginning of the initial invasion when the Banu Qasi submitted to Musa ibn Nusayr in 714. Now the defeat of Zaragoza by Alfonso appeared to be achievable. In 1118, the Battler attacked the city and lay siege to it. The Almoravid governor Abd Allah ibn Mazdali hastened from Córdoba to relieve the besieged populace only to be killed in battle there in November 1118. Zaragoza fell to Alfonso I of Aragon in December of that year, and the campaign moved on to Tudela which fell in February 1119 (Reilly *The Contest* 145). The heart of the Muslim Upper March, which had been governed by Muslims for more than four centuries had now fallen under the control of the crown of Aragon.

The fall of Zaragoza paved the way for the conquest of the entire region that was under the rule of the former *taifa* of Zaragoza. On June 17, 1120, Alfonso of Aragon defeated a major Almoravid army at Cutanda, about sixty-five miles south of Zaragoza. Following this loss, the Almoravids were no longer able to defend the Upper March, and shortly thereafter, Calatayud and Daroca surrendered to the Battler. In this same year, Alfonso agreed to a three-year extension of the truce with León-Castile (Reilly *The Contest* 149). He was fully occupied with organizing the administrative controls of his recent territorial gains. In 1122, Alfonso established a fraternity of military knights at Belchite, some twenty miles southeast of Zaragoza. The purpose of this fraternity was for its members to dedicate their entire existence to the defense of the frontier against the Muslims. The confraternity of Belchite continued its activity during the lifetime of Alfonso but perished shortly after the Battler's demise. Again in 1123, the truce between León-Castile and Aragon was extended for an additional three-year period during which time the Battler had designs on conquering Muslim-held Lérida. His military advances against that city were derailed, because Lérida was paying *parias* to Ramon Berenguer III and was under his protection. In 1125 and 1126, Alfonso I of Aragon embarked on a nine-month raid against al-Andalus (O'Callaghan *A History* 220). By the time that he had finished his campaign, Queen Urraca of León had died and her son had been installed as the King Alfonso VII of León-Castile.

Young Alfonso VII and the Elder Battler in Contest: 1126–1134

Alfonso Raimúndez ascended the throne of León-Castile as Alfonso VII (1126–1157) following the death of his mother Urraca on March 8, 1126. He had exercised authority over Toledo since 1117 under the guidance of Archbishop Bernard of Toledo, and he had been on his own since the bishop's death in April of 1125. With the death of Urraca, the opposition in Galicia to the crown of León dissolved, for the Galicians had sided with the queen's son all along. Now with the unified support of the magnates of Galicia and León-Castile, Alfonso VII broke the peace with Aragón, which had been renewed in three-year increments since 1117. The young monarch mounted an offensive against the positions of Alfonso the Battler in León-Castile. Alfonso VII seized control of the Battler's garrisons along the pilgrimage route, such as Carrión de los Condes, and by April 30, 1127, portions of Castile around Burgos were again under the authority of León.

To address this threat, Alfonso the Battler of Aragón advanced an army into Castile and encountered the opposing army of Alfonso VII near Castrojeriz in late July of 1127. A battle was averted when two French nobles at the scene negotiated an agreement whereby Alfonso of Aragón agreed to surrender the locations which belonged to the crown of León-Castile by hereditary right and to discontinue using any titles which implied a claim to the crown of León. This was a wise decision for the Battler. Even if he had won the battle, he could not have controlled the territory whose counts, magnates, and prelates were now clearly supportive of the young Alfonso VII. Yet he was reluctant to yield the territories of Old Castile, La Rioja, and Basque Álava to the northeast of Burgos, and by agreement, they remained under his control. In November of that same year, Alfonso VII married Berenguela/Berenguera, the daughter of Ramon Berenguer III, to forge an alliance with the count of Barcelona and at the same time to strengthen his position against Alfonso I of Aragon (Reilly *Alfonso VII* 21–3).

In 1129 and 1130, Alfonso VII turned against the powerful Lara family that had been supportive of his mother but troublesome for him. He revoked the countships of both Rodrigo González of Asturias and of Pedro González of Castile, the former lover and consort of his mother Urraca. Their tenuous support of his authority was no longer needed (Reilly *Alfonso VII* 31–3).

With the loss of some of his western holdings, the Battler was intent on expanding his authority down the Ebro to the east. Specifically, he was desirous of capturing Lérida and Tortosa. These cities were part of the heritage of the ibn Hud family, and during that time, these cities either recognized the authority of the Almoravids or alternatively paid *parias* to the count of Barcelona, whoever provided greater protection for them. In 1133 and 1134, Alfonso I the Battler of Aragón targeted two smaller strongholds, Mequinenza and Fraga, near the Segre River which provided an avenue of supplies needed for a siege of Lérida. However, on July 17, 1134, he was surprised by an Almoravid attack near Fraga and was unpredictably routed. Some of his nobles including the Viscount Centulle of Bigorre and several bishops all perished in the defeat, and Alfonso I the Battler himself was wounded. He later died on September 7, 1134, from the wounds he received at Fraga. Alfonso I of Aragon left no heirs, not even any illegitimate ones. He had a will and testament drawn three years earlier, and as he lay on his deathbed on September 4, he reaffirmed his testimony, which specified that his kingdom be left to an assortment of religious military orders. Alfonso's testament was indeed problematic for the future governance of Aragon, and for the purpose of his successor, his will would be ignored (Reilly *The Contest* 171–3).

The Reign of Ramiro II and the Union of Aragon and Catalonia: 1134–1137

Alfonso I of Aragon had left neither son nor offspring to continue his line of inheritance. His marriage to Alfonso VI's daughter Urraca in 1109 not only failed to produce an heir but resulted in eight years of civil war before a truce was called in 1117. His last will and testament bequeathed his entire realm to three religious orders: the Holy Sepulcher, the Hospitallers, and the Templars. These final wishes were not only unprecedented but were problematic for the orderly succession of the crown. More specifically, the will that he had specified in 1131 deviated from the customary practices of the time which recognized the accession of the eldest son, or if none, the rights of male siblings. A sovereign realm governed by three religious military institutions was impractical if not inconceivable at the time. For the purposes of determining the future governance of Aragon, Alfonso's will and testament was effectively ignored.

Alfonso I of Aragon descended from the illegitimate line of Sancho Garcés III (1004–1035) of Navarre. Indeed, Alfonso was the great grandson of Sancho. Those who descended from Sancho's legitimate line, including Alfonso VII of León-Castile and

Alfonso Enríquez of Portugal as well as many other lesser nobles, may have had a genuine claim to the crown of Aragon. Further, if anyone were to recognize the validity of the marriage agreement between Alfonso and Urraca, the domains of Alfonso I would pass on to her and to her son, Alfonso Raimúndez, since he did not produce a son from that union as stipulated in the marriage contract. All that considered, two pretenders to Alfonso I's inheritance immediately presented, each with substantial partisan support.

Within weeks of Alfonso's death, the magnates and prelates of Aragon assembled at Jaca and recognized Alfonso's brother Ramiro II (1134–1137) as their next king. Ramiro certainly had a claim to the crown, since he was now the sole surviving son of Sancho Ramírez (1063–1094) (See Chart 11). Yet it is curious that Ramiro had spent his entire adult life as a monk and had served the crown only in a religious capacity. Nonetheless, Ramiro II, the monk, was installed as the monarch of Aragon, Sobrarbe, and Ribagorza, with the remaining portions of the Battler's realm still in dispute.

By contrast, the people of Navarre elected García Ramírez (1134–1150), the castellan of Monzón and Tudela, as their king. García was the grandson of Sancho Garcés of Uncastillo, the illegitimate son of García Sánchez III (1035–1054) of Navarre (See Chart 13). García took the title of king of Pamplona *rex pampilonensium*, and the people of Navarre conferred on him the epithet of *el Restaurador* "the Restorer" in reference to the fact that they were deprived of their own king in 1076 when Sancho Garcés IV (1054–1076) *el de Peñalén* was assassinated by his brother and sister, resulting in the division of the kingdom of Navarre between Aragon and León-Castile (Ubieto Arteta *Historia* 200+).

As a great grandson of Sancho Garcés III, Alfonso VII of León-Castile had his own claims to the territories left by Alfonso I. By November of 1134, Alfonso VII appeared with his forces at Nájera. The populace of that city had already declared allegiance to García Ramírez, but that declaration would not endure. Alfonso took possession of the entire west bank of the Ebro in La Rioja, the area that became part of Castile in 1076 after the death of Sancho Garcés IV of Navarre, *el de Peñalén*. Further, Alfonso VII proceeded to take control of Zaragoza, which Ramiro II of Aragon was powerless to prevent. In January of 1135, Ramiro of Aragon and García of Navarre concluded the pact of Vadoluengo which recognized the regal status of García and confirmed the boundary between their respective domains. In addition to Navarre, García's realm included the Basque areas of Álava, Vizcaya, and Guipúzcoa (Ubieto Arteta *Historia* 206–8).

By May 1135, Alfonso VII returned to La Rioja and met with García. Alfonso acknowledged him as the rightful king of Navarre and recognized his rule over the east bank of the Ebro down to and including Zaragoza. Ramiro II was left in a debilitated position. To prevent a further erosion of his authority and to reassure the populace of his remaining realm, Ramiro concluded a two-year truce with ibn Ganiya, the Almoravid governor of Valencia and Murcia, who defeated Alfonso I the Battler at Fraga. Furthermore, Ramiro II, the monk, set aside his religious vows and took a bride in November of 1135. Agnes, the daughter of Duke William IX of Aquitaine and widow of Viscount Aimery of Thouars, immediately became pregnant which reassured Ramiro's supporters that the regal lineage would be continued. In August of 1136, Ramiro's wife Agnes gave birth to the heiress Petronilla of Aragon. She was not expected to rule on her own, so the question arose as to whom she would marry in order to perpetuate the dynastic line. The following year when Petronilla was just one year old, she was betrothed to Count Ramon Berenguer IV (1131–1162) of Barcelona. The agreement of August 11, 1137, unconditionally ceded the entire realm of Aragon to Ramon upon the death of Ramiro II even if Petronilla predeceased her father and if the marriage produced no children. The marriage of Petronilla and Count Ramon eventually took place in 1150 when she became of age. The arrangement of 1137 gave birth to a new, united kingdom of count-kings reigning over Aragon and the eastern counties now called Catalonia. The union created a dynastic power that endured into the fifteenth century. Thus in 1137, Ramon Berenguer IV replaced Ramiro II as the monarch of Aragon with the consent and cooperation of the local magnates; Ramiro II returned to monastic life until his death in 1158; and Ramiro's wife Agnes returned to France.

Alfonso VII of León-Castile did not interfere with the agreement between Aragon and Catalonia. Moreover, he reversed an earlier donation of Zaragoza to García in the fall of 1135 by taking it back and yielding it to his brother-in-law Ramon Berenguer in August of 1136. Alfonso then turned his attention to Navarre in order to settle some issues with García Ramírez. After a brief campaign against Navarre, the Basque territories of Álava, Guipúzcoa, and Vizcaya were returned to the crown of León-Castile (Reilly *The Contest* 185–7).

In summary, the untimely death of Alfonso I of Aragon, the Battler, precipitated the brief and unexpected ascension of his brother Ramiro II, the monk, to the crown of Aragon and led to the subsequent union of Aragon and Catalonia. These circumstances also resulted in the re-birth of the kingdom of Navarre with García Ramírez as its *Restaurador* and in the recovery of territories by the crown of León-Castile that had been lost to Alfonso I during his war with Urraca.

The Re-Alignment and Stabilization of Four Christian Realms: 1137–1143

The re-alignment of the Christian realms following the death of Alfonso I of Aragon produced four sovereign rulers. In Aragon and Catalonia, Ramon Berenguer IV (1131–1162) remained as count of Barcelona and in addition became *princeps* of Aragon. García Ramírez (1134–1150) *el Restaurador* resuscitated the kingdom of Navarre and became the *rex pampilonensium*. Alfonso Enríquez (1139–1185) continued to rule as count of Portugal after the deposition and exile of his mother Teresa in 1128 and later was recognized as king. However, King Alfonso VII (1126–1157) of León-Castile remained the pre-eminent monarch in the peninsula, and on May 25, 1135, he had himself crowned as emperor and demanded vassalage from the other three rulers. While his superiority existed in principle, he exercised in practice much less control over them (Palenzuela 353).

Before and after Alfonso's imperial coronation, skirmishes between Portugal and the crown of León foreboded Portuguese independence. Early in 1137, the Portuguese invaded the territory of Limia on the border of León. The truce reached after this skirmish was ineffective, and from 1139 through 1140, Alfonso VII was compelled to returned to Galicia to restrain the advances of Alfonso Enríquez. Finally, the intervention and mediation of the Holy See in 1143 brought recognition of the regal status of King Alfonso I of Portugal in return for his homage to Alfonso VII.

Alfonso VII faced similar unrest on his eastern border. García Ramírez of Navarre was dissatisfied with losing authority over Zaragoza which had been transferred from his realm to Ramon Berenguer. Border skirmishes between Navarre and Castile arose in 1137, which prompted Alfonso VII to undertake military action on both eastern and western fronts. Hostilities subsided with an arrangement of marriage in 1140 between García's daughter Blanca and Alfonso's son Sancho, the future Sancho III (1157–1158) of Castile. Under the brokered peace agreement, Alfonso VII retained authority over La Rioja, while García continued to control the east bank of the Ebro down to Tudela. An additional alliance was struck in June 1144 with the second marriage of García Ramírez to Alfonso's daughter Urraca born of Alfonso's paramour Guntroda Pérez. (Palenzuela 355). During these same years, Navarre was also engaged in border clashes with Aragon, and peace between them was more elusive. A truce of 1141 did not stop their intermittent border skirmishes until 1146 (Reilly *The Contest* 188+).

Alfonso VII found time in 1137 to stage raids through al-Andalus all the way down to the environs of Cádiz. Further, the leadership of the Almoravids was stretched thin in 1137 when Emir Sir called his half-brother Tashfin back to North Africa, which left their brother ibn Ganiya in charge of operations in Iberia. Alfonso VII immediately took advantage of this void by attacking the Muslim fortress of Colmenar de Oreja about thirty-five miles to the northwest of Toledo, a castle which posed a continual threat to that city. In 1142, Alfonso lay siege to Coria in Extremadura aimed at eliminating the threat to the western flanks of Toledo. In June of that year, Coria fell to Alfonso (Reilly *The Contest* 208–9). The power of the Almoravids in Iberia and in North Africa was clearly in decline. However, the rising power of the Muslim Almohads in North Africa was waiting in the wings to supplant the Almoravids on both sides of Gibraltar.

The Rise of the Almohads

The birth and rise of the Almohad sect in some ways repeats the genesis of the Almoravid movement. In each case, a young man leaves home in search of learning and knowledge and returns filled with religious zeal and with a mission to lead his tribe to the rightly guided path of Islam. The founder of the Almohad movement was Muhammad ibn Tumart who was born around 1080. He left his village of Igiliz in the Sous Valley of the high Atlas Mountains around 1106 in search of learning and became one of the many wandering scholars of the era. He is said to have traveled to Córdoba and then to Egypt, Syria and perhaps Bagdad to seek out the most famous teachers of the day. He travelled back through Tunisia and Algeria and returned to the Maghreb around 1119 and began preaching his own brand of fundamental Islam.

Ibn Tumart's brand of Islam did not conform to the other Islamic sects of the day. Instead he proclaimed a form of Islam that would complete the call of the Prophet and restore a "true" form of Islam (Fromherz 137). As a fundamentalist, he interdicted worldly pleasures such as alcohol, music, poetry, and dance and practiced strict segregation of the sexes, but his guiding principle stressed the unity of God. While all Islamic sects observed one God, the Almohad version affirmed that God had no observable traits nor any anthropomorphic characteristics. From this basic tenet, the followers of ibn Tumart became known as the *Muwahhidun*, "those who affirm the unity of God," and this epithet was subsequently Hispanicised as the *almohades*, the Almohads (Kennedy *Muslim Spain* 198).

It is surprising that ibn Tumart's initial attempts at preaching against the Almoravids did not result in his immediate demise. He is said to have railed through the markets of Fez, smashing wine jugs and musical instruments. He openly criticized the Almoravid emir, Ali ibn Yusuf, and reportedly pulled the emir's daughter from her horse, because she was not wearing a veil (Fletcher *Moorish Spain* 119). Further, he characterized the Almoravids as feminine because of their tradition of wearing a veil, while permitting their women to appear in public without one.

Ibn Tumart achieved little success among the Almoravid centers and very shortly gravitated to his home in the Atlas Mountains. In the foothills of his homeland at Tinmal, he converted the Berber tribes of the region to his view of religion and in 1121 proclaimed himself as Mahdi, that is the rightly guided one sent by God to restore righteousness before the day of judgement (Fromherz 60). Unlike the Almoravids whose leadership was tribal and familial, ibn Tumart installed a chain of command among his followers as they began to take military action against the Almoravids. The Almoravid campaigns of Emir Ali ibn Yusuf against the mountainous strongholds of the Almohads went for naught. The desert tactics of the Almoravids were no match for the Almohads accustomed to maneuvering in mountainous terrain. Over the next decade, the military strength of the Almohads crescendoed and did not cease with the death of ibn Tumart in 1130. He was succeeded by a very capable commander, Abd al-Mumin, who advanced the legacy of ibn Tumart.

The weakening Almoravid empire, as it continued to maintain operations on both sides of Gibraltar, was further devastated by the death of the aging Emir Ali ibn Yusuf in January of 1143. Ali's son, Tashfin ibn Ali, had been called back from al-Andalus to North Africa to address the growing threat of the Almohads, and now with his father deceased, he became emir of the empire and commander of their military. The Almohads now saw a chance to defeat and replace the Almoravids. In 1145, Abd al-Mumin attacked Tlemcen, Tunisia and forced Tashfin ibn Ali to retreat to Oran, a North African citadel on the Mediterranean. The Almohads trapped Tashfin and his allies at that citadel by the sea and set fire to it as the refugees waited for ten ships to sail them to the safety of Iberia. In a desperate attempt to escape the conflagration, Tashfin fled on horseback in the dead of night and was thrown from his horse into a ravine and killed. The Almoravids were now without a strong leader, and that same year the Almohads continued their assault by laying siege to Fez. After seven months, that city fell, and the Almohads moved immediately to assail Marrakesh where the heir to Tashfin's Almoravid empire was seated. Tashfin's heir apparent was his son Ibrahim ibn Tashfin, who was only ten years old and too young to rule effectively. Consequently, the tribal elders opted for Ishaq ibn Ali, the grandson of the first emir, Yahya ibn Umar, although Ishaq was also very young and untested. Abd al-Mumin made a ceremonious entrance into a conquered Marrakesh at the end of March 1147. The recently appointed emir of the Almoravids, Ishaq, was denied mercy and was beheaded, putting an end to the Almoravid empire (Messier 164–8). The supremacy of the Almohads in North Africa was secured. They were now free to turn their attention to al-Andalus.

The Christian North Confronts a New Power in al-Andalus: 1143–1157

The death of the Almoravid emir, Ali ibn Yusuf, in late January 1143 of natural causes induced a chain of events which unraveled the Almoravid Empire and subsequently set in motion a succession of changes of power in Iberia. Emir Ali ibn Yusuf had designated his son Abu Muhammad Sir as his successor, but the governance of Iberia lay in the hands of two other sons. Ibn Ganiya was governor of Valencia, and Tashfin ibn Ali was seated in Seville. However, by the time of the death of Ali ibn Yusuf, Abu Muhammad Sir was killed in a situation of domestic violence, and his half-brother Tashfin was called to North Africa and placed in command of the Almoravid armies to counter the rising power of the Almohads (Lagardère 300). Consequently, ibn Ganiya remained in charge of the entire Almoravid operation in al-Andalus.

In 1143, the Almoravids in Iberia faced assaults on three fronts. The Christians campaigned incessantly from the north; lack of defense and security fomented unrest and revolt within al-Andalus; and the rising power of the Almohads threatened their North African empire. Alfonso VII of León-Castile campaigned with impunity through al-Andalus, while Alfonso Enríquez of Portugal pushed unsuccessfully to the south against Lisbon, and Ramon Berenguer IV of Barcelona ravaged the Muslim-held countryside around Lérida and Tortosa. In June 1144, Alfonso VII arranged the marriage of his daughter Urraca to King García Ramírez of Navarre and continued his raids against Almoravid positions. The death of Ali ibn Yusuf as well as the inability of the Almoravids to defend against the incursions of the Christian north led to a general revolt throughout al-Andalus. In the summer of 1144, a revolt against Almoravid authority erupted in the Algarve in southwest Iberia, followed immediately by an insurrection in Córdoba in late 1144 and early 1145. Ibn Ganiya was successful in restoring his authority over the Algarve and Córdoba, but the eastern portion of al-Andalus including Murcia, Málaga and Granada were all declared independent. The collapse of Almoravid authority produced a new generation of *taifa* states such as those that were prevalent following the disintegration of the Umayyad caliphate. Alfonso VII's response was swift. In May 1146, he attacked Córdoba and forced ibn Ganiya to become his vassal (Reilly *The Contest* 210–2). While the Almoravids were losing ground in Iberia, the struggle between the Almoravids and the Almohads continued in North Africa. The Almohads led by Abd al-Mumin attacked Tlemcen, Tunisia in 1145 and defeated Emir Tashfin ibn Ali. Within two years, the Almoravid empire in North Africa was defunct.

Almohad forces landed at Algeciras in 1146 and established a position at Jerez de la Frontera where the Muslim population welcomed them. They proceeded to march through the rebellious Algarve and obtained a tentative submission from the cities of Niebla, Mértola, Silves and then moved north to Badajoz. The following year in 1147, the Almohads attacked the Almoravid center of Seville and took that city after a great show of resistance and loss of life. Later that same year, ibn Ganiya, who was still in charge of Córdoba, rejected the vassalage that he had just recently pledged to Alfonso VII and surrendered the towns of Córdoba and Jaén to the Almohads. Ibn Ganiya sought asylum in Granada where he died the following year. The initial campaign of the Almohads during 1147 and 1148 had secured the entire southwest portion of al-Andalus from the Algarve to Badajoz and eastward including Córdoba and Seville. However, in the eastern half of al-Andalus, the new *taifa* rulers not only replaced the authority of the Almoravid regime, but they resisted the Almohads as well. The most powerful among the independent rulers was ibn Mardanish, known to Christian sources as *el rey lobo* "the wolf king," who rose to power in Valencia in 1147. Ibn Mardanish quickly established relationships with the Christians and began to pay *parias* to Ramon Berenguer IV for security against the Almohads. He subsequently negotiated a ten-year trade agreement with Genoa for the ports of Valencia and Denia and agreed not to attack Almería (O'Callaghan *A History* 229–32).

While the Almohads were busy claiming positions formerly held by the Almoravids, the Christians were not idle. In a winter campaign of January 1147, Alfonso VII conquered the Almoravid stronghold at Calatrava la Vieja. The Christian campaigns then turned into crusades after Pope Eugenius III issued a bull which designated Iberia as an area of crusade. As a part of this effort, Alfonso VII agreed to participate in an attack of the Almoravid pirate port of Almería. The attack was supported by Alfonso VII, Ramon Berenguer IV of Barcelona, García Ramírez IV of Navarre and was assisted by a fleet sent from Genoa with a host of crusaders. No assistance was forthcoming from Muslim partisans, and the city surrendered on October 17, 1147. Almería became a vassal city of the Genoese commune (Kennedy *Muslim Spain* 190). By agreement with Ramon Berenguer, the combined forces that had conquered Almería turned their sights in 1148 on the coveted city of Tortosa at the mouth of the Ebro River. The siege was joined by the Templars, Hospitallers, and Christian forces from the south of France. The city was forced to surrender in December of 1148. Ramon Berenguer then continued his assault on the Ebro Valley in 1149, and with the assistance of the count of Urgell and Christian troops from the south of France, he was finally able to take control of Lérida and neighboring Fraga and Mequinenza. By the end of that year, the entire territory of the former *taifa* of Zaragoza including the Ebro Valley all the way down to Tortosa was in Christian hands (Reilly *The Contest* 215).

Meanwhile on the western front, Alfonso Enríquez of Portugal attacked the Muslim town of Santarém that protected Lisbon from the north. He immediately put that city under siege while he traveled north to Oporto to meet with a fleet carrying German, English and Flemish crusaders on their way by sea to the Holy Land. Alfonso Enríquez offered the crusaders the spoils of Lisbon and future trading privileges if they would join in the attack on Lisbon. That city finally surrendered to the combined Christian forces on October 24, 1147 (Lomax 92). Alfonso Enríquez now controlled the entire stretch of Portugal from south of the Minho River down to and including Lisbon on the Tajo.

In 1150 Alfonso VII resumed his offensive against the Almohads. Aided by King García Ramírez (1134–1150) of Navarre and Count Ermengol VI (1102–1154) of Urgell, he lay siege to Córdoba and skirmished with Almohad forces in the area without significant results. Later that year on November 21, 1150, García Ramírez died and was succeeded by his son Sancho VI (1150–1194), *el Sabio*, without challenge.

In 1151 Alfonso VII and Ramon Berenguer signed the treaty of Tudején which agreed on a division of Navarre. The agreement went on to state that Ramon would hold the eastern territories south of Catalonia down through Valencia, Denia, and Murcia in fief at such time that they were conquered. This agreement may have been optimistic or premature, since ibn Mardanish of Valencia was well in control of these domains and was paying Ramon for protection to maintain that status. Further, Sancho VI was not unseated from his authority in Navarre. The agreement of Tudején, therefore, had no effect (Palenzuela 360–1). In July and August of that year, Alfonso VII lay siege to Jaén near the Sierra Nevada. On the western front, Alfonso Enríquez attacked the Almohads at Alcácer do Sal in the Algarve. Neither Christian expedition produced favorable results. The following year, Alfonso VII again made a failed attempt to control the small *taifa* of Guadix, which perhaps prompted his respite from campaigning during 1153 and 1154. During that time, the Almohads strengthened their southern position by overcoming the independent *taifa* of Málaga. During his haitus from campaigning, Alfonso VII negotiated the marriage of his daughter Constanza to King Louis VII of France, and the union was consummated in 1154 (Reilly *The Contest* 219–20; Reilly *Alfonso VII* 119–20).

Alfonso VII finally succeeded in advancing into Andalucia by taking Andújar on the Guadalquivir in 1155, as well as Santa Eufemia and Pedroche to the north of Córdoba. But the following year as the king of León-Castile fell ill, the Almohads launched a major offensive, taking the *taifa* of Granada. They then continued to regain the recently controlled Christian positions at Santa Eufemia, Pedroche, and Montoro to the northeast of Córdoba (Lomax 93).

In 1157, the Almohads, under the leadership of ibn Saïd, the son of Emir Abd al-Mumin, lay siege to Almería. Alfonso VII led a relief force against the siege, but when he was unable to break through enemy lines into the city, he decided to attack Granada as a diversionary tactic. The assault was aborted, and as Alfonso VII made his way back to Toledo, he succumbed to illness just after passing through the pass of Despeñaperros in the Sierra Nevada range on August 21, 1157 (Reilly *The Contest* 222–3). The fifty-two-year-old monarch left a will that divided his kingdom between his two sons Fernando II (1157–1188) and Sancho III (1157–1158) (See Chart 10). The struggle against the new Almohad threat would be resumed by Alfonso's heirs.

CHAPTER 8

The Division of León-Castile and the Decline of the Almohads: 1157–1214

The Division of León-Castile and the Regency of Alfonso VIII: 1157–1169

The death in 1157 of the ailing monarch of León-Castile, Alfonso VII, resulted in the division of his realm between his two sons. Sancho III (1157–1158) the elder received the kingdom of Castile, and Fernando II (1157–1188) inherited the kingdom of León (See Chart 10). The partitioning of authority was not sudden. Alfonso VII had referred to his sons using the title of king as early as 1148, and they had been issuing royal documents in their own names (Linehan *Spain* 7). The realization of this division in 1157, however, provoked decades of mistrust and conflict, not only between these two realms, but it precipitated power struggles over territorial control and expansion among all the Christian monarchs. The feud over the border regions between León-Castile would not be resolved until the re-unification of the bifurcated kingdom was finalized in 1230.

The succession of Sancho III and Fernando II aroused immediate apprehension throughout the Christian realms. Soon after Fernando hastened to León to take possession of his inheritance, Alfonso I (1139–1185) of Portugal arrived to meet with the new monarch to affirm that the relationship between Portugal and León would not change, even though there were unresolved boundary disputes. Similarly, Sancho III had barely assumed the throne of Castile when he received a visit from Sancho VI (1150–1194) of Navarre at Soria in November 1157. The two Sanchos reaffirmed the vassalage of Navarre to Castile, and they agreed on the marriage of Sancho VI with the Castilian princess Sancha, the sister of Sancho III. Yet to be settled was the intent of Ramon Berenguer IV (1131–1162) to seize the territory of Navarre despite the treaty of Tudején, which specified a division of Navarre between Aragon and Castile in the event that Sancho VI was not able to secure the throne. In February of 1158, Ramon and Sancho III met at Nájima near Osma to discuss their respective borders and to reaffirm the treaty of Tudején. The meeting between the two monarchs further recognized Ramon's authority over Zaragoza in return for Ramon's homage to Castile (Palenzuela 368–9). We can only wonder how the issue of Navarre was treated, since the installment of Sancho VI as king of Navarre was already an accomplished fact. A division of Navarre between Castile and Aragon was not a realistic expectation at that time.

Three months later in May 1158 at Sahagún, the brothers Sancho and Fernando formulated their own pact. They vowed mutual aid against all aggressors, except against their uncle Ramon Berenguer IV. They further agreed not to sign an agreement with Alfonso I of Portugal without the consent of the other. Any territories acquired from Portugal were to be partitioned equally between them. As for the expansion into Muslim territories, Fernando would have the rights to lands from Niebla to Lisbon, and Sancho would expand into the remaining Muslim lands. Seville and its environs would be shared between both. The brothers also agreed on terms regarding the jurisdiction of the *tierra de campos*, the fertile, flat high plain on the northern boundaries of Zamora, Valladolid, and Palencia, formerly known as the *campos goticos*, where many Goths settled during their migration from the Toulouse region. Sancho acknowledged Fernando's claim to the *tierra de campos* with the stipulation that the Castilians in the disputed area be allowed to retain their holdings (Palenzuela 365–70). Despite the agreement reached by Fernando II and Sancho III at Sahagún, the *tierra de campos* would be fought over until after the death of Sancho's son Alfonso VIII (1158–1214).

The untimely death of Sancho III on August 31, 1158, after an abbreviated rule of just over 12 months left an infant successor, Alfonso VIII, barely three years old, whose mother Blanca of Navarre died in childbirth. Sancho III granted custody of the young king to his tutor Gutierre Fernández de Castro, but the power of regency was given to Manrique Pérez de Lara. The long minority of the child-king engendered a power struggle between these influential Castilian families that had a history of enmity. A few months after Sancho's death, the tutorship of Alfonso was wrested from Gutierre Fernández and given to García Garcés, who was aligned with the Laras. Consequently, open hostilities erupted between the two families in March 1160, provoking the Castros to align and conspire with Fernando II of León. Their joint conspiracy of 1162 succeeded in transferring the governance of Toledo from Castile to León with Fernando Rodríguez de Castro as its governor. Meanwhile, the care of the young Alfonso VIII was entrusted to Manrique Pérez de Lara, making him the guardian and regent for the boy-king (Linehan *Spain* 26+).

In July 1164, the power struggle between the Castros and the Laras culminated in a battle at Huete between their private armies, led by Fernando Rodríguez, the governor of Toledo, and Manrique de Lara, the king's guardian, who was killed in the fray. This egregious activity was terminated by the bishops of the kingdom of Castile who called a synod at Segovia in 1166 and issued decrees declaring the Peace of God. All the inhabitants of Castile were required under the threat of excommunication and other penalties to defend the kingdom against any invader. In August of that same year, the citizenry of Toledo took matters into their own hands by overthrowing Governor Fernando Rodríguez, who fled to al-Andalus, whereupon they returned the city to the king of Castile (Linehan *Spain* 29–31).

While Castile sorted out its internecine difficulties, it lost territories to both León and Navarre by 1161. Fernando II of León had seized control of several Castilian towns on its western border, and Sancho VI (1150–1194) of Navarre did the same for several border locations in the east of Castile. Also in 1161, Fernando II diverted his attention from Castile to the establishment of a stronghold at Ciudad Rodrigo in the Extremadura, which attracted settlers from Ávila and Salamanca, thereby impeding the expansion of the Portuguese into that region (O'Callaghan *A History* 236; Linehan *Spain* 28–9).

With the death of Alfonso VII of Leon-Castile in 1157, Ramon Berenguer IV (1131–1162) became the most powerful leader in Iberia. Through his marriage to the child-queen Petronilla of Aragon, he ascended as monarch of that realm, all the while retaining an overlordship as count of the eastern counties now recognized as Catalonia. By the treaty of Tudején in 1151, Alfonso VII recognized Ramon's right to expand southward into Valencia and Murcia. Ibn Mardanish, the Muslim king of these territories, had already begun paying tribute to Ramon for military assistance when needed. Ramon completed a truce with Sancho VI (1131–1162) of Navarre in 1159 that ended their border disputes. Ramon Berenguer IV also acted as protector of his nephew, Count Ramon Berenguer of Provence, and in 1162 successfully negotiated the title to that realm, which recognized his nephew's legitimate inheritance to it. Ramon Benenguer IV died unexpectedly in Piedmont in August 1162 and left an heir of five years named Ramon. The boy's right to the succession of Aragon and Barcelona was confirmed at Huesca in October 1162 with the magnates of Aragon and Catalonia present. Subsequent documents changed the boy's name from Ramon to Alfonso II (1162–1196) of Aragon and Alfons I of Catalonia (Bisson 35; Reilly *The Contest* 226). Petronilla, the mother of Alfonso II, surrendered all her rights to him in 1164, and two years later, he inherited Provence from his cousin Ramon, which included overlordship of Béziers, Carcasonne, Narbonne, and Montpellier (O'Callaghan *A History* 236) (See Chart 14).

The Almohad Emir Abd al-Mumin (1130–1163) came to al-Andalus in 1160 and ordered the construction of a town and fortification at Gibraltar. He left his son Abu Yaqub Yusuf (1163–1184) in charge of dealing with ibn Mardanish and with re-claiming the Muslim positions formerly held by the Almoravids and now under the control of ibn Mardanish. In 1162, Yusuf routed ibn Mardanish near Granada and regained control of Jaén, Ubeda, Baeza, Carmona, and Ecija. When Abd al-Mumin died in 1163, Yusuf increased the pressure on ibn Mardanish and defeated him near Murcia in 1165. Thereafter, the Almohads gained ground city by city, and before ibn Mardanish died in 1172, he had advised his son to make peace with the Almohads, which effectively surrendered Valencia and the remaining portions of al-Andalus to them (O'Callaghan *A History* 237).

The relationship between Fernando II of León and Alfonso I of Portugal remained tenuous. Despite their meeting at La Cabrera to the north of Madrid at the end of November 1158 to discuss matters of border disputes and despite their treaty of Lérez in 1165, which included an agreement of marriage between Alfonso's daughter Urraca with Fernando II, expansionary efforts of Portugal impinged on the expansionary designs of Fernando II. The Leonese response to Portuguese expansion into the Extremadura was the taking of Alcántara in 1166. As early as 1158, Alfonso I of Portugal captured Alcácer do Sal, just below Lisbon south of the Tajo River. Furthermore, several conquests were made on Alfonso's behalf by the military adventurer Geraldo Sem Pavor, the Fearless. During the years from 1165 to 1168, Geraldo captured Evora, Trujillo, Cáceres, Montánchez, Serpa, and Juromenha. He became known to some as the Portuguese Cid. His most successful attempt included an attack on Badajoz in May 1169.

He breached the walls, controlled the town, and then called Alfonso I to assist him in taking the inner fortification. The entrance of the Portuguese into Badajoz prompted the intervention of Fernando II of León, who considered Extremadura as an area reserved for his own expansion. Fernando immediately staged an attack on Badajoz. The Portuguese led by Alfonso I and Geraldo were put to flight and captured. However, during the melee, Alfonso I broke his leg and thereafter was unable to mount a horse. Alfonso I and Sem Pavor were released only after agreeing to yield to León the border territories of Toroño and Limia in addition to surrendering the recently acquired locations in Extremadura. Badajoz was returned to the control of the Muslims with a stipulation of vassalage to León. Upon the departure of the Christians, the Muslims immediately repudiated the agreement, and the city walls were opened to the Almohads. Geraldo then defected and spent some time in the service of the Almohads until he was accused of conspiring with Alfonso I of Portugal in 1174 and was beheaded (Palenzuela 373).

While Fernando II of León was preoccupied with border problems with Alfonso I of Portugal, and even as border disputes between Castile with León and Navarre dragged on, Alfonso VIII of Castile (1158–1214) attained the age of majority on November 11, 1169, and began to rule on his own without a regent. Later in November, he called the first curia of his reign at Burgos, and before year's end, he married Leonora, the ten-year-old daughter of King Henry II of England.

Almohad Campaigns During the Early Reign of Alfonso VIII: 1169–1188

Alfonso VIII (1158–1214) of Castile became of age in November 1169 and was knighted to mark his passage into manhood. He would now be dealing with the other monarchs of Iberia on his own behalf. At the time of Alfonso's ascendance, there were four other Christian monarchs, and confusingly two others were also named Alfonso. His cousin, Alfonso II (1162–1196) of Aragon was still under age and influenced by his regent, Seneschal Guillem Ramon in concert with the bishop of Barcelona, Guillem de Torroja. Alfonso II became of age in 1174 and married Sancha of Castile, the daughter of Alfonso VII with his second wife Rica. Sancha was therefore the half-sister of Fernando II of León. Sancho Garcés VI (1150–1194) of Navarre was still in possession of borderlands confiscated from Castile during Alfonso VIII's minority, and similarly, Fernando II (1157–1188) of León held properties that were claimed by Castile. Alfonso I (1139–1185) of Portugal was now well established as king and had recently expanded his realm into Muslims locations to the south.

In June 1171, the Almohad threat intensified as Emir Abu Yaqub Yusuf (1163–1184), known also as Yusuf I, arrived in Iberia to campaign against the Christians. He had been the leader of the Almohads since the death of his father Abd al-Mumin (1130–1163) eight years earlier, and now he settled in at Seville and remained there while he planned his campaign. The following spring, news arrived that ibn Mardanish had died of natural causes on March 8, 1172. Ibn Mardanish had already lost most of his support, and the Muslim population of his kingdom now submitted to Almohad rule. With all al-Andalus now under Yusuf's authority, the emir was free to focus his attention on the Christians. The newly recruited men from ibn Mardanish informed Yusuf I that Huete was an ideal target for an attack against the Christians, because it was recently settled and inadequately fortified. Huete did not have natural fortifications. It had a citadel on a hill with a lightly fortified suburb below next to a small stream.

The emir left Seville in June 1172 by way of Córdoba, and as he approached Huete, he was leading a formidable force of Almohads and Arabs from North Africa supplemented by the Muslims of al-Andalus. On July 12, an assault of the suburb of Huete caused its defenders to flee to the citadel for refuge. A direct assault on the citadel failed, forcing the Almohads to settle down for a siege. The inadequate provisioning of the Almohad army began to show as parties were dispatched to the countryside to forage in vain for food. The emir ordered siege engines to be built, but construction was impeded on the fourteenth when violent storms, unusual for July, interrupted all activity. News arrived on the July 22 that Alfonso VIII was on his way with a large army to relieve the siege. With this news, the emir ordered the siege engines to be burned and to load the bells from the tower of the suburb onto pack animals. He further ordered his forces to break camp and head for Cuenca, the nearest Muslim town some thirty-three miles to the east. In the confusion, the Christians from the citadel attacked the departing camp, slaughtering the weak and ill. On July 25, the Almohad army camped near Cuenca on the banks of the Júcar River, and supply problems became more appreciable. The next day, the Almohads learned of the approach of Alfonso VIII and his army, and the emir again gave the order to transfer the camp to the safety of the other side of the Júcar. Again, there was much confusion and chaos as when the camp at Huete was broken. On July 28, a small band of Almohads skirmished with the Christian forces on the other side of the river, but when the Almohads finally decided to fully engage on July 29, the Christian army had departed, and the Almohads did not pursue. The population of Cuenca was left to its own devices without a garrison, and Yusuf I departed for Murcia in desperate need of food. By August 17, the emir was in Murcia after temporary stops in Buñol and Valencia, and with most of his army disbanded, he returned to Seville in October with all the accolades befitting of the Almohad leader. In fact, however, Huete was still controlled by the Christians; Cuenca was left for future conquest by them; and the strength and leadership of the Almohad emir were left in question (Kennedy *Muslim Spain* 223–31).

The Almohads unleashed a ferocious attack on Extremadura in September 1173. In the following year, Alcántara and Cáceres fell, and many Christian positions south of the Tajo were evacuated. The Christians assembled at Ciudad Rodrigo and withstood the Almohad menace until a relief force arrived. Fernando II succeeded in driving off the Almohad armies from the environs of Ciudad Rodrigo in October of 1174, but effectively all the Leonese positions in Extremadura south of the Tajo were lost (Palenzuela 380).

In the beginning of 1176, Emir Yusuf I returned to North Africa. His campaign in Iberia had not produced any decisive victories against the Christians, but he did succeed in annexing the Muslim occupied territories around Valencia into the Almohad empire. Further, he reinforced the Muslim borders to block the advances of Castile and Portugal. This maneuver induced these two Christian realms to petition for a five-year truce that left Fernando II alone to combat the Almohads. In the final analysis, Yusuf had blocked the advance of León into the Extremadura and had pushed its population to the north of the Tajo. (Kennedy *Muslim Spain* 230).

The internal court in León was in turmoil. A papal decree had deemed the marriage of Fernando II and Princess Urraca of Portugal illegitimate by reason of consanguinity. Fearing excommunication, Urraca left the marriage in June 1175 and retired to a convent. However, the future King Alfonso IX, born to the couple on August 15, 1171, at Zamora, was legitimate and began to figure into the official documents of the realm. In search of another queen, Fernando negotiated a marriage with Teresa Fernández de Traba, recently widowed from Nuño Pérez de Lara, who was killed in battle at Cuenca. Through this marriage, Fernando intended to strengthen his relationships with both his wife's powerful Galecian family as well as with the house of Lara. However, his strategy proved to be ephemeral as Queen Teresa of León died in childbirth in 1180, and the child died shortly afterwards. To further thwart his relationships, the king's half-sister Estefanía, the wife of Fernando Rodríguez de Castro, also died, severing the king's direct affiliations with another important family (Palenzuela 381–2).

Yusuf I's departure from the peninsula encouraged the northern kings to take military action, even though the five-year truce between Yusuf and Castile and Portugal had not yet expired. In 1177, Alfonso VIII of Castile, Alfonso II of Aragon, and Fernando II of León convened at Tarazona to discuss future action against the Almohads. That very summer following the meeting, Fernando II campaigned as far south as Jerez. In September, Alfonso VIII conquered Cuenca, and for his part, Alfonso II staged an attack on the lands around Murcia.

In early 1179 Alfonso VIII and Alfonso II again convened to resolve open issues between their realms, specifically those which related to the expansion of their respective territories. They also discussed a strategy to deal with Sancho VI, who had not delivered on previous territorial agreements. Specifically, Sancho VI of Navarre and Alfonso VIII of Castile agreed in August of 1176 to submit their border disputes to be arbitrated by Henry II of England, Alfonso's father-in-law. Henry's finding was that the borders between Navarre and Castile were to be re-established as they were at the time of death of Alfonso VII in 1157. Alfonso VIII of Castile and Alfonso II of Aragon met on March 20, 1179, at Cazola, today an uninhabited location near Ariza (Palenzuela 383), to sign an agreement for the rights of future expansion. Castile recognized the right of Aragon to expand into Valencia, Biar, Játiva and Denia and as far as Calpe. However, the domains of Murcia and to the south including the province of Alicante would be reserved for Castilian conquest. Further, Aragon would be released from its vassalage to Castile. The treaty of Cazola effectively modified the treaty of Tudején of 1151 in two major ways. First, it released Aragon from its vassalage to Castile, but more significantly, Aragon lost its right to expand into the domains of Murcia. The exclusion of Navarre from the discussion at Cazola exerted pressure on Sancho VI of Navarre to reconsider the arbitration decision of Henry II concerning the boundary disputes between Navarre and Castile. A few days later, Alfonso VIII and Sancho VI met near Logroño, and Sancho accepted the arbitrated decision with modifications. In the end, Sancho returned the locations that he occupied in La Rioja, and Alfonso returned the locations that he occupied in Navarre. Guipúzcoa and Álava were defined to be in the borders of Navarre, although Alfonso VIII still considered them part of his realm (Palenzuela 383–4).

In March of 1181, Fernando II and Alfonso VIII met at Medina de Rioseco, some 25 miles to the northwest of Valladolid, and signed an agreement which in principle would resolve the border issues between León and Castile that dated from the death of Alfonso VII. The agreement was eventually finalized two years later in 1183, but it also required a unified action against the Almohads. The two monarchs fulfilled their campaign commitments in the ensuing years. In the spring of 1182 while Yusuf I was still in North Africa, Alfonso VIII launched a raid into the Muslim environs of Córdoba, Seville, Málaga, and Granada and kept a garrison for several months at Setefilla, near the Guadalquivir to the north of Seville. In January 1184, Fernando II lay siege to Cáceres for six months but failed to take it.

Emir Yusuf came back to the peninsula in May 1184, and Fernando fell back to the safety of Ciudad Rodrigo. After a short stop at Badajoz, the emir struck at Santarém, laying siege to that city. Fernando decided to direct a relief force toward Santarém, and when the emir was informed of Fernando's impending arrival, he lifted the siege and departed in great disarray, just as he had done previously at Huete. Fernando struck while the Almohads were disorganized, and during the ensuing battle, Yusuf was mortally wounded and died a few days later. The Almohads retreated to Seville and the new Emir Abu Yusuf Yaqub al-Mansur (1184–1199) succeeded his father. The death of the emir provoked uprisings within the Almohad empire and drew the attention of the new emir, Abu Yusuf, away from the peninsula for a hiatus of nearly ten years, permitting increased aggression from the Christians. In 1186, Alfonso VIII seized Júcar and Cabriel and strengthened his positions at Trujillo and Plasencia (Palenzuela 385).

On December 6, 1185, Alfonso I of Portugal died of natural causes. The long and illustrious reign of Alfonso elevated the status of the *terra portucalensis* from a county in nominal subservience to León-Castile into a separate, independent kingdom. In 1128, the young Alfonso had overthrown his mother Teresa and her Galician paramour to take control of the region. By about 1139, he began referring to himself as king, and a letter from Pope Alexander III dated May 23, 1179, recognized Alfonso as *rex portugalensium* which confirmed Portugal as an independent monarchy. Alfonso was succeeded by his son Sancho I (1185–1211), who in 1174 married Dolça, the sister of Alfonso II of Aragon (See Chart 15).

A little more than two years after the death of Alfonso I, Fernando II died at his villa at Benevente on January 22, 1188. His son Alfonso was traveling to Limia when the news of his father's death reached him. He immediately hurried to claim his inheritance and to have his father buried at Compostela. Alfonso IX (1188–1230) ascended to the crown of León at just seventeen years of age.

The Almohads Successfully Contest Christian Aggression: 1189–1195

The death of Fernando II (1158–1188) in 1188 and the ascension of his son Alfonso IX (1188–1230) to the throne of León left Alfonso VIII (1158–1214) as the senior, most powerful and influential Christian monarch of the peninsula. Sancho VI (1150–1194) of Navarre sought territorial expansion to the north of the Pyrenees after being hemmed in by Alfonso VIII to the west and by Alfonso II of Aragon to the east. In Portugal, Sancho I (1185–1211) had inherited the kingdom just three years earlier from his father Alfonso I and was still untested. The rising power and territorial expansion of Alfonso VIII of Castile eventually provoked the other peninsular kingdoms to align against him.

The young and inexperienced Alfonso IX faced a daunting task to establish himself against his neighbors in Portugal and Castile, who were ready to expand their borders at his expense. To establish his own footprint on the realm of León, Alfonso called a *curia* in León in the spring of 1188. Usually only prelates and magnates of the realm attended the king's court, but Alfonso deviated from this practice by summoning representatives from the towns as well. This event set a precedent for the establishment of parliaments elsewhere in Europe. At his first court, Alfonso declared his intention of recovering the rights and properties that his generous father had conceded. At the same time, he pledged to uphold the existing laws of his predecessors and to restore order throughout his realm (O'Callaghan *A History* 241). A few months later, Alfonso IX attended the court of Alfonso VIII held at Carrión at which time the Castilian monarch knighted his Leonese cousin and received homage from him in an obvious demonstration of supremacy (Palenzuela 400). Additionally, Alfonso IX agreed to a future marriage to Urraca, Alfonso VIII's daughter. Alfonso IX would later repudiate these accords.

In 1189, the Christians took advantage of internal revolts in the Almohad empire and launched attacks into Muslim al-Andalus. That year, a Castilian expedition raided the countryside around Córdoba and Seville, laying siege to the castle at Almenara and returning with considerable booty and captives. In Portugal, Sancho I benefited from the pope's decree of a crusade. He convinced fleets of crusaders on the way to the Holy Land to campaign against the Almohads on their way. One fleet stopped at Alvor on the southern coast of today's Portugal and plundered the city, killing its inhabitants. Another fleet arrived at Lisbon in July 1189 and was persuaded by Sancho I to join an attack on Silves not far from Alvor. Sancho's army marched to the south while the crusaders sailed along the coast then plundered the outlying areas of Silves before uniting with Sancho for a siege of the city. Silves fell on September 1, 1189, and the crusaders resumed their pilgrimage loaded with booty (O'Callaghan *A History* 241).

The retaliation of the Almohads did not take long. On April 23, 1190, Abu Yusuf Yaqub al-Mansur (1184–1199) crossed from North Africa to Tarifa and ordered his governor at Seville to assemble an army. By June 5, he was camped outside the walls of Silves awaiting the arrival of siege engines and equipment that were delivered by boat on July 5. While Silves held strong against the siege, the emir campaigned through the Algarve, burning crops and destroying vines as far north as Torres Novas north of Santarém. That location surrendered under terms, and the men were permitted to leave. Nonetheless, the walls of the fortification were destroyed. The Muslim army moved on to Tomar that was defended by the Templars. The Muslims were not prepared to endure a protracted siege, and their destruction of the countryside left nothing in the area to forage. The army began to suffer serious food shortages, and the men were plagued with hunger and then dysentery. They returned to Seville on July 26, 1190 (Kennedy *Muslim Spain* 241–2).

In the summer of 1190, a truce was called between the Castilians and the Almohads. Furthermore, Abu Yusuf al-Mansur renewed his truce with León, which left him free to retaliate against the Portuguese in the Algarve. After wintering in Seville, al-Mansur undertook a siege of Alcácer do Sal, south of Lisbon on the coast, in April 1191. The initial assault was unsuccessful, but after siege weapons arrived by sea, the position fell. Al-Mansur decided to establish a permanent garrison at this strategic location. The Muslims then marched southward to attack Silves on June 27, 1191, and caught the city by surprise. The survivors were granted safe conduct, and the location was once again under Muslim control. Satisfied with his success, the emir crossed the Strait on October 6 and returned to Marrakesh (Kennedy *Muslim Spain* 243).

That same year, the relations between the Christian monarchs became embroiled and embattled. On February 15, 1191, at Guimarães, Alfonso IX of León married his first cousin Teresa, the daughter of Sancho I of Portugal. While this marriage strengthened Alfonso IX's relationship with Portugal, it violated his agreements with Castile. However, the alliance between León and Portugal drew the support of Alfonso II of Aragon, and Castile found itself isolated and surrounded by hostile neighbors. In the spring of 1191, Alfonso II of Aragon and Sancho VI of Navarre invaded the territories around Soria. The military aggression between Christians drew the disdain of the pope, who wanted Christian aggression directed against the Muslims rather than against each other. The pope sent a legate to the peninsula early in 1192 to quell the impending conflicts and mediate a truce. The papal legate, Cardinal de Santangelo, first secured a peace agreement between Castile and Aragon. Then in April 1194, Alfonso VIII and Alfonso IX signed an agreement regarding the *tierra de campos*. Alfonso VIII rendered the castles at Alba, Luna, and Portilla to the kingdom of León, and upon his death the remaining castles captured by Castile since 1188 would be returned and then destroyed. Portugal agreed to give back to León the castles that were part of the marriage agreement of Teresa and her cousin Alfonso IX at the time that the marriage would be annulled (Palenzuela 400–1).

Hostilities among the Christians had been laid to rest. However, Alfonso VIII's truce with the Almohads had expired, and he quickly decided to dispatch an expedition against them through Calatrava in 1194. From there, the campaign moved on to raid the environs of Córdoba and Jaén, reaping large amounts of booty. The renewal of aggression triggered the return of Emir Abu Yusuf Yaqub al-Mansur to the peninsula. On June 1, 1195, al-Mansur journeyed to al-Andalus by way of Tarifa and stopped at Seville to prepare his army. The emir left Seville on June 22, 1195, with the intention of destroying the southernmost positions in Castile around Alarcos and Calatrava. The Castilian army under Alfonso VIII hastened to challenge the Almohads and established themselves at the newly constructed castle at Alarcos. On July 13, 1195, the Muslim army prepared for battle on the plains near Calatrava. Alfonso VIII of Castile chose not to wait for reinforcements from León. On July 17, the Muslim army advanced slowly and engaged the Christians on the open plains near Alarcos. The initial charge of the Castilians inflicted severe damage to the vanguard of the Muslims, whose counterattack, however, routed the Christians. Some fled to the castle at Alarcos while another contingent with Alfonso VIII hurried back to the safety of Toledo. The Christian losses were enormous, and the castle of Alarcos surrendered a few days later, soon followed by the castles of Malagón, Benavente, and Calatrava. The emir did not pursue Alfonso VIII, possibly because he remembered suffering food shortages on other campaigns, such as at Huete and at Torres Nova. Instead, al-Mansur chose to retreat to Seville where he arrived on August 7. The Castilians lost a sparsely populated region, but one which served to protect Toledo from hostile incursions. Alarcos represented an embarrassing defeat for Alfonso VIII, which not only depleted his military strength, but also diminished his prestige, and left him vulnerable (Kennedy *Muslim Spain* 245–6).

A Defeated Alfonso VIII Triumphs at Las Navas de Tolosa: 1196–1212

At his worst moment after the defeat at Alarcos in 1195, Alfonso VIII found no respite from the Muslims nor from his Christian neighbors, who once again began to lay claims to his domains. Alfonso's attempt to negotiate a truce with al-Mansur was futile. To the contrary, the Almohads struck an alliance with Alfonso IX of León, which enabled them to campaign together against the western frontier of Castile. Alfonso IX lay waste to the *tierra de campos*, and combined Leonese and Almohad forces conquered Montánchez, Trujillo, and Santa Cruz without any resistance. Only Plasencia offered resistance before it fell. On their retreat, the Almohads devastated the regions around Talavera, Santa Olalla, Escalona, Maqueda and Toledo. In the spring of 1197, the Almohads returned to raid the already devastated fields of Talavera and Maqueda, before laying siege to Madrid for a short time and then pillaging their way back to Córdoba through Guadalajara, Alcalá, Oreja, Huete, Uclés, Cuenca, and Alarcón. Similarly, Sancho VII (1194–1234), who ascended to the throne of Navarrre upon the death of Sancho VI in 1194, resumed his father's attempts to annex La Rioja (See Chart 13). Only Alfonso II of Aragon aligned with Alfonso VIII, but Alfonso II died shortly afterwards on April 25, 1196. Alfonso II left the kingdom of Aragon and Catalonia to his oldest son Pedro II (1196–1213), who continued his father's alliance with Alfonso VIII. However, Alfonso II bequeathed Provence and related territories to his second son Alfons. This division marked the permanent end to the union between Catalonia and Provence (See Chart 14).

Unhappy with the attacks of Alfonso IX on his Christian neighbors, Pope Celestine III excommunicated the king of León and offered indulgences to anyone who took up arms against him just as if he were a Muslim. An eventual solution to the dispute of the territorial boundaries between Castile and León was suggested by Queen Leonor of Castile. She proposed a marriage between her daughter Berenguela and Alfonso IX. The wedding of October 1197 in Valladolid brought a dowry of the disputed fortresses held by Alfonso VIII. Nevertheless, the marriage agreement did not bring peace. The Holy See was against the marriage for reasons of consanguinity, and the local magnates were dissatisfied with the rendering of castles. So, hostilities resumed, only to be resolved in later years (O'Callaghan *A History* 244–5). Between 1196 and 1199, Sancho I (1185–1211) of Portugal attempted to take advantage of Alfonso IX's excommunication by seizing locations on the western border of León. Further attempts were foiled when the Portuguese suffered a devastating rout near Pinhel, which ended their aggression (Palenzuela 401).

By the spring of 1198, al-Mansur had not been seriously challenged by the Christians, but he was faced with insurrections in Majorca and Tunisia, which induced him to agree to a truce with Castile. On March 30, he crossed the Strait for North Africa and was journeying to Marrakesh when his ill health became apparent. By January 1199, al-Mansur died of natural causes. He was succeeded by his son and designated heir, Muhammad al-Nasir (1199–1213), who was only seventeen at the time (Kennedy *Muslim Spain* 246). Truces with the Almohads produced a long period of peace between the Christian realms and the Muslims. Only the military Orders maintained a presence along the Muslim borders. The Order of Calatrava lost their base of operations during the defeat of Alfonso VIII at Alarcos in 1195. In 1198, however, the Order captured the castle at Salvatierra and used it to launch raids into Muslim territories. The Order of Santiago defended the eastern frontier from their base at Uclés with additional advanced positions at Cuenca and Alarcón. On the western front, the Order of Monfragüe provided a buffer of resistance, and The Hospitallers defended the central front from their castle at Consuegra (Palenzuela 406).

Despite the excommunication of Alfonso IX, he and Berenguela remained together until 1204 and produced several offspring including the future Fernando III (1217–1252). Their separation in that year released the couple from ecclesiastical censures, but animosity over the disputed territories was re-ignited. Finally, on March 26, 1206, the treaty of Cabreros recognized the future Fernando III of León-Castile, as the rightful lord over the disputed territory, since he was the son of the king of León and the grandson of the king of Castile. After the peace was secured between León and Castile, Alfonso VIII turned his attention to the expulsion of Sancho VII from the disputed lands on his eastern border with Navarre. Alfonso VIII seized control of the Basque provinces of Guipúzcoa and Álava and completed a truce with Navarre in 1207 that formally assigned these domains to the realm of Castile once again. A similar treaty was agreed by Navarre and Aragon the following year. Next, an agreement of continuing peace was renewed between León and Castile in 1209, resulting in peace at last between all Christian realms of Iberia (O'Callaghan *A History* 245).

While the Christian monarchs were busy settling differences among themselves, the conflict between Christians and Muslims was muted. Nonetheless, the clergy incited a renewal of hostilities against the infidels. Specifically, Bishop Rodrigo Jiménez de Rada, the archbishop of Toledo, at the behest of Pope Innocent III, urged the Castilian King Alfonso VIII in 1209 to initiate a crusade. Even before the end of the truce, Alfonso VIII sent an expeditionary force as far south as Jaén in 1209 and then began to fortify his frontier and repopulate Béjar. The pope applauded the positive response from Castile and encouraged the other monarchs to follow suit by threatening excommunication of any king who attacked his neighbor and by granting indulgences for joining the crusade. Pedro II of Aragon needed no such encouragement. In response to a Muslim attack against the coast of Catalonia in 1210, Pedro responded with a campaign against Valencia, conquering Ademuz and Castielfabib (Palenzuela 406–7).

Emissaries from al-Andalus were dispatched to al-Nasir in North Africa in 1210 and convinced him that action needed to be taken against the Christians. He left Marrakesh on February 6, 1211, and sojourned in Seville until June while he planned his attack on Salvatierra, the southernmost outpost in Muslim territory that the Order of

Calatrava used to stage its raids. The large Almohad army, well-equipped with siege engines, began their encirclement of Salvatierra on June 15. Alfonso VIII was at Talavera but did not want to risk a confrontation. The siege dragged on for fifty days until the garrison was given permission to surrender, and the Almohad army retreated to Seville in triumph (Kennedy *Muslim Spain* 254). The loss of Salvatierra was compounded a month later by the death of the Infante Fernando, the heir apparent of Alfonso VIII of Castile, who succumbed to a fever in Madrid.

Al-Nasir's decision to return to Córdoba for the winter afforded the Christians the opportunity to proclaim an allied crusade. The pope and Archbishop Rodrigo as well as many other bishops recruited crusaders from Italy, France, and even Germany. The kings of Aragon and Navarre committed their assistance to the effort, but the kings of León and Portugal were still engaged in their own border disputes. In March 1211, King Sancho I of Portugal died and was succeeded by his son Afonso II (1211–1223). Afonso's ascendance was troubled by his father's quarrels with the local bishops and even with the pope for delaying tribute to the Holy See. Further, Afonso contested the will of his father, that gave portions of the royal domains to two other daughters. Meanwhile Alfonso IX of León viewed this turmoil as an opportunity to assail the new Portuguese king. Alfonso IX launched a raid and routed the Portuguese at Valdevez (O'Callaghan *A History* 246–7).

During the spring of 1212, an amalgamated army, absent the Portuguese and Leonese, began to assemble at Toledo, and the crusaders who departed on June 20, 1212, were divided into three contingents. The vanguard consisted of troops from above the Pyrenees. The main body was led by Pedro II of Aragon, and the rearguard, which included the bishops from the peninsula and the military orders, was led by Alfonso VIII. On June 24, the vanguard of the crusading army attacked the castle at Malagón and overwhelmed the garrison stationed there. The army then moved on to Calatrava and lay siege to the former fortress of that military order. The small garrison surrendered after a brief siege and was permitted to leave unharmed. At this juncture, the crusaders from above the Pyrenees left the campaign. Reports are divided as to whether they were suffering from the heat or whether they were dissatisfied with the lack of booty. Nevertheless, the campaign moved on to take Alarcos, Piedrabuena, Benavente, and Caracuel, but skirted Salvatierra to avoid an extended siege. At the encampment at Alarcos, Sancho VII brought knights from Navarre to join the fight. July 13 found the crusaders at rest at Las Navas de Tolosa.

The Almohads left Seville in the spring of 1212 with a mix of fighters from al-Andalus and from North Africa. They camped on the plain of Las Navas de Tolosa, in front of a narrow pass giving access to the plain. The Christians entered on to Las Navas by a little-known pathway and waited for the opposing army to deploy. The two armies engaged on July 16, 1212, with Sancho VII of Navarre commanding the left flank for the Christians. Diego López de Haro led the center, and Pedro II of Catalonia took the right flank. Alfonso VIII and the military Orders maintained the rear guard. It was the charge of Alfonso VIII and his rear guard that broke through the enemy lines and destroyed their unity, and it was Sancho VII who succeeded in advancing to the emir's tent and caused him to flee well in advance. The loss of Muslim lives was enormous, and the booty was immense. The tapestry banner of the Almohad emir was recovered and sent to the nunnery of Las Huelgas just to the west of Burgos, founded by Alfonso VIII at the behest of his wife Leonora (O'Callaghan *A History* 248).

The immense booty from this victory allowed the Christian army to campaign further, taking the castles at Vilches, Ferral, Baños, and Tolosa in a single day. Their arrival at Baeza the following day found the city abandoned, and so the crusaders destroyed the city walls. From there, they lay siege to Úbeda for three days. When the populace surrendered, they were all taken prisoner, and the city walls were razed. Amid sickness and rowdiness of the troops, the army was then directed back to Toledo (Palenzuela 408). Las Navas de Tolosa was the first major defeat suffered by the Almohads in the peninsula and marked the beginning of their decline and extinction.

The Death of Three Leaders and the End of an Era: 1213–1214

After leading a tactical wing at Las Navas de Toloso under Alfonso VIII in 1195, Pedro II (1196–1213) of Aragon, also known as Pere I of Catalonia, suffered a mortal defeat at Muret near Toulouse when he was drawn into the Albigensian crusade. The Albigensian heresy, which supposed a primeval conflict between light and darkness and which represented Satan as coeternal with God, was prevalent in southern France and was raging in Pedro's domains at the time that he ascended to the crown. Early in his reign, Pedro published a law in 1197 that banned heresy under pain of confiscation of property and death at the stake. While Pedro had taken a firm opposition to the heretics, his vassals in Languedoc, namely Count Raymond VI of Toulouse, and Raymond Roger Trencavel, Viscount of Béziers and Carcassonne, and others, failed to act against the religious deviants.

To promote closer ties with Catalonia, Raymond VI married Pedro's sister Leonor in 1200, and four years later Pedro II married Maria of Montpellier, which made him the lord of Montpellier and also produced their son and heir, Jaume, in 1208. Pedro travelled to Rome in 1204 to renew the feudal agreement between Aragon and Rome that was established by King Sancho Ramírez (1063–1094) in 1068. Pedro offered his kingdom to the pope and became his vassal. In return for his sworn fidelity and payment of an annual tribute, Pedro received the pope's protection from any intrusions into his sovereign domains.

By 1208, the pope called for a crusade against the Albigensians, no doubt prompted by the assassination of a papal legate in January of that year. The pope accused Count Raymond VI of the murder and urged good Christians to rise up against him, which invited opportunism among northern French warriors to enrich themselves at the expense of the counts of Languedoc. The crusaders invaded Béziers and Carcasonne in 1209 and slaughtered many while deposing Raymond Roger Trencavel, who died shortly afterwards. As a leader of this initial attack, Simon de Montfort was installed as the viscount over the confiscated territories. De Montfort then intended to attack Count Raymond VI, the Count of Toulouse. Pedro II did not intervene in the conflict; he had two conflicting duties. On one hand, he had an obligation to protect his vassals, but on the other, as a vassal of the pope, he could not oppose the crusade. At first,

Pedro II refused the vassalage offered by de Montfort for Béziers and Carcasonne, but in an attempt to resolve his conflicting interests, he subsequently reversed his decision in 1211 and accepted de Monfort's offer. Additionally, he arranged the marriage of his son Jaume, only three years old at the time, to the daughter of de Montfort. Jaume was delivered to the custody of de Montfort to assure that the agreement would be fulfilled. Despite these accommodations, de Montfort resumed his intentions to conquer Toulouse. After his campaign at Las Navas de Tolosa, Pedro II appealed to Innocent III, claiming that de Montfort was planning to attack the count of Toulouse who was a good Christian. The pope ordered a suspension of military activity, but Pedro II finally decided to act. On September 12, 1213, Pedro II rallied his vassals from Languedoc, including Count Raymond VI and allies from Foix, Comminges, and Béarn, and attacked the castle of Muret near Toulouse. De Montfort mustered a relief force of far superior numbers and hastened to Muret. Despite being outnumbered, Pedro II opted to give battle and died in the fray. The vision of a future Catalonia, which would have extended across the French Midi, was forestalled with the death of Pedro. The Languedoc would pass into the hands of the Capetian dynasty a few years later. Jaume I (1213–1276), still under the supervision of de Montfort inherited the crown of Aragon-Barcelona at the age of five years (O'Callaghan *A History* 249–53).

After his humiliation at Las Navas de Tolosa, Emir Muhammad al-Nasir (1199–1213) ignominiously departed for Marrakesh and apparently left no provisions for the continued defense of al-Andalus. The administrative structure of the Almohad hierarchy remained in place to govern but without a central plan or direction. Neither al-Nasir nor his successors returned to the peninsula to lead a Muslim counterattack against the Christians. He died at Marrakesh at the hands of assassins on December 25, 1213, at age 32. Al-Nasir was succeeded by his son and designated heir, Abu Yaqub Yusuf II, al-Mustansir (1213–1224), only about ten years old at the time. Too young to rule effectively, Yusuf II was controlled by his paternal uncles and relatives, and the Almohad empire morphed into an oligarchy with Yusuf as its titular ruler (Kennedy *Muslim Spain* 256–9).

During the months following Las Navas de Tolosa, the Castilians continued to skirmish against the Muslims. The governors of al-Andalus, left to their own wiles, harassed the newly won Christian positions without success. The following year, however, they were successful in taking a few positions on the Castilian eastern front, only to lose them again by year's end. In November of 1213, Alfonso VIII lay siege to Baeza, which had been reconstructed since being destroyed after Las Navas. The city was fiercely defended, and because of a lack of provisions during a period of drought, Alfonso lifted the siege. A truce was agreed in 1214 that endured for ten years. Shortly afterwards on October 5, 1214, Alfonso VIII died at the small village of Gutierre Muñoz near Ávila. His first-born son Fernando had died of a fever in 1211, so his younger son Enrique (1214–1217) ascended to the throne at just eleven years of age (Palenzuela 456–7). Three major leaders at the battle of Las Navas de Tolosa, Pedro II of Aragon, Muhammad al-Nasir, and Alfonso VIII of Castile, died within two years of that event, and they were all succeeded by underage inheritors. The long truce negotiated by Alfonso in 1214 and perpetuated until 1224 allowed the young Christian monarchs to become established, but the Almohad successor did not return to Iberia.

CHAPTER 9

The Age of the Great Christian Conquests and the Era of Alfonso X: 1214–1284

The Unfortunate Reign of Enrique I and the Ascendance of Fernando III: 1214–1224

The death of Alfonso VIII (1158–1214) in 1214, followed shortly thereafter by the death of Queen Leonor, left the crown of Castile to Alfonso's youngest son, the eleven-year-old Enrique I (1214–1217), under the guardianship of his much older sister Berenguela, the ex-wife of Alfonso IX, whose marriage had been annulled for reasons of consanguinity. Alfonso VIII's oldest son and heir apparent, Fernando, had died of a fever in Madrid in 1211, so Enrique was the only son remaining. As Enrique ascended, the nobles of Castile insisted that the boy-king be put under their tutelage, and consequently, Berenguela was prevailed upon to release him to the custody of Count Álvaro Núñez de Lara in May 1215 (Ballesteros 20–4).

After taking possession of Enrique, Álvaro and his brothers Gonzalo and Fernando Núñez began to usurp royal power by attacking and confiscating the assets of the Church, which resulted in Álvaro's excommunication. Moreover, Álvaro meted out similar treatment against other nobles of Castile, which caused them to align against the de Laras and to appeal to Berenguela for support. Further, to reinforce his support against all opposition, Álvaro Núñez attempted without success to arrange the marriage of Enrique to a much older Mafalda of Portugal. When that agreement failed, he then attempted to match Enrique with Sancha of León, the oldest daughter of Alfonso IX with his first wife Teresa (See Chart 10).

In late 1216 and early 1217, Berenguela began initiatives to remove Enrique from the tutelage of Álvaro. She and her sister Leonor had left Las Huelgas and were sojourning in Autillo, the castle of their ally Gonzalo Ruiz Girón, when hostilities erupted. Álvaro departed Valladolid with a group of supporters and attacked the environs of Autillo and moved on to ravage other positions in the area before retreating to the episcopal palace of Palencia with Enrique I in tow. It was there that the fatal accident involving the king occurred on June 6, 1217. While playing with some boys his own age, a roof tile fell and struck the king in his head, mortally wounding him (Palenzuela 459).

Hearing of the unfortunate news, Berenguela and the nobles at Autillo who supported her agreed that she was the rightful heir to the crown. They further planned to wrest Berenguela's son Fernando from León, where he was staying with this father Alfonso IX, and bring him to Castile. Accompanied by Gonzalo Ruiz Girón and Lope Díaz, Alfonso IX's brother-in-law, Berenguela successfully regained custody of Fernando and made her way from León to Valladolid where the culmination of her plans unfolded. At an assembly convened at Valladollid, Berenguela was recognized as queen and immediately ceded her rights to her son Fernando. On July 2, 1717, Fernando III ascended to the throne of Castile at the age of sixteen.

Alfonso IX, sensing a missed opportunity to unite León and Castile under his own authority, retaliated by laying waste the *tierra de campos* and then by attacking without success a well-defended Burgos. Finding no support in Castile for his cause to reunite the two realms under his name, he returned to León. Similarly, Alvaro attempted to avenge his loss of control over the kingdom of Castile by taking castles by force and by robbing and destroying the countryside. In short order, however, he was surprised by Alfonso Téllez and taken prisoner, putting an end to his malevolent behavior. The following year, the father and son made peace and agreed to join the forces of León and Castile against the Muslims. In 1218, Berenguela arranged Fernando III's marriage to Beatrice, the daughter of Philip of Swabia and granddaughter of Frederick Barbarossa. The marriage was performed in Burgos in November of 1219, which gave their son, the future Alfonso X born two years later, a presumptive claim to the Holy Roman Empire. The realm of Castile remained under a truce with al-Andalus until 1224 when King Fernando III decided, in agreement with the nobles of the realm, to resume military activity against the Muslims (Palenzuela 458–61).

The Early Years of Jaume I of Aragon-Barcelona: 1213–1228

Following the death of Pedro II of Aragon (1196–1213) at Muret, Jaume or Jaime I (1213–1276) inherited the crown when he was just five years old. Sadly, his mother Marie de Montpellier predeceased Pedro II by a few months, which left Jaume in the custody of Simon de Montfort, his intended future father-in-law and the slayer of his father at Muret. The Aragonese nobility petitioned Pope Innocent III to have the boy-king released to the custody of a papal legate, who then convened an assembly at Lérida in August 1214 to determine the boy's future. The nobles and clergy assembled there recognized Jaume as the rightful heir to the crown and appointed his great-uncle Sanç, the Count of Roussillon, as regent. The custody and education of Jaume was entrusted to Guillem de Montrodon, the master of the Knights Templar at Monzón where the boy was lodged for the next four years. Sanç and Jaume's uncle Ferrando both had their own designs on the crown, but the general court at Lérida ratified the Peace of Catalonia, and all in attendance swore an oath of loyalty to the king, thereby foiling the intentions of the pretenders to the crown.

The authority of Jaume's regency did not function well. The remission of taxation agreed to at Lérida led to fiscal problems, and Jaume's uncle Ferrando, excluded from the regency, fomented unrest in Aragon. The responsibility for fiscal issues was transferred to Guillem de Montrodon, since Count Sanç had become embroiled in the struggles of Languedoc. Sanç's preoccupation there led to his resignation in 1218. Fiscal shortages began to improve when a *bovatge* "tax" was levied in a general court at Monzón in June of 1217. During his youth, Jaume overcame minor uprisings in Aragon and prevailed over baronial politics concerning the lordship of Urgell. In February 1221, Jaume became of age, was knighted, and married Leonor of Castile, the daughter of Alfonso VIII and Leonor of England (See Chart 10). By 1225 at age seventeen, Jaume was finally in control of public order and fiscal administration. He was a young man experienced beyond his years.

In 1228, Aurembiaix, the daughter of Ermengol VIII (1184–1209) laid claim to the county of Urgell and appealed to Jaume for assistance in the matter. Guerau de Cabrera, based on his descendance from Ermengol VII (1154–1184), was permitted to retain the rights to Urgell on the condition that he yield these claims if Aurembiaix were to return from Castile. In that year, Aurembiaix had her marriage to Álvaro Pérez de Castro annulled, and she did return to Catalonia. Presenting herself before Jaume, Aurembiaix swore fealty to him on the condition that he recover the county of Urgell for her. In October of 1228, Jaume campaigned against the castles of the lower Urgell and rendered them to Aurembiaix. She further agreed to become Jaume's concubine with the understanding that any son born of that relationship would inherit Urgell. With domestic matters firmly under control, the nineteen-year-old Jaume turned his attention to thoughts of territorial expansion (Bisson 58–63).

The Reign of Afonso II of Portugal: 1211–1223

Afonso II (1211–1223) inherited the crown of Portugal when his father Sancho I (1185–1211) died in 1211. Afonso was the eldest son of Sancho and his wife Urraca of Castile, the daughter of Alfonso VIII of Castile and Leonor of England. When Afonso ascended, the monarchy was embroiled in disputes with the large land holders of the realm, both lay and ecclesiastical, over property rights conceded by his father. These privileges negatively affected the property rights and revenues of the crown. Further, Afonso contested the provisions in his father's will, which bequeathed certain domains to Afonso's sisters. Afonso viewed his inheritance as an indivisible royal patrimony.

Shortly after his ascension, Afonso II called a *curia* at which he drew a fine distinction between the economic privileges given to his sisters compared to administrative privileges which he reserved for the monarchy. The three daughters of Sancho I, Teresa the former wife of Alfonso IX of León, Mafalda, and Sancha were further disgruntled by Afonso's ruling, and the realm was thrown into turmoil when Alfonso IX of León came to the aid of his ex-wife Teresa by attacking and routing the Portuguese at Valdevez (Palenzuela 466). All-out war was averted on the eve of the battle of Las Navas de Toloso when Pope Innocent III intervened to declare peace among Christian realms and a common cause against the Muslims. Shortly after Las Navas, the two Alfonsos of Leon and of Castile and Afonso of Portugal signed a truce agreement at Coimbra which pledged mutual aid against the Muslims. By 1216, Afonso II had resolved the dispute with his two sisters over inherited lands. The lands were agreed to be the property of the crown in exchange for a lifetime income guaranteed to the sisters. During the remainder of his reign, Afonso II focused his attention on strengthening the resources of the monarchy. He undertook a series of *inquirições* "inquests" aimed at verifying the origin and rights of landowner claims including those of the Church. These challenges into the rights of large land holders as well as challenges to the churches and monasteries brought him into conflict with the Church and precipitated his excommunication by the Archbishop of Braga (O'Callaghan *A History* 337).

With Afonso's attention diverted from military activities and focused on internal issues, campaigns against the Muslims fell to the initiatives of the military Orders spurred on by the clergy. Military activity in Portugal against the Muslims proceeded without the involvement of Afonso II. A fleet of crusaders from Germany and Frisia arrived at Lisbon in July 1217 and were persuaded by Bishop Sueiro to join an attack on Alcácer do Sal, which had been turned into a Muslim stronghold by Abu Yusuf Yaqub al-Mansur (1184–1199) in 1189. The crusaders attacked the fortress on July 30, 1218. The Portuguese, who were led by the bishops of Lisbon and Evora and assisted by the military Orders, joined the crusaders three days later. A Muslim relief force was dispatched from Seville, Córdoba, and Jaén, but the Christians repulsed them on September 11. Alcácer surrendered on October 18, 1218, leaving the path to the Algarve open.

Afonso's quarrels with the Church over land holdings and rents that led to his excommunication were still not settled when he died of leprosy on March 25, 1223. Sancho II (1223–1248) succeeded his father Afonso II at the age of about twelve years. He made amends with the Church, and the archbishop lifted the sentence of excommunication of his father, which allowed the deceased king to be buried in consecrated ground. However, the disputes over the rights and privileges of the magnates and prelates lingered throughout Sancho II's reign and led to his ultimate demise two decades later (Palenzuela 467–8).

The Almohad Empire in Disorder and the Renewal of Christian Offensives: 1224–1230

On January 4, 1224, the young caliph of the Almohad empire, Abu Yaqub Yusuf II, al-Mustansir (1213–1224), died unexpectedly, reportedly from being gored to death by a pet cow (Kennedy *Muslim Spain* 260). This event threw the Almohad leadership into disarray and provided an opportunity for the Christians to take advantage of a divided al-Andalus.

The Almohad oligarchy in Marrakesh recognized Abu Muhammad Abd al-Wahid I al-Makhlu (1224) as the successor to the empire, but the Muslim governors of al-Andalus did not universally accept this nomination. The governor of Valencia, Zayd Abu Zayd, remained loyal to Marrakesh, while the other governors of al-Andalus rejected al-Wahid I in favor of Abd Allah al-Adil (1224–1227), the governor of Murcia, who proclaimed himself as caliph. Decidedly in support of al-Adil was his brother Abu al-Ala Idris, the governor of Córdoba and Granada and later caliph from 1229 to 1232. Meanwhile the governor of Seville, Abu Muhammad Abu Abd Allah, known as al-

Bayyasi, the one from Baeza, was forced to relinquish the governorship of that favored city and was replaced by al-Adil's brother al-Ala. In exchange, al-Bayyasi received the governorships of Córdoba, Jaén, in addition to Baeza, where he had family connections and support. Unhappy with this apparent demotion, al-Bayyasi shortly thereafter declared his independence from the Almohad regime, which prompted a campaign against him from Abu al-Ala in the spring of 1224. Al-Ala's army re-gained the authority over most locations that recognized al-Bayyasi, reducing his control to the region around Baeza itself. At this juncture, al-Bayyasi was left with few options and proposed an alliance with Fernando III of Castile. He offered to become his vassal (Lomax 137+).

During the decade following their success at Las Navas de Tolosa in 1212, the Christian monarchs were, for the most part, at peace with the Muslims. Only Alfonso IX of León (1188–1230) attempted military campaigns against them, since he was not constrained by a peace treaty. Alfonso's siege of Cáceres from October through December of 1218 failed to overcome the resistance of the city, and the king returned to León before Christmas. The following year, Alfonso commanded an expeditionary campaign into the environs of Seville and demonstrated his military superiority against Muslim forces near Tejada by routing them and reaping considerable booty. Then in the spring of 1222, he attempted a new siege of Cáceres which endured through June and July. Just when it seemed that the city was about to propose an offer of surrender, serious illnesses among his troops induced Alfonso to lift the siege and return to León. Alfonso's military exploits during this period successfully harassed and weakened Muslim positions but resulted in no territorial expansion. Meanwhile, Afonso II of Portugal (1211–1223) was preoccupied with internal quarrels, so it was left to the military Orders, clergy, and a fleet of crusaders from northern Europe to dislodge the Muslims from their stronghold at Alcácer do Sal in 1218. In Catalonia, Jaume I (1213–1276), the young king of Aragon and count of Barcelona, was still establishing his influence within the realm during this period, and he would postpone territorial expansion for a few more years. In Navarre, Sancho VII (1194–1234) was at peace and had not campaigned since Las Navas. However, the Muslim civil strife, the expiration of Castile's truce with them, and an appeal for assistance from al-Bayyasi provided an opportunity for Fernando III of Castile to resume the struggle against al-Andalus. In July 1224, Fernando called a *curia* at which the magnates of Castile supported the resumption of crusades against the Muslims. He assembled an army at Toledo, and in early September of that year, he crossed through the pass at Despeñaperros into Muslim territory where he united with al-Bayyasi and accepted him as his vassal (Martínez Díez *Fernando III* 75–6).

The combined forces of Fernando III and al-Bayyasi campaigned in September of 1224 against the city of Quesada, which had not remained loyal to al-Bayyasi. The location was sacked, and many captives were enslaved. Nevertheless, the town was left unoccupied, and Fernando returned to Toledo in October. In retaliation, Abu al-Ala launched an unsuccessful attack against Baeza. The city not only held strong, but the combined Christian and Muslim forces garrisoned at the city sent the attackers into flight.

In September of 1224, Abd al-Wahid, the Almohad caliph in Marrakesh, was deposed and executed, which opened the possibility for al-Adil to leave al-Andalus and take possession of the empire. He left Almohad operations in al-Andalus in the hands of his brother Abu al-Ala. The ascendance of al-Adil produced a change in loyalties for the government of al-Andalus and opened the door for renewed aggression from the Christians. Zayd Abu Zayd, the governor of Valencia, Alcira, Játiva, and Denia, who was also the brother of al-Bayyasi, was pressured no doubt by these changing political and military events. He decided to break with the Almohads and align with Castile by joining his brother al-Bayyasi as a vassal of Fernando III. Abu Zayd's change of heart drew a rapid response from Jaume I of Aragon, who understood that by previous agreement with Castile, Valencia and its environs were reserved for the territorial expansion of Aragon. On April 28, 1225, Jaume I attacked the Muslim positions held by Abu Zayd, which induced him to reconsider his vassalage to Fernando III. Under the threat from Aragon, he immediately negotiated a treaty and began paying tribute to Jaume (Palenzuela 462; Martínez Díez *Fernando III* 76).

In the summer of 1225, Fernando and Abd Allah al-Bayyasi resumed their campaign around Jaén, Martos, and Priego. At Jaén, they ravaged the countryside, but their siege proved ineffective against the city's superior fortifications. Leaving Jaén, they pushed peacefully past Martos, which recognized al-Bayyasi's authority, and then moved on to attack Priego, which did not support al-Bayyasi. After an attack of two days, the outer city had been taken and the residents were massacred, while the survivors sheltered in the inner citadel negotiated for terms and were permitted to leave. Fernando's army moved on to storm the city of Loja where he destroyed both the citadel and its inhabitants. Approaching Granada, he found the town of Alhama abandoned, and before he reached Granada, the Christian knight Álvar Pérez de Castro, then in service to the Muslims of Granada, proposed the release of some 1,300 Christian captives in exchange for a peaceful retreat. Fernando accepted Álvar's proposal. On his return to Baeza, Fernando's army destroyed Montejícar and several other small cities as he went. In return for Fernando's military assistance, al-Bayyesi surrendered the castles of Martos and Andújar to Christian garrisons as promised, and Fernando withdrew to Toledo.

The Christian army, now under the command of Álvar Pérez de Castro, who had changed sides and sworn allegiance to Fernando III, launched raids from the newly-acquired strongholds at Martos and Andújar into the countryside around Córdoba, Tejada, Jerez, and even Seville. The Muslim army from Seville, which had engaged them in October of 1225, was soundly defeated. To relieve themselves of the Christian onslaught, the populace of Córdoba deposed their Almohad governor and recognized the authority of Abd Allah al-Bayyasi. At the same time, Castilian forces under the direction of Alfonso Téllez and the bishop of Cuenca conducted raids eastward in the direction of Murcia (Martínez Díez *Fernando III* 80).

In exchange for Fernando's continued support, al-Bayyasi had agreed to yield the fortress of Capilla and two others; however, the population of Capilla rose up against al-Bayyasi and resisted the establishment of a Christian garrison in their city. Consequently, Fernando launched his third campaign in June of 1226, laying siege to that location. The Muslims proposed a truce of eight days, during which time they expected Abu al-Ala of Seville to come to their aid. Failing that assistance, they would surrender the city and leave with any belongings that they could carry. At the end of the term, Fernando took possession of the city and escorted its citizens safely to the next town. During the siege of Capilla, news arrived in the summer of 1227 that the people of Córdoba had turned against al-Bayyasi and assassinated him for colluding with Fernando. Following the death of al-Bayyasi, the Muslims of Baeza no longer supplied the Christian garrison with food and attempted to drive them out with the assistance of the Muslim Governor of Jaén and his militia. The Christian garrison held out long enough so that the threat of a counter-attack from Fernando induced the Muslims to evacuate the city. This scenario was also repeated at the other Castilian outposts of Martos and Andújar.

In 1227, Abu al-Ala staged an ineffective attack against Martos and had returned to Seville by the end of the summer. By mid–September he had proclaimed himself caliph of the Almohad empire, despite the fact that his brother al-Adil was still reigning in Marrakesh. The premature proclamation of al-Ala may have foretold al-Adil's tenuous relationship with the Almohad power structure, for on October 4, 1227, in Marrakesh, al-Adil was assassinated. Rather than recognizing Abu al-Ala, the conflicted Almohad regime elected Yahya al-Mutasim (1227–1229), the sixteen-year-old brother of Abu Yaqub Yusuf II, al-Mustansir (1213–1224), whom the Almohad oligarchy could easily manipulate. Back in Seville, al-Ala negotiated a truce with Fernando III for the winter of 1227–8 that included tribute payments (Lomax 139; Martínez Díez *Fernando III* 89–93).

Amid the confusion and ineffectiveness of the Almohad regime, another rebel by the name of Abu Abd Allah Muhammad ibn Yusuf ibn Hud al Yudami, or simply ibn Hud, raised the banner of revolt against Abu al-Ala, the self-proclaimed Almohad caliph in Seville. Ibn Hud descended from the *taifa* rulers of Zaragoza and was serving in the militia of Murcia at the time that he rebelled in Ricote to the northwest of Murcia in the late spring of 1228. The people of al-Andalus had grown tired of the Almohad's inability to provide a defense against Christian attacks, and they were drawn to ibn Hud's anti–Almohad campaign. Ibn Hud not only slaughtered the Almohads and their allies at every opportunity; he repudiated their religious ideology and aligned himself with the Abbasids, pledging allegiance to the caliph in Bagdad. Abu al-Ala launched a campaign against ibn Hud that proved to be ineffective. Although he defeated ibn Hud at Lorca, he was repelled at Murcia when the people of that city rose up in support of ibn Hud. As the caliph returned to Seville in November of 1228, ibn Hud's following crescendoed, and his authority was recognized throughout the Iberian Levant. Shortly after his return to Seville, Abu al-Ala planned his return to Marrakesh to seize control of the debilitated empire. He crossed the Strait, probably in November, with the remaining contingent of Almohads and a Christian mercenary force of 500 knights. He would displace his young rival Caliph Yahya in 1229. Al-Ala's departure marked the end of Almohad rule in al-Andalus, but the Almohad empire would survive for another forty years until being replaced entirely by the Merinid dynasty (Kennedy *Spain* 264–6; Martínez Díez *Fernando III* 89–93).

Meanwhile, military campaigns in Extremadura resumed. Alfonso IX of León finally succeeded in taking Cáceres in the summer of 1227 and advanced to lay siege to Mérida, which surrendered in March 1230. Alfonso then followed the river Guadiana to Badajoz, which capitulated after a brief siege. Farther to the west, the Portuguese knights loyal to Sancho II advanced to Elvas and found the city abandoned by its Muslim defenders. The knights moved on to Juromenha and seized it without difficulty.

In Aragon, an experienced, twenty-year-old Jaume I was fully secure with the command of his realm. Moreover, the maritime enterprise of Barcelona had matured but was being threatened by Muslim piracy centered in Majorca. In December of 1228,

Jaume called a court session in Barcelona to propose the conquest of that den of piracy. The assembly supported his proposal with the passage of a *bovatge* or tax to fund this undertaking. The Catalan fleet set sail on September 5, 1229, and was immediately threatened by a furious storm. Landing safely a few days later at the bay of Palma, the Catalans lay siege to the city. Negotiations for surrender stalled in December, and the Christian assault on Palma resulted in a disastrous loss of Muslim lives. The Catalans took possession of Palma on the last day of 1229, and the remainder of the island was subjugated by the spring of 1230. The Muslims who surrendered peacefully were permitted to migrate to other islands or back to North Africa, thereby facilitating the partitioning of land among the Catalans (Bisson 63–4).

Back on the peninsula, Fernando III lay siege to Jaén for three months during the summer of 1230 without successfully penetrating the city's robust fortifications. The Castilian monarch was returning from this campaign when he learned of the death of his father Alfonso IX on September 24, 1230. This event marks the end of a six-year period of complicated military alliances, a confusing exchange of Muslim loyalties, and the beginning of a re-unified León-Castile under the leadership of Fernando III.

Relentless Strikes from a Reunited León-Castile: 1231–1235

Fernando III (1217–1252) of Castile was proclaimed king of León on November 7, 1230, following the death of his father Alfonso IX (1188–1230), thereby reuniting the realms of León and Castile that had been partitioned in 1157 after the death of Alfonso VII (1126–1157). To obviate any possibility of resistance to his ascendance, Fernando toured Extremedura, Asturias and Galicia for seven months in order to gain the favor of the nobles of these regions. Further, he forestalled potential claims to the crown by his half-sisters, Sancha and Dulce, by offering monetary considerations in exchange for a renunciation of their regal aspirations.

While Fernando III was occupied with matters of state, the relentless assaults on al-Andalus continued. He authorized the bishop of Toledo, Rodrigo Jiménez de Rada, to campaign against Muslim positions to the southeast of Toledo. The city of Quesada was being rebuilt since its destruction by Fernando in 1224, and the bishop with a substantial military drove out the Muslims not only from Quesada but also from numerous other smaller fortifications such as Toya and Lacra until by 1233 the Christians were maintaining garrisons at more than thirty locations in the region that were previously held by Muslims (Martínez Díez *Fernando III* 123–4). While Bishop Jiménez was sent to occupy the region around Quesada, Fernando III dispatched Álvar Pérez of the house of Castro, accompanied by the eleven-year-old future Alfonso X, to attack the environs of Córdoba and Jerez, which recognized the authority of ibn Hud. Early in 1231, Alvar Pérez lay waste the fields of Córdoba and raided southward. Passing Seville, he then destroyed the districts around Jerez. Ibn Hud issued a call to arms and assembled a substantial force of Muslim faithful, but the response proved to be futile. Álvar Pérez and the Christian invaders routed the counterattack, killing many and reaping a large booty.

The failure of ibn Hud to defend against the Christian onslaught drew disdain from the Muslim populace and weakened his standing as emir. Discontent quickly grew to rebellion at Andújar when in April 1232 yet another self-proclaimed emir rose with the support of influential families of the region around Jaén. Muhammad ibn Yusuf ibn Nasr ibn al-Ahmar rejected the leadership of ibn Hud and established a relationship with Abu Zakariya, the first Hafsid leader in Tunis, whom he recognized as his sovereign. Al-Ahmar immediately negotiated a truce with the Christians, which produced an ephemeral respite from their offensives. Seville rejected the authority of ibn Hud, and by the end of 1232, only Córdoba still recognized him.

In 1233, Fernando III personally led the siege against Úbeda. After prolonged resistance and with starvation looming, the city negotiated a peaceful and safe surrender in July of that year. The entire population was permitted to exit with a secure escort. Meanwhile, ibn Hud negotiated a treaty with Fernando III, so that he could direct his efforts towards reunifying al-Andalus under his authority. Safe from northern incursions, he sought to bring Seville under his control by siege. However, he was driven off by al-Ahmar, who was called in to assist the town militia. Moreover, al-Ahmar had his own plans. In a betrayal of town leaders, he summoned them to his camp outside the city walls where he assassinated them in an attempt to seize control of the city. In a total reversal of support, the town militia now rejected al-Ahmar and realigned with ibn Hud. Over in Niebla to the west, the local ruler ibn Mahfuz declared his independence and sought the protection of Fernando III. As Fernando's vassal, he was sheltered from outside influence.

By 1234, the internecine wars between competing Muslim emirs left al-Andalus fragmented into quarters. In Valencia, Zayyan had dethroned Abu Zayd as governor. Muhammad ibn Nasr al-Ahmar was recognized in Arjona, Jaén, and Granada. He established the line of Nasrid rulers who controlled al-Andalus from Granada until their expulsion in 1492. Ibn Mahfuz ruled in Niebla, while ibn Hud exercised control over Córdoba, Seville and the remaining Muslim territories (Martínez Díez *Fernando III* 130–3).

From his first military efforts in 1224, Fernando's campaigns were unbridled successes. Fortune had smiled on the king and his family. Queen Beatriz did not normally accompany Fernando on his missions; she busied herself with matters of the family. However, the unexpected occurred at Toro on November 5, 1235, when Beatriz suddenly died without warning at the young age of thirty-seven. During their sixteen years of marriage, she had given birth to ten children of whom eight survived her. The heir apparent, the future Alfonso X, was approaching fourteen; Fadrique was thirteen; Fernando nearly twelve; Berenguela seven; Enrique five; Felipe almost four; Sancho two; and Manuel just a year old. Two other daughters, María and Leonor died very young. The queen lay at rest at the monastery of Las Huelgas until her son Alfonso had her entombed next to Fernando III in the cathedral of Seville forty years later. Finding little time to grieve, Fernando was soon called to duty with the news that his forces had begun an assault on Córdoba (Martínez Díez *Fernando III* 123–40).

Jaume I of Aragon Advances on Valencia: 1232–1238

When Jaume I (1213–1276) ascended to the crown of Aragon, its southern boundary extended to Teruel in the west and to the mouth of the Ebro River in the south. In

1229, Abu Zayd, the Almoravid governor of Valencia, was overthrown and replaced by the Muslim ruler Zayyan. Abu Zayd's removal prompted his negotiations with Jaume I in that year. The deposed governor offered several castles in exchange for a share in Christian conquests. Having concluded his campaigns in the Balearic Islands, Jaume entertained Abu Zayd's proposal and took locations at Peñíscola, Morella and Burriana in 1232 and 1233. These conquests opened a pathway to Valencia, but other domestic matters led to a hiatus in Jaume's campaign.

The aging Sancho VII of Navarrre died in 1234, and Jaume was desirous of reuniting Navarre and Aragon. Jaume had persuaded Sancho to leave him the crown of Navarre, although Sancho's sister Blanca was the rightful heir to the kingdom. Jaume's anticipated inheritance was thwarted by the appearance of Thibault I (1234–1253) of Champagne, the son of Blanca, whom the Navarrese preferred to either Jaume or to Fernando III of Castile. Both monarchs, while eager to annex Navarre, declined to countermand the acceptance of Thibault by the Navarrese people. With this transition, the crown of Navarre passed into the hands of the Champagne dynasty. The following year (1235), Jaume married his second wife, Violante, the daughter of King Andrew II of Hungary; his first marriage to Leonor of Castile had been dissolved in 1229. However, by 1236 with domestic matters settled, Jaume renewed his commitment to conquer Valencia and obtained approval for the campaign at the court in Monzón in October of that year.

Jaume began the assault on Valencia in 1237 by positioning a garrison on the Puig de Cebolla about 15 kilometers north of the city. The Valencians attempted to dislodge the Christian invaders from their promontory, but the garrison maintained its position until Jaume arrived with a larger army to drive off the Muslim attack. In 1238, Jaume succeeded in having the campaign against Valencia declared a crusade, which attracted fighters from Languedoc and beyond. The siege of the city began in April. Valencia appealed to Abu Zakariya, the Hafsid emir of Tunis, for assistance. However, the fleet carrying food and arms from North Africa was blocked by Catalan vessels and failed to complete its mission. Nearing starvation, Valencia capitulated on September 29, 1238, and Jaume made his entrance into the city on October 9. In accordance with the terms of surrender, citizens desiring to leave the city could exit with any movable possessions, and the main mosque was converted into a cathedral. As Jaume brought the towns and villages south of Valencia into submission, he honored the limits of Aragonese expansion as agreed to by Alfonso II of Aragon and Alfonso VIII of Castile in the treaty of Cazola of 1179. With the annexation of Valencia and the surrounding territories in 1238, the peninsular expansion of the kingdom of Aragon was complete. Jaume and his successors would have to look overseas for future conquests (Bisson 65–7).

Córdoba and Its Environs Fall to the Crown of Castile: 1235–1241

In the years from 1224 until 1235, Fernando III had waged a war of attrition against the Muslim population. He had cleared a path through La Mancha and Extremadura with raids, destruction, and harassment, leaving the Muslim population discouraged, impoverished, and starved. Many inhabitants withdrew to safer locations. He had vanquished major outposts and protective fortifications, but the major Muslim centers were yet to be conquered.

As Fernando was attending to matters of state in the kingdom of León following the loss of Queen Beatriz, news arrived that a contingent of Castilians had successfully staged a surreptitious attack on a section of Córdoba called Ajarquía. The Castilian raiders had captured a Muslim, who formerly had taken refuge in the city and was familiar with that district. They learned from him the layout of the fortifications and the lack of vigilance in some of them. The captive led them to believe that the walls could be scaled under a veil of darkness. The Castilians implemented their plot by constructing ladders and then waited for the next dark night occurring on December 24, 1235. The first marauders, dressed as Muslims, scaled one section of the walls and surprised the sleeping guards in the adjacent tower. They opened one of the gates, permitting the Castilians to surprise the citizens and take command of Ajarquía.

The Muslim citizens who escaped this unexpected affront found refuge within the inner city, and the Christian intruders in Ajarquía faced a hailstorm of projectiles from the citadel. The Christians dispatched a messenger to Álvar Pérez de Castro in Martos and another to King Fernando for assistance. Álvar Pérez was first to arrive with a body of knights and brothers of the military Orders who reinforced the Christian position. The messenger from Córdoba found Fernando to the north of Zamora from where he departed in mid–January, collecting town militias to his cause as he hastened to Córdoba. He established his camp outside the walls of the city on February 7, 1236, and prepared for a lengthy siege.

Meanwhile ibn Hud, the recognized emir for most of al-Andalus including Córdoba, assembled an army at Ecija for a counterattack. However, he opted to retire to Seville when informed that Fernando commanded a superior force. The demoralized population of Córdoba held on as best they could until a shortage of food supplies forced them to bargain for terms of surrender. They were permitted to leave safely with any moveable possessions. Fernando made his formal entrance into the city on June 29, 1236, and immediately had the main mosque consecrated as a cathedral. He then ordered the return of the bells taken from Santiago de Compostela by Almanzor in 998. The bells were to be transported to Compostela by Muslim captives, since they had been carried to Córdoba by Christian prisoners. Fernando disseminated an announcement throughout his realm that the city of Córdoba was empty and needed to be repopulated. Soon the number of Christian immigrants outnumbered the houses available for them. When Fernando departed Córdoba at the end of 1236, the city was populated with Christians and garrisoned by a contingent of soldiers and combatants from the military Orders (Martínez Díez *Fernando III* 146–51).

On a personal level, Fernando at the age of thirty-five had now been without a queen for a year. His mother Berenguela began searching for an eligible partner and eliminated most of the Hispanic princesses because of close parentage. Together with her sister Blanca of France, Berenguela selected Juana of Ponthieu, who travelled to Burgos for the wedding in the fall of 1237. Fernando's marriage to Juana produced five children: Fernando, Leonor, Luis, Simon, and Juan. The latter two died very young, and the eldest Fernando also predeceased his father. Leonor went off to marry the English Prince Edward, and Luis lived his entire life in Castile. Of course, Fernando's first born and future heir, Alfonso X, overshadowed all the other fourteen siblings. Fernando's new marriage and ill-health confined him to Castile for the next two years, while his faithful militias took charge of the castles and fortifications in the province surrounding Córdoba.

The fall of Córdoba, once the crown jewel of the Umayyad empire, diminished the authority of ibn Hud and aroused discontent among his subjects. His incompetence provided an opportunity for his rival emir, Muhammad ibn Nasr al-Ahmar of Jaén, to seize possession of Granada in the spring of 1237. In an attempt to regain authority over Granada, ibn Hud travelled to Almería to solicit the assistance of its governor. However, instead of support, ibn Hud found hostility and was assassinated on January 12, 1238. The death of ibn Hud led to further fragmentation of al-Andalus. Ibn Nasr al-Ahmar was now recognized in Jaén, Granada, Almería, Málaga, Guadix, and Baza. A local magnate Aziz ibn Khattab immediately seized possession of Murcia, but on April 19 its citizens offered the governorship to ibn Zayyan, who had recently been expelled from Valencia by Jaume I. The people of Seville were now left to their own devices and petitioned the Almohads in Marrakesh to send a governor. The arrival of an Almohad governor nominally re-established Seville as a territory of the Almohad empire. The petty King Mahfuz of Niebla remained independent from the other three Muslim *taifa* states and continued as a protected vassal of Fernando III.

By 1240 Fernando III realized that his personal attention was needed to organize the hamlets and villages in the countryside around Córdoba to bring them under his authority. The new inhabitants of Córdoba lacked a supply chain capable of supporting them, although Fernando had twice sent them monetary infusions. In February of 1240 Fernando, accompanied by his sons Alfonso and Fernando, departed for Córdoba despite his ill health. He began a fourteen-month program to incorporate dozens of Muslim cities and villages into his kingdom. Local governors and leaders yielded castles and fortifications to the king and began to pay tribute in the same amount as they paid their emirs. It was further agreed that the inhabitants were free to go wherever they chose and to take their belongings with them. They were also free to remain in their houses and to practice their own religion. Justice was to be exercised on their own terms. In the spring of 1241, Fernando withdrew to Burgos, after meeting his family briefly in Toledo. The governance of the province of Córdoba had been established and placed under the authority of the crown of León-Castile (O'Callaghan *A History* 344–5; Martínez-Díez *Fernando III* 154–6).

The Fall of Murcia, Jaén and the Vassalage of Granada: 1243–1246

In March of 1243, the armies of Fernando III were assembling at Toledo in preparation for an offensive on the southeast of al-Andalus when a messenger arrived with a peace offering from the Muslim king of Murcia. Following the death of ibn Hud in 1238, the kingdom of Murcia was governed in swift succession by a local magnate, Aziz ibn Khattab, and then by Zayyan ibn Mardanish, the former king of Valencia, and finally by ibn Hud's son, Muhammad ibn Yusuf ibn Hud. In a short period, Muhammad ibn

Hud (the son) had restored the unity of the kingdom of Murcia which included Orihuela, Lorca, Cartagena, and Mula, and he now offered to become the vassal of Fernando III to obviate threats not only from Aragon and Castile but also to thwart the expansionary designs of ibn Nasr al-Ahmar, the king of Jaén and Granada.

The twenty-one-year-old Alfonso, Fernando III's eldest son, accepted Muhammad ibn Hud's offer on behalf of his father, who was in Valladolid at the time. As a consequence of his son's acceptance, Fernando later directed the Castilian army towards Murcia instead of campaigning against ibn Nasr al-Ahmar of Granada as originally planned. Alfonso met with the representatives of ibn Hud at Alcaraz in early April and negotiated a pact in which the kingdom of Murcia recognized the sovereignty of Fernando III and pledged a remittance of one half of the revenue of the kingdom. In exchange, the people of Murcia would maintain their properties, religion, and local governance. On May 1, 1243, the Castilians took possession of the alcazar in Murcia.

Several locations, notably Mula, Lorca, and Cartagena, had second thoughts about complying with the agreement made at Alcaraz. These cities resisted occupation by Castilian garrisons, but they finally capitulated in 1244 and 1245 under pressure from Christian sieges. By 1244, Castilian forces under the direction of Infante Alfonso, were also taking control of locations around Játiva, which was north of Biar and part of the lands destined for Aragon as defined in the treaties of Tudején and Cazorla. In retaliation, Jaume I incorporated locations around Villena, which were designated to become part of Castile. All out warfare between Castile and Aragon was averted when Alfonso and Jaume met at Almizra to arrive at an understanding regarding the border. They agreed that Biar and its environs including a line to the east and all to the north of that line including Játiva and Denia were reserved for the crown of Aragon. On the other hand, everything south of Biar, including Villena and Alicante were reserved for the crown of Castile. The treaty of Almizra signed on March 26, 1244, avoided hostilities between these two Christian realms and established the limits of Aragonese territorial expansion in the peninsula, which Jaume I had already observed after taking Valencia a few years earlier.

The submission of ibn Hud of Murcia in 1243 had delayed Christian attacks on the kingdom of Granada ruled by Muhammad ibn Nasr ibn al-Ahmar, who also controlled Jaén, Arjona, Málaga, and Almería. Early in the following year, Fernando III concluded his convalescence in the north and resumed his plan of attacks on the kingdom of Granada by systematically destroying the cultivated fields around Arjona. He did the same for the crop lands around Jaén before returning to Arjona to lay siege to the city. The citizens under siege recognized the hopelessness of the situation and capitulated after just two days. They were permitted to leave freely as the monarch took possession of the interior fortification. The lesser locations of Mengíbar and Pegalajar easily fell prey to Fernando, who then dispatched his troops to ravage the fertile lands around Granada before resting comfortably in Córdoba for the winter of 1244–1245.

In June of 1245, Fernando's legions once again lay waste the grain fields, vineyards, and orchards around Jaén. The city's food supply was depleted. The Christian army met no resistance as they moved on to destroy what had been renewed of the fields of Granada. The ample cavalry of ibn Nasr remained behind the city walls. As the winter of 1245 drew near, Fernando decided to return to Jaén and to place it under siege. The encirclement dragged on throughout the winter, and ibn Nasr al-Ahmar came to realize that the trapped citizens of Jaén no longer had the means to survive. This time Fernando was not going to relent. To relieve his subjects from destruction, ibn Nasr elected to submit to Fernando's authority. He left Granada to meet face to face with the Castilian monarch and offered to become his vassal. Under the agreement, the vassalage obligation would pass to Fernando's successors and to ibn Nasr's. Further, the realm of Granada was obligated to serve faithfully in peace and in war against any enemy of Castile. Finally, the king of Granada would pay an annual tribute but would retain control over all his territory, except for Jaén that was already considered lost. With most of the population of Jaén evicted, Fernando III made his formal entry into the city in March 1246 (O'Callaghan *A History* 351–2; Martínez-Díez *Fernando III* 166–194).

After the submission of ibn Nasr, only the kingdom of Seville remained independent of the authority of León-Castile. The other Muslim kingdoms of Murcia, Granada, and small Niebla had all become vassals of Fernando and were paying tribute to him for protection.

The Deposition of Sancho II and Portugal's Advance on the Algarve: 1245–1249

As the crowns of Castile and Aragon campaigned against Muslim positions in the center and east of the peninsula, Sancho II (1223–1248) of Portugal extended the Christian march in the west down into the Algarve. Mértola was taken in 1238 and Ayamonte on the east bank of the Guadiana River fell soon afterwards. Tavira just to the west of the river surrendered the following year. The swath cut down the Guadiana by the Portuguese effectively isolated the Muslims on the southwest tip of the peninsula from their coreligionists in Niebla to the east of the river.

Sancho's control over the magnates and prelates of Portugal was tenuous. His quarrels with them over rights and privileges dated from the time of his father and grandfather. These disputes limited his effectiveness as a ruler, and ultimately abbreviated his reign. On one hand, the prelates complained that royal agents violated ecclesiastical privileges and abused the clergy. On the other hand, the magnates and nobles continued to contest the crown's attempt to recover royal rights and revenues. Moreover, bishops and magnates alike competed for usurpation of the rights of the monasteries. For decades, the bishops complained to the papacy about alleged injustices, and the new Pope Innocent IV (1243–1254) was induced to act against Sancho despite the monarch's record of achievement against the Muslims.

At the General Council of Lyons in March 1245, an incredible indictment was levied against Sancho, accusing him of "destroying the property of the realm; of allowing men, women, and children, clergy and laity, to be killed with impunity; of tolerating incest, rape, extortion, incendiarism, profanation of churches; in a word, of encouraging the spread of anarchy throughout the realm" (O'Callaghan *A History* 350). A few months later, the Portuguese bishops reported to the pope that conditions had not improved. Consequently, the pope declared that, for the good of the people, the governance of the realm should be entrusted to the king's brother Afonso. The arrival of Afonso, who had been living in France and married to the Countess of Boulogne, Matilda, provoked anarchy. With little support remaining from any segment of the population, Sancho was compelled to flee to Toledo into exile where he died on January 4, 1248. Sancho left no children and was succeeded by his brother Afonso III (1248–1279). With the support of the people and more specifically of the military Orders, Afonso continued the Portuguese advance to the sea. After Faro and other locations to the extreme south were conquered in March 1249, the entire Algarve fell under the control of the Portuguese, and the boundary between Portugal and Castile (except for a few later modifications) was established.

The Conquest of Seville and the Last Days of Fernando III: 1246–1252

After the fall of Jaén and the submission of al-Ahmar of Granada to Fernando III, Seville became more vulnerable. It remained isolated from the rest of the Muslim world. It found no support from within the peninsula, and there was little chance that substantial reinforcements from the Almohads in Marrakesh or the Hafsids in Tunis could be procured. The conquest of Seville was imminent.

Early in October 1246, Fernando launched his first expedition against Seville which targeted the localities to the east of the city to sever its sources of food. The Christian army first devastated Carmona, wasting the crops and taking many captives from the city. In fulfillment of his obligation as a vassal, al-Ahmar, the king of Granada, assisted the Christian army with a contingent of Muslim cavalry. The joint forces moved to Alcalá de Guadaíra, which submitted to Fernando to avoid the destruction of their fields. One group under the leadership of Fernando's brother, Alfonso de Molina, was sent to attack Aljarafe, a rich storehouse for Seville. A second group, led by the king's son, Infante Enrique, along with the cavalry from Granada, destroyed the region around Jerez. Fernando then discharged ibn Nasr al-Ahmar from his military obligation, and the Muslim knights returned to Granada.

While Fernando was rebuilding the fortifications of Alcalá de Guadaíra, the sad news arrived that the queen mother Berenguela had died on November 8, 1246, at Burgos. The death of Berenguela left a void in the administration at Burgos, and although Fernando recognized the need for administrative leadership, he hesitated to abandon the campaign against Seville. A withdrawal from the campaign would permit the region to recover from its debilitated condition. Consequently, he decided to dispatch his brother Alfonso de Molina to Burgos to take control of administrative matters and to return with additional forces for the siege of Seville.

Fernando understood that a naval force was necessary to prevent Seville from being supplied from the Guadalquivir. He summoned Ramón Bonifaz from Jaén and instructed him to raise a fleet from the Bay of Biscay and bring it to the mouth of the Guadalquivir. Fernando also sent for an additional number of land combatants and additional money to supply them. These were necessary measures for a well-prepared siege of Seville. In the meantime, Fernando continued his relentless assault on the outlying locations surrounding Seville during the spring of 1247. He began with Carmona and forced the capitulation of nearly a dozen other smaller cities. The Christians now controlled the northern and eastern reaches of Seville.

The arrival of the Castilian fleet at the mouth of the Guadalquivir in July 1247 was challenged by a Muslim flotilla from Tangier and Ceuta, but Ramón Bonifaz and his well-provisioned sailors drove off their attackers. Fernando directed the fleet to come farther up the river closer to his encampment so that he could protect the ships with soldiers on both banks. However, a full siege was impossible without additional manpower which would not arrive for several months. In the meantime, a war of attrition was waged on both sides of the river, while defending the ships that blockaded the arrival of supplies by river.

The campaign was transformed into a siege when the king's son, Infante Alfonso, returned to the front with a substantial army of Castilians, Leonese, Galicians, Portuguese, and even Aragonese. The entire city of Seville was now encircled, and Fernando had enough manpower to relieve and reinforce the vigilant combatants on the right bank to the west of the city. Only the bridge of Triana now gave access to Seville from the fortress on the west side of the Guadalquivir. To tighten the noose around Seville, a plan was devised to destroy the pontoon bridge across the river, which consisted of heavy oak and iron chains. Under the command of Ramón Bonifaz, two of the largest and strongest vessels in the fleet charged the bridge under full sail and weathered a hailstorm of arrows from both banks. The first boat smashed the bridge head on but failed to break through. The second vessel piloted by Bonifaz immediately inflicted a second blow which broke the bridge and sailed cleanly beyond. The bridge of Triana was destroyed on May 3, 1248, and the next day, Fernando ordered an attack on the castle at Triana. The initial assault failed to take the fort, but under a longer siege, the lack of provisions forced the castle to surrender. The Muslims at Triana were permitted to take refuge in the city of Seville.

The loss of Triana induced the Muslims of Seville to consider offering terms of surrender to the Christian monarch. Their leader Axaçaf proposed three increasingly generous offers, which Fernando rejected in succession; the Castilian wanted the entire city without condition. Axaçaf finally acquiesced when Fernando offered to give him other locations in the area, after they would be conquered by the Christian army. The final rendition of Seville included the entire city. The alcazar was immediately placed under Christian control, and the citizens of Seville were given one month to evacuate with any riches, arms or other belongings that they could transport. On November 23, 1248, Fernando III entered the alcazar. His entrance terminated a seventeen-month struggle that began when his army left Córdoba in June of 1247. The campaign had cost innumerable lives and misery in the process, but the jewel of al-Andalus was again under Christian rule after more than five centuries of Muslim control. Nevertheless, much remained to be done to restore order and administration to the deserted city. Seville needed to be repopulated with Christian inhabitants. Furthermore, the valley of the Guadalquivir from Seville to the ocean needed to be brought under Fernando's control (Martínez Díaz *Fernando III* 203–39).

Fernando's immediate concern of was the administration and distribution of wealth from the recently conquered domains of Jaen, Córdoba, and Seville. These tasks prevented him from taking a respite from his regal duties despite the ill health that plagued him. At various stages during his reign, infirmity had restrained him from taking personal command of his armies. Nevertheless, he now pressed on to establish his authority and administration over the newly conquered territories. By agreement, the territories in the east and west of Iberia were ruled by Catalonia and Portugal respectively. The remaining Muslim kingdoms of Niebla and Granada were his vassals and paid tribute to him. The rest of the peninsula was under the rule of León-Castile. However, Fernando's aspirations for his kingdom were not yet fulfilled as he prepared for an invasion of North Africa. The three Muslim empires across the Strait of Gibraltar, the Almohads in Marrakesh, the Marinids in Fez, and the Hafsids in Tunis, were weakened and divided from warring against each other. The time for conquest was propitious. Nonetheless, Fernando's dream of conquest in North Africa was dashed by his unexpected death on May 30, 1252, at the age of 50. His eldest son, Alfonso X, would claim the rights to a greatly expanded kingdom of León-Castile

The Early Reign of Alfonso X: 1252–1275

Alfonso X (1252–1284), known as *el Sabio*, the Wise or Learned, ascended to a vastly expanded and lavishly wealthy crown of León-Castile in 1252 at the age of thirty. He was experienced in warfare and well educated in history, the letters, and law. Along with the inheritance of his father's conquered territory came the responsibility of distributing the spoils. Alfonso was generous in sharing the riches among the nobles and combatants who participated in the recent conquests, but additional settlers were needed to colonize abandoned sectors. Christian immigrants were welcomed from all corners of Iberia, and the list of grants and estates given to both nobles and immigrants by Alfonso's decree were recorded in the *Libro del Repartimiento*.

In the year following his ascendance, Alfonso X disputed with Afonso III (1248–1279) of Portugal over the rights to the territories to the east of the Guadiana that Portugal had conquered. Moreover, Alfonso X laid claim to the Algarve to the west of the Guadiana that Portugal also controlled. Several factors clouded the claims of rights over these lands. The earliest agreement to the division of these regions dated from the time of Fernando II (1157–1188) of León and Sancho III (1157–1158) of Castile as they proposed to disinherit Alfonso Enríquez (later Alfonso I of Portugal). Of course, the overthrow of Alfonso Enríquez never happened, and Portugal was recognized as a sovereign realm. There was more recent evidence that Sancho II (1223–1248) of Portugal had ceded the rights to the Algarve to Castile during the time of Fernando III (1217–1252) in exchange for Castile's assistance against Sancho's deposition. Further, there was the claim that the rights to the Algarve were granted to León-Castile by the king of Niebla while in vassalage to Fernando III. To set aside their disputes and to avert warfare, the pact of 1253 postponed the complete resolution of this issue while committing to closer family ties between Portugal and Castile. Afonso III agreed to marry Alfonso X's illegitimate daughter Beatriz, even though Afonso's estranged first wife Matilda of Boulogne was still alive (Ballesteros 74–7; O'Callaghan *The Learned King* 156–62). The two monarchs would resume negotiation of this issue more than a decade later.

Thibault I (1234–1253) of Navarre died in 1253, and Alfonso X attempted to impose his authority over that kingdom by invoking the commitment of García Ramírez (1134–1194) of Navarre, who had agreed to pledge homage to Alfonso VII (1126–1157) of Castile in 1134. The new King Thibault II (1253–1270) of Navarre rejected Castilian authority, and consequently, Alfonso dispatched Castilian troops to the Navarrese border. Alfonso X abandoned his designs on Navarre when his father-in-law, Jaume I (1213–1276) of Aragon, pledged to support Navarre against Castile.

About that same time, Alfonso X received an appeal for help from the disgruntled nobility of Gascony, who felt mistreated by their monarch Henry III of England. Alfonso X invoked a presumptive claim to Gascony, recalling that his great grandmother Leonor, married to Alfonso VIII (1158–1214), was the daughter of Henry II of England. The issue was laid to rest with a treaty at Toledo in April 1254, wherein Alfonso X yielded any claims to his half-sister Leonor, who was to marry Henry's son, the future Edward I of England.

Of greater importance to Alfonso X than the affairs of Navarre and Gascony was his quest for the crown of the Holy Roman Empire. Alfonso lay claim to this right because his mother, Beatrice of Swabia, was the granddaughter of Frederick Barbarossa. Indeed, this effort preoccupied him for most of his reign and diverted his attention from matters of state. Alfonso spent vast sums of money throughout western Europe to support his claim and his candidacy as a member of the Hohenstaufen family. Nevertheless, his hopes were dashed when Richard of Cornwall, a brother of the English king, went to Germany to receive that distinction. Alfonso would continue to aspire to that office, even though his aspiration created a distraction from his duties of state and imposed an additional tax burden on his realm (O'Callaghan *A History* 361–2).

Alfonso X inherited a broadly expanded realm that reached far into territories that were overwhelmingly populated by Muslims. The *mudéjares*, the Muslims living under Christian rule, far outnumbered their conquerors. They were permitted to practice their own religion and to preside over their own laws, but they were subjected to the nominal authority of a Christian king and were required to pay tribute to him. The possibility of insurrection from within al-Andalus as well as intervention from North Africa still posed a menace. A new power arose in North Africa represented by the Merinid dynasty, also known as the Banu Marin or Benimarines. Whereas the Almoravids and the Almohads were both founded by religious reformers who rose to political power, the rise of the Merinids promoted no divergent Islamic ideology. Their bent was strictly tribal supremacy. The Merinids were Zenata Berber while the Almoravids and Almohads were Sanhaja and Masmuda Berbers respectively. From their base in Fez, the Merinids challenged the rule of the Almohads in Marrakesh. Moreover, the Hafsid dynasty in Tunis further divided control over the region. Alfonso X recognized the division as an opportunity for an invasion of North Africa, and in 1260 he resumed his father's dream of conquest there by preparing a fleet and appointing an *adelantado de la mar*, an admiral in charge of sea operations. That same year, the Castilians regained control over Cádiz. That city had previously been conquered under Fernando III, but since then had broken from Castilian authority. The resumption of Castilian control provided access to an additional naval base.

Just as Castilian naval capabilities strengthened, Alfonso received a request for assistance from the Governor Yaqub of Salé on the Atlantic coast of present-day Morocco about sixty miles north of Casablanca. Yaqub intended to declare independence from the Marinid Emir, Abu Yusuf Yaqub ibn Abd al-Haqq (1258–1286). In response, Alfonso dispatched a Castilian fleet that arrived without warning and easily gained access to the city. In betrayal of the Muslim governor's plea for help, the Castilians began to pillage and plunder. When Abu Yusuf hastened to rescue Salé, the Castilians retreated to their ships and departed on September 21. The assault on Salé failed to establish a Christian foothold in North Africa. However, it did succeed in reaping a considerable amount of booty in goods and slaves, and it aroused the ire of the Merinids (O'Callaghan *The Learned King* 172–4).

Alfonso's effort to command the Atlantic ports west of Gibraltar continued in 1262. Niebla was formerly a vassal state of Castile, but Alfonso removed the Muslim governor and assumed total authority of the city in that year. Huelva on the Atlantic coast was overcome as well. Alfonso then demanded al-Ahmar of Granada to cede the ports of Gibraltar and Tarifa. However, the king of Granada refused Alfonso's request, realizing that if he lost control of the Strait of Gibraltar, the Muslims of al-Andalus would be severed from the assistance of their co-religionists across the Strait.

Al-Ahmar continued to pay annual tribute to Alfonso X, but the king's attempt to gain control of the Strait provoked a conspiracy among the Muslims of al-Andalus. Al-Ahmar devised a surreptitious plan to stage a simultaneous revolt in the towns throughout al-Andalus. Around May 1264, the towns rejected Castilian authority and proclaimed al-Ahmar as their king. A substantial contingent of Merinid volunteers assisted al-Ahmar's venture. Only Alfonso's absence from Seville during the uprising thwarted a planned attempt on his life. Totally surprised by this event, Alfonso began immediate efforts to regain control. One by one the major locations were recaptured, which induced many Muslims to migrate to Granada or to North Africa to escape reprisal. Fortunately for Alfonso, the governors of Málaga, Guadix, and Comares belonged to the Banu Ashqilula family and supported Alfonso against al-Ahmar. The uprising ended when Alfonso X invaded the environs of Granada in the spring of 1265. The attack on al-Ahmar's capital threatened his regime and prompted his request for a truce in August of that year. He pledged an additional annual payment in reparations and agreed to assist in the subjugation of Murcia.

The revolt of the *mudéjares* presented such a widespread menace that Alfonso X felt compelled to appeal to his father-in-law, Jaume of Aragon, for help in subduing this threat. After overcoming the reluctance of the nobles and prelates of Catalonia, Jaume led an army into the kingdom of Murcia in the fall of 1265. By the end of January 1266, Murcia and the surrounding towns had surrendered to Christian control. The Muslims were permitted to remain and keep their property. Jaume's only demand was that the main mosque be converted into a cathedral. The Aragonese monarch remained true to the treaty of Almizra of 1244 by relinquishing this territory to the Castilians. However, many Catalans remained to settle there, which converted this part of the Castilian kingdom into a predominantly Catalan speaking region. As the number of Christian settlers increased, the Muslim population decreased and migrated to Granada.

During the *mudéjar* uprising, Alfonso not only appealed to his father-in-law for military support, but he also solicited the assistance of his son-in-law Afonso III of

Portugal. In exchange for Afonso's help, Alfonso X was willing to negotiate a settlement of the boundary dispute between Portugal and Castile. A decade earlier, the two monarchs had deferred an agreement on territorial boundaries and chose to strengthen their relationship with the marriage of Alfonso's daughter Beatriz to Afonso III. However, the issue of boundaries was not settled. So, on September 20, 1264, after the Muslim uprising, Alfonso X yielded administrative control of the Algarve to Portugal in exchange for the service of fifty Portuguese knights and other considerations. Subsequently, on February 16, 1267, the two monarchs met again at Badajoz. Alfonso X expressed his gratitude for Portuguese assistance during the *mudéjar* revolt and demonstrated his love of his grandson, the future Dinis I of Portugal, by surrendering all rights to the Algarve. He agreed on the boundary between their respective realms along the Guadiana, which effectively set the present-day limits. The boundary was modified again only slightly during the reign of Dinis I (Ballesteros 420–5; O'Callaghan *A History* 368–9).

A major administrative initiative of Alfonso X was the implementation of a uniform set of laws across the kingdom of León-Castile. His pursuit to impose a *Fuero Real*, a uniform code of municipal law, and the *Espéculo de las leyes*, an earlier version of the the *Siete Partidas*, intended to implement a uniform code throughout the realm. However, his effort met with serious opposition from nobles and townsmen alike. Alfonso's codes were based on Roman law. They varied from the medieval notion of the balance between the sovereign and his subjects, each having their respective rights and obligations. The nobility vigorously challenged Alfonso's authority to upset this balance, and the townsmen were fearful of any change. Furthermore, the towns objected to the heavy taxation imposed on them to fund the king's quest for the crown of the Holy Roman Empire. They were also being asked to underwrite the lavish wedding of his son Fernando de la Cerda to Blanche, the daughter of Louis IX of France, in November 1269.

On one hand, Alfonso succeeded in accommodating the petitions of the townsmen by confirming the local *fueros* of the municipalities instead of the *Fuero Real*. In exchange for modifying the uniform royal law to allow traditional customs, the towns granted the king an additional tax levy until his pursuit of the crown of the Empire was concluded. On the other hand, Alfonso's negotiations with the nobles was less fruitful. The discontent of the magnates mounted, and the king's brother Felipe led them in a plot against Alfonso. In 1272, the nobles confronted the king regarding their demands for a reinstatement of rights, but the king's attempt at conciliation with them was unsuccessful. As a consequence of this impasse, Felipe and other nobles decided to go into exile to Granada, where King al-Ahmar welcomed them with the thought of promoting opposition to Alfonso. However, in a stroke of fate later that year, the king of Granada and founder of the Nasrid dynasty, Muhammad I ibn Nasr al-Ahmar (1238–1272) died unexpectedly. His son Muhammad II (1273–1302) succeeded him in early 1273 after overcoming some resistance to his ascendance. Meanwhile, Alfonso's negotiations with the Christian rebels and with the new king of Granada resumed. Muhammad II renewed the pledge of vassalage with an annual payment of tribute, and Alfonso confirmed the old *fueros* and acceded to other demands of the Christian rebels. With his offer accepted, the king welcomed the rebellious nobles back to Castile.

Putting the rebellion of the nobles behind him, Alfonso continued his pursuit of the crown of the Empire. At the end of 1274, he set out to meet with Pope Gregory X in May 1275 at Beaucaire, France. Upon arrival, however, he learned that the pope had already recognized Rudolph of Hapsburg as emperor (O'Callaghan *A History* 371–4). Alfonso's dream of empire was crushed once and for all. As an additional obstacle, the king's return to Castile was delayed by a severe illness that prevented him from traveling. Later diagnosed by historians as a brain cancer, this chronic malady had been tormenting the king for several years and caused severe episodes throughout the remainder of his reign. To compound matters, a new threat from the Merinids awaited the king upon his return.

The Final Years of Alfonso X: 1275–1284

Alfonso X returned from France in late 1275 and found the realm of León-Castile under attack from the Merinids. The Merinid Emir Abu Yusuf had taken advantage of the death of the last Almohad caliph, Abu al-Ula (Abu Dabbus) Idris II al-Wathiq (1266–1269), to expand his kingdom eastward. He now controlled all of Morocco as far east as Tlemcen where the Hafsids still reigned. The success of Abu Yusuf prompted the new king of Granada, Muhammad II (1273–1302), to appeal to the Merinid emir for assistance in overthrowing Christian rule in al-Andalus. As a condition of the campaign, Abu Yusuf demanded control of the ports of Algeciras and Tarifa. These naval bases permitted the invaders to cross the Strait in May 1275, and the emir himself followed in August. They pushed on to destroy the river valley along the Guadalquivir as far as Córdoba, while from Granada the Nasrids ravaged the countryside around Jaén.

During Alfonso's sojourn in France, his first-born son and heir, Fernando de la Cerda, was appointed regent in charge of the realm. As the Merinid invasion unfolded, Fernando hastened to assemble a counterattack but suddenly fell ill and died at Villa Real (Ciudad Real) on July 25, 1275. The leadership of the Castilian troops then fell to Nuño González de Lara, who as head of the frontier forces, gave battle to Abu Yusuf near Ecija on September 7. Nuño's forces were sorely beaten, and he was decapitated in the battle. The king's second-born son Sancho subsequently took command of an army that assembled in Córdoba to defend the frontier. Alfonso X returned from France at the end of the year and negotiated a truce that lasted until the spring of 1277, at which time Abu Yusuf returned and raided the territories around Seville, Córdoba, and Jerez. Despite the destruction, Alfonso did not give battle but remained on the defensive. In the summer of 1278, Alfonso sent a fleet to block the port of Algeciras. The Merinids succeeded in breaking the blockade, but afterwards Abu Yusuf retreated to Morocco to address more pressing problems there (O'Callaghan *A History* 375–6). Yusuf's departure brought relief to the battered Castilians.

The death of Fernando de la Cerda in 1275 raised the issue of succession to the crown and ultimately caused a break between Alfonso X and his son Sancho. Custom dictated that a king's surviving son should take precedence over the rights of the children of the first-born son, and Sancho asserted his rights based on that custom. The recently drafted code in the *Espéculo* confirmed that the throne should pass to the eldest son and then to his grandchildren. However, the new code was silent on what should occur when the eldest son predeceased the monarch. To further complicate Alfonso X's decision, Philip III of France, whose daughter Blanche was Fernando's widow, was pressuring Alfonso to recognize the rights of Fernando's children, for they were the grandchildren of Philip III just as they were the grandchildren of Alfonso X. At a court in Segovia of 1278, Alfonso finally (and perhaps reluctantly under pressure from prelates, magnates, and townsmen) concurred that Sancho was his rightful heir (O'Callaghan *The Learned King* 236–9, 246–7).

Alfonso X also faced political pressure from France as he attempted to claim rights to the kingdom of Navarre. The political intrigue began with the death of Henry I (1270–1274) of Navarre, who left his kingdom to his two-year-old daughter Jeanne I (1274–1305). Both Castile and Aragon were eager to depose her and to claim that kingdom as their own, but Henry I's widow, Blanche of Artois, appealed to Philip III (1270–1285) for protection. Philip's solution was to propose the marriage of Jeanne to his son, the future Philip IV of France. With this agreement, Navarre fell under the rule of the kings of France for several generations (See Chart 13; Chart 16).

Meanwhile in Catalonia, Jaume I (1213–1276) set out on June 27, 1276, to put down a revolt of the Muslim rebels of Valencia, inspired by the invasion of the Merinids into Castile. Before he could complete his mission, he fell ill and died after a reign of sixty-three years. Jaume had made a final decision in 1262 to divide his kingdom between his two legitimate sons, Pere and Jaume. Their inheritance excluded territories previously held by the crown of Aragon in southern France. Back in 1258, Jaume I had signed the treaty of Corbeil with Louis IX, whereby he renounced any claim to the Languedoc, and in return, Louis IX as the descendant of Charlemagne renounced all claims to the former Spanish March that comprised the counties of Catalonia. That same year, Jaume I relinquished his rights to Provence to Queen Margaret of France, the daughter of Ramon Berenguer V. Therefore, with respect to Jaume I's remaining legacy, the elder Pere received Aragon, Catalonia, and Valencia, while Jaume inherited Roussillon, Cerdagne, Majorca, and the lordship of Montpellier (Bisson 69).

After his coronation, Pere, known as Pedro III of Aragon but Pere II of Barcelona, immediately addressed the revolt in Valencia. After ravaging the lands around the city and laying a six-month siege, the rebels acquiesced and presented no further difficulties. However, Pere's relations with Castile and France were more delicate. In January 1278, Pere's sister Queen Violante, the wife of Alfonso X, arrived in the Catalan court, accompanied by Blanche, the widow of Fernando de la Cerda, and her two sons Alfonso and Fernando. Leaving her sons in the custody of the king of Aragon, Blanche departed for France to petition her brother Philip III for intervention into the rights of inheritance for the young Alfonso and Fernando. Alfonso X found himself deserted by his wife, his daughter-in-law, and his grandchildren. He was further pressured by Philip III into making concessions for the inheritance of Alfonso and Fernando. Alfonso X proposed a counteroffer in 1280 to establish a vassal kingdom of Jaén for the Infante Alfonso, the son of Fernando de la Cerda. This offer was rejected by Philip III and opposed by Alfonso's son, the future Sancho IV, who objected to any division of his future inheritance. The following year Alfonso X and Pere II agreed to an alliance in which they proposed to partition the kingdom of Navarre that was ruled *in absentia* by Jeanne I (1274–1305) and her betrothed, the future Philip IV of France. Meanwhile Pere kept the Infantes de la Cerda in his custody to be used as leverage against either Castile or

France. Pere further insured against future hostilities from Castile through a marital alliance with Portugal in 1281 by offering the hand of his daughter Isabel to the twenty-year-old King Dinis (1279–1325).

The final years of Alfonso X were marked by rebellion, disloyalty, and a break with family members. At the *Cortes* at Seville in 1281, he again tried the patience of his people by proposing the coinage of new monies rather than imposing yet another tax. He further alienated his son Sancho when he announced his intention to resume discussions with the king of France concerning the rights of inheritance of the Infantes de la Cerda. After heated words, Sancho left Seville and summoned a *Cortes* in Valladolid in April 1282 where he voiced his grievances against his father. With the support of the nobility, townsmen, and military Orders, he effectively took charge of the administration of the realm without assuming the title of king. Queen Violante and other family members, along with support from Dinis of Portugal and Pere II of Aragon, were all drawn to Sancho's cause against Alfonso X.

Grasping for support from wherever he could find it, Alfonso X appealed to his former enemy, the Merinid Emir Abu Yusuf. The two leaders met in the summer of 1282 near Seville, and Abu Yusuf lent the king 100,000 gold dinars and accepted as collateral the gold crown that Alfonso X and his father had worn. The Merinids then proceeded to ravage the regions loyal to Sancho, including the countryside around Córdoba and Toledo and as far north as Madrid. The raids for booty continued the following spring until the emir returned to Morocco at the end of summer (O'Callaghan *A History* 378–80).

Alfonso X gained little by permitting the destruction of his own kingdom, and Sancho drew only fickle support from the nobility. Realizing the folly of their actions, the father and son attempted a reconciliation that was perfunctorily aborted by the death of Alfonso X at Seville on April 4, 1284. As soon as he learned of his father's death, Sancho IV (1284–1295) successfully claimed the inheritance of the entire realm, despite the last will of Alfonso X, which left the kingdom to his grandson, Alfonso de la Cerda, and created vassal kingdoms at Seville and Murcia for two of his younger sons, who were still loyal to him.

While the final years of Alfonso X's reign were marred by tragedy, his accomplishments were remarkable. As a patron of scholarship, he provided funds for the survival of the University of Salamanca. He had works supporting the *trivium* and *quadrivium*, the traditional curricula of medieval study, translated into vernacular Spanish. In law, he promulgated three sets of codes throughout his realm, known as the *Fuero Real*, *Espéculo*, and *Siete Partidas*. In history, he had the *Estoria de Espanna*, a history of Iberia, and the *General Estoria*, a world history, written in the vernacular. In science, he brought a knowledge of astronomy and astrology to the educated masses through translations of Arabic treatises into Castilian. In literature, he drew praise as a poet by composing some of the works found in the *Cantigas de Santa María*, a collection of several hundred poems and hymns praising the miracles and intercessions of the Virgin Mary. As a result, Alfonso X would be known as *el Sabio*, the Wise. However, all this activity did not come without a cost. Alfonso X was criticized for his largesse in support of scholars and troubadours as were his extravagant expenditures in quest of the crown of the Holy Roman Empire. Moreover, his renown as a learned scholar may have come at the expense of his ability to unify the internal politics of his realm. Consequently, his heir Sancho IV would struggle to rectify the political disunity of León-Castile.

CHAPTER 10

A Rebellious Nobility During War, Plague and Famine: 1284–1369

The Reign of Sancho IV (1284–1295)

Sancho was in Ávila when he learned that his father Alfonso X had died at Seville on April 4, 1284. He immediately claimed the rights to the crown of León-Castile and hastened the plans for his coronation in the cathedral of Toledo. In attendance were the bishops of Burgos, Cuenca, Coria, and Badajoz. Noticeably absent was the archbishop of Toledo, Gonzalo Pérez Gudiel. The archbishop's absence reflected, no doubt, the censure of Pope Martin IV, who considered Sancho's marriage to María de Molina as incestuous. The pope had excommunicated the couple for that reason, even though the marriage had been approved by the Castilian clergy.

It was at Toledo in June of 1282 that Sancho married María de Molina, the daughter of Alfonso de Molina, the brother of Fernando III (1217–1252). His marriage to his first cousin was a total rejection of Alfonso's plan for Sancho's betrothal to Guillerma de Moncada, daughter of Gaston, the Viscount of Moncada. Years earlier at barely twelve years of age in April of 1270, Sancho was subjected to an arranged marriage of convenience with Guillerma. This marriage was the only one recognized by the Church during Sancho's lifetime, even though it was never consummated and was performed with the two parties *in absentia*. The French Pope Martin's declaration of Sancho's marriage to María as incestuous probably reflected his close political alignment with the French King Philip III, who favored the rights of his grandchildren, the Infantes de la Cerda. The declaration of Sancho's marriage as illegal diminished the rights of Sancho's children and increased the opportunities for Philip III's grandchildren (Nieto Soria 24–5, 49).

As Sancho ascended to the crown of León-Castile in 1284 at nearly twenty-six-years of age, he faced internal challenges compounded by external threats on his northern and southern borders. Internally, the Castilian nobility had grown extremely rich and powerful during the reign of his father Alfonso X, and Sancho was pressed to win their acceptance. The spoils of war that increased the wealth and power of the noble families intensified the jealousies and rivalries that existed between them. Their own self-interests hampered Sancho's attempt to unify them under his authority. Externally, he had to maintain a delicate balance between his relations with France and Aragon who were on the brink of war over Aragon's annexation of the French kingdom of Sicily (discussed in greater detail in a later section). On the southern front, the Merinids of North Africa, who still controlled a base at Tarifa, threatened attacks on the basin of the Guadalquivir, and the Nasrids of Granada were poised to take advantage of any Castilian weakness.

Sancho began his reign on friendly terms with his uncle Pere III of Aragon, and they met at Ciria, to the east of Soria, in February of 1285 to form an alliance. Sancho agreed to assist Pere against an imminent attack from Philip III of France over the annexation of Sicily. However, Sancho failed to dispatch troops to aid Pere when Philip III invaded Aragon in the spring of 1285 and took Girona. Sancho was consumed by the Merinid threats on his southern border. The French attack on Aragon, supported by Pope Martin, was short and without consequence. The three leaders perpetrating this conflict all died in the following months. Pere III of Aragon was succeeded by his son Alfonso III. Philip IV of France replaced his father Philip III, and Honorius IV became the new pontiff, replacing the deceased Martin IV. The new pope decided that the sanctions against Sancho and María de Molina no longer served a purpose. He lifted the order of excommunication against them in November of 1286, but he remained silent regarding the legitimacy of the marriage.

Meanwhile, the threat from the Merinids escalated. From their peninsular stronghold at Tarifa, Emir Abu Yusuf mobilized his forces early in 1285 and launched an offensive aimed at Jerez and the surrounding areas. The city was put under siege, and the countryside was destroyed. Sancho's relief army of nobles and military orders did not arrive until July 1285, but it forced the siege of Jerez to be lifted in August. The presence of the Christian army and the arrival of a Castilian fleet outside of Tarifa threatened the Merinid position, and the Muslim army conceded withdrawal. More importantly, however, the lack of supplies caused by the rampant devastation throughout the area constrained a successful campaign for either side. Sancho came to an agreement with Abu Yusuf on October 21, 1285, without giving battle. The truce permitted the Muslim army to retreat and gave Sancho considerable monies in reparation. The death of Abu Yusuf on March 20, 1286, at Algeciras afforded the Castilians a respite from Muslim attacks and led to the planning of the eventual conquest of Tarifa. In the meantime, the future Fernando IV was born in Seville on December 6, 1285, while his father Sancho was at Badajoz (Nieto Soria 60-5).

Sancho IV continued to rely on the nobles who supported him against his father Alfonso X. He gave them broad administrative powers and delegated his authority to them. Notably, Gómez García, the abbot of Valladolid, was an early supporter of Sancho. However, the abbot abused his administrative position in the city to expand his responsibilities beyond legitimate fiscal and judicial authority. Alerted to García's overreach and, perhaps, monetary misappropriation, Sancho ordered an audit of the abbot's financial affairs. The unfavorable findings of the investigation spoiled the political ambitions of the abbot. However, there were others who also usurped the king's authority. The rise to power of Lope Díaz III de Haro presented an even greater threat to the king. Lope descended from a powerful family line that served the crown of Castile from the early twelfth century and whose power climaxed under Sancho. Lope exercised authority over Sancho IV's royal household and finances, and he held the royal castles of Castile under his custody. For some time, Lope's rise to power had provoked dissension in the royal court, and his influence was finally challenged at a meeting convened by Sancho at Alfaro on June 8, 1288. Sancho had gathered the prelates, magnates, and other royal counselors to determine whether Castile should ally with Philip IV of France, who was politically in lock step with the pope, or else join with Alfonso III of Aragon against France and the pope. On one side, Lope and the Infante Juan, Sancho's brother who had married María de Haro, favored an alliance with Aragon. On the other side, the remainder of the counselors, including Queen María de Molina, opted for an alliance with France. The queen understood that favor with France and the pope could encourage recognition of her marriage as legal. That determination would also recognize her children as legitimate heirs. In a heated discussion during the meeting at Alfaro, Lope de Haro attempted to impose his will in opposition to the king and queen. In rebuke, the king demanded that Lope return all the royal castles that were under his command. An enraged Lope charged towards Sancho with dagger in hand. Responding quickly, a king's guard severed the hand with the clutched dagger, and a second guard struck Lope in the head with a mace, killing him instantly. The king's brother, the Infante Juan, who was aligned with Lope and who had his own pretensions to the crown, was immediately imprisoned at the castle in Burgos.

On July 13 Castile reached an agreement with Philip IV, which stipulated that France renounce any rights to the crown of Castile. It also created the kingdoms of Murcia and Ciudad Real for the Infantes de la Cerda, which they rejected as an insufficient substitute for their claim to the crown. Alfonso III of Aragon saw an opportunity to leverage Infante Alfonso de la Cerda against Castile. He provoked a civil war by inciting the disgruntled Castilian nobility to rally around Alfonso de la Cerda with the promise of restoring the honors and privileges that they enjoyed under Alfonso X in 1281. Alfonso III's connivance was implemented at Jaca in September 1288. In the presence of a confederation of Castilian nobles favoring the deposition of Sancho IV, Alfonso de la Cerda was sworn in as king of Castile (Nieto Soria 82–6).

Open hostilities erupted in April of 1289. Supplemented with Portuguese troops, Sancho IV amassed his forces on the borders of Aragon. The main bodies of the Castilian and Aragonese armies did not meet in open combat, but rather skirmished and damaged the properties of their opponents. The greatest lost to the Castilians occurred at Cuenca when Diego López de Haro in service to King Alfonso III of Aragon badly defeated Rui Páez de Sotomayor serving Sancho IV. This confrontation witnessed the death of several Castilian nobles and friars of the military Orders. Hostilities were neutralized on April 5, 1290, by an additional agreement between France and Castile in which France renounced completely any pretensions to the crown of Castile. Moreover, the alliance effectively abandoned the interests of the Infantes de la Cerda. This development sounded a death knell for the cause of the Infantes and dashed the hopes of their supporters, who sought the deposition of Sancho IV.

The agreement with France dampened Sancho's troubles on his eastern front, but internal dissension was not entirely repressed in Galicia. Juan Alfonso de Albuquerque was encouraging insurrection there. De Albuquerque was an ally of Juan Núñez de Lara and a supporter of the imprisoned Infante Juan, the king's brother. Sancho visited various locations in Galicia in 1291 to pacify the region, and he subsequently ordered the release of Juan on August 24 of that year as an offer of peace. With domestic issues mended, Sancho enhanced his relationship with Portugal by arranging the marriage of his son, the future Fernando IV, with Constanza, the daughter of King Dinis of Portugal. Constanza was not yet two years old at the time, and the marriage was not formalized until 1299 after the death of Sancho. Meanwhile, the king of Granada was disposed to a peace treaty with Castile. The Nasrid King Muhammad II had become increasingly fearful of the Merinids, who had launched raids throughout the environs of Jerez and Seville in 1291 before returning to North Africa in September of that year.

In Aragon, Jaume II (1291–1327) ascended as king on June 16, 1291, after the death of his older brother Alfonso III. The new king of Aragon continued to reign over Sicily, which drew opposition from the French royal family and from the pope. To reduce the possibility of a threat from Castile, Jaume chose to establish a friendship with Sancho. By befriending Castile, he would benefit from one less opponent. Furthermore, Jaume and Sancho both preferred to direct their military efforts against the Merinids. On November 29, 1291, the two monarchs signed the treaty of Monteagudo, which promised mutual defense and established a collaborative fight against the Muslims. Jaume also promised to marry Sancho's daughter Isabel, only eight years old at the time. He would later repudiate this part of the agreement.

By 1292, Sancho found himself at the zenith of his political influence. He had established a peace agreement with France, and he had signed cooperation agreements with Portugal and Aragon, involving the marriage of his daughters. Muhammad II of Granada, fearing a threat from the Merinids, had aligned with Sancho, and the formerly disgruntled Castilian nobility seemed to be pacified for the moment. The time was now propitious for Sancho to secure his southern border that was constantly under threat from the Merinids garrisoned in Tarifa and Algeciras.

In the spring of 1292, Castilian forces began amassing at Seville in preparation for an attack on Tarifa. Towards the end of May, newly-built ships from Galicia and Cantabria arrived with additional troops, adding to ships sent from Aragon. Sancho considered launching his first attack on Algeciras, but he later chose to follow the advice of his counselors to attack Tarifa, which was the narrowest point across the Strait. By mid–June, Castilian forces were in full siege of Tarifa. By agreement, the king of Granada supplied food and rations to the Christian attackers, while harassment of the besieged city continued day and night and resulted in its capitulation on October 13, 1292.

Muhammad II of Granada harbored the notion that Tarifa would be returned to his regime after eviction of the Merinids. However, Sancho had expended vast resources in the conquest of that location and had no such intention. The disappointed king of Granada realigned with the Merinids, and they jointly attacked Tarifa from late 1293 until mid 1294. Only adequate preparation and a fierce defense by the Christians prevented the loss of the city. The arrival of naval reinforcements in August of 1294 along with plague and starvation among the Muslims caused their retreat.

Throughout his reign, Sancho suffered from consumption, and his intense campaign against Tarifa only aggravated his illness. His condition progressively worsened until his death three years later. Succumbing to his illness, Sancho died at his birthplace in Toledo on April 25, 1295, leaving his wife, María de Molina, and a nine-year-old heir Fernando IV (Palenzuela 605–7).

The Reigns of Pere III (1276–1285), Alfonso III (1285–1291), and Jaume II (1291–1327) of Aragon

During his short eleven-year reign, Sancho IV (1284–1295) of Castile witnessed three consecutive rulers in Aragon who charted a new course for that monarchy. Decades earlier, Jaume I (1213–1276), dubbed the Conquerer, had expanded the limits of Aragon as far south as possible. After the conquest of Valencia in the fall of 1238, the federation of Aragon, Catalonia, and Valencia had completed its peninsular expansion. It was hemmed in by Castile to the south and west and by Navarre and other French holdings in the north. It now made sense for the monarchy to support the burgeoning maritime commerce of Barcelona and Valencia by expanding control and influence over the Mediterranean. Pere III, and his two sons Alfonso III and Jaume II set a new course for the overseas expansion of the crown of Aragon.

Pere III (1276–1285) succeeded his father Jaume I, the Conqueror, in 1276. When the Conqueror died, Pere (ruling as Pero (Peter) III in Aragon and Pere II in Catalonia) was away subduing a Muslim revolt in Valencia that dragged on until 1277. In the interim, he traveled to Zaragoza where he was crowned in November 1276. Two years later, the Catalan nobility rose up against him. The nobles objected to the imposition of a *bovatge* "tax," which had not been approved by the Catalan *Corts*. Pere countered the objections of the leader of the insurrection, the viscount of Cardona, by winning the support of the cities. Nonetheless, Pere III quickly reconciled with the malcontents, so that he could gain their approval for the funding of a maritime fleet. The purported intention of the fleet was for commercial purposes and for use against the Muslims of Tunis. However, as it turned out, Pere would use the fleet to take the island of Sicily that had recently been wrested from the Hohenstaufens by Charles of Anjou.

Under the Emperor Frederick II, Sicily had secured a prominent position of influence in the Mediterranean. After the emperor's death, combined French and papal forces forcefully took command of the island against the will of the people. The friction between the new rulers and the populace came to a head on March 30, 1282, as the citizens of Palermo were celebrating the Easter holiday. A young Sicilian woman was on her way to vespers when a French soldier began to abuse her. The incident quickly escalated from a local violent reaction into full scale uprising, known as the Sicilian Vespers, in which the French were massacred and ejected from the island. This disaster presented the perfect opportunity for the intervention of Pere III, who had stationed his fleet off the coast of Tunis. Pere arrived on the island and found a welcoming populace at Palermo in early September. The Catalans repulsed a counterattack from the French naval force and thereby secured the continuation of their authority. Dissatisfied with this turn of events, Pope Martin IV excommunicated Pere in November of that year and declared him deposed from Aragon. He proffered Philip III's brother, Charles of Valois, as a replacement for Pere.

Back in Aragon the following year, Pere called a *Corts* at Tarazona in September of 1283 to muster support for his overseas plans. The Aragonese nobility protested that they had not been consulted about the Sicilian affair and that they were being taxed unlawfully. The king's rebuttal did not satisfy the nobles, and the following month at Zaragoza, he was obliged to confirm their privileges and agreed not to enact laws without the approval of the *Corts*. He was thereby compelled to recognize the influence of the *hermandad* or Union which the Aragonese nobility had formed as a show of power. The Catalans acted in like fashion. At an assembly convened at Barcelona in December of 1283, the barons and towns demanded that a general *Cort* be assembled annually and that any legislation including tax levies should have their consent (Bisson 85–90).

In retaliation for the confiscation of Sicily, the French Pope Martin IV authorized a Crusade, and Philip III of France attacked Catalonia by land and sea in the spring of 1285. Pere's younger brother Jaume II of Majorca proved to be disloyal to the crown of Aragon and sided with the French. The invading French army successfully infiltrated Empordà and captured Girona on September 7. However, the French fleet was defeated by the Catalans at the Bay of Roses, the northernmost location on the Catalan coast. Because of the naval defeat, the French army at Girona could not be sustained, and Philip III ordered a retreat from the city. King Philip died soon afterwards on October 5. Pope Martin IV's death had preceded Philip's in late March as did Charles of Anjou's demise even earlier in the year. Pere intended to retaliate against his brother Jaume II of Majorca for being disloyal and for supporting the French, but Pere died as well on November 11. He would not witness the execution of his vengeful plan against his brother. Before his death, Pere took possession of the Infantes de la Cerda when his sister Violante abandoned her husband Alfonso X of Castile and fled to Barcelona along with her daughter-in-law, Blanche of France, and her two sons, the Infantes Alfonso and Fernando. Later, Pere and his sons used the custody of the Infantes and their claims to the crown of Castile as political leverage against Sancho IV of Castile. Before his death in 1285, Pere also arranged the marriage of his daughter Isabel with King Dinis (1279–1325) of Portugal.

As the eldest son of Pere III (1276–1285), Alfonso III (1285–1291) began his reign at the age of twenty after the sudden death of his father in 1285. Pere's testament gave the peninsular holdings of Aragon, Catalonia, and Valencia to Alfonso, while Alfonso's younger brother, the future Jaume II (1291–1327), was installed as king of Sicily. At the time of his father's death, Alfonso was laying siege to Palma in Majorca as part of his father's plan to exact revenge on Jaume II of Majorca for supporting the French invasion of Catalonia. The campaign successfully took Majorca and resulted in the later surrender of Ibiza. Menorca would then fall to the Catalans in 1287.

Alfonso III returned to Aragon and attended the *Cort* in Zaragoza in April of 1286, where he met the protests of the Union, established during the time of his father. The Union demanded more control over the officials who governed throughout Aragon. Alfonso was reluctant to agree to their demands, but fearing the possibility of deposition or civil war, he finally granted privileges to the Union on December 28, 1287. More specifically, he agreed to hold a general *Cort* in Zaragoza annually at which time the *Cort* would have the power to elect counselors, who would govern and administer throughout the kingdom.

On the international front, the hostilities of the pope and of the French king still loomed over Alfonso, and the alliance between France and Sancho IV of Castile added to the menace. However, Alfonso still controlled the fate of the Infantes de la Cerda. As a countermeasure to the plans of Castile and France, he proclaimed Alfonso de la Cerda as king of Castile at Jaca in 1288. This proclamation nullified Sancho's agreement with France to cede Murcia and Ciudad Real to the Infantes and led to border skirmishes between Castile and Aragon. Edward I of England mediated a tentative agreement at Tarascon in February 1291, whereby Alfonso pledged loyalty to the new Pope Nicolas IV (1288–1292) and agreed to withdraw support for his brother Jaume in Sicily. In exchange, the pope would rescind his donation of the crown of Aragon to Charles of Valois. Nonetheless, Jaume and the citizens of Sicily did not consent to the agreement made elsewhere, and the island remained under the crown of Aragon. Moreover, the sudden death of Alfonso III in June of 1291 at the age of twenty-five nullified the peace of Tarascon (Bisson 90–4; O'Callaghan *A History* 392–6; Palenzuela 616–7).

Alfonso III left neither wife nor child, and so his brother Jaume II (1291–1327) hastened to accept the crown of Aragon after governing Sicily for the previous six years. In turn, Jaume left his younger brother Frederico as viceroy of Sicily. Aragon's possession of Sicily put Jaume at odds with the pope and with the French, and he attempted to mollify this opposition by aligning with Sancho IV of Castile through the treaty of Monteagudo in November of 1291. The two monarchs pledged friendship and mutual assistance, and Jaume agreed to marry Sancho's daughter Isabel, only about eight years old at the time. However, when Sancho made overtures of friendship to France to promote the legitimization of his own marriage, the relationship with Aragon was severed, and the Infanta Isabel was returned to Castile in February of 1295.

After Sancho died later that same year, Jaume attempted to reconcile with France over the issue of Sicily. The treaty of Anagni of June 1295 ceded the island of Sicily to France in exchange for the rights granted by Pope Boniface VIII (1294–1303) to the conquest of Corsica and Sardinia. Jaume also agreed to return Majorca to his uncle Jaume II of Majorca, who would remain a vassal of Aragon. Finally, Jaume agreed to marry Blanche of Anjou to solidify the arrangement. With respect to the rendition of Sicily, however, neither Jaume's brother Frederick of Sicily nor the populace of the island concurred. Frederick not only refused to comply, but instead he was proclaimed king, which established a cadet branch of the house of Aragon that went on to conquer additional domains in the eastern Mediterranean (Bisson 92).

During Jaume's long reign, he vacillated several times between friendship and enmity with Castile. He began by establishing a good relationship with Sancho IV, but by 1295, he reversed course. Not only did he reject his proposed marriage to Isabel, but he advanced the cause of Alfonso de la Cerda as king of Castile. During the regency of Fernando IV of Castile, he intervened in the Castilian civil war and in some respects fanned its flames. Moreover, he wrested Murcia from the Castilians before the end of the decade. Jaume later reconciled and cooperated with Castile during the majority of Fernando IV and into the minority of Alfonso XI of Castile (more details in later sections) until his own death in 1326.

The Reign of Fernando IV (1295–1312)

Fernando IV was proclaimed king of León-Castile at the age of nine on April 26, 1295, in Toledo with his mother María de Molina as the regent acting on his behalf. During the minority of Fernando, the crown was beset with civil war. Some of the high nobility sought to take advantage of the under-aged king to aggrandize their own wealth and power. The ambitions of the nobility, that had been enriched and empowered through the conquest of Andalucia Baetica, threatened the authority of the crown, but there were other menaces as well. The intervention of Jaume II of Aragon in support of the rights of the Infantes de la Cerda, and the invasion of King Dinis of Portugal into the realm of León-Castile presented additional perils during the minority of Fernando IV.

During the month following his ascension while the new king and his mother were still in Toledo, the rumor arrived that the Infante Juan, the brother of Sancho IV, was preparing to have himself proclaimed as king. At the same time, Diego López de Haro, the brother of Lope Díaz slain in 1288 by Sancho's guards when he attempted an assassination of the king, was leading an army from Aragon to reclaim the lordship of Viscaya that had been confiscated from his brother. Meanwhile the Infante Enrique, the brother of Alfonso X and son of the great Fernando III, aligned with the house of de Lara, namely Juan Nuñez, to forcefully compete for their own self-interests (González Mínguez 25). At the *Cortes* in Valladolid of 1295, Fernando IV's mother María drew no support from the nobility, who acted on their own behalf to the detriment of Sancho's son Fernando. To garner the support from the town councils to recognize Fernando IV as king, María bestowed large concessions. She granted the cities the right to collect taxes and to control fortresses in their respective locations in exchange for their support in recognition of her son as the rightful king. Maria's briberies eventually extended to nobles, church officials, and urban allies. These indulgences reduced royal authority but gained the support needed for Fernando IV.

Jaume II (1291–1327) of Aragon was on friendly terms with Castile during the early reign of Sancho IV, but later he intended to depose Fernando IV in favor of Alfonso de la Cerda, who was still under his control. While preparations for an Aragonese invasion of Castile were underway, Fernando's uncle, the Infante Juan, met with Alfonso de la Cerda on January 21, 1296, at Bordalba near Ariza to agree on the division of León-Castile. Alfonso would rule Castile, Toledo, Córdoba, Murcia and Jaén, while Juan would receive León, Galicia, and Seville. The Aragonese invaded Castile and captured several locations in the *tierra de campos* and lay siege to Mayorga. The city was well fortified, and the attack dragged on for several months until a sudden plague struck and killed many of the besiegers, causing their retreat. Meanwhile, the Infante Juan had himself crowned in León and established his own claims to the kingdom (González Mínguez 31–40). To the east, Jaume II of Aragon initiated an invasion of Murcia. He first took Alicante then Elche and entered Murcia on August 2, 1296. Only Alcalá, Lorca, and Mula resisted.

The forces loyal to Fernando lay siege to Paredes de Nava, a short distance to the northwest of Palencia from October 1296 to mid–January of 1297. The partisans of Don Juan held strong without offering combat, and the siege was lifted without effect. Later in July of that year, María found out that Juan Núñez, a staunch supporter of Infante Juan, was staying at Ampudia near Palencia. María immediately lay siege to the village and ordered it to continue until Juan Nuñez was either captured or dead. When the rebel found this out, he fled during the night with a few horsemen.

On the western front, King Dinis (1279–1325) of Portugal took advantage of this delicate situation by invading the western reaches of León. He aligned with the opponents of Fernando IV, such as Infante Juan, Alfonso de la Cerda, and Jaume II of Aragon, and in 1296 he occupied the region along the Côa River. However, the skillful negotiations of María de Molina in September 1297 swung the allegiance of Dinis over to Fernando's side with the promise of marital agreements and the concession of territories. Fernando IV agreed to marry Constanza, the daughter of Dinis. Fernando's sister Beatriz was promised to the son of Dinis, the future Afonso IV of Portugal (See Chart 15). The treaty of Alcañices firmly established the boundaries between Castile and Portugal which have endured to the present day and are purported to be the oldest international boundaries in western Europe. The locations of Serpa, Mouro, and Mourão, south of Badajoz and to the east of the Guadiana were confirmed to belong to Portugal. Similarly, the Riba-Côa region, that is the valley of the Côa River which flows north into the Duero including locations from Sabugal up to Castel Rodrigo, were established as Portuguese territory (O'Callaghan *A History* 401).

By the beginning of the new century, the resources of the nobility as well as those of the crown were drained, and both sides were looking for reconciliation. At a *Cortes* in Valladolid on June 26, 1300, news arrived that the Infante Juan was prepared to abandon his quest for the crown and enter the service of Fernando IV. The perpetuation of Fernando's reign appeared to be inevitable, and importantly, Infante Juan had lost the support of Juan Nuñez de Lara, his most powerful ally. Infante Juan yielded the city of León which had been his seat of power, as well as other locations that he had seized during the civil war, but he was granted other locations as compensation. Three months later in September 1301, María de Molina finally received a communication from Pope Boniface VIII which legitimized her children, Fernando IV, Felipe, Pedro, Isabel, and Beatriz (See Chart 16). The announcement also declared a dispensation for the close parentage of Fernando and Constanza of Portugal so that they could be married. Their vows were celebrated in January 1302. Fernando IV reached the age of majority at sixteen on December 6, 1301, leading to the debasement of his most influential detractors. With the rapid succession of these events, unrest in León-Castile had been quelled, and the quarrelsome nobility had accepted the reign of Fernando IV. However, the claim of Alfonso de la Cerda with the support of Jaume II of Aragon still presented a nuisance.

Early in the fourteenth century, the political landscape of the peninsula was turning its own page. Muhammad II (1273–1302) of Granada, who had unsuccessfully attacked Tarifa in 1296, died in April 1302 and was succeeded by his son Muhammad III (1302–1309). Don Enrique, the last surviving son of Fernando III, died on August 11, 1303, at the age of seventy-three at Roa. His death freed the crown of an incorrigible meddler. As an erstwhile ally of María de Molina, he often strove to direct the crown according to his own vision, which at times countermanded the wishes of the queen. The following year, Jaume II of Aragon was willing to entertain negotiations over Murcia, which he had seized from Castile by force during Fernando's minority. The agreement of Torrellas was reached on August 8, 1304. Consequently, most of Murcia was restored to Castile, except for Alicante, Elche, and Orihuela, and the territory north of the river Segura. The lands around Murcia to the south of that river, were given back to Castile. This agreement also compelled Alfonso de la Cerda to renounce his rights to the crown of

Castile in exchange for several towns and castles (O'Callaghan *A History* 402). The quarrel over Murcia was settled, and Aragon and Castile turned their attention to Muhammad III and to the kingdom of Granada.

On December 19, 1308, Jaume II and Fernando IV concluded an alliance at Alcalá de Henares for the future partition of the kingdom of Granada. Previous treaties between the two kingdoms reserved all of Granada for Castile, but the new agreement allotted the port of Almería and its environs to Aragon. Muhammad III of Granada captured the port of Ceuta in 1306 to take advantage of turmoil among the Merinids and to control maritime activity in the Strait. By 1309, however, Muhammad faced an internal rebellion of his own, which resulted in the accession of his brother Abu al-Juyush Nasr (1309–1314) and the recapture of Ceuta by the Merinids (Palenzuela 608–9).

The Christians began their offensive against Granada in July 1309. Fernando besieged Gibraltar and Algeciras while Jaume II attacked Almería by land and sea. Fernando was successful in taking Gibraltar, the only major military conquest of his reign. The attack of Algeciras went differently. Infante Juan and Infante Juan Manuel, who oversaw the operation, failed to complete their mission and retreated along with their troops. The siege of Algeciras was lifted in January 1310. Left to his own wiles, Jaume II of Aragon lifted the siege of Almería and retreated.

Fernando's plans to rein in the excessive power of the nobility and restore the rights of the crown were aborted by his premature death from an apparent heart attack on September 7, 1312, at Jaén as he prepared for battle against Nasr (1309–1314) of Granada. Fernando was survived by his wife and two children. Infanta Leonor was born in September 1307, and the future King Alfonso XI was a little over one year old.

The Minority of Alfonso XI: 1312–1325

The premature death of Fernando IV at Jaén on September 7, 1312, renewed the political instability in the realm of León-Castile. Fernando was in the course of unleashing a new offensive against Nasr, the king of Granada, when he died suddenly at just twenty-six years of age of an apparent heart attack in his sleep. His infant successor, Alfonso XI, only twenty days past his first birthday inherited the crown under a very contested and contentious guardianship and regency. Fernando had not expressly named the guardians for the boy, and therefore they were to be elected by the prelates and members of the nobility as specified in the *Partidas*. This situation opened the door once more for an opportunity of the nobility to usurp the power of the crown.

The nobility split into two factions, each vying for control of the infant king and his regency. Additionally, the factious groups gave rise to *hermandades*, fraternities or brotherhoods, represented by the cities and ecclesiastical bodies, which attempted to aggregate power in their own interest and away from the powerful nobility. Maria de Molina, the grandmother of Alfonso XI, and her son Pedro led one group of nobles, while a second group, led by Sancho IV's brother Juan and his supporter Juan Núñez de Lara, competed for control. A court was called in April of 1313 in Palencia to agree on the regent or regents, but the factions were so contentious that they met in separate locations in the city so that each group could impose its own decision. An assembly with the partisans of Infante Juan nominated him as regent, allowing the custody and upbringing of Alfonso to his mother and grandmother. The second assembly elected María de Molina and Infante Pedro as regents. These results only provoked increased hostilities. The following year, another *hermandad*, consisting of church prelates and bishops was convened in the monastery of Palenzuelos near Valladolid. This assembly was convened to stop the abuses and lawlessness against the Church, but it also resulted in the nomination of a regency shared between Infante Juan and Infante Pedro. The assembly at Palenzuelos assigned custody of the child king to María de Molina, since the boy's mother, Constanza of Portugal, had died in the fall of 1313. A court held at Burgos in July 1315 ratified the proposal of Palenzuelos and additionally established a general *hermandad* supported by hundreds of knights and villages throughout León, Castile, Toledo, Galicia, Extremadura, and Asturias. The *hermandad* was deemed to be necessary to combat the lawlessness and lack of governance during the regency and to control the damage being done by powerful men. Moreover, the court established a commission of twelve members to watch over the action of the regents and to report or prevent their malfeasance (Palenzuela 611–4).

On June 24, 1319, both regents Juan and Pedro died in combat against the Muslims at Elvira on the frontier of Granada. Once again political rivalries escalated as nominations for the regency were debated. The three most viable candidates were Juan Manuel; Felipe, the brother of Fernando IV; and Juan *el Tuerto* "one-eyed," the son of the deceased regent of the same name. Juan Manuel was eager to snatch the regency at all costs. As the son of Manuel of Castile, Juan Manuel was the nephew of Alfonso X and the grandson of Fernando III. His legacy derives from his renown as the writer of works such as *El Conde Lucanor*. The city of Ávila supported Juan Manuel as regent, which aroused the ire of Felipe and gave rise to open hostilities. The *Cortes* held at Valladolid in 1322 only fanned the flames of dissent by proclaiming a shared regency. Furthermore, the unity of the *hermandades* broke down when they split their support among three different candidates. Old Castile favored Juan *el Tuerto*, while Murcia and locations in Extremadura supported Juan Manuel. Felipe drew the concurrence of Galicia, of the frontier, and of those councils that remained loyal to his mother María (Sánchez-Arcilla 89–109). Nothing was settled; hostilities escalated; and civil disorder and violence continued until the minority of Alfonso XI ended in 1325.

Leadership Changes in Portugal, Navarre, Aragon, and Granada in the 1320's

Alfonso XI (1312–1350) reached the age of majority in 1325, and in the next few years, he witnessed a rapid succession of monarchs throughout the peninsula. Afonso IV (1325–1357) succeeded Dinis I (1279–1325) in Portugal; that same year, Muhammed IV (1325–1333) succeeded Ismail I (1314–1325) as king of Granada; Alfonso IV (1327–1336) replaced his father Jaume II (1291–1327) in Aragon; and finally, Jeanne II (1328–1349) wrested control of Navarre away from the French crown with the support of the Navarrese people.

The reign of Afonso IV of Portugal largely coincided with the majority reign of Alfonso XI of León-Castile. Afonso followed the lengthy career of his father Dinis, the grandson of Alfonso *el Sabio* of Castile through his mother Beatriz, the daughter of Alfonso X and the wife of Afonso III (1248–1279) of Portugal. Afonso IV's accomplishments pale by comparison with his father's, and in the end, he even led an opposition to the policies of Dinis.

During the long reign of Dinis I, the realm had largely been at peace, but the king also faced internal political friction. The Portuguese nobility and clergy opposed Dinis for his continued policy to strengthen the authority of the monarchy at the expense of the nobility. He resumed the practice of *inquirições* "inquiries" that were initiated during the reign of his grandfather Afonso II (1211–1223). Performed by the royal administration, these inquiries, consisted of cadastral surveys into property rights and revenues. Through this process, the king required the nobles to prove their rights. Dinis also promoted commerce. He was known as the *rey labrador* "the labor king" for his interest in improving agriculture to increase production and exports. His construction of a navy contributed to internal and external commerce. In 1295, Dinis supported the intervention of Jaume II of Aragon on behalf of Alfonso de la Cerda, but he later reversed his support and aligned with María de Molina and Fernando IV of Castile when he agreed to the treaty of Alcañices of 1297. Dinis later supported the treaty of Torrellas in 1304, which ended the civil war in Castile and recognized Fernando IV as the legitimate king. On the cultural side, Dinis created the *Estudo Geral em Lisboa*, which promoted education in the Portuguese language and obviated the need to send students to foreign universities. In 1319, however, his son and heir, Afonso, began to impinge upon his authority. From age 28 in 1319 until 1325, the future Afonso IV led the Portuguese nobility in a confrontation against his father that morphed into a civil war. Dinis died at Santarém on September 7, 1325, disheartened by the conflict with his only legal son (Palenzuela 620–2).

As Afonso IV (1325–1357) of Portugal came to power, his relationship with the young King Alfonso XI of Castile turned sour. Alfonso XI was betrothed to Juana Manuel, the daughter of his cousin Juan Manuel, but he rejected her in favor of marriage to Maria of Portugal, the daughter of Afonso IV. While remaining married to Maria, Alfonso preferred the relationship of his life-long paramour, Leonor de Guzmán, who bore him ten children and spawned the illegitimate line of the Trastámaras. Afonso of Portugal was outraged by the public display of infidelity and dishonor bestowed on his daughter, and he plotted against Alfonso XI with the ever-conspiring Juan Manuel, whose daughter, Constanza Manuel, was then married to Afonso's son, the future Pedro I (1357–1367). In later years, Pedro shunned Constanza in favor of a beautiful lady of the court, Inés de Castro. The feuds between Afonso IV and Alfonso XI were suspended only long enough to join forces in their mutual defense against the invading Merinids (more in the next section).

In Granada, a young Muhammad IV (1325–1333) rose to power in 1325 when his father Ismail I (1314–1325) was assassinated by a cousin, apparently over a personal grudge. Ismail himself had forcefully overthrown his predecessor Nasr (1309–1314), who aroused opposition from the ruling class for his alliances with Castile. The deposed Nasr continued his relationship with Castile during the reign of Ismail and into the minority of Alfonso XI. He encouraged Castile to launch attacks against the frontiers of Granada and motivated the Infantes Pedro and Juan, who were the co-regents for Alfonso XI, to undertake a major offensive against Granada in 1319. That year at the battle of the Vega, the Castilians were soundly defeated, resulting in the death of both regents, and Ismail claimed the greatest victory the Nasrids ever won over the Castilians. He went on to recover Baza and Martos from the Castilians in 1324 and 1325 before his assassination. The young successor Muhammad IV was not his father's equal and fell under the control of the Banu Abi al-Ula, who constituted the major military force in Granada. When Muhammad attempted closer ties with the Merinids, his assassination brought his short, unremarkable rule to an end and ushered the ascension of his brother Yusuf I (1333–1354) (Kennedy *Muslim Spain* 286–9). The lengthy reign of Yusuf placed him in direct competition with Alfonso XI and other Christian leaders (more detail in the next section).

Alfonso IV inherited the crown of Aragon in 1327 and reigned just a short nine years in stark contrast to the reign of his father Jaume II of thirty-six years. In Catalan, Alfonso was known as *el Benigne* "the kind or gentle" possibly because he avoided confrontation with the nobility regarding internal politics. He protected Catalan interests in Sardinia, while he repulsed attempted advances from Granada, and he assisted the Castilians in defending maritime interests in the Strait. His first wife, Maria d'Entença bore him a son and rightful heir, the future Pere IV (1336–1387), in September of 1319. His second wife, Leonor of Castile, the sister of Alfonso XI, proved to be more problematic. She constantly dogged her husband to recognize the rights of her own son Ferran (Fernando) over her stepson Pere. Consequently, the kind King Alfonso acquiesced by granting Ferran property rights around Valencia. Under protest from the local nobility whose rights had been violated, Ferran was compelled to relinquish the land grants. The incident provoked a mutual hatred between Leonor and her stepson Pere, and after his coronation in 1336, he attempted to have his stepmother arrested. His attempted seizure sent her in flight back to her brother in Castile. Pere's animosity endured throughout his reign as he sided with Juan Manuel and with the enemies of Alfonso XI of Castile (O'Callaghan *A History* 410–411).

The ascension to the crown of Navarre of Jeanne II (1328–1349) and her husband Philip III d'Évreux (1328–1343) restored local governance in Navarre and continued the bloodline which descended from Sancho III (1004–1035), the Great, down through García Sanchez III (1035–1054). The bloodline was perpetuated through the illegitimate branch of the family from García Ramírez (1134–1150) down to Jeanne II (See Chart 7 and Chart 13). Back in 1274, the inheritance of a one-and-a-half-year-old Jeanne I (1274–1305) was safeguarded by betrothing her to the future Philip IV of France. From that time until the time of Jeanne II, the kingdom of Navarre was ruled *in absentia* by the French monarchs. After the death of Jeanne I in 1305, her son Louis X (1305–1316) ruled *in absentia*. Louis was succeeded both in France and in Navarre by his brother Philip V (known as Philip II in Navarre 1316–1322). The next French monarch to rule in Navarre was their brother Charles The Bald (1322–1328). After the death of Charles, the people of Navarre at last recognized and supported the inheritance of Jeanne II, the daughter of Louis X and Margaret of Burgundy and granddaughter of Jeanne I. She inherited a troubled relationship between Navarre and Castile that would be settled with Alfonso XI later in her reign (Palenzuela 623–625).

The Majority of Alfonso XI: 1325–1350

During the minority of Alfonso XI, the authority of the monarchy had been seriously weakened by overreach and abuses of the nobility and by the establishment of *hermandades,* which sought to bring order to an otherwise lawless realm. When Alfonso XI became of age on August 13, 1325, he immediately abolished the general *hermandad* and looked for support of his regime among those who united with his uncle Felipe and his grandmother María de Molina. The nomination of Alvar Núñez Osorio, Garcilaso de la Vega, and Yuçaf de Écija, as Alfonso's principal lieutenants in his staff, established a counterbalance to the powerful influence of Juan Manuel, the nephew of Alfonso X, and Juan *el Tuerto,* the son of Alfonso XI's great-uncle Juan and María Díaz de Haro. Noticeably, Alfonso's nominations excluded Juan Manuel and Juan *el Tuerto.* Their separation from the monarchy only exacerbated their opposition and alienation.

To placate Juan Manuel, Alfonso offered to marry Juan's daughter Constanza and then named him as *adelantado* or person in charge of the frontier as an additional dividend. The marriage between Alfonso XI and Constanza was not immediately consummated because of Constanza's young age. As for Juan *el Tuerto,* the king discovered that the one-eyed noble was plotting against him and sent Alvaro Núnez to Burgos to lure *el Tuerto* to Toro with an offer of marriage to Alfonso's sister Leonor. Arriving at Toro, the king had *el Tuerto* and his close allies murdered on All Saints day in 1326. Learning of the death of *el Tuerto* and considering the king's hesitation to marry his daughter Constanza due to her young age, Juan Manuel decided to depart for his possessions in Murcia, leaving the king without a commander of forces on the frontier. Without the assistance of an *adelantado,* the young king left for Seville to mount an offensive against the Muslims for himself, and by mid-summer of 1327, he had returned after conquering several small castles such as Pruna, Aimonte and Alfaquín.

To relieve tensions with the kingdom of Portugal, Alfonso XI arranged his marriage with Afonso IV's daughter María, displacing his earlier offer to Constanza Manuel. This maneuver incited Juan Manuel to arouse rebellion in cities such as Valladolid, León, Toro and Zamora against Alfonso XI's regime. Furthermore, Juan Manuel drew support against Alfonso XI from an alliance with Alfonso IV of Aragon which proved to be ephemeral. In 1228, following the death of his wife Teresa d'Entença, Alfonso of Aragon agreed to marry Alfonso XI's sister Leonor. This marriage clearly drew Alfonso IV of Aragon closer to his Castilian brother-in-law and away from Juan Manuel. Deprived of external support from Aragon, Juan Manuel was compelled to put down his arms and swear allegiance to King Alfonso XI (Palenzuela 630). His oath would not endure. By 1332 the ever-plotting Juan Manuel had abandoned his service to Alfonso XI and convinced Afonso IV of Portugal to arrange the marriage of his son Pedro to Constanza Manuel. At the same time, Juan Manuel conspired with the king of Granada, promising his assistance against Castile. Meanwhile, Juan Manuel and his ally Juan Núñez de Lara assembled rebellious factions to attack locations loyal to Alfonso XI. While the Castilian king was preoccupied with subduing threats to the crown in the north of his realm, a second menace was mounting in the south.

The early success of Alfonso XI in taking frontier positions from Granada in 1327 drove Muhammad IV (1325–1333) to appeal to the Merinids of North Africa for intervention. As Alfonso fended off skirmishes with Juan Manuel and Juan Núñez in the north, he learned of the entry of the Merinids in the south. Emir Abu al-Hassan had sent his son Abd al-Malik to campaign with Muhammad IV of Granada against Alfonso. Muhammad attacked the frontier regions of Castile, while Abd al-Malik lay siege to Gibraltar. Alfonso faced the dilemma of leaving Castile to the unmerciful assaults of Juan Manual or abandoning the fortress of Gibraltar to a Muslim siege. After several failed attempts to reconcile with Juan Manuel and to persuade him to rally against the Muslims, the increasingly desperate situation in the south finally convinced Alfonso to muster his forces at Seville in June of 1333 for the rescue of Gibraltar. Unfortunately, the relief force was still three days from Gibraltar when the news arrived that the fortress had surrendered. Arriving too late to prevent the fall of Gibraltar, Alfonso attempted a futile siege that devolved into a standoff. Thus, Alfonso negotiated a four-year treaty and conceded withdrawal. Alfonso was leading his troops back to Seville when word arrived that Muhammad IV had been assassinated at the hands of those who did not agree with the truce. A young, fifteen-year-old Yusuf I (1333–1354) had been installed as leader of the Nasrids of Granada (Sánchez Arcilla 152–63).

The truce with the Muslims allowed Alfonso to address the assaults on his authority from Juan Manuel and Juan Nuñez de Lara. Towards the end of March 1334, Alfonso planned a counterattack on Juan Nuñez who was then besieging Cuenca de Campos. Learning of Alfonso's approach, Juan Nuñez abandoned his forces and fled to the safety of his fortress at Lerma. Alfonso then assigned a contingent of men to entrap Juan at that location, while the king employed his remaining troops to captured and kill Juan's revolutionaries. The confiscation of Juan Nuñez's properties as well as those of his relatives compelled the subversive to swear allegiance to Alfonso. The Castilian monarch now needed to deal with his greatest enemy, Juan Manuel.

Alfonso's marriage to María of Portugal and the birth in 1334 of a son and heir, the future Pedro I of Castile, produced a short period of tranquility between Castile and Portugal. However, that amity was challenged when Alfonso met the beautiful Leonor de Guzmán. Enraptured by her charms and beauty, the king repudiated his wife and embarked on a relationship that produced ten offspring and spawned the bastard line of the Trastámaras. In view of the public disgrace and humiliation of María, the renewed friendship between Portugal and Castile evaporated and devolved into hostility.

Meanwhile the ever-cunning Juan Manuel continued to make deals. In 1336, he aligned with Pere IV of Aragon (1336–1387), who succeeded his father Alfonso IV that year. Pere was embroiled in a feud with his stepmother Leonor, the sister of Alfonso XI. Leonor had persuaded Pere's father Alfonso to endow her children Ferran (Fernando) and Joan (Juan) with land grants, which reduced the rightful inheritance of Pere. Although the grants were nullified by the angry voices of the local landlords, the attempted endowment established Leonor and Pere as bitter enemies. As soon as he received the power of the crown, Pere attempted to arrest Leonor, who escaped to the safety of her brother's court in Castile. Fearing reprisals from Alfonso XI, Pere was all too willing to support Juan Manuel's machinations against the Castilian king. On the western front, Juan Manuel then took advantage of the estrangement between Portugal and Castile by arranging the marriage of his daughter Constanza to Afonso's heir, the future Pedro I (1357–1367) of Portugal. Alfonso XI reacted by besieging Juan Manuel in his castle at Peñafiel. Meanwhile, Afonso IV of Portugal, resentful of Alfonso's treatment of his wife María and encouraged by Juan Manuel, attacked Castile. The Portuguese engaged the Castilians at Villanueva de Barcarrota, but were sorely defeated. In the end, Juan Manuel was devoid of resources and reluctantly submitted to Alfonso in 1337. Alfonso's triumph extinguished the uprising of the nobility and established the primacy of his royal authority. At the end of the year, a letter from the pope compelled a truce between Castile and Portugal (Palenzuela 631).

At Burgos in the spring of 1338, Alfonso XI promulgated an ordinance designed to eradicate the hostilities and abuses of the nobility. First, he pardoned all the past transgressions not only of the nobility but also of the peasants and vassals who committed killings and robberies on behalf of the nobility. Going forward, the ordinance specified severe penalties for acts of violence. Further, in order to equip soldiers for combat against the Muslims, the ordinance also specified monetary allowances for the combatants as well as the equipment required of each soldier (Sanchez Arcilla 163). The ordinance of 1338 marked an additional triumph of Alfonso XI over the Castilian nobility, an elite class that had become increasingly lawless and abusive in proportion to the escalation of their wealth and power since the time of Fernando III.

As Alfonso was conducting a *Cortes* at Madrid in 1339 and mustering support for the resumption of campaigns against the Muslims, the Merinid troop count at Algeciras was rising. The truce with the Nasrids and Merinids had expired, and Abd al-Malik, the son of the Merinid Emir Abu al-Hasssan, had returned to plunder the valley of the Guadalete and the lower Guadalquivir. During one of these raids, Abd al-Malik was surprised in his camp by a contingent of military Orders on patrol from Seville. The unexpected strike delivered a fatal blow to the son of the Merinid sultan, but his death did not deter the flow of Muslim ships with additional combatants from North Africa. The Castilian Admiral Jufré Tenoria had thus far mastered the control of the Strait, but on April 8, 1340, his fleet was defeated by a large Muslim flotilla. The admiral's loss abandoned these waters to the control of Abu al-Hasssan and exposed Tarifa to attack. Abu al-Hassan himself then crossed the Strait and mounted an attack on Tarifa. After weeks of fighting, the struggle morphed into a longer siege of starvation. The Muslim menace now appeared to be more than Castile alone could handle (Sánchez Arcilla 205+).

All Christian monarchs of the peninsula were rallied to the threat of the Muslim invasion. Portugal and Aragon provided additional naval power, and more significantly, Alfonso XI and his father-in-law Afonso IV of Portugal set aside their differences long enough to plan the Christian counterattack. The two monarchs met at Seville and each sent a message to Abu al-Hassan announcing their intentions to liberate Tarifa, while ships sent from Aragon arrived to patrol the waters of the Strait. In response, the Merinid sultan and the king of Granada broke camp at Tarifa and accepted the challenge of the Christian kings. When the two armies engaged at the Río Salado on October 30, 1340, the Muslims suffered an overwhelming defeat. Abu al-Hassan and Yusuf I fled to the safety of Algeciras and from there, they boarded separate ships back to their own realms.

The defense of Tarifa did not appease Alfonso; he decided to take the offensive by conquering Alcalá la Real and other frontier locations in 1341. In the summer of 1342, he began preparations for the siege of Algeciras, which was key to preventing the reentry of the Merinids into the peninsula. In the fall, he established his camp near Algeciras and protracted a war of attrition into 1343. As the siege dragged on, the lack of supplies afflicted the Christians as well as the Mulsims of Algeciras. However, in mid–March of 1344, word arrived from Yusuf I that he was willing to render the city with the promise of safe conduct of its citizens. Alfonso took possession of Algeciras on March 27, 1344 (Palenzuela 636).

After Alfonso had successfully defended his realm and secured Algeciras, he turned his attention to internal affairs. One of his major accomplishments was the enactment of the Ordinance of Alcalá de Henares of 1348. This ordinance promulgated the book of the *Siete Partidas*, that his great-grandfather Alfonso X *el Sabio* had promoted but never fully enacted throughout the entire realm. The Ordinance improved and reorganized the administration of justice and established the juridical norm in León-Castile for centuries to come.

In the summer of 1349, Alfonso initiated the siege of *el Peñón*, the Rock of Gibraltar. His father Fernando IV had conquered Gibraltar in September 1309, but Alfonso had lost this fortress in 1333 when he arrived too late to protect it. His priority at the time was to defend the northern regions from a rebellious nobility. During the siege of the Rock, the Black Death struck the Christian camps, and Alfonso became one of its victims on March 27, 1350. Alfonso XI again failed to regain his father's conquest. With the seizure of Algeciras and the death of Alfonso XI at Gibraltar, the territorial expansion of León-Castile was suspended for more than one hundred years, while its monarchs struggled with famine, plague, and civil turmoil.

The Reign of Pedro I, *el Cruel* (1350–1369)

As Pedro accompanied the body of his deceased father Alfonso XI from Gibraltar to Seville in September 1350, his claim to the crown of León-Castile at the age of fifteen years and seven months was unchallenged. He was the only legitimate son of Alfonso and María of Portugal, and yet his father's mistress, Leonor de Guzmán, had borne ten illegitimate offspring, on whom the deceased king had bestowed land grants and honors in disregard for his legitimate wife and son. The Trastámaras, as the bastard line was known, derived its name from their brother Enrique, who held the title of Count of Trastámara (= trans–Tamaris "across the Río Tambre"). In order of birth, the illegitimate children of Alfonso XI and Leonor de Guzmán were: Pedro de Aguilar (1330), Sancho el Mudo (1331), twins Enrique (1333) and Fadrique (1333), Fernando (1336), Tello (1337), Juan (1340), Sancho (1341), Juana (1342), and Pedro (1345). (Note: Some of the birth dates may lack precise documentation, Díaz Martín 285.) The king's favoritism to his illegitimate family created a political power that, after many years of conflict, would prove to be Pedro I's nemesis.

It was understandable, therefore, that Pedro I of Castile leaned toward his mother's side of the family when he elected Juan Alfonso de Albuquerque, a wealthy and influential cousin of his mother, as his chancellor. Albuquerque descended from the bastard line of the Portuguese King Dinis and had served as counselor to María of Portugal and as tutor to Pedro. The new king quickly negotiated a peace with the Merinids and the Nasrids that lasted from July 17, 1350, and until January 1357. Yusuf I (1333–1354) of Granada agreed to pay annual *parias* in addition to supplying Pedro with a cavalry that would remain faithful to his command.

The following February, Pedro and his royal retinue moved northward to conduct a *Cortes* in Burgos, but not before delivering Leonor de Guzmán into the custody of María of Portugal. The queen exacted her revenge on the king's mistress by having Leonor executed, which entrenched the opposition of the Trastámaras and intensified their political propaganda all the more. Arriving at Burgos, the king dealt rapidly and severely with an armed opposition to his authority. The leader of the uprising, Garcilaso de la Vega, was immediately captured and killed. His cadaver was dragged through the streets and mutilated by stampeding bulls. Thus, the northern territories were abruptly pacified, and Pedro I and his second in command Juan Alfonso de Albuquerque set about the task of governing the kingdom. At Palenzuela in May, Pedro I met with Tello, one of the sons of Leonor de Guzmán, and the young Trastámara pledged his fidelity to the king's authority. At this juncture, Leonor's son Enrique appeared to be the only offspring who refused to recognize Pedro's rightful authority (Díaz Martín 56). After visiting with his grandfather, Afonso IV of Portugal, Pedro I decided to pardon the revolutionary transgressions of his half-brother Enrique. However, Enrique had attracted a rebellious following and had ensconced himself in a fortress at Gijon. On June 24, 1352, Pedro lay siege to the fortress and after two days obtained a pledge of loyalty from Enrique and his promise to refrain from further subversive activity (Díaz Martín 78). The promise would not be kept.

Throughout the summer of 1352, a contract was being finalized for the marriage of Pedro with Blanche de Bourbon which offered a sizable dowry in gold from the king of France Jean II (1350–1364). The marriage between Pedro I and Blanche was scheduled for June 3, 1353, in Valladolid. Unexpectedly and uninvited, Tello and Enrique de Trastámara arrived with a sizable armed force and requested to attend the ceremony. It was Albuquerque who negotiated with them and permitted their attendance along with a small number of their followers. He even granted Enrique and Tello a role in the ceremony by assigning them the honor of holding the reins of Blanche's horse. Three days after the marriage, Pedro abruptly abandoned Blanche, never to see her again. He subsequently banished her to the alcazar in Toledo. Pedro blamed Albuquerque with deceit and betrayal over the entire affair, and as an additional affront, the dowry did not accompany the bride upon her arrival. Leaving Valladolid, Pedro reunited with his paramour María de Padilla and her relatives. María had already given birth to their first daughter Beatriz (O'Callaghan *A History* 420; Palenzuela 649).

The marriage scandal provided fodder for the political ruminations of the Trastámaras; the influence of the bastard family was mounting. Enrique had aggrandized his lineage and heritage by marrying Juana Manuel, the daughter of Juan Manuel. Tello had married into the de Lara family and became inheritor of the lordship of Viscaya, and Fadrique had become master of the Order of Santiago. Their campaign of denunciation of the king provoked an increasingly hostile nobility that forcefully compelled Pedro I to relinquish his authority and to surrender the royal seals that empowered him. He remained powerless until September 1356 when he regained a military following and compelled his opponents to surrender at Toro, thereby dissolving the resistance of the nobility. Enrique de Trastámara went to Aragon; his half-brother Fadrique of the Order of Santiago submitted to Pedro's authority; and the outrage of the nobility was neutralized for the moment (Ruiz 78–81).

On the eastern front, animosity swelled between Pedro I of Castile and Pere (Pedro) IV of Aragon (1336–1387). Each monarch harbored the enemies of the other. Pere sheltered Enrique de Trastámara, while Pedro's court provided sanctuary to Ferran (Fernando) and Joan (Juan), his own cousins who were also the half-brothers of Pere. When Pere ascended to the crown of Aragon in 1336, he attempted to incarcerate his stepmother Leonor, the sister of Alfonso XI, but she fled to Castile. Leonor's sons Ferran and Joan followed her to evade the wrath of their half-brother Pere. Open hostilities erupted in 1356 which began as a disagreement over Aragonese ships impeding Genoese commercial traffic in Castilian waters around Cádiz. The quarrel escalated into war over territories on the frontier of Murcia that had been ceded to Aragon in 1304 during the reign of Fernando IV, Pedro's grandfather. Enrique de Trastámara aligned with Pere IV, while the half-brothers of Pere IV, in asylum in Castile, pledged vassalage to Pedro. Pedro attacked the frontier around Valencia and took Tarazona in March 1357, while Pere and Enrique countered by strengthening their defense with the support of disgruntled Castilian nobles. Pedro I enlisted support from Muhammad V (1354...1391) of Granada, from Afonso IV of Portugal, and subsequently from Pedro I of Portugal (1357–1367) (O'Callaghan *A History* 421).

Pedro I of Portugal was a direct descendent of Sancho IV of Castile and was the cousin of his namesake Pedro I of Castile. The new Portuguese king had some aspirations to the crown of Castile and aligned with his namesake against Aragon until taking a more neutral position in 1363. Pedro of Portugal married Constanza Manuel, the daughter of Juan Manuel in 1340, but he became enraptured with a beautiful lady of the court, Inés de Castro, of Galician nobility. Constanza died in 1345, but not before giving birth to the future Fernando I (1367–1383) of Portugal. Inés was the niece of Teresa, the widow of the bastard Alfonso Sánchez, the disliked half-brother of King Afonso IV (1325–1357). For reasons of parentage to his disinherited half-brother, King Afonso had Inés banished from the court on June 7, 1355, and later had her assassinated. The irate future Pedro I rose up against his father but soon reconciled. When Afonso died in 1357, Pedro declared that he had secretly married Inés, thereby legitimizing her children. He then proceeded to seek out and exact revenge on her assassins (Palenzuela 657–8).

Soon after the war with Aragon began, Pedro I of Castile initiated an internal purge of suspected conspirators. He accused Fadrique, the master of Santiago and the twin of Enrique de Trastámara, of treason and had him killed. Similarly, the Infante Joan of Aragon met the same fate, because his brother Ferran had changed sides and swore allegiance to Pere IV. But there was more to Pedro's rampage. He assassinated his own aunt Leonor, the mother of the Infantes Ferran and Joan, as well as Juana de Lara, the wife of the bastard Tello de Trastámara.

In September of 1359 Enrique de Trastámara launched a campaign against Castile and won a decisive surprise victory at Araviana, to the east of Soria, defeating and killing Juan Fernández de Hinestrosa, one of Pedro's key counselors and the uncle of María de Padilla. Fearing reprisals, Enrique retreated to the safety of Aragon. There he rallied the exiled Castilians against Pedro and amassed recognition as the legitimate heir to crown of Castile. This maneuver alienated Enrique from the Infante Ferran (Fernando), Pedro IV's half-brother, who harbored his own aspirations. Meanwhile, Pedro I of Castile exacted revenge by executing Enrique's brothers Juan and Pedro. The following year, Enrique was not as successful. At the head of a contingent of Aragonese and Castilian exiles, Enrique was soundly defeated by Pedro at Nájera on April 24, 1360, and sought refuge within the city walls. Inexplicably, Pedro withdrew to Seville rather than laying siege to the city and ridding himself once and for all of his bastard brother.

The close ties between Castile and Portugal during this time produced an exchange of prisoners. Rebellious Castilian nobles who were exiled in Portugal were returned to Castile and executed. The Portuguese nobles who sought refuge in Castile, namely those who were involved with the assassination of Inés de Castro years earlier, were returned to Portugal and met the same fate (Palenzuela 659).

A peace was signed between Castile and Aragon at Terrer (Soria) on May 13, 1361. Pedro I agreed to render most of the Aragonese locations that he had conquered, and Pere IV agreed to remove Enrique from his service, which sent the count of Trastámara into exile across the Pyrenees. The short hiatus in combat against Aragon afforded Pedro I the opportunity to restore his ally King Muhammad V (1354–1359, 1362–1391) of Granada to power. In 1359, Muhammad was overthrown by Ismail II (1359–1360) who, in turn, was overthrown by Muhammad VI (1360–1362). Pedro raided and destroyed numerous locations along Granada's frontier, which brought Muhammad VI to submission. To gain relief, Muhammad offered large quantities of jewels, gold, and other booty for a guarantee of peace, and traveled to Seville to present his offering. Pedro accepted the booty, but summarily killed Muhammad and the horsemen who accompanied him (O'Callaghan *A History* 422). Pedro's ally Muhammad V was restored in Granada and continued to rule until 1391 (See Lists: Nasrids of Granada).

In the same year (1361) at an undetermined date, Pedro I ordered the execution of his legitimate wife Blanche of Bourbon at the age of twenty-five at Medina-Sidonia where Pedro had her transferred to distance her from the war. Also in July of that year, María de Padilla died of natural causes, possibly of the plague. In Seville at a *Cortes* in the spring of 1362, Diego García de Padilla and several other attendees swore that Pedro and María were married prior to the ceremony with Blanche, thus invalidating the latter marriage and legitimizing María's children and their rights of inheritance. Alfonso, the youngest and only son of Pedro and Maria, would have become king had he not died in infancy shortly afterwards (Díaz Martín 196).

Pedro's offensives against Aragon resumed in 1362 by taking Alhama, Ariza, Ateca and the even Calatayud. Castile had aligned with England and had convinced Charles II (1349–1387) of Navarre, at least for the moment, to side with them. Despite his earlier treaty with Castile, Pere IV enlisted the services of Enrique de Trastámara and supported Enrique's ascendance to the crown of Castile over his own half-brother Ferran. From the success at Calatayud, Pedro advanced towards Valencia, which demonstrated the military superiority of Castile and induced Pere IV to petition for the treaty of Murviedro on July 2, 1363. Pere's half-brother Fernan died under mysterious circumstances shortly thereafter. However, by 1364 the political winds had again changed direction. Charles II of Navarre, who whimsically had gone over to Pere IV's side, returned to negotiations with Pedro, but the pope now financed the efforts of Enrique, who enlisted French mercenaries under the command of Bertram du Guesclin.

In the early months of 1366, Enrique de Trastámara, at the command of French mercenaries, invaded Castile. After taking Calahorra, he proclaimed himself king of Castile and pressed on to Burgos. There, Enrique was met by a welcoming populace, and he had himself crowned at Las Huelgas. This event is sometimes noted as the first reign of Enrique. On the other hand, Pedro I was rejected by most of the nobility and abandoned by his troops. He retreated to the south with his remaining loyal followers, hoping in vain that Portugal would lend support. As a last resort, Pedro made his way to Libourne, France near Bordeaux to contract with Edward, the Prince of Wales, known as the Black Prince for the armor that he donned. Edward agreed to campaign with Pedro in exchange for territories in Vizcaya as compensation. Charles II of Navarre also received the promise of Guipúzcoa, Álava, and locations in the Ebro Valley for his support of safe passage of the English troops through Navarre (Palenzuela 663).

On April 3, 1367, Enrique once again engaged the forces of Pedro I at Nájera and again met with defeat. The advanced tactics and the English archers sent Enrique into flight back to France. Pedro was incapable of paying the English soldiers, and he failed to keep his promise of land grants to Edward. Thus, the Black Knight returned to Libourne empty handed (Ruiz 80–1).

The resolute Enrique de Trastámara was not yet finished. Most of the regions in Castile favored him, and only Galicia and some areas on the southern frontier preferred Pedro. Once again, Enrique returned to Castile in the fall of 1367, and by April of the following year, he was laying siege to Toledo, which had remained faithful to Pedro. France remained supportive of Enrique by dispatching Bertram du Guesclin back to Castile with a new army early in 1369. To raise Enrique's siege of Toledo, Pedro assembled an ineffective army that was routed at Montiel in La Mancha in March of that year. Pedro was trapped in the castle at Montiel without egress. In desperation, he sent a messenger to du Guesclin, offering bribes to facilitate his escape. Instead, Pedro was lured into a meeting with du Guesclin on the night of March 22–23. Entering the conference tent, Pedro came face to face with his half-brother Enrique, who delivered the knife blows that ended the life of *el Cruel* (Palenzuela 665). In the court at Seville the following summer, Enrique de Trastámara was formally established as the king of Castile. His inauguration marked the triumph of the bastard line of Alfonso XI and Leonor de Guzmán, that dominated the Castilian monarchy into the reign of the Catholic Monarchs, Isabel of Castile and Fernando of Aragon, who were both cousins from the House of Trastámara.

CHAPTER 11

The Age of the Trastámaras: 1369–1479

The Reign of the First Trastámara, Enrique II (1369–1379)

Enrique's long and arduous struggle for the crown of León-Castile ended with the fratricide of King Pedro I (1350–1369) during the night of March 22 to 23, 1369 at Montiel. Nonetheless, the recognition of Enrique as king did not entirely subdue his opposition. Within León-Castile, the supporters of Pedro I, the *petristas*, continued their subversive activity. Pockets of resistance remained in Galicia and in the cities of Carmona, Ciudad Rodrigo, and Zamora. Furthermore, the monarchs of Granada, Portugal, Navarre, and Aragon all grew increasingly hostile to Enrique. Despite the challenge of suppressing his remaining opponents, Enrique recognized the need to compensate the Castilian nobility and the French mercenaries who were invaluable in the overthrow of Pedro I.

Enrique bestowed generous grants and favors on the partisans who assisted in his rise to power. His close family and relatives were among the first to benefit from his generosity. His brother Sancho became the count of Albuquerque, a title previously held by Juan Alfonso de Albuquerque, a favorite of Pedro I. Brother Tello received the lordship of Viscaya, Lara, Aguilar, and Castañeda. His bastard son, Alfonso Enríquez, received the villas Noreña and Gijón. The French General du Guesclin was awarded Soria, Almazán, and Atienza, which he later gave back to Enrique in exchange for monetary considerations to facilitate his return to France. Nobles who battled with Enrique were given lesser rent-producing villas. Even the nobles who came to his side late in the campaign were rewarded with grants. From 1369 to 1371, the number of concessions mounted to such a degree that the towns assembled at the Cortes of 1371 asked for a limit on these favors (Ruiz 81; Valdeón *Trastámaras* 32–3).

Outside of his realm, Enrique was challenged on all borders. Muhammad V of Granada raided the border towns along the Castilian frontier and took Algeciras in July 1369. Fernando I (1367–1383) of Portugal blockaded the entrance to the Guadalquivir. The Portuguese king had his own designs on the crown of León-Castile and drew the support of the *petristas* of Galicia and Zamora. Moreover, Fernando legitimized his own claim to Castile, because his great-grandfather Dinis (1275–1329) was the grandson of Alfonso X, *el Sabio*, and his paternal grandmother Beatriz, the wife of Afonso IV (1325–1357) of Portugal, was the daughter of Sancho IV (1284–1295) of Castile (See

Chart 15; Chart 19). With Navarre, Enrique's relationship was tenuous; Charles II (1349–1387) of Navarre still held locations in La Rioja such as Logroño and Vitoria that he annexed in 1368 during the Castilian civil struggle. From Aragon, Pere IV (1336–1387) demanded the surrender of properties, notably Murcia, that Enrique had promised in exchange for Pere's military support against Pedro I. Furthermore, Pere supported Fernando I's claims to the crown of Castile and promoted a coalition of Portugal, Navarre, and Aragon against Enrique. The new king of León-Castile faced a formidable convergence of challenges (Palenzuela 682).

One by one, Enrique overcame each of his opponents. From July through October 1369, he campaigned in Galicia from Santiago down into northern Portugal to subdue resistance and opposition to his authority. In 1370, the king of Granada agreed to a peace treaty. In August of that same year, a Castilian flotilla under the command of Ambrosio Bocanegra routed the Portuguese at Sanlúcar de Barramedo, ending the blockade at the mouth of the Guadalquivir and leading to peace talks. The subsequent negotiations between Castile and Portugal concluded with an agreement at Alcoutim on March 31, 1371, in which Fernando I renounced his claims to the crown of Castile and agreed to marry Enrique's daughter Leonor. The marriage was not consummated, and the peace did not last long (Valdeón *Enrique II* 111). Fernando chose to marry Leonor Teles de Meneses.

Meanwhile Enrique resumed efforts to vanquish the remaining *petristas*. Early in 1371, Enrique's army conquered Zamora, a stronghold of the *petristas* that was supported by Portuguese troops. Upon the arrival of the Castilians, the Portuguese deserted the city and abandoned it to a siege of starvation. Zamora yielded in February of that year. Resistance at Carmona was suppressed on May 10, and a blow to Galician resistance was delivered when Enrique sent Pedro Ruiz Sarmiento to rout the forces of Fernando de Castro, the final menace of Galician rebellion.

In the summer of 1371, Enrique dispatched troops to the Castilian locations that Charles II of Navarre had annexed in 1368. The Castilians were welcomed at Salvatierra and Santa Cruz de Campezu, which sounded an alarm for the Navarrese monarch and persuaded him to negotiatiate with Enrique. In November, an agreement was reached to cease hostilities and to submit their differences to the pope and to the king of France for arbitration (Valdeón *Enrique II* 112). The Christian realms of the peninsula were now at peace, but a new menace appeared as John of Gaunt, the Duke of Lancaster, made claims to the crown of Castile.

In September 1371, Duke John of Gaunt married Constanza, the daughter of Pedro I of Castile and María de Padilla. Constanza and her sister Isabel were exiled in England along with other Castilian nobles who opposed Enrique de Trastámara. The following January, the British Council recognized John of Gaunt as the legitimate king of Castile and held a reception to recognize Constanza as queen. Additionally, Edmond, the Duke of Cambridge, wedded Constanza's sister Isabel on July 11 of that year. John of Gaunt wasted no time in establishing a chancellery to complete his pretensions (Valdeón *Enrique II* 137+). In July 1372, he negotiated a mutual assistance pact with Fernando I of Portugal, which specified that if he attacked Castile through Navarre, Fernando I would enter Castile from the west, and if Fernando attacked Castile first, Duke John of Lancaster would lend assistance.

Apprised of the threat posed by his neighbor to the west, Enrique decided to launch a preemptive strike against Portugal in December 1372, and by year's end, he had taken several locations in Lusitania including Viseu. The advance of the Castilian army met little resistance and cut through Coimbra and Santarém within weeks. Lisbon was captured on February 23, 1373. Assistance from the Duke of Lancaster did not arrive, and Fernando was left powerless and petitioned for peace. Fernando agreed to provide ships for assistance to the Castilians in support of France against England, and he sent hostages to make sure that his promises were kept. He also agreed to expel the partisans of the deceased Pedro I of Castile who sought political asylum in Portugal. Finally, several marriage arrangements were struck between the Portuguese royal family and the Trastámaras, but only one was completed. In April of that year, Enrique's brother Sancho married Fernando's sister Beatriz. This marriage produced a daughter Leonor, known as *la ricahembra*, who became the wife of the future king of Aragon, Fernando de Antequera, yet another Trastámara (Valdeón *Enrique II* 141+).

With negotiations between Portugal and Castile settled, Enrique pressed on to Santo Domingo de la Calzada to resolve his differences with Charles II of Navarre. Enrique demanded that Charles return the cities of Vitoria and Logroño in La Rioja that had been annexed in 1368 during Enrique's war with Pedro I. The king of Navarre could not approximate Enrique's military strength and quickly met his demands. The two monarchs pledged mutual friendship, the return of the disputed cities to Castilian control, and a matrimonial union between Enrique's daughter Leonor and Charles II's son, the future Charles III (1387–1425) of Navarre.

Meanwhile, John of Gaunt had not abandoned his plans to claim the crown of Castile in the name of his wife Constanza. Supported by King Edward III of England, John crossed the channel to Calais towards the end of July 1373 with the intention of launching an attack on Castile from Bordeaux. The difficult four-month passage through French territories into English held possessions in southwest France reduced the troop count of his army by almost one half and seriously debilitated his intentions. His plans were further thwarted by Enrique's conquest of his erstwhile ally Fernando I. Additionally, Gaunt's negotiations for military assistance with Pere IV of Aragon broke down in the fall of 1373, and by April of the following year, Duke John of Lancaster suspended his campaign and returned to England.

After a long chain of exchanges between the Castilian and Aragonese monarchs, the peace of Almazán was agreed on April 12, 1375, which specified the return of Molina and Requena to the authority of Castile and a quantity of money advanced to Aragon as compensation. Further, Aragon would make no addition territorial claims of Enrique, and Pere IV's daughter Leonor would marry Enrique's son, the future Juan I (1379–1390) of Castile. At Soria in 1375, two marriages took place which united the Trastámaras to Navarre and Aragon. On May 27, Leonor of Castile and the future Charles III of Navarre were wed, and Leonor of Aragon married the future Juan I of Castile on June 18 (Valdeón *Trastámaras* 44).

Despite the familial ties between Castile and Navarre, hostilities again erupted when Enrique II instructed his son Juan to assemble as many companies as possible to attack Navarre and do as much damage and destruction as he could. Evidently, Enrique discovered that Charles II was again plotting to give the English access to Castile through

Navarre, and the Castilian king was having none of it. This military action resulted in the peace treaty of Briones signed on March 31, 1379, which confirmed that Navarre could not be used by the enemies of Castile and which brought Navarre closer into the political sphere of Castile (Valdeón *Trastámaras* 46).

Two months after the treaty of Briones on May 29, 1379, Enrique II of Castile died at Santo Domingo de la Calzada at the age of forty-six, succumbing to a painful illness of twelve days. His ten-year reign triumphed over all opponents and assured the successful continuation of the line of the Trastámaras.

Juan I (1379–1390) of Castile and the Failed Annexation of Portugal

The unchallenged succession of Juan I of Castile was celebrated at his coronation at Las Huelgas on July 25, 1379, assuring the continuation of the line of the Trastámaras established by his father Enrique II (1369–1379). During the last days of his father's reign, Juan had invaded Navarre to suppress a threat of an English invasion through that realm. The resulting agreement with Charles II of Navarre brought peace among all four monarchs of the peninsula. At the same time, a new schism within Christianity divided the politics of western European rulers and challenged the kings of Iberia to decide between two popes, which in turn determined the friendship or enmity between nations.

Following the death of Pope Gregory XI in 1378, an assembly of cardinals in Rome elected Bartolome Prignano as Pope Urban VI. The election of the new pope was hastily agreed and conducted under pressure from the local people who wanted an Italian pontiff and a return of the seat of Christianity to Rome. However, the immediate reforms of Urban VI contradicted the preferences of the cardinals, who met again within months to rescind the selection of Urban VI and to elect Roberto de Ginebra as Clement VII, who maintained the seat of the papacy at Avignon (O'Callaghan *History* 529). To evaluate the schism and to determine the course of action for the peninsula, Juan I convened an assembly of prelates at Medina del Campo in November of 1380. A majority of the prelates at the assembly favored the recognition of Clement VII, which concurred with the opinion of France and opposed the recognition of Urban VI by England. The following May, Juan announced his support of the pope at Avignon.

Fernando I of Portugal openly sided with Castile in support of Clement VII. Surreptitiously, however, he agreed to an alliance with England to replace Juan I with John of Gaunt, the Duke of Lancaster, as king of Castile. Signed in June of 1380, Fernando's agreement permitted English troops to attack Castile by entering through Portugal. Juan I learned of this plot from the Portuguese Infante João, the son of Pedro I of Portugal and Inés de Castro, who was exiled in Castile at the time. Informed of the imminent threat from the west, Juan I staged a preemptive assault of the border of Portugal, while his ships harassed the Portuguese coast and blocked the mouth of the Tajo at Lisbon. Nonetheless, the English vessels broke the blockade and became an army of occupation that the Portuguese populace resented. The English occupation in the summer of 1381 threatened the economy of the cities, while the war with Castile blocked trade routes and imposed heavy demands on agriculture. Fortunately, a peaceful resolution between Portugal and Castile was reached at Elvas in August of 1383, which included an exchange of prisoners and the return of locations in Portugal that were occupied by Castile. Additionally, the agreement arranged a marriage of Fernando's daughter Beatriz with Juan's second son Fernando, later known as *el de Antequera*, who was only two at the time. However, the death of Juan I's wife Leonor of Aragon on September 13, 1382, at age twenty-four modified the agreement entirely. In April 1383, Juan I accepted a proposal to marry the ten-year-old Beatriz himself. The royal wedding was celebrated at the cathedral of Badajoz on May 13, 1383 (Palenzuela 690–3).

The provisions of the marriage agreement had a profound impact on the future of Portugal and its relationship with Castile. Fernando I of Portugal was too ill to participate in the marriage negotiations himself, but his delegates were instructed to stipulate that if he died without a son, the children of Juan and Beatriz would inherit his realm, and his wife, Queen Leonor, would act as regent until the child monarch's fourteenth birthday. If there were no children from the marriage, Juan would inherit Portugal. In any case, the realms would remain separate (Palenzuela 692). The ill health of Fernando sustained him only another few months. He died on the twenty-second of the following October. Queen Leonor Teles de Meneses immediately proclaimed herself regent for the new queen and king, Beatriz and Juan. At the same time, Juan demanded that Leonor recognize Beatriz as the kingdom's sovereign. This recognition would thereby empower Juan I as the proxy of Beatriz.

In December 1383, Juan I entered Portugal with a substantial army to claim the sovereign rights to the crown of Portugal. He took Santarém in January and asked the regent Leonor to yield to him the powers of state and to divest herself of the regency. He moved on to lay siege to Lisbon in May where he met an unexpected resistance. While the nobility was less eager to oppose Juan, anti–Castilian sentiments had exploded in the large cities such as Lisbon and Oporto, signaling that the general populace was not prepared to accept a Castilian king. Resistance rallied around João, the master of the military Order of Avis, who was the illegitimate son of Pedro I (1357–1367) of Portugal and his mistress Teresa Lourenço and therefore the half-brother of Fernando I. João directed the resistance in Lisbon while another military leader, Nun Alvares Pereira, diverted Castilian attention with guerrilla tactics and defeated them in a skirmish at the Atoleiros (Fronteira, 60 km west of Badajoz) on April 6. Meanwhile, Portuguese ships from Oporto breached the Castilian naval blockade of Lisbon harbor and replenished the city's food supply. Finally, an outbreak of the plague devastated Juan's army and compelled him to retreat to Castile in September 1384 (Valdeón *Trastámaras* 61–2).

The departure of the Castilians afforded an opportunity for the Portuguese to unify their politics. On April 6, 1385, a *Cortes* at Coimbra, consisting of prelates, nobles, scholars, and citizens, recognized the master of Avis as King João I (1385–1433) of Portugal. The convocation rejected the claims of Beatriz and Juan I of Castile as well as those of João and Dinis, the sons of Pedro I and Inés de Castro and half-brothers to the new King João I (See Chart 19). João I's elevation maintained a direct line of inheritance from Alfonso I (1139–1185), the first king of Portugal, but for the first time, inheritance was redirected to an illegitimate branch. João's politics brought closer relations with England and supported John of Gaunt as king of Castile (Palenzuela 696). His political direction also proclaimed Portugal's obedience to the Roman Pope Urban VI.

In view of the depressed economic state of Portugal and its lack of resources, Juan I decided to mount a new invasion to break resistance and gain control of that realm. With a new army and a dominant naval force to blockade Lisbon, Juan I entered Portugal at Guarda and descended the Mondego River. He bypassed Coimbra and was heading toward Santarém when the Castilians encountered João's well-rested forces perched on a hill near Aljubarrota. On August 14, 1385, the Castilians, who were already enervated from the armored march in the summer heat, staged an uphill attack against the Portuguese and were sadly beaten. The losses were great and included many Castilian nobles. Juan I fled for his life and managed to escape to the safety of the boats in Lisbon harbor, which carried him back to Seville (Palenzuela 697).

Following the overwhelming success of the Portuguese at Aljubarrota, João I set out to recover locations that were recently occupied by Castile. He successfully drove out remaining Castilians from the north and to the east in Extremadura but failed to expand his borders. Despite their military debacle, the Castilians remained strong and reinforced the army of the Consejo Real in December of 1385.

Meanwhile, John of Gaunt persisted in his quest for the crown of Castile. With funding from the English king, he invaded A Coruña in July of 1386. Supported by the remaining *petristas* in Galicia, he occupied Santiago de Compostela, where he was crowned king of Castile. He then moved on to establish his court at Ourense. In November of 1386, João I met with Duke John to strengthen their relationship. João agreed to marry the duke's daughter Felipa, and the ceremony was celebrated at Oporto in February of 1387. The duke's initial success and acceptance was checked by severe resistance and political rejection by the local people of Castile as his military campaign advanced eastward. He attacked Benavente and Valderas in March of 1387, but when he advanced to the small village of Cea, he found that the citizens had destroyed their own belongings rather than have them fall into English hands. Moreover, the naval superiority of Castile choked off the duke's communication with England. Sensing the hopelessness of his operation, the Duke of Lancaster sought to reach an agreement. In April, Juan I agreed to compensate the duke's wife in exchange for her renunciation of any rights to the crown of Castile. Additionally, Juan's son, the future Enrique III of Castile, would marry Catalina (Catherine), the duke's daughter and the granddaughter of Pedro I of Castile, thereby uniting the line of the assassinated Pedro I, *el Cruel,* with the line of the Trastámaras. The wedding was celebrated at Palencia in September of 1388 (Valdeón *Trastámaras* 66).

On October 9, 1390, the life of Juan I came to an abrupt and unexpected conclusion. As he left Alcalá de Henares after Mass, his horse was galloping through a recently plowed field and threw the king violently from his saddle, breaking his body as he landed. A young, eleven-year-old Enrique III was proclaimed king of Castile (Suárez Fernández *Historia* 389–90).

The Reign of Enrique III (1390–1406) of Castile

The sudden death of Juan I (1379–1390) from a fall from his horse on October 9, 1390, elevated his son Enrique III (1390–1406) to the throne of Castile just four days past his eleventh birthday. The young monarch was too young to rule in his own name, and his step-mother, Queen Beatriz, at age seventeen was incapable of controlling his regency.

Archbishop Pedro Tenorio of Toledo took immediate control of the situation to protect the rights of the young monarch. He first concealed the death of Juan for a few days until an orderly transition could be assured. He then called a *Cortes* for October and promoted the establishment of a small Regency Council that he could control. The small council proved to be temporary, and a second convocation was arranged for January 1391, which established a Regency Council of more than a dozen prelates, nobles, and town procurators. This arrangement proved to be not only unmanageable, but it inflamed rivalries among noble families, who were interested in protecting and aggrandizing their own powers. Further, several relatives of Enrique III had designs of controlling the monarchy. Among them were Fadrique of Benevente, an illegitimate son of Enrique II and uncle of Enrique III; Pedro, Count of Trastámara; and Leonor of Navarre, Enrique III's aunt (Valdeón *Trastámaras* 78; Suárez Biblao 7-30). The Council was quickly disregarded in some parts of the kingdom as local authorities assumed control. Despite the disorder in Castile, a peace treaty with Portugal was signed in May 1393.

During the minority of Enrique, the preaching of the Archdeacon Fernando Martínez of Écija against the Jews escalated to disastrous proportions. Juan I had admonished the archdeacon, which kept the minister's reckless teachings in check. However, after Juan's death without a viable authority to control the archdeacon's behavior, nothing restrained his harassment of the Jews. Complaints to the courts about Jewish usury and their use as tax collectors had been festering for years. Compounded by poverty and the Black Death, the Christian population was easily led to believe that the Jews were responsible for their woes. Incited by the hateful sermons, the resulting pogrom massacred thousands of Jews in the ghetto of Seville and spread throughout the southern towns including Córdoba, Écija, Jaén, and others. The violence continued northward up to Burgos and even into Aragon. The Jews of Valencia were murdered, and the synagogue was converted into a church. Many Jews became *conversos*, converts to Christianity, to avoid being slain. A contemporary chronicler reported that most of the malfeasance and murder was perpetrated out of a quest for plunder rather than out of a thirst for piety (O'Callaghan *History* 537). Indeed, this was the darkest of days for the Jewish community in Iberia.

The political free-for-all among the regents vying for power ended with the premature proclamation of Enrique's age of majority. On August 2, 1393, at Las Huelgas, a full two months before Enrique's fourteenth birthday, Archbishop Juan García Manrique of Santiago de Compostela on behalf of the Regency Council proclaimed that the king was capable of ruling in his own name. The regency was squelched. Enrique quickly formed an alliance with the lesser nobles, who put themselves in direct service to the new king and opposed the increasing power and abuses of the titled nobility, represented principally by the king's relatives. The two competing factions nearly caused a civil war. The lesser nobles, represented by the families of the Mendoza, Velasco, Guzmán, Stúñiga, and Manrique in support of the king, displaced the political power of the high nobility, who then decided to pay homage to the king. Only a few remained dissident. Fadrique, the Duke of Benavente, and Leonor of Navarre, the king's aunt and wife of King Charles III of Navarre, were both taken prisoner. She was later delivered safely to her husband with a friendly reception at the border. However, Count Alfonso Enríquez of Noreña remained in defiance of the king. An initial siege of Gijon in September 1394 followed by a more successful attack in the summer of 1395 caused Alfonso and his wife Isabel to flee to the English ports on the coast of France. Enrique had the castle at Gijon destroyed, and the opposition from his relatives was finished (Valdeón *Trastámaras* 85+).

In 1404 while Enrique III was preoccupied with duties in the north, alarming news arrived from the southern border that the kingdom of Granada was building its military strength. Granada and Castile had been at peace for decades dating back to the restoration of Muhammad V (1354–1359; 1362–1391) in 1362. From that point, peace continued through the reigns of Enrique II (1369–1379) and Juan I (1379–1390) and into the regency and reign of Enrique III. The peace-loving Muhammad died in 1391. Yusuf II (1391–1392) succeeded his father, but he too died of natural causes the following year. After Yusuf II's untimely death, his younger son Muhammad VII (1392–1408) seized power from an older brother Yusuf and had him imprisoned. The elder brother Yusuf would later be elevated to Yusuf III (1408–1417) when Muhammad VII died in 1408 (Kennedy *Muslim Spain* 293–4). By 1404 after ruling Granada for a dozen years, Muhammad VII was beating the drums of war against Castile.

In anticipation of an impending threat, Enrique set in motion the plans to mount an attack against the Muslims. Nonetheless, the preparations came too late. Muhammed VII (1392–1408) acted first by taking Ayamonte (also known as Carastas Castle at Olvera, Cádiz) in 1405, and Muslim skirmishes continued all along the border in 1406. A truce signed on October 6 was meaningless, and the violence persisted. In December of 1406, a *Cortes* was convened at Toledo with a principal objective of raising the funds to put a stop to the Muslim incursions, but the ill health of Enrique aborted his retaliation. The young king died on Christmas Day in 1406 at the age of twenty-seven years. Enrique was known for his fervent piety and for his passion for constructing monasteries and palaces, among which include the Palace of the Pardo near Madrid and the Miraflores in Burgos. His successor Juan II (1406–1454) was born at Toro on March 6, 1405, less than two years earlier.

The End of the Male Line in Aragon: 1387–1410

The death of Pere IV (Peter), "the Ceremonious" (1336–1387), of Aragon in 1387 concluded a long and successful reign that spanned four Castilian monarchs from Alfonso XI (1312–1350) through Pedro I (1350–1369), Enrique II (1369–1379) and Juan I (1379–1390). During most of his reign, Pere was at odds with the crown of Castile. As he ascended the throne, his quarrels with his step-mother Leonor drove her back to her brother Alfonso XI of Castile. Later, Pere supported the rise of Enrique II over Pedro I but subsequently opposed Enrique when promises of territorial concessions to Aragon were not kept. As Pere's days ended, he was at peace with Castile as his daughter Leonor of Aragon was married to Juan I of Castile. As we shall see, this union ultimately provided a male heir for the crown of Aragon, since Pere's sons Joan (John 1387–1396) and Martí (1396–1410) failed to produce sons that survived them.

When Pere IV died in 1387, his son Joan acted quickly to claim his rights to the crown despite a life-long illness, probably epilepsy. Joan was highly experienced in governance. His father gave him the title of Duke of Girona as a child, and he had led military forays as early as age thirteen. He was broadly educated in several languages but preferred the art of the hunt to his duties of governance. Joan married Mata of Armagnac in 1373 at Barcelona. In rapid succession, she produced five children, four of whom died in infancy. Leonor was the only child to outlive her parents. Mata died in 1378, and Joan was now approaching forty years of age without a male heir. Rejecting the encouragement of his father and step-mother, Sibilla de Fortiá, to marry candidates of their choosing, Joan married an ambitious fifteen-year-old Yolanda of Bar at Perpignan in 1380. Of the six children that Yolanda birthed, only the eldest Yolanda survived them. Yolanda married Louis II of Naples in 1400.

Despite his experience, Joan lacked the patience necessary for effective governance. Early in his reign, he clashed with the *Corts* and was unwilling to concede the administrative changes that they were proposing. Later he paid little attention to defending Valencia against Muslim incursions. To his credit, he reacted favorably to the outbreak of violence against the Jews in June 1391. Like other monarchs in the peninsula, the crown of Aragon employed Jews in their governmental services and depended on them for administrative functions. The sudden violence against the Jews produced massacres in Valencia and then spread to Barcelona and even to Majorca before Joan could react. He was in Zaragoza when the news reached him, and he immediately denounced the killings and ordered that the Jews be protected throughout the kingdom.

As the ruler of the kingdom, Joan was unproductive. The concerns of the *Corts* as well as those of the peasants went unattended as did the anti–Catalan resistance in Sardinia and Sicily. While pursuing his favorite pastime of hunting, he fell from his horse, probably of a heart attack, and died on May 19, 1396. Since he was still without a male heir, his brother Martí, "the Humane" (1396–1410), was proclaimed the rightful heir of Aragon (Bisson 121–5).

At the time of his nomination to the crown, Martí was in Sicily, assisting his son Martí the Younger and his daughter-in-law María of Sicily, the heiress to Frederick III, establish control of the island. María was not only Martí's daughter-in-law, but she was also his niece, since his half-sister Constança was Frederick III's wife and María's mother (See Chart 14). The Catalonian *parlament* investigated the estate of the deceased King Joan and dispatched ambassadors to Martí with a substantial subsidy on the condition that he return to Catalonia to accept the crown. Martí remained a short time to secure Sicily and returned in 1397 to assume control. In the interim, his wife since 1372, María de Luna, acted as regent on behalf of her husband.

Martí proved to be much more politically astute than his brother Joan. He was well received by the Catalans in Barcelona and immediately confirmed their rights and privileges, while not neglecting to support his son's success in Sicily with financial support and military resources. After a few months in Barcelona, he journeyed to a ceremonial reception in Zaragoza and confirmed the *fueros* of Aragon as his father Pere IV had done in 1348 (Ruiz 75). His visit to Valencia in 1402 was deferred due to an outbreak of the plague that year.

Early in his reign, Martí worked diligently to restore the fiscal domains of the crown that his father and brother had depleted through sales or pledges. He restored jurisdictional rights and directed the administration of the tenancies of these properties. During the papal schism, Martí remained supportive of Pope Benedict XIII, his wife's relative, and when the pope refused to resign in order to resolve the dual papacy, Martí provided a pontifical seat for him in Barcelona.

The wife of Martí the Younger, María of Sicily, died in 1401, and the elder negotiated a second marriage for his son with Blanche of Navarre in 1402. Martí had concluded a peace agreement with Navarre just three years earlier. Throughout his entire reign, Martí had to deal with unrest in Sardinia, which was being undermined by Genoese commercial and shipping interests. In 1409, Martí supported an expedition against Sardinia led by his son Martí the Younger, who prevailed against the island's rebels in June of that year. However, the younger Martí died of malaria just one month later, leaving the elder without an heir and the island without a firm controlling authority (Bisson 125–30).

The elder Martí had been a widower since 1406, and when his only son died, he quickly married Margarita de Prades in September 1409, no doubt with the hope that he could sire another male heir. His intentions went unfulfilled as he expired on May 31, 1410, just two months short of his fifty-fourth birthday. The death of Martí brought to an end the direct line of male rulers of Barcelona who descended from Guifré I, "the Hairy" (870–897), and from the earliest counts installed in the Spanish March at Barcelona after 801. A female heiress in Catalonia was unprecedented, but as the search for a new monarch was initiated, a male descendent from the daughter of Pere IV, Leonor, with her husband, Juan I of Castile, was accepted after a lengthy process (discussed in the next section). The son of these Castilian monarchs, Fernando de Antequera, from the house of Trastámara was recognized as Fernando I of Aragon.

The Minority of Juan II of Castile and the Rise of Fernando de Antequera: 1406–1419

Juan II (1406–1454) was a little more than twenty-one months old when his father Enrique III (1390–1406) died of natural causes in Toledo on Christmas Day in 1406 as he was preparing to respond to Muslim incursions on the border of Castile. The deceased king's testament named his wife, Queen Catalina, and his brother, the Infante Fernando, as co-regents. The queen would govern Castile in the north, and Fernando would control Andalucia to contain the imminent aggression of the Nasrid King Muhammad VII (1392–1408) of Granada. Muhammad had broken decades of peace between the two realms by taking Ayamonte in 1405 and by raiding areas around Baeza the following year. The regents officially took charge of their duties on January 15, 1407 (Valdeón *Trastámaras* 121–2).

From Seville in September 1407, Fernando initiated an offensive against Setenil and locations to the north of Ronda. Zahara was taken using canons for the first time. Setenil was placed under siege, but when an assault tower broke down, the siege was lifted. As Fernando retreated to Seville for the winter, the campaign accomplished little and was neutralized by a counteroffensive from Granada. All in all, the campaign proved to be ineffective. The spring of 1408 brought a truce that would continue until mid–November. However, the death of Muhammad VII on May 13 elevated Yusuf III (1408–1417) as king of Granada. Yusuf had been incarcerated by his younger brother Muhammad, who had usurped power in 1392. Now released from confinement, the new king was granted an extension of the truce until March 1409. Nonetheless, a misunderstanding broke the peace in September when Fernando granted permission to occupy and re-populate the fortress of Priego that was abandoned upon his retreat the previous year. Yusuf III understood that Priego was still in his domain and sent an army to eject the interlopers (Porras 46). As the year concluded, the location was still in dispute.

With funding and resources for the war secured, Fernando initiated a new campaign in February 1410 and arrived in Córdoba in early April to learn that the Nasrids had retaken Zahara. Without delay, Fernando lay siege to the small but well-fortified position of Antequera, despite the fact that siege engines from Seville had not yet arrived. In response, the king of Granada mobilized a large relief army, which after several skirmishes, attacked a Christian division led by Bishop Rojas, who was stationed on the other side of Antequera from Fernando's main division. Day-long fighting on May 6 resulted in a standoff until Fernando's main contingent arrived to scatter the enemy. The Muslim losses were devastating, and Fernando denied Yusuf III's attempt to negotiate a two-year truce. Fernando considered granting Yusuf's request only on the condition that Granada become the vassal of Castile. He also demanded that they pay *parias* and that they release all Christian captives. Siege engines were prepared over the following month to facilitate a general assault on the walls. In the interim, raiding parties were dispatched to the surrounding countryside and as far as the outskirts of Málaga. Through the month of August, the siege tightened, and finally by mid–September, the Castilians succeeded in breaching a wall with a siege tower, driving the defenders to the inner castle. The breach compelled the people of Antequera to petition for terms of surrender. Approximately 2500 men, women, and children were permitted to leave with movable possessions, and all Christian prisoners were released. Infante Fernando and Bishop Rojas took possession of Antequera on September 24. Upon his victorious return to Seville in early October and with his acclaim trumpeted throughout the realm, Fernando became known as *el de Antequera* (Porras 50–54; Kenedy *Muslim Spain* 294). The following month, a truce of seventeen months was agreed, allowing both sides a respite from the violence.

While the siege of Antequera was playing out during the summer of 1410, Fernando received a letter from his uncle, King Martí of Aragon, inviting him to Zaragoza to broach the subject of succession to the crown of Aragon. Given Fernando's commitment to the siege, the meeting was an impossibility. Even so, his departure would have been futile, for just a few days later, news arrived that King Martí had died. The deceased king was the brother of Queen Leonor of Castile, the mother of Fernando and the grandmother of Juan II of Castile. Consequently, Fernando's name was in consideration for the crown of Aragon along with others, notably Count Jaume of Urgell, the brother of Pere IV (1336–1387) and the great-uncle of Fernando. The *Corts* of Aragon agreed to nominate a commission of nine persons, three each from Aragon, Catalonia, and

Valencia, to rule on which candidate had rights to the crown. Dissatisfied with the process of a commission, Count Jaume attempted to commandeer the crown by force with the assistance of Gascons and his Valencian partisans. The count's army was overwhelmingly defeated by Castilian troops dispatched from Cuenca. Meanwhile, the Commission of Caspe allowed twenty days to hear the arguments in favor of the potential candidates. On June 29, 1412, the Commission announced its findings that the grandson of Pere IV, Fernando de Antequera, had the right to become Fernando I of Aragon. Despite the recognition of Fernando I as king, Count Jaume rose up in protest until he was besieged and captured at Balenguer on October 29, 1413. The count was stripped of his possessions and incarcerated for life (Porras 54–63). It wasn't until February 10, 1414, that a formal coronation of Fernando was performed at the Aljafería palace in Zaragoza, following an announcement a year earlier that the dual regency in Castile would continue.

Fernando strengthened the bonds of the Trastámaras by arranging the marriage of his son, the future Alfonso V of Aragon, with María of Castile, the sister of Juan II, on June 12, 1415, in the cathedral of Valencia. Their marriage had been preordained in the last testament of their mutual grandfather Enrique III of Castile, and the ceremony was performed by the schismatic Antipope Benedict XIII, who also gave them a dispensation for their close parentage as first cousins.

The papacy of Benedict XIII was nearing an end. On January 5, 1416, Fernando I of Aragon withdrew his support of Benedict, which concluded the final chapter in the schism of the western Church that began in 1387 with the installation of Clement VII at Avignon as a second pope. Pedro de Luna had succeeded Clement VII as Pope Benedict XIII at Avignon in 1394, but he had resisted attempts at deposition by the French monarch and others until only the crown of Aragon supported him. When Aragon's recognition was finally withdrawn, Pedro de Luna spent his remaining days in reclusion at Peñíscola under the protection of the crown of Aragon until his death in 1422. The deposition of Pope Benedict paved the way for the resignation of two other papal claimants and permitted the Council of Constance to elect Oddone Colonna as Pope Martin V in November 1417. The Church returned to the recognition of a single pope.

Fernando's tenure as monarch was short. He died of natural causes at the town of Igualada twelve miles west of Barcelona on April 2, 1416. His eldest son was recognized as Alfonso V (1416–1458) without contest, and his death left Queen Catalina as the sole regent for Juan II of Castile. In April of the following year, the queen granted King Yusuf III (1408–1417) of Granada an extension of a truce for two years, but her days as regent were numbered as well. On the morning of June 2, 1418, Queen Catalina was found dead in her bed at the age of fifty years. Twelve days later, Juan II issued a notification that he would take charge of the kingdom in his own name, since both regents had deceased. But the Council in service to the crown had other ideas. They intended to continue as a group. In the interim, Juan II celebrated his betrothal to María of Aragon, the daughter of Fernando I, the following October. By the end of the year, a *Cortes* was convened in Madrid to acknowledge the fact that Juan II was approaching his fourteenth year and would govern in his own name. On March 7, 1419, the day after his fourteenth birthday, Juan II's majority was recognized.

The Majority of Juan II of Castile: 1419–1454

The age of majority of Juan II in 1419 marked the beginning of a power struggle for control over the weak-willed monarch that endured throughout his reign. Competing forces vied for influence. Alvaro de Luna, the king's favorite, exercised the most leverage over Juan II by being his closest confident. The Infantes of Aragon, especially Enrique and Joan, challenged the king's authority for more than two decades, while the aristocratic nobility wielded the greatest economic power of the day. The nobility's support at the Royal Council determined the direction and fate of the monarchy.

From his first appearance at the Castilian court in 1410, Alvaro de Luna, Juan II's favorite, won the trust and heart of the young monarch. The five-year-old Juan grew so emotionally attached that he needed the constant presence of Alvaro, even demanding that they sleep in the same room. Early in his reign, Juan II named Alvaro as Constable in charge of military operations and as steward of the royal household. In effect, he ruled in the king's name.

The children of Fernando I of Aragon, *el de Antequera*, known collectively as the Infantes of Aragon, derived enormous wealth and power not only from their vast estates in Castile but also from their marriages into royal families throughout the peninsula. Alfonso V (1416–1458) of Aragon succeeded his father Fernando as king and married his first cousin María, the sister of Juan II of Castile. Infante Joan (designated in this section with his Catalan name to avoid confusion with his cousin Juan II of Castile) married the heiress to the crown of Navarre and ruled as king of that realm on behalf of his wife, Blanche I (1425–1441). He also served as his brother's deputy in Aragon, and ascended as Joan II (1458–1479) of Aragon after his brother's death. Infante Enrique married his cousin Catalina (Catherine), the sister of Juan II of Castile, and battled for the control of Castile until his death. Infanta María married her cousin Juan II of Castile, and Infanta Leonor married King Duarte of Portugal. Less influential, Infante Pedro fought alongside his brothers in Castile and in Italy (See Chart 14; Chart 15; Chart 17; Chart 18). Collectively and individually, the Infantes vied for control over Juan II of Castile until the defeat of Infantes Joan and Enrique at the battle of Olmedo in 1445.

The Royal Council that advised, and indeed controlled, the decisions of the king had morphed into an instrument of the high nobility that held sway over the monarch's authority. Influential nobles had replaced the seats on the Council that were formerly held by procurators from the cities. To be sure, each noble family acted in its own interest, and all families rarely acted in a unified block. Nonetheless, the power of the nobility served as a counterweight to the overreach of Constable Alvaro and to the Infantes of Aragon, vacillating in alignment now with one, now with the other.

Shortly after the majority of Juan II began in 1419, Infante Joan received an offer to marry the future Blanche I (1426–1441) of Navarre, the daughter of Charles III (1387–1425) and widow of Martí the Younger of Aragon. Joan took leave of the Castilian court in the summer of 1420 to celebrate his marriage at Pamplona. During Joan's absence from Castile, Infante Enrique, in an unprecedented affront to royal authority, staged an overthrow of King Juan II. In the small hours of the morning of Sunday, June 14, 1420, Enrique entered the palace of the king at Tordesillas with a small armed group and rudely awakened Juan II and Alvaro, who was sleeping at the foot of the king's bed.

Enrique took possession of the king and commandeered his authority under the pretext of defending the crown and of removing all the evil lieutenants of the king. Under Enrique's supervision, the fifteen-year-old King Juan II was quietly married two months later on August 4, 1420, to Infanta María, Enrique's sister and Juan's first cousin. To weave an even larger web of influence, Enrique quietly married the Infanta Catalina, the sister of Juan II and his own first cousin, at Talavera the following November. The lordship of Villena that he received as a dowry expanded his wealth and power all the more.

At the end of November, Enrique's good fortune would take a turn for the worse. Taking advantage of a hunting expedition, Alvaro and the king escaped to the castle of Montalbán where the king's partisans arrived to negotiate his freedom from the pursuit of Enrique. The foiled Infante then retreated to Ocaña to await his fate for the failed coup (Suárez Frenández *Nobleza y Monarquía* 119–26). Infante Enrique remained at large until the summer of 1422 when he was compelled to appear before the king in Madrid and was sentenced to incarceration at the castle of Mora. He and his partisans were stripped of their properties. With the demise of Enrique, influence over the king passed to Alvaro. Furthermore, the remaining high nobles including Infante Joan of Navarre aligned with Alvaro de Luna, who was elevated to the position of Constable in charge of royal military operations. Alvaro also served as steward of the royal household and was rewarded with the lordship of San Esteban de Gormaz.

King Alfonso V of Aragon, "the Magnanimous," returned to the peninsula from Italy and was determined to free his brother Enrique from prison. In September 1425, Alfonso summoned his brother Joan to a meeting near Tarazona and berated him for not supporting Infante Enrique. As the two brothers plotted the release of their sibling, news arrived from Olite on September 8 that Charles III of Navarre had died, and his daughter, now Queen Blanche I (1425–1441), sent the royal banner of the kingdom of Navarre to her husband Joan in recognition of his ascendance as king of Navarre (See Chart 18). Under threat of war from Alfonso V of Aragon and Joan of Navarre, Juan II agreed to release Infante Enrique from his prison at Mora on Sunday, October 7. Further, Enrique's properties were restored. The return of influence of the Infantes of Aragon led to a reorganization of the king's Royal Council. The noble families began to take sides either with the Infantes or with Constable Alvaro de Luna. The pendulum then swung in favor of the Infantes. They convinced a majority of the Council of Alvaro's abuse of power, and the Constable was ordered to leave the Court for a period of eighteen months. However, the sentence did not hold. The Constable's absence resulted in chaos and lack of governance. Altercations between nobles erupted and destroyed the administration of justice throughout the realm. The civil disorder precipitated a recall of Alvaro only four months later and brokered a realignment of the Royal Council that again favored the Constable over the Infantes of Aragon.

In the late spring of 1428, rumors of a Muslim invasion drew the attention of Alvaro, and consequently, Infante Enrique was dispatched to the border of Andalucia. At the same time, members of the Council opined that it was not fitting to have two kings in Castile and that the king of Navarre was no longer welcomed there. As fortune would have it, King Joan's wife Blanche I sent for him, indicating that he was needed in Navarre (Porras 145–6). Castile was temporarily rid of the two powerful Infantes of

Aragon, but they had not yet abandoned their quest for political control of the realm. Furthermore, their absence did not last long. To settle the rivalries between Infante Enrique and Joan of Navarre, Alfonso V of Aragon arranged a meeting at Chelva to the west of Valencia to hatch a common strategy for the Infantes of Aragon. By the spring of 1429, Alfonso V of Aragon and Joan of Navarre crossed the borders of Castile from the east, proclaiming the liberation of Juan II from the control of Alvaro. Infante Enrique threatened the interior, while Infante Pedro menaced from the castle at Peñafiel. However, neither Castile nor Aragon was eager for all-out war. In the summer, the Aragonese retreated from their advances on Sigüenza and Hita, and Infante Enrique was again stripped of his patrimonial properties, which provoked Infantes Enrique and Pedro to ravage Extremedura. They took, among others, the castles of Trujillo and Albuquerque. The Castilians countered by placing Trujillo under siege, which resulted in a standoff until Enrique asked his brother-in-law Duarte of Portugal, to have King João I (1385–1433) intervene. Peace was achieved when Enrique agreed to surrender the castles that recognized his authority and to forfeit his properties. Both Enrique and Pedro were delivered to Lisbon and travelled on to unite later with their brother Alfonso V in Italy. Navarre and Aragon signed the treaty of Majano with Castile in July of 1430 for a period of five years. The departure of the Infantes of Aragon left Castile in the hands of an oligarchy of noble families headed by Alvaro de Luna, who rose to great power and abuse. During the peace among Christian realms, Castile now directed its attention toward the Muslims of Granada (Palenzuela 737–9).

Castile had been at peace with the kingdom of Granada since 1410 when Fernando defeated them at Antequera. Juan II's mother Catrina acting as regent before her death agreed to an extension of truce in 1417. Similarly, Juan II granted another extension in 1421. Nonetheless, the Nasrids had their own internal disputes. Dominant families of Granada feuded to install their own choice of emir. Yusuf III (1408–1417) died in 1417 and left an eight-year-old Muhammad VIII as his successor, who was placed under the tutelage of Ali al-Amin. A rival family of the Banu Sarraj (known as *Abencerrajes* in Castilian) plotted against the al-Amin family and staged a coup in 1419. A cousin of the deceased Yusuf III was installed as Muhammad IX, who went on to serve no less than four separate episodes as ruler of Granada until he died in 1453 (See List: Nasrids of Granada). Meanwhile, the dethroned Muhammad VIII was held in captivity and was later restored to power between 1427 and 1429 by a popular uprising. This revolt drove the Banu Sarraj and Muhammad IX in exile to Tunis, only to return two years later with a force supplied by the Hafsid ruler of Tunis and a promise of assistance from Juan II of Castile. Muhammad IX returned to power for the second time (1430–1431) and had Muhammad VIII killed in captivity in 1431. Meanwhile, the Castilians launched a punitive campaign against Muhammad IX for not recognizing Juan II as his overlord. Assisted by Muslim dissidents, the Castilians succeeded in taking enough cities so that the dissident allies were able to proclaim their candidate Yusuf IV (1432) as ruler of Granada on January 1, 1432. The generous treaty that Yusuf made with the Castilians was wildly unpopular with the general populace of Granada, and by April 1432, Yusuf was besieged in the Alhambra and assassinated. Muhammad IX (1432–1445) was established for the third time (Kennedy *Muslim Spain* 295–6).

Meanwhile, the truce with Navarre and Aragon ended in 1435, and the Infantes of

Aragon began negotiations to indemnify their losses in Castile. An agreement was reached on September 22, 1436, at Toledo which provided small monetary compensations for the loss of rents, but it did not authorize the return of the Infantes to Castile, nor did it return their estates. However, the agreement stipulated the marriage of Prince Enrique, the son of Juan II of Castile born in 1425, to Blanche, the daughter of Joan of Navarre and Blanche I (1425–1441). The ceremony would take place four years later when the bride and groom would be sixteen and fifteen years old respectively. Notably, Blanche would receive as a dowry all her father's former properties along the Duero. She also acquired the marquisate of Villena, that Joan of Navarre would administer for her (Palenzuela 739). This ruse enabled Joan of Navarre to reintegrate himself into the politics of Castile.

The return of the Infantes of Aragon to Castile in 1437 coincided with unrest among the Castilian nobility. The noble families were growing increasingly hostile to the abuses and illegal actions of the king, which is to say of Alvaro. Rebellion broke out in 1437 in the town of Medina de Rioseco in the domains of the Enríquez family, who then united with the Infantes in common cause against the government of the king. As an intended remedy to the unrest, Alvaro opened discussions, which marked his decline and the rise of the nobility and of the Infantes. The accords of Castronuño in the fall of 1439 heralded the expulsion of Alvaro from the court and from the Royal Council. The aristocratic families of Castile in league with the Infantes, who recouped their economic privileges, assumed control of the government. The Infantes and the nobility now commanded the greater military strength and invaded the court of Juan II at Medina on the night of July 28–29, 1441. They took possession of the king, and Alvaro fled to the safety of Escalona to re-establish his power base. During the following year, however, some of the nobility grew increasingly less supportive of the Infantes Joan and Enrique, whose actions were uncontrollable. In July of 1443, for example, Joan ordered the incarceration of the members of the Royal Council who remained supportive of Alvaro, and then he turned Juan II into a veritable prisoner (Valdeón *Trastámaras* 135). This *coup d'état* produced a break in unity with the nobility, who realized that they had exchanged one authoritarian usurper for another. To compensate his loss of support from the nobles, Joan of Navarre strengthened his ties with the powerful Enríquez family by marrying Juana Enríquez, who became the mother of the future Fernando the Catholic. His first wife Blanche I of Navarre had died in 1441.

Juan II escaped from house arrest in March of 1444 and found refuge at Dueñas. He then conferred the Principality of Asturias to his son Enrique and made Juan Pacheco, the favorite of Enrique, as his majordomo. The rents from Asturias funded the resistance of Prince Enrique and Juan Pacheco, who united with Alvaro against the Infantes. By March of 1445, Infantes Joan and Enrique had joined forces at Olmedo. The united forces of Alvaro and Prince Enrique met the Infantes in open-field combat on May 19, 1445, and soundly defeated them. Infante Enrique was severely wounded and died, probably from infection, several days later at Calatayud. Joan fled to the safety of Aragon, never to return to Castile (Palenzuela 742–3). He continued to act as his brother's deputy in Aragon, and at the same time, maintained his position as king of Navarre, denying his son Charles IV (1441–1461), Prince of Viana, his rightful inheritance. Alfonso V of Aragon was pre-occupied with his enterprise in Naples, and Pedro died in combat at Naples in 1438. Both Queen María of Castile and Queen Leonor of Portugal had died earlier. Finally, the influence of the children of Fernando de Antequera in the kingdom of Castile had been nullified.

As conflict subsided in Castile, internal turmoil escalated in the kingdom of Granada. Muhammad IX had again caused enough dissatisfaction among the populace that his nephew, the governor of Almería, succeeded in overthrowing him and was recognized as Muhammad X. The Banu Sarraj fled to the Castilian frontier and once again established their own rival claimant as Yusuf V (1445–1446). Back in Granada, Muhammad X still claimed power until 1447–8 when Muhammad IX was again re-established in his fourth reign until his death in 1453. Muhammad IX's testament nominated the son of his cousin Muhammad VIII, who was elevated as Muhammad XI (1453–1454) (Kennedy *Muslim Spain* 296–8).

In August of 1447, Juan II married his second wife, the Infanta Isabel of Portugal. His first wife, María of Aragon had died two years earlier. This second marriage produced the future Catholic Queen Isabel, born on April 22, 1451, and the Infante Alfonso, born on November 15, 1453 (See Chart 17). Significantly, the influence of his new wife and the appreciation of his son Enrique drew the king's attention away from his favorite, Alvaro de Luna. In fact, the enmity between Alvaro and Enrique was growing, and the king's new wife Isabel lent no support to Alvaro either. By 1449, Juan was overwhelmed with complaints of tyranny against Alvaro, which gave rise to a rebellion in Toledo that year. The ever-increasing complaints against Alvaro caused Juan II to lose confidence in his constable. When accusations of conspiracy of murder in Burgos were levied, Juan had Alvaro imprisoned in April 1453. Afterward, doctors of law convinced Juan II of Alvaro's culpability and attested that he had been usurping the king's authority for years. Juan II was finally persuaded to sign the order of execution for his former favorite. In the plaza of Valladolid on June 3, 1453, the Constable Alvaro de Luna was beheaded, and his head was displayed above the scaffold for nine days (Valdeón *Trastámaras* 141+). A little more than a year later, Juan II was overcome with a fever and died at Valladolid on July 21, 1454, at the age of forty-nine. His legacy portrayed the image of a weak, disinterested leader.

The Reign of Enrique IV (1454–1474) of Castile

Enrique ascended to the throne of Castile at the age of twenty-nine on July 23, 1454, just a year after Constantinople fell to the Ottoman Turks and as the monarchs of western Europe were pressed by Pope Calixtus II to respond to this Muslim incursion. Amid this atmosphere, Enrique sought conciliation with the rebellious elements of the high nobility of Castile and announced his intentions to take the offensive against the Muslims of Granada rather than entertaining the idea of dealing with the Turks.

The Muslims of Granada were embroiled in their own turmoil. Muhammad IX died in 1453 ending his fourth reign and had designated as his successor the son of his cousin Muhammad VIII, who was elevated as Muhammad XI (1453–1454), known to the Christians as *el Chiquito*. Once again, the Banu Sarraj divided the kingdom by designating their own rival candidate in the name of Abu Nasr Sad (1454–1464). Sad controlled the outlying regions of Granada while Muhammad XI held the Alhambra. Enrique IV launched his campaign against the Nasrids in the spring of 1455 with a war of attrition and devastation. However, this style of warfare proved to be unsatisfying to the nobility, since they derived little glory and no territorial reward from the effort. On the other hand, the Christian raids caused enough division among the Muslims that Sad successfully wrested the Alhambra from Muhammad XI, who fled but was invited back by popular demand when Sad struck an overly generous agreement with the Christians. On his return to Granada, Muhammad was ambushed and killed by Sad's partisans, leaving Sad in sole command of the Muslim kingdom until his own deposition in 1464. The Castilians resumed their offensive in 1456 and took Estepona and Jimena de la Frontera. A brief two-year truce was agreed in 1459, and thereafter Enrique delegated the campaign to Enrique de Guzmán, Duke of Medina-Sidonia, and Rodrigo Ponce de León, Marquis of Cádiz, who succeeded in capturing Gibraltar in 1462 (Kennedy *Muslim Spain* 298).

When Enrique ascended to the throne, he was childless and had no successor. His first marriage in 1440 to Blanche of Navarre, the daughter of Joan II and Blanche I (1425–1441), was arranged as part of a settlement which indemnified Joan II and the other Infantes of Aragon against the loss of their estates in Castile. The marriage was never consummated, and thirteen years later, Enrique IV obtained an annulment by claiming that he was impotent only with Blanche but not with other women. This maneuver cleared the way for his marriage to the Portuguese Princess Joana (Juana), the daughter of King Duarte (1433–1438) and the sister of King Afonso V (1438...1481), at Córdoba in March 1455 (Valdeón *Trastámaras* 197). The Infanta Juana was born to Enrique and Juana of Portugal in 1462, seven years after their marriage (See Chart 17; Chart 19).

With King Enrique's indulgence, his favorite, Juan Pacheco, acting in his own self-interest, had become the wealthy and powerful Marquis of Villena. He was the driving force in Castilian politics, which proved to be unpalatable for some nobles. In the summer of 1459, a confederation of nobles gathered to assure the protection of their property rights, and the following year, it grew into a League that championed the "good of the kingdom." The dissents in Castile drew the attention of Aragon. After the death of Alfonso V in 1458, Joan of Navarre was elevated as King Joan II of Aragon. Joan announced his support of the League that was contesting the authority of the Castilian monarchy. Enrique's angry rebuttal to this affront was to declare his support for Prince Charles of Viana, who was asserting his right to the crown of Navarre and opposing the authority of his father Joan II. In December 1460, Joan II had his son Charles imprisoned, which prompted Enrique IV to dispatch an army to assist the *beaumontes* partisans that supported Charles. Then Prince Charles of Viana was released shortly thereafter on February 25, 1461, but he unexpectedly died the following September (Valdeón *Trastámaras* 198–200). His death triggered the eruption of internal problems that burgeoned into civil war in Aragon (more in the next section).

Meanwhile in 1461, Enrique concluded an agreement with the League, which pacified the realm but which marked a split with Juan Pacheco. The Marquis of Villena grew increasingly out of favor with Enrique as Beltrán de la Cueva assumed the role of the king's favorite. Beltrán had risen to the post of master of Santiago as a reward for campaigning against Granada. For taking Archidona in 1462, he was rewarded with the countship of Ledesma. By 1462, Enrique's approval was at its zenith. At least temporarily, he had pacified the nobility. He had campaigned successfully against the Nasrids, and at last he had produced an heiress to the crown. Princess Juana was born to Enrique and Juana of Portugal on February 28 of that year. Furthermore, the rebellion against Joan II of Aragon added to Enrique's recognition. The *Generalitat* of Catalonia, rising up against Joan, proclaimed Enrique IV as their king. Enrique welcomed the proposition of expanding his monarchy into Catalonia. However, the Castilian nobility and specifically Juan Pacheco voiced disfavor to the annexation. The situation drew the attention of Louis XI of France, whose mediation at Bayonne in 1463 convinced Enrique to reject the annexation of Catalonia and settle for the jurisdiction of Estella in Navarre as compensation. Thereafter, Enrique's image began to fade.

Juan Pacheco's support of Enrique turned to opposition. The Marquis of Villena had grown powerful enough to contest the very authority of the king. At an assembly of rebellious nobles at Burgos in September of 1464, Villena accused the king of protecting the infidels, of demeaning the Catholic clergy, of devaluing the currency, of intervening in Navarre and Catalonia without right, and of destroying justice. A further accusation alleged that the king's daughter Juana was illegitimate and had no right to accede to the crown. He declared that the king's half-brother Alfonso should inherit. While the king's counselors advised him to react forcefully to this affront, the weak Enrique dithered. The pressure from the hostile nobility induced the resignation of Beltrán de la Cueva as master of Santiago, and he was distanced from the court. To add to the insult, Pacheco took custody of the king's half-brother, Infante Alfonso, just eleven years old at the time. On June 5, 1465, the disgruntled opponents of Enrique assembled on the plains outside of Avila to enact a theatrical deposition of the king. An effigy of King Enrique was seated on a platform, ridiculed, and declared deposed. The Infante Alfonso was then brought to the stage and proclaimed king of Castile. This event, dubbed as the farce of Avila, marked a low point in the history of the medieval Castilian monarchy (Valdeón *Trastámaras* 203–7).

Despite the farce of Avila, Enrique IV was still king and still in power, so the rebels resorted to open confrontation in the summer of 1465. On the other hand, the king was not yet devoid of resources. The powerful Mendoza family and others remained loyal to him, and Beltrán de la Cueva returned to the court. Armed confrontation broke out during 1467 and culminated in another battle near Olmedo, pitting revolutionary and royal armies against each other. Although details are absent, it appears that the king's forces were once again victorious. However, the fatal blow to the insurrection was dealt by the death of the Infante Alfonso. The presumptive new King Alfonso died on July 5, 1468, at Cardeñosa near Avila, probably from the plague that was ravaging the region.

The death of Infante Alfonso left two names in contention as Enrique's successor. The League dismissed Infanta Juana as a candidate because of the rumors that tarnished her legitimacy. She was whispered to be the daughter of the king's favorite, Beltrán de la Cueva, and was labeled *la Beltraneja*. Queen Juana's notorious misconduct supported this accusation (Ruiz 99). A second candidate, the king's half-sister Isabel born on April

22, 1451, at Madrigal de las Altas Torres, aspired to the throne, but she was not disposed to assume a partnership with the rebel factions to achieve that goal. Instead Isabel chose to meet with her half-brother Enrique IV to resolve the issue of inheritance. This meeting led to the announcement of los Toros de Guisando of September 18, 1468, whereby the king recognized Isabel as the legitimate heiress on the condition that she marry someone of their mutual choice. This decision relegated Infanta Juana to a subordinate role. After considerable negotiations but without her brother's consent, Isabel chose Fernando, the heir to the crown of Aragon, as the most suitable husband. The couple were married at Santa María la Mayor in Valladolid on October 18, 1469, and would later be remembered as the Catholic Monarchs.

Feeling betrayed and under the influence of the partisans led by Villena, King Enrique declared jointly with Queen Juana in October of the following year that their daughter, Infanta Juana, was legitimate. The announcement effectively reversed the agreement of los Toros de Guisando and rejected the ascendancy of Isabel. Isabel responded immediately with the accusation that Enrique and the queen were perjuring themselves.

The following years were thrown into anarchy as nobles and townsmen alike aligned with either Isabel or Juana. To add to the misery, economic recession and monetary inflation inflamed and promoted small feudal wars throughout the kingdom. Juan Pacheco, the Marquis of Villena, died in October 1474. Two months later, during the night of December 11–12, 1474, Enrique IV died in the alcazar of Madrid. The official report indicated that the king experienced a "discharge of blood." His daughter Juana later asserted that he was given herbs and poisons before his death (Valdeón *Trastámaras* 215–7). Isabel and Fernando faced a formidable challenge to rectify the failed monarchy.

Civil War in Navarre and Aragon During the Reign of Joan II: 1441–1472

The death of Queen Blanche I (1425–1441) of Navarre in April 1441 at Santa María de Nieva (Almería) should have opened the door to the ascension of her son Charles. Nearly forty years old at the time of his mother's death, Charles was endowed with the title of Prince of Viana by his grandfather Charles III (1387–1425) of Navarre. While the queen's testament left the kingdom and all other possessions to Charles, it also stipulated that the prince should assume the title of king only with the kind consent and blessing of his father King Joan. The queen's testament went on to declare that if Charles died without any descendants, her daughter Blanche would inherit, and absent these conditions, her daughter Leonor and her descendants would inherit Navarre. While King Joan did name Charles as his deputy in Navarre, he maintained the title of king for himself and continued to control the finances of the realm, which effectively deprived the Prince of Viana of meaningful control.

The rift between father and son escalated from 1445 through 1449 as Joan used the *Cortes* of Navarre to fund his own interests. These efforts denied the rights of Charles and deprived him of the funds needed for his own regime. As the rift widened, support of the powerful families of Navarre, began to choose sides. The family of Jean of Beaumont and his partisans, the *beaumonteses,* sided with Charles. The Gramont family, the *agramonteses,* sided with Joan II. The most combative member of this group and the strongest ally of the king was Pierres de Peralta. The feuds between these two groups, that had been rivals and enemies with each other for years, exploded into a civil conflict that compounded the quarrel between father and son and precipitated the prince's self-exile into Guipúzcoa in July 1450. The following year, Joan launched an offensive against the rebellion that led to the incarceration of Charles from 1451 to 1453. Two years later, the *beaumonteses* again rose up in favor of Charles, which prompted Joan to disinherit his son and install his daughter Leonor, the wife of Gaston de Foix, as his deputy and heiress, although Queen Blanche's testament gave Joan no authority to do so. A *Cortes* at Estella officially recognized Leonor as heiress in 1457.

Meanwhile the death of Alfonso V of Aragon, "the Magnanimous," without leaving any legitimate children, complicated the inheritance of the Prince Charles of Viana all the more. Joan II succeeded his brother Alfonso as the rightful heir to Aragon in July 1458 at the age of sixty. However instead of recognizing Charles as his primogenital heir, the king named his son Fernando as his successor. Fernando was born in 1452 to Joan's second wife Juana Enríquez. The young Fernando would not only inherit Aragon after the death of Joan, but he would later marry Isabel of Castile. Together they would be recognized as the Catholic Monarchs.

Charles openly contested his father's decision in Barcelona, and consequently, he was again forceably detained, which gave the anti–Joan partisans of Catalonia a reason to revolt. The aristocratic groups, dissatisfied with the governance of Joan during the time that he served as his brother's deputy, judged that the detention was arbitrary. They now had an excuse to detonate their revolution. Joan disregarded the complaints lodged against him, and consequently, the *Consell del Principado* that convened on February 7, 1461, proclaimed Charles of Viana as heir to Catalonia. Menaced by insurrection and pressured to capitulate, Joan declared the liberation of his son on February 25. The *Capitulación de Villafranca del Penedés* of June 1461 prevented Joan from entering the territory of Catalonia without prior authorization. Furthermore, the agreement recognized Charles as Joan's irrevocable deputy in Catalonia and, as a default, Joan's young son Fernando (Valdeón *Trastámaras* 240). The death of Charles of Viana on September 23, 1461, from a pulmonary disease nullified this nomination. Two months later, Fernando at age nine was recognized as heir to the crown of Aragon.

The insurrection burgeoned into civil war the following year as the *Consell del Principado* voted on March 5, 1462, to raise an army to defend against the farmers of the *remença* (Catalan serfdom), who objected to the abuse that their overlords were inflicting on them. Meanwhile, civil disorder in Barcelona induced Juana Enríquez and Fernando to flee to the safety of Girona. The civil war in Catalonia separated two opposing political convictions. On one hand, the nobles and the wealthy, known as the *Biga,* promoted a constitutional oligarchy. On the other hand, the merchants, craftsmen, guildsmen, and the country farmers, known as the *Busca,* supported a strong monarchy. The army of the *Consell* lay siege to Girona where Queen Juana and Fernando were sheltered. To counter this attack, Joan II aligned with Louis XI of France. In exchange for French military support, Joan mortgaged the sovereign rights to Rosellón and Cerdaña until the army's expenses were repaid. A relief force of French mercenaries arrived at Girona to rescue the queen and her son from a six-month siege.

In the early summer of 1462, Joan violated the agreement of Villafranca by entering Catalonia and occupying Balaguer and then moving on to defeat rebel forces at Rubinat. This violation prompted the *Consell* to petition Enrique IV of Castile for military aid, and later that summer, Catalonia deposed Joan II and recognized Enrique as their sovereign. On September 12, Joan initiated a siege of Barcelona with the assistance of French mercenaries, but the effort failed after a few weeks in the face of staunch resistance from the city. In April of the following year, Louis XI persuaded Enrique to renounce his planned annexation of Catalonia in exchange for sovereignty over the territories around Estella in Navarre. The pacification of Navarre followed in September 1464 when Jean de Beaumont, the leader of the Navarrese group that had supported Charles of Viana, became dissatisfied with the politics of the rebels in Catalonia and came over to the side of Joan II. His pact with Joan II marked the end of the *beaumonteses* opposition in Navarre.

For the remainder of the decade, the aging Joan II, enabled by the funding provided to him by the *Cortes* of Aragon, relentlessly overcame rebellious locations one at a time. Realizing the futility of their cause and the devastation to the economy, the aristocracy returned to the king's allegiance. By 1472, only Barcelona remained as the last holdout of the rebellion. Barcelona finally yielded to a royalist siege on October 16, 1472, concluding a civil war of more than ten years (Valdeón *Trastámaras* 248–55). Yet as the war ended, Rosellon and Cerdaña were still mortgaged to France; Joan II had not repaid the expenses of the French troops enlisted earlier in the conflict.

Portugal Under Duarte (1433–1438) and Afonso V (1438…1481)

João I (1385–1433) of Portugal rose to power after the death of his half-brother, Fernando I (1367–1383). João repelled the invading forces of Juan I of Castile in 1384 and subsequently routed Juan's invasion at Aljubarrota in August of the following year. João's recognition as king established a new dynasty, the House of Avis, that promoted legal scholars, bureaucrats, and lesser nobles within its administrative structure. Furthermore, the new king endowed his sons with positions of wealth and authority. His son Pedro was named as Duke of Coimbra, and Enrique (Henry, the Navigator) became the Duke of Viseu in addition to accepting the master of Cristo, the richest of the orders. Son João was appointed as master of the wealthy religious Order of Santiago, while son Fernando rose as the master of Avis. His administration, staffed with loyal functionaries, and his sons, endowed with wealth and military strength, served as a counterbalance to the landed nobility, who although few, commanded wealth and power through the ownership of the great estates (Oliveira 128–30).

Later in his reign, João searched for economic opportunity beyond his borders, and accordingly, attacked and conquered Ceuta in 1415. Nonetheless, Portuguese plans for additional conquests lay dormant until after his death in 1433, when Duarte inherited the Portuguese crown and renewed his father's territorial ambitions for Africa. Infante Fernando proposed an assault on Tangiers to gain control of the Strait of Gibraltar, but brothers João and Pedro expressed opposition due to the costs and dangers. Nevertheless, Duarte consented to the project, and in August of 1437, Enrique and Fernando set sail from Lisbon to Ceuta. Their westward advance overland from the city was cut off by the Africans on October 6, and the Portuguese were forced to surrender. Their petition for terms permitted their departure by leaving Fernando, the master of Avis, as a hostage to be released only on the surrender of Ceuta to the Muslims. The surrender of Ceuta was considered as an alternative to a second military expedition, but the decision was not yet finalized when Duarte fell victim to the plague the following year on September 9, 1438. Ceuta remained under Portuguese control, and Fernando died in captivity eleven years later.

The crown of Portugal was inherited by Duarte's six-year-old son Afonso V (1438...1381) under the regency of his mother Leonor, Infanta of Aragon and sister to Alfonso V of Aragon. Pedro, the Duke of Coimbra, and his brother João, the master of Santiago, opposed the regency of Leonor, and in the *Cortes* of 1438 proposed to share the regency with the queen. The proposal was supported by Lisbon and other major cities but was opposed by Afonso, the powerful count of Barcelos and bastard son of João I. The following year in the absence of the queen and Count Barcelos, Infante Enrique, Duke of Viseu, proposed a compromise to allow the queen to retain guardianship of her son and control of the finances. Furthermore, the proposal offered Pedro the responsibility for the defense of the realm. In rejection of shared control, the *Cortes*, instead, recognized Pedro as the sole regent. Count Afonso's opposition to Pedro as regent persisted until he was rewarded with the title of Duke of Bragança in 1442. Meanwhile with her own security at risk, Queen Leonor exiled herself to Castile where she died in 1445 (O'Callaghan *History* 566).

Afonso became of age in January 1446 and asked his uncle Pedro to continue governing the realm. Further, the young king married Isabel of Coimbra, the daughter of uncle Pedro. However, Duke Afonso of Bragança was not yet finished. He continued in a role as chief royal counselor to the king and used that position to strengthen his influence to the detriment of Pedro, whose supporters and friends were removed from important governmental positions. The Duke of Bragança began spreading damaging rumors against Pedro, even alleging that Pedro had poisoned his brother King Duarte. With the loss of authority, Pedro was resigned to rebellion. In an armed confrontation against the king's allies, Pedro was defeated and killed at Alfarrobeira in 1449 along with most of his followers (Oliveira 131–2). This event elevated the Bragança family to the highest rank of Portuguese nobility with the lands, titles, and favors that they obtained as rewards for themselves and their friends.

The papal call for crusades against the Turks after the fall of Constantinople in 1453 induced Afonso V to attack the Muslims closer to Portugal. He and his uncle Enrique the Navigator set sail from Setúbal in September 1458 to attack Alcácer Seguir on the west coast of Africa. The Portuguese landed successfully on October 21 and scaled the city walls, forcing a same-day surrender. The king of Fez attempted two subsequent assaults to recover his losses but was driven back. Alcácer Sequir was the second victorious conquest of the Portuguese in Morocco after Ceuta (O'Callaghan *History* 569). Tangiers was captured two years later, only to be lost, regained, and lost. It proved to be too difficult to hold. In 1471, the king renewed his African exploits by capturing Ariza and then re-captured Tangiers for good. Afonso's hard-won victories earned him the sobriquet of "Afonso the African."

In the interim, Enrique the Navigator pursued the exploration of the African coast, including the Canary Islands, Madeira, and others until his death on November 1460. Afterwards, Afonso postponed the quest for exploration and devoted the remainder of his reign to competing for the crown of Castile (more in the following section).

Isabel and Fernando Struggle for Unity and Pacification: 1474–1479

Isabel's ascension to the throne of Castile after the death of her half-brother Enrique IV in December 1474 failed to achieve complete acceptance. She immediately proclaimed herself queen of Castile, and two weeks later on December 27, 1474, in Segovia, the proclamation was formalized before a confederation of her supporters, including Diego Hurtado de Mendoza, Admiral Alonso Enríquez, the Count of Benevente, Beltrán de la Cueva, and others. An overwhelming majority of noble houses and major cities supported her as a means of achieving peace in Castile. Nevertheless, formidable opponents rallied around the cause of Enrique IV's daughter of dubious parentage, Juana *la Beltraneja*. Her supporters included the Marquis Diego López Pacheco of Villena, the Stúñiga family, and their partisans. Furthermore, pockets of support for Juana persisted in important cities such as Burgos and Madrid (Palenzuela 783). The realm was now divided between those who supported Juana's claims and those who rallied behind Isabel and her husband Fernando.

Pacheco, the Marquis of Villena, proposed Juana's betrothal to Afonso V of Portugal. King Afonso viewed this proposal as an opportunity to expand his authority into Castile and, at the same time, to eliminate the dynastic threat of the union between Castile and Aragon. Afonso hastened to Palencia in May 1475 to meet his thirteen-year-old niece, Juana, and to celebrate their marriage on the twenty-ninth. The following day Juana announced that she was the legitimate heiress of her father Enrique IV, and Afonso claimed his rights to the crown of Castile on her behalf. Their supporters in Palencia recognized them as the monarchs of Castile. Meanwhile, Portuguese troops crossed into Estremadura and advanced toward the Duero. They were well received at Arévalo, Toro, and Zamora where support for the cause of Juana prevailed. In the fall, the Portuguese army, assisted by Castilian partisans of Juana, the Archbishop Carrillo and the count of Ureña, took Baltanás on September 18, 1475, on the way to control Burgos, where an uprising favored their cause. In a sudden reversal, however, the Portuguese monarch aborted his advance and returned to Arévalo, apparently from fear of being cut off from Portugal and his allies to the west. In January 1476, both Burgos and Madrid accepted Isabel and Fernando, while Zamora remained in contest. On March 1, the Castilian army under the command of Fernando pursued Afonso V on the way to Toro and bested the Portuguese invaders, sending them in flight to Castronuño and dashing Afonso's aspiration for the crown of Castile. Zamora fell to the Castilians on March 19 (Palenzuela 783).

The next month in April, a *Cortes* was convened at Madrigal de las Altas Torres, the queen's birthplace, for the purpose of presenting a plan for the pacification and ordering of the kingdom. An essential component of the monarchs' plan was the re-creation of the *Hermandad General*, a general brotherhood, that was intended to exact rapid justice on a local level while it operated under the auspices of the monarchy. Additionally, the *Ordenamiento de Madrigal* of April 19, 1476, set forth the details of a procedure for the judicial ordering of the realm (San Miguel 105). The ordinance addressed the re-establishment of public order and lay down the guidelines for royal power. This political mission became known as the "New Monarchy."

During the first two years of their reign, Isabel and Fernando competed for unification in the northern half of their kingdom. Military operations continued to snuff out pockets of resistance to their authority. In the following two years, the monarchs effected the unification of Estremadura and Andalucia, where they campaigned to negotiate and pacify unruly elements of the nobility, who had obstructed public peace for decades. While at Seville, Isabel gave birth on June 30, 1478, to her son Juan, named after both of his grandfathers. Juan's birth assured the realm of a male heir.

After his defeat at Toro, Afonso V of Portugal travelled to France in September 1476 to petition Louis XI to intervene on behalf of Juana's cause. Failing both in his battle for Castile and in his solicitation for French assistance, he informed his son João (1477...1495), who had been acting as his regent in the interim, that he intended to go on a pilgrimage and enter religious life. He effectively abdicated his reign to his reluctant son. In a turnabout of intentions, Afonso returned to Portugal on November 20, 1478, just five days after his son had been crowned (Edwards 33–4). As an additional disgrace, Afonso's marriage to his niece Juana had been declared illegitimate by Pope Sixtus IV. Juana chose to spend her remaining days in the convent of Santa Clara in Coimbra until her death in 1530. Afonso returned to the throne but soon delegated his duties to his son and retired to the monastery of Sintra where he died in 1481.

With the crown of Portugal in a weakened state and with the monarchs of Castile on a rise, Isabel and her aunt Beatriz of Bragança met in Alcántara in March of 1479 to initiate negotiations for peace. Direct discussions through the spring and summer of that year led to the accords of Alcaçobas and Trujillo the following September (San Miguel 143). These agreements ended the Portuguese claims on the crown of Castile and confirmed the existing boundaries between Portugal and Castile.

The aging Joan II of Aragon died on January 19, 1479, at the age of eighty after experiencing a severe illness for several weeks. Joan left the kingdom of Aragon along with Valencia, Catalonia, Majorca, Sardinia, and Sicily to his son, who ascended as Fernando II of Aragon in addition to holding the title of Fernando V of Castile with his spouse, Queen Isabel. Moreover, Joan's death returned control of Navarre to his wife's rightful heirs. Following his wife's death in 1441, Joan refused to grant the title of king or queen to her children. He maintained the title of king for himself and permitted his son Prince Charles of Viana and subsequently his daughter Leonor to rule, in turn, as his deputy. His unfortunate daughter Blanche was denied this recognition and was assassinated on December 2, 1464, by partisans of her sister Leonor. With the passing of Joan II, Leonor claimed the crown of Navarre, but she outlived her father by less than a month, expiring on February 12. Leonor's testament left the kingdom to her eleven-year-old grandson Francisco Febo (1479–1483). The withdrawal of Afonso V of Portugal from active governance and the (second) formal coronation of his son João in 1481 set a new stage for the peninsula, and the Catholic Monarchs, Isabel and Fernando, were poised to spearhead a new approach in its history.

CHAPTER 12

The Catholic Monarchs and the Conquest of Granada: 1480–1492

A New Order in Iberia and an Escalation of War with Granada: 1480–1486

The first half of the decade of the 1480's heralded a new order for the Iberian Peninsula. Isabel and Fernando were now the monarchs of an expanded realm that included both Castile and the crown of Aragon. To solidify the pacification of Castile that they struggled to realize in recent years, the monarchs convened the *Cortes* of Toledo in 1480 to restore power to the crown of Castile and to reorganize the administration of justice. The *Ordenamiento de las Cortes de Toledo* established two objectives: (1) to reform the administration of justice and (2) to specify the elements of legislation necessary for a "New Monarchy." Under a major provision of the Ordinance, the *Consejo Real* or Royal Council, whose members were appointed by the monarchs, served as the administrative arm of the monarchy. This provision placed control of the legal system in the hands of the crown and reduced the influence of the nobility. Elsewhere in the peninsula, Afonso V of Portugal, whose influence and prestige had been destroyed in his defeat at Toro at the hands of Fernando V, died in 1481. His son João II (1477...1495) created a more congenial relationship with Castile. In Navarre, the boy-king Francisco Febo (1479–1483) died on January 29, 1483, leaving the crown in the hands of his sister Catherine I (1483–1518). The influence of France over the crown of Navarre abated with the death of Louis XI on August 30 of that same year. The passing of the young king of Navarre presented an opportunity to unite Navarre and Castile through the marriage of Prince Juan of Castile, born in 1478, to Catherine of Navarre, born in 1468. Marriage negotiations between Queen Isabel and Cardinal Pedro de Foix at Santo Domingo de la Calzada through the summer months of 1483 proved to be unsuccessful. The fate of Navarre remained tenuous.

As for Granada, the Castilian monarchs had been at peace with the Nasrid kingdom for several years. During the Castilian monarchs' preoccupation with the pacification of their own realm, the queen had signed a truce with Emir Abu l-Hasan Ali (1464...1485), known to the Castilians as "Muley Hacén," in 1475 and extended it in 1476 for another five years. Despite the truces, local violence continued. The Marquis of Cádiz captured Garciago in 1477, and the Granadans responded by taking Cieza (Murcia), each resulting in deaths and captured prisoners (Edwards 101). On January 17, 1478, the monarchs signed a new treaty with Abu l-Hasan for a period of three years. However, the new decade engendered a new policy. Following the fall of Otranto on the southeast coast of Italy to the Muslims in 1480, the pope proclaimed new indulgences for a Crusade. Consistent with this initiative, the monarchs envisioned their own plan for the conquest of the Nasrid kingdom. However, the Nasrid emir acted first. In the final days of 1481, as the peace agreement was coming to an end, the Muslims attacked and captured the fortress of Zahara. This loss was particularly painful to Fernando, because that location had been conquered in 1410 by his grandfather Fernando I of Aragon, *el de Antequera*. Abu l-Hasan's opening volley at Zahara marked the beginning of the end for the kingdom of Granada.

Without delay, Fernando initiated military preparations by installing the knights of Santiago under Alfonso de Cárdenas at Ecija and the Order of Calatrava under Rodrigo Tellez Girón at Jaén. He also alerted the guardians of the southern frontier, the Duke of Medina-Sidonia, the Marquis of Cádiz, the Lord of Aguilar, and the Count of Cabra, to prepare for war. Under his own initiative, Rodrigo Ponce de León, the Marquis of Cádiz, repaid the loss of Zahara with the conquest of Alhama that was strategically placed between Ronda, Málaga, and Granada. In the night hours between February 27–28, 1482, Rodrigo's men scaled the walls of that elevated fortress, previously thought to be impregnable, and overcame an inattentive guard. The gates were opened to permit access to the marquis and his men, and the Christians commandeered the inner citadel. Abu l-Hasan immediately launched a counterattack and lay siege to his former stronghold. Fortunately for the Christians, messengers had been dispatched to summon a relief force. The first few to arrive were driven back, but the arrival of a larger force, including the Duke of Medina-Sidonia, the Lord of Aguilar, and the Count of Cabra, succeeded in temporarily beating off the forces of the emir, who made two additional but futile attempts to recover the fortress in April and in the following August (Villapalos 151). The loss of Alhama severely damaged the prestige of Abu l-Hasan, and diverted popular sentiment in favor of his sons Muhammad, "Boabdil," and Yusuf.

In his eagerness to capitalize on the success at Alhama, Fernando hastily prepared an army for an attack on Loja, a fortress located about thirty-three miles to the west of Granada. The Castilians left Córdoba on June 1, perhaps delayed while Fernando awaited the birth of his daughter Infanta Maria on June 29. Sadly, her twin sister died two days later (Villapalos 152). Fernando's arrival at Loja met with unanticipated resistance. The town's governor Ali al-Attar was forewarned and fiercely defended his position, while Abu l-Hasan arrived with a relief force to scatter the royal army. A considerable amount of equipment and artillery were lost, and Rodrigo Téllez Girón, the master of Calatrava, was killed in the retreat (Edwards 106). Meanwhile as the battle at Loja was unfolding, Emir Abu l-Hasan faced another problem. Back in Granada, his son Abu Abd Allah Muhammad, "Boabdil," deposed the aging Nasrid emir. With the help of the Banu Sarraj, who were dissatisfied with the performance of Abu l-Hasan, Boabdil staged a bloody coup and established himself as Muhammad XII. The deposed emir and his partisans took refuge in Málaga with Muhammad, al-Zagal, the emir's brother, later to recognized as Muhammad XIII. This overthrow marked the beginning of an internecine struggle that weakened the Nasrid kingdom's unity and persisted for the duration of the conflict.

In March of 1483, the Castilian magnates of the southern frontier under the command of Alonso Cárdenas, including the Count of Cifuentes, the Marquis of Cádiz, and Alfonso de Aguilar, attempted a campaign into the Ajarquía, the fertile region to the northeast of Málaga. However, the inhabitants of the region were all on alert and rose up to surprise the Christian intruders on the night of March 22–23. The Marquis of Cádiz escaped under cover of darkness as did other leaders. The Count of Cifuentes was not as fortunate. He was captured and delivered to Abu l-Hasan in Málaga. More than two-thirds of a total force of three thousand Christians were either killed or captured.

The Muslim victory in the Ajarquía was led by Boabdil's uncle al-Zagal, Abu l-Hasan's brother. Perhaps to overshadow his uncle's military success or else to justify his ascendance, Boabdil, who then controlled Granada, Guadix, Baza, and other locations, decided to attack the Christian fortress of Lucena on the border of Córdoba, that was defended by Diego Fernández de Córdoba. Apprised of the advance of the Muslim army, Diego solicited the assistance of other near-by governors and was well prepared when the attackers arrived on April 20, 1483. Boabdil's forces were easily driven back, and as they opted to destroy the fields around Montilla and collect booty, Diego and the Count of Cabra mounted a counterattack. Boabdil's troops were scattered, and he was taken prisoner. With Boabdil in captivity in the tower of Porcuna, negotiations were opened for terms of his release. Boabdil offered to become a vassal of the Christian king and to wage war against his father, while his mother offered a sizable monetary tribute and the release of prisoners as well as Boabdil's own son as a hostage. The agreement drew the disgust of the religious jurists of Granada, who issued a *fatwa* denouncing him as a rebel against the faith. Upon his release, Boabdil set up headquarters at Guadix, since his support in Granada was now weakened, and his father had regained a majority of support in the capital city. Abu l-Hasan, debilitated with age, continued to attack the regions around Morón and Utrera but was badly beaten by the Marquis of Cádiz. Exhilarated by his success, the marquis decided to take back the castle of Zahara. This symbolic fortress returned to Christian possession on October 29, 1483 (Villapalos 154–6).

In the spring of 1484, Fernando ordered the Castilians to destroy the fields and crops in the region around Málaga to prevent supplies from reaching the city. Fernando returned to Córdoba in May to confer with his commanders and to develop a plan of attack for the remainder of the year. They agreed to target the strategic fortress of Álora on the right bank of the Guadalhorce River forty kilometers northwest of Málaga. The campaign, that included more than 5000 horsemen and foot soldiers, featured the first field hospital. The Marquis of Cádiz lay siege to the fortress on June 10 and produced a capitulation ten days later. The inhabitants were guaranteed their personal safety and were permitted to keep their belongings. Importantly, this location extended Castilian control farther into Muslim territory. The next ambitious siege targeted Setenil, an impregnable fortress that Fernando de Antequera himself had failed to conquer. The marquis lay siege to Setenil on September 6, and the constant bombardment of the fortress brought the defenders to the point of negotiation within days (Villapalos 158–60).

After the fall of Setenil, the king and queen wintered in Seville. In the final weeks of 1484, the *Ordenanzas Reales de Castilla*, the ordinances that had been commissioned in the *Cortes* of Toledo of 1480, were finalized for publication (San Miguel 178). Moreover, administrative and financing measures needed attention. From the onset of the war against Granada, the monarchs took advantage of several measures to assure its financing and support. The papal Bulls of Sixto IV in 1479 and of Innocence VIII in 1483 granted plenary indulgences and other spiritual benefits which attracted combatants from locations in western Europe. Pontifical rents were also attached to the Crusade. Finally, loans from nobles and other wealthy sources as well as tributes required of Jews and Muslims under Castilian rule contributed to the funding of the war.

Early in 1485, Muhammad, al-Zagal, intended to supplant his brother Abu l-Hasan, who was in poor health. While the latter lived on for nearly a decade, he was effectively deposed this time by his brother. Al-Zagal took command of the king's army and attacked Almería, where his nephews, Boabdil and Yusuf were stationed. Yusuf was killed, and Boabdil escaped to continue as the presumptive vassal of the Christian monarchs. During this same period, Fernando assembled knights from all sectors of his realm to stage a major offensive on Málaga by first capturing the surrounding fortresses that protected it. The king launched his campaign on April 15 at the head of 25,000 foot soldiers, 11,000 lancers, and 1,000 artillery wagons (Villapalos 162). Benamaquex was the first village to feel the pain of the Christian assault. The inhabitants who survived the attack were thrown into slavery. The cities of Coín and Cártama surrendered in quick succession and fell under Christian control. News arrived that on May 8 the Marquis of Cádiz had initiated a siege of Ronda with intense bombardments. Interrupting his march toward Málaga, the king hastened to facilitate the fall of that city. After its water supply was cut off, surrender followed two weeks later. Some of the citizens were permitted to leave with their movable goods. Others departed for North Africa, and the remaining population was subjected to serfdom as *mudéjares*, Muslims living under Castilian rule. The capture of Ronda was significant and led to the fall of smaller locations in the area without contest. The Castilian army moved in the direction of Málaga and took Marbella without the use of heavy artillery. Nevertheless, a significant loss at Mijas signaled that it was wiser to return to Córdoba rather than to attack Málaga at that time (Edwards 111).

Fernando retreated to Córdoba during the month of July to cure a fever, while the army remained in readiness in Andalucia. The Count of Cabra with his nobles from Córdoba attempted a risky assault on Moclín, about thirty kilometers from Granada and was severely punished for his effort on September 3 by al-Zagal. The Christians lost 1,000 combatants. This minor success of al-Zagal did not elevate his stature in the eyes of the Muslim populace. Once again, the partisans of Boabdil succeeded in controlling the Albaicín sector of Granada. Abu l-Hasan, weakened with illness, was now completely out of the picture and sought refuge in Almuñécar. Back in Alcalá, the queen gave birth to Catalina, the future queen of England, on December 15, 1485.

At the beginning of 1486, the Muslims of Granada were effectively in a state of civil war. One group in the Albaicín quarter of Granada rose up in favor of Boabdil, who was safely residing in Loja. The other group supported his uncle Muhammad XIII, al-Zagal. On the Christian side, Fernando strengthened the flotilla on the southern coast and ordered his army to prepare for a systematic campaign against Loja, Íllora, Moclín, Montefrío, and Colomera. His double objective was to destroy the fertile Vega of Granada and to subjugate the defensive fortresses around its perimeter. The siege of Loja began on May 21, and the Castilians prepared their artillery placements. Heavy artillery bombardment began on the twenty-eighth, and the city surrendered only a day later. Boabdil was captured once again, but Fernando forgave him on the condition that he return to the obedience of the Christians. The king was not willing to recognize Boabdil as emir but rather offered him a lordship over a reduced area consisting of Guadix, Baza, Vera, Mojácar, Vélez Blanco, and Vélez Rubio. Moreover, Boabdil was an asset in maintaining the rift in Muslim civil disputes. Baobdil's partisans in the Albaicín district welcomed him back to Granada in September 1486, and Fadrique of Toledo was sent along with him to provide military assistance against al-Zagal. After the fall of Loja, additional locations yielded to the punishment of the Castilian artillery in rapid succession. Íllora fell on June 9, 1486, and Moclín, Colomera, and Montefrío followed within days (Villapallos 164; Palenzuela 889). After the fall of Íllora, Fernando sent for Queen Isabel to come to Loja to lift the morale of the troops. The queen subsequently witnessed the fall of Moclín and Montefrío in the early summer before leaving for Galicia to address administrative abuses in that area (San Miguel 191–2).

The Fall of Málaga, Eastern Andalucia, and Granada: 1487–1492

Málaga, the economic and strategic centerpiece of the Nasrid kingdom, had remained out of the grasp of the Castilian monarchs. They had succeeded, however, in occupying numerous fortresses that protected the perimeters of both Málaga and Granada, and they had weakened the economic value of the surrounding agriculture. Further, the Nasrid kingdom was fractured by its own internecine quarrels. Málaga was ripe for the picking.

To clear a path to Málaga, Fernando targeted the city of Vélez-Málaga. Through the late winter months of 1487, he assembled a formidable army of 40,000 foot soldiers and 13,000 horsemen that departed from Córdoba in the direction of his target on April 7. As the Castilians approached Vélez-Málaga in mid–April, their artillery bogged down in the heavy spring torrents and became vulnerable to Muslim attacks. Al-Zagal had assembled an equally large but less skilled force from the militias of Guadix, Baza, Almería, Salobreña, and Almuñécar and unsuccessfully attacked the Castilians on April 25 and 26. Al-Zagal's withdrawal from the confrontation before a decisive victory could be claimed by either side, led to the capitulation of Vélez-Málaga on May 3 (Villapalos 168–9). Furthermore, al-Zagal's engagement with the Castilian army permitted Boabdil to assert his authority over Granada and install himself in the Alhambra. After Vélez, the smaller, surrounding villages surrendered without contest, and a direct path to Málaga was cleared. Al-Zagal no longer challenged the Christian advance. Rather he abandoned Málaga and sought refuge in Almería, since he could not return to Granada, which was now controlled by Boabdil.

The siege of Málaga began in early May. Fernando's army severed the distribution of food from the interior, and the flotilla of the Count of Trivento blocked the flow of supplies from the sea. In the city, Berber garrisons from North Africa encouraged a strong resistance. The Berbers and other contentious elements in the city prevented the city's governor, Hermete Zeli, from negotiating a peaceful surrender. The Christians drove the defenders into the inner castles and then began to construct earthen and timber shelters for artillery, cavalry, and infantry, which soon encircled the city (Edwards 113–5; Palenzuela 889–90). As plague broke out in the Christian camp, morale declined and desertion was prevalent. To bolster the courage of the Christians, Fernando encouraged Isabel to leave Córdoba and join the troops in the field. Life in the Christian camp was difficult, but the citizens within the city had it worse. As the siege dragged on, conditions inside Málaga grew desperate. While a more conciliatory faction of citizens offered to become subjects of the king, an uncompromising contingent remained combative. The city finally capitulated in August, and because of the prolonged resistance, favorable terms were not granted. Few were given guarantees of safe conduct. One-third of the citizens were designated for exchange of Christian captives in North Africa. The remaining captives were sold to defray the costs of the war.

As the year 1488 began, Boabdil was firmly established as the Nasrid emir of Granada yet as a presumptive vassal of the Christian king. Al-Zagal took advantage of the winter months to fortify Baza, Guadix, and Almería. Consequently, an assault on Baza by Fadrique of Toledo early in the year only resulted in a loss of men and equipment. In April, Fernando and Isabel opted to focus their attention on the submission of the eastern portion of Andalucia that had thus far been distanced from the conflict. Fernando established a base of operations at Lorca and sent the Marquis of Cádiz to attack the city of Vera that quickly fell on June 10 after only three days of resistance. Cuevas capitulated the same day, and Mojácar followed only two days later. An overwhelming show of force effected the peaceful surrender of Vélez Blanco, Vélez Rubio, Níjar, Huéscar and others. The conditions of surrender without violence permitted the citizens to practice their religion and to remain exempt from participation in the war (San Miguel 199–200). The campaign of 1488 established the occupation of the eastern regions of Andalucia. These recently subjugated locations were garrisoned under the command of Luis Fernández Portocarrero, while the Marquis of Cádiz was left in charge of the western portion of Andalucia from Málaga to Jaén. The well supplied and important fortress of Baza on the eastern front, defended by al-Zagal's brother-in-law, Yahya al-Nayyar, would be targeted the following year.

By 1489, al-Zagal and his partisans controlled Baza, Guadix, Almuñécar, Salobreña, and Almería. Boabdil still clung to Granada. His previous agreements with Fernando stipulated that he would become the vassal of the Castilian monarch in exchange for the lordship over an area in eastern Andalucia. These locations had recently been subdued by the king. Nonetheless, Boabdil was recognized by his partisans in Granada as the legitimate emir of the Nasrid kingdom. Boabdil's relationship with the Castilian king would be resolved later. For the moment, Fernando focused his attention on the conquest of Baza. During the winter months of 1488–9, he readied men and supplies in expectation of a lengthy siege. He launched his campaign from Jaén in May by neutralizing the lesser location of Zújar before encircling his primary objective in the middle of June. Al-Zagal's commander at Baza, Yahya al-Nayyar, refused to surrender and compelled Fernando to employ his artillery. Well-established supply lines maintained an extended siege of more than five months against a city that was also well-nourished. However, as winter approached, the Castilians' plight worsened as make-shift housing failed and seasonal rains deteriorated supply routes. At that point, the citizens of Baza were hopeful that their attackers would retreat for the winter, but the arrival of the queen guaranteed the continuance of provisions and ignited the morale of the Christian army (Edwards 116). Muslim hopes for the departure of the royal army were dashed, and Yahya decided to negotiate. Baza capitulated on November 28 and the final agreement of December 4 included a generous settlement for Yahya and his family. He converted to Christianity and took the name of Pedro de Granada, rising to the post of mayor of that city. The remaining great leader of the Nasrid resistance, al-Zagal, realized that his resources were depleted and that the end was near. His awareness of the generous terms given to Yahya induced him to consider terms for himself. He surrendered Almería and Guadix towards the end of December, and the rendition of Almuñécar and Salobreña followed during the first few days of 1490. Despite the generous offer of a lordship and monetary considerations, al-Zagal opted to leave for North Africa. The fall of Baza and the surrender of al-Zagal left the entire eastern front down to the coast in the hands of Castile.

While negotiations began with Boabdil for the rendition of Granada, the monarchs undertook measures to shore up the maintenance of their new possessions. They named Diego López Pacheco as lead commander in charge of the frontier, and then reinforced the coastal flotilla to prevent any intervention from North Africa. Finally, they obtained an extension of the papal Bull for the Crusade against the Muslims of the peninsula. In family matters, they had reached an agreement on March 29, 1489 with Henry VII of England for the betrothal of Infanta Catalina to Arthur, Prince of Wales. The eldest daughter of the monarchs, Infanta Isabel, married Prince Afonso of Portugal in 1490.

The monarchs now demanded the rendition of the Alhambra. Boabdil sent Abu-l-Qasim al-Mulih to negotiate terms, but stubborn partisans of resistance influenced Boabdil to hold out. On one hand, Boabdil was feigning surrender. On the other, his actions demonstrated resistance. Boabdil slipped away to occupy the coastal town of Adra, from where he could receive assistance from North Africa. In May 1490, Fernando left Seville with the intention of laying waste the Vega of Granada. Boabdil successfully attacked Alhendin, but failed to take Almuñécar or Salobreña that were defended by Christian garrisons. In September, Boabdil attempted to re-take some of the former strongholds of al-Zagal in the eastern front, but his success was aborted by the intervention of Fernando's troops. Through the winter months, Fernando prepared for an all-out siege of Granada. As he left Seville in April 1491, he rebuffed the negotiators sent by Boabdil. By April 26, the king's army was just a few miles outside of Granada. Fernando ordered not just the establishment of a camp, but the construction of a veritable city named Santa Fe. On June 8, the king ordered the destruction of the Vega, which sparked a counterattack from the Granadan cavalry, who were badly beaten. Negotiations for the surrender of Granada began in earnest in August and continued until terms were signed on November 25. Boabdil agreed to transfer the sovereignty of his domains over to the monarchs, who agreed to respect the religion and liberties of the Muslims. Local administration and commerce remained under Muslim control, but fortifications were controlled by the Christians (Edwards 117–8). During the hours after midnight of January 2, 1492, Christian forces under the command of Gutierre de Cárdenas entered the Alhambra, and Boabdil handed over the keys to the palace. The Catholic monarchs entered the city, and the pendant of King Fernando flew over the Alhambra. Boabdil later departed for North Africa. Nearly eight centuries of Muslim rule in the Iberian Peninsula had run its course, and sovereign authority was once again placed in the hands of the Christian monarchs.

Appendix I: Lists

Visigothic Rulers

Alaric I (395–410) led the sac of Rome.
Athaulf (410–415)
Sigeric (415) murdered Athaulf and was then promptly assasinated.
Wallia (415–419)
Theoderic aka Theodoric I (419–451)
Thorismund (451–453)
Theodoric II (453–466)
Euric (466–484)
Alaric II (484–507)
Gesalic (507–511)
Amalaric (511–531)
Theudis aka Theodoric III (531–548)
Theudigisel aka Theodisclus (548–549)
Agila I (549–554)
Athanagild (554–568)
Liuva I (568–573)—Septimania
Leovigild (569–586)—Iberia
Reccared I (586–601)
Liuva II (601–603)
Witteric (603–610)
Gundemar (610–612)
Sisebut (612–621)
Reccared II (621)
Suinthila (621–631)
Sisenand (631–636)
Chintila (636–639)
Tulga (639–642)
Chindasuinth (642–653)
Reccesuinth (649–672)
Wamba (672–680)
Ervig (680–687)
Egica (687–702)
Wit(t)iza (698–710)
Roderic (710–711)

Umayyad Governors, Emirs, Caliphs 632–1031

Rashidun (rightly guided) Caliphs

Abu Bakr (632–634)
Umar ibn al-Khattab (634–644)
Uthman ibn Affan (644–656)
Ali ibn Abi Talib (656–661)

Caliphs of Damascus

Muawiya I (661–680), Umayyad founder
Yazid I (680–683)
Muawiya II (683–684)
Marwan I (684–685)
Abd al-Malik (685–705)
Al-Walid I (705–715)
Sulayman (715–717)
Umar II (717–720)
Yazid II (720–724)
Hisham (724–743)
Al-Walid II (743–744)
Yazid III (744)
Ibrahim (744)
Marwan II (744–750)

Muslim Governors of al-Andalus

Musa ibn Nusayr (711–714)
Abd al-Aziz ibn Musa (714–716)

Ayyub ibn Habib al-Lakhmi (716)
Al-Hurr ibn Abd al-Rahman al Thaqafi (716–718)
Al-Samh ibn Malik al-Khawlani (718–721)
Abd al-Rahman ibn Abd Allah al-Ghafiqi (721)
Anbasa ibn Suhaym al-Kalbi (721–725)
Udhrah ibn Abd Allah al-Fihri (725–726)
Yahya ibn Salama al-Qalbi (727)
Hujefa (728) six months
Uthman ibn Abi Nasah (728) four months
Al-Haythan ibn Ubayd al-Kilabi (729–730)
Muhammad ibn Abd Allah al-Ashjai (730)
Abd al-Rahman al-Ghafiqi (730–732)
Abd al-Malik ibn Qatan al-Fihri (732–734)
Uqba ibn al-Hajjaji al-Saluli (734–740)
Abd al-Malik ibn Qatan (740–741) restored
Balj ibn Bashr al-Qushayri (741–742)
Abu al-Kattar (743–745)
Thalabah ibn Salamah aka Tawaba (746–747)
Yusuf ibn Abd al-Rahman (747–756)

Emirs of Córdoba

Abd al-Rahman I (756–788)
Hisham I (788–796)
Al-Hakam I (796–822)
Abd al-Rahman II (822–852)
Muhammad I (852–886)
Al-Mundhir (886–888)
Abd Allah ibn Muhammad (888–912)
Abd-al-Rahman III (912–929) as Emir

Caliphs of Córdoba

Abd-al-Rahman III (929–961) as Caliph
Al-Hakam II (961–976)
Hisham II al-Hakam (976–1009)
Muhammad II al-Mahdi (1009)
Sulayman ibn al-Hakam (1009–1010)
Muhammad II al-Mahdi (1010) restored
Hisham II al-Hakam (1010–1013) restored
Sulayman ibn al-Hakam (1013–1016) restored
Ali ibn Hammud (1016–1018) non Umayyad
Abd al-Rahman IV (1018)
Al-Kasim ibn Hammud (1018–1021) non Umayyad
Yahya ibn Ali ibn Hammud (1021–1023)
Al-Kasim ibn Hammud (1023) restored
Abd al-Rahman V (1023–1024)
Muhammad III (1024–1025)
Yahya ibn Ali ibn Hammud (1025–1027) restored
Hisham III (1027–1031)

Almoravid and Almohad Leaders

Almoravid Leaders

Yahya ibn Ibrahim (founder)
Yahya ibn Umar
Abu Bakr ibn Umar
Yusuf ibn Tashfin (1071–1106)
Ali ibn Yusuf (1106–1143)
Tashfin ibn Ali (1143–1145)
Ishaq ibn Ali (1145–1147)

Almohad Leaders

Muhammad ibn Tumart (1121–1130) born c. 1080
Abd al-Mumin (1130–1163)
Abu Yaqub Yusuf or Yusuf I (1163–1184)
Abu Yusuf Yaqub al-Mansur (1184–1199)

Muhammad al-Nasir (1199–1213)
Abu Yaqub Yusuf II, al-Mustansir (1213–1224)
Abu Muhammad Abd al-Wahid I al-Makhlu (1224)
Abd Allah al-Adil (1224–1227)
Yahya al-Mutasim (1227–1229)
Abu al-Ala Idris I al-Mamun (1229–1232)
Abu Muhammad Abd al-Wahid II al-Rashid (1232–1242)
Abu al-Hassan Ali al-Said (1242–1248)
Abu Hafs Umar al-Murtada (1248–1266)
Abu al-Ula (Abu Dabbus) Idris II al-Wathiq (1266–1269)

The Nasrids of Granada

The beginning and end dates for some reigns are challenged by rival claimants.

Muhammad I ibn Nasr (1238–1272)
Muhammad II al-Faqih (1273–1302)
Muhammad III (1302–1309)
Nasr (1309–1314)
Ismail I (1314–1325)
Muhammad IV (1325–1333)
Yusuf I (1333–1354)
Muhammad V (1354–1359)
Ismail II (1359–1360)
Muhammad VI (1360–1362)
Muhammad V (1362–1391) restored
Yusuf II (1391–1392)
Muhammad VII (1392–1408)
Yusuf III (1408–1417)
Muhammad VIII (1417–1419)
Muhammad IX (1419–1427)
Muhammad VIII (1427–1429) restored
Muhammad IX (1430–1431) restored
Yusuf IV (1432)
Muhammad IX (1432–1445) restored
Yusuf V (1445–1446)
Muhammad X (1446–1448)
Muhammad IX (1448–1453) restored
Muhammad XI (1453–1454)
Abu Nasr Sad (1454–1464)
Abu l-Hasan Ali, "Muley Hacén" (1464–1482)
Abu Abd Allah Muhammad XII, "Boabdil" (1482–1483)
Abu l-Hasan Ali, "Muley Hacén" (1483–1485) restored
Abu Abd Allāh Muhammad XIII, "al-Zagal" (1485–1486)
Abu Abd Allah Muhammad XII, "Boabdil" (1486–1492) restored

Appendix II: Maps

Boundaries for all maps are approximate.

Map 1: Roman Provinces.

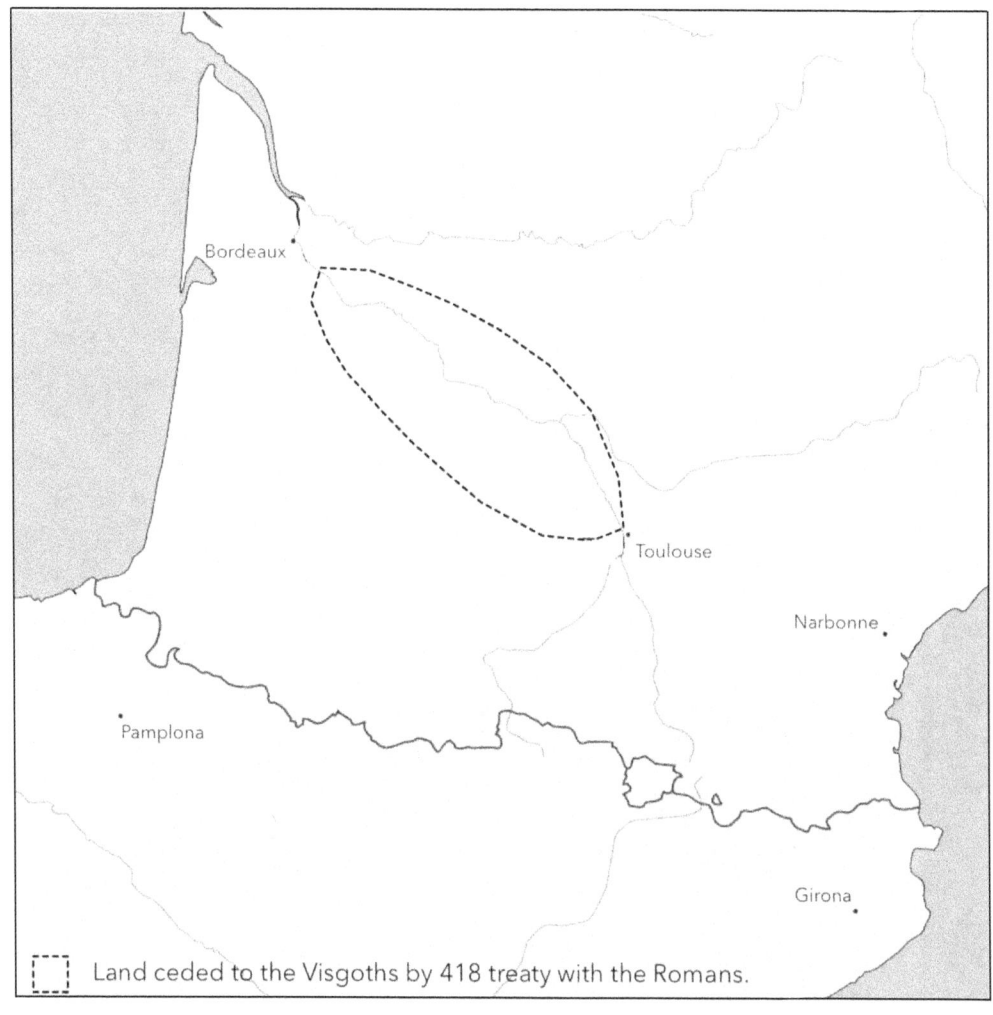

Map 2: Visigothic Settlement Between Bordeaux and Toulouse.

APPENDIX II: MAPS

Map 3: Visigothic Conquests Under Leovigild, Sisebut and Suintila.

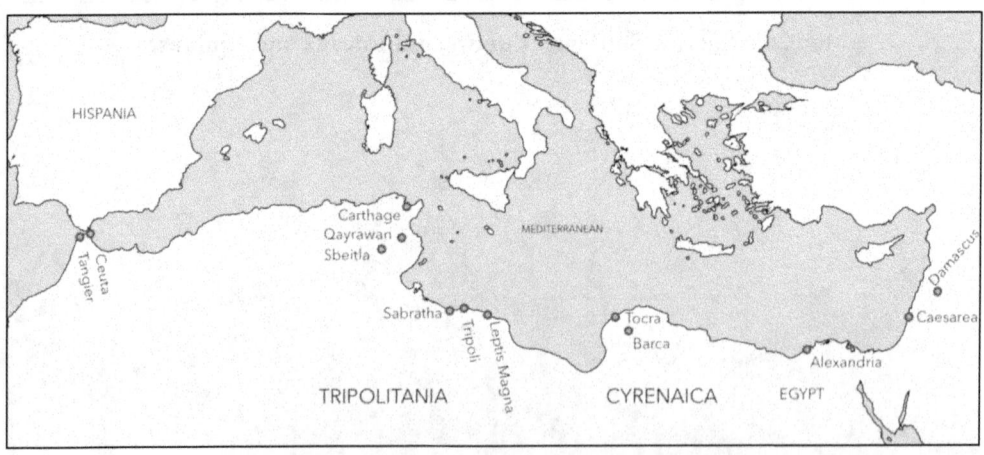

Map 4: The Muslim Conquest of North Africa.

Appendix II: Maps

Map 5: Muslim Invasion Routes in Iberia: 711–714.

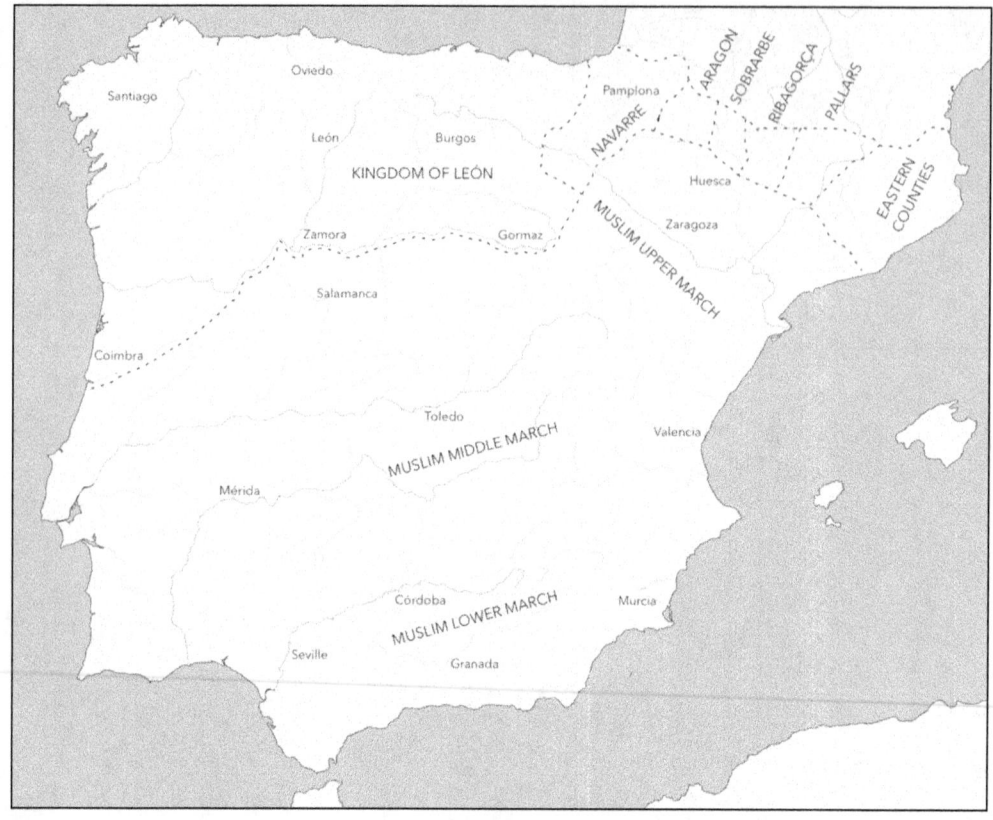

Map 6: Iberia, circa 930.

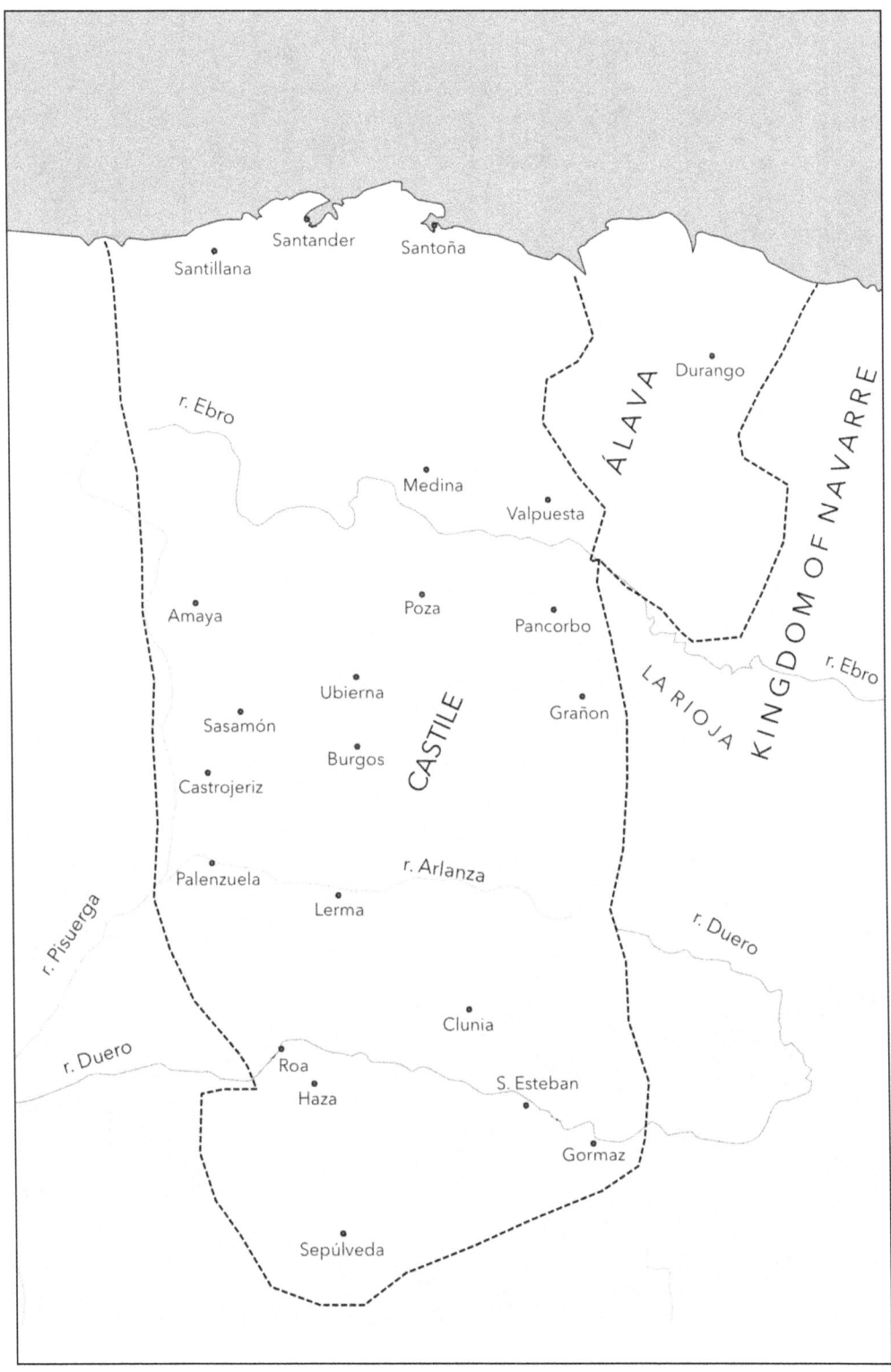

Map 7: The Early County of Castile.

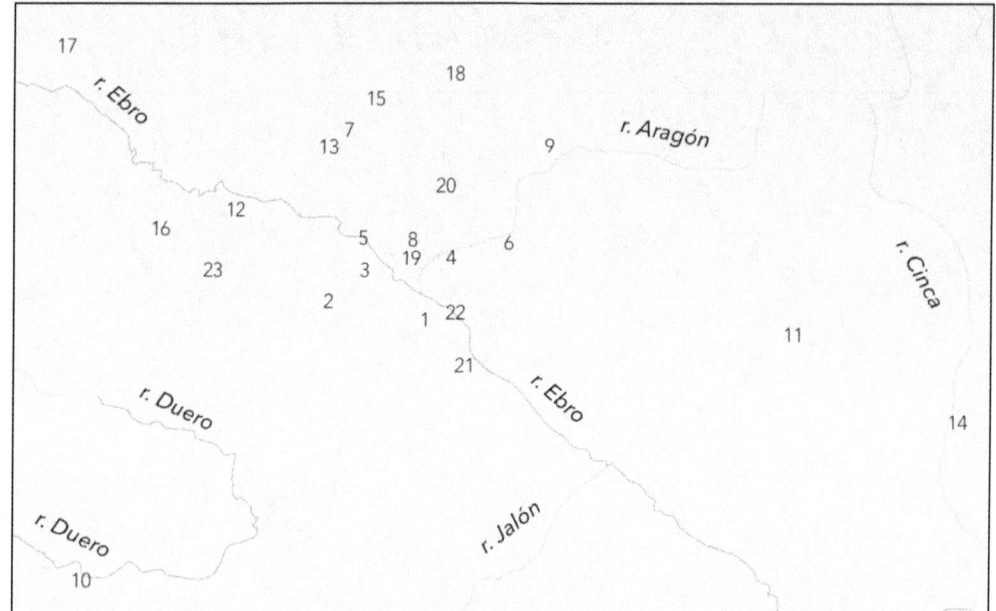

1. Alfaro; 2. Arnedo; 3.Calahorra; 4. Caparroso; 5. Cárcar; 6. Carcastillo; 7. Estella; 8. Falces; 9. Foz de Lumbier; 10. Gormaz; 11. Huesca; 12. Logroño; 13. Monjardín;14. Monzón; 15. Muez; 16. Nájera; 17. Miranda de Ebro; 18. Pamplona; 19. Peralta; 20. Tafalla; 21. Tudela; 22. Valtierra; 23. Viguera

Map 8: Locations in La Rioja.

Map 9: Christian Advances by 1076, 1086, 1157, 1230, and 1252.

Appendix III: Genealogical Charts

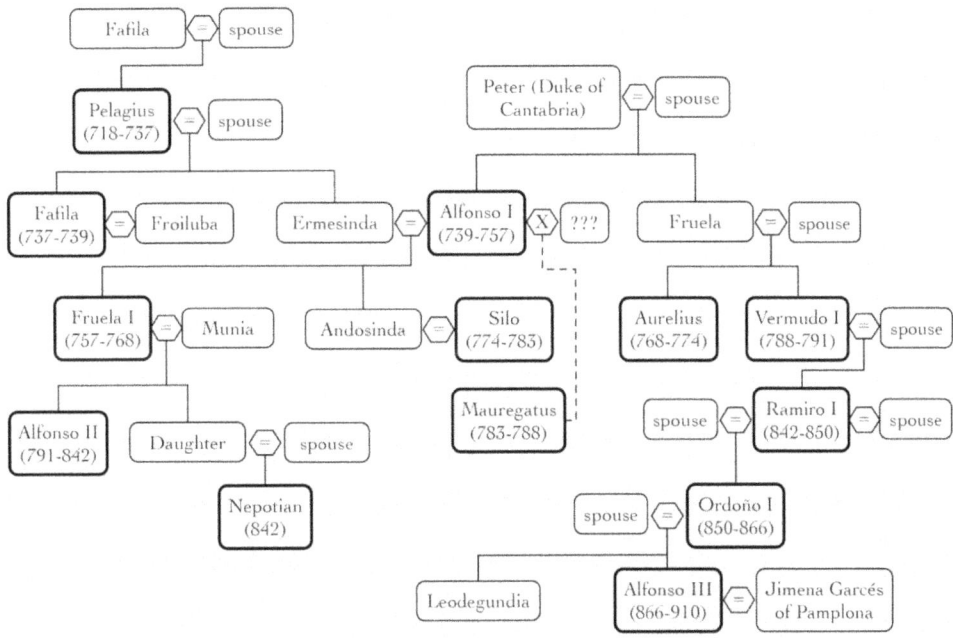

Chart 1: The Kings of Asturias: 718–910.

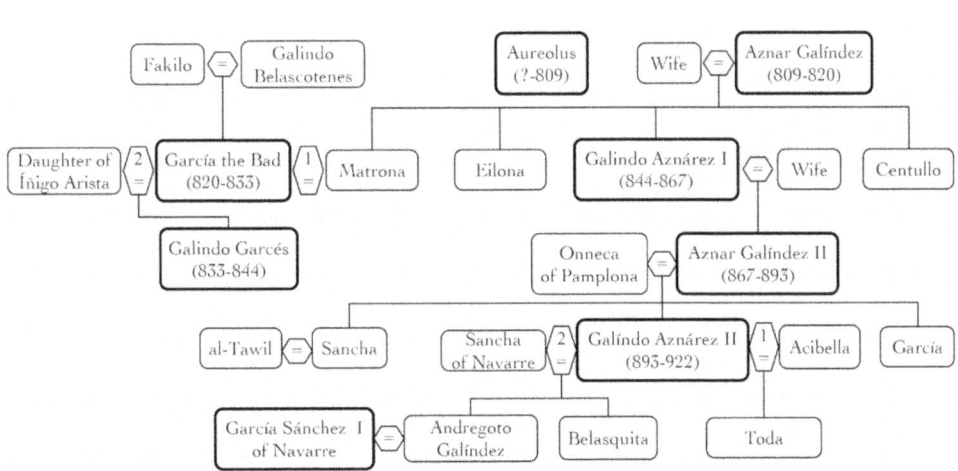

Chart 2: The Counts of Aragon: 809–922.

APPENDIX III: GENEALOGICAL CHARTS

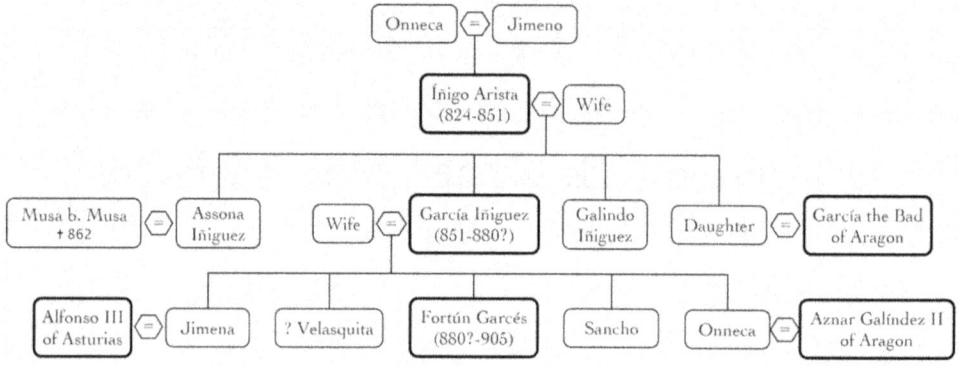

Chart 3: The Kings of Pamplona: 824–905.

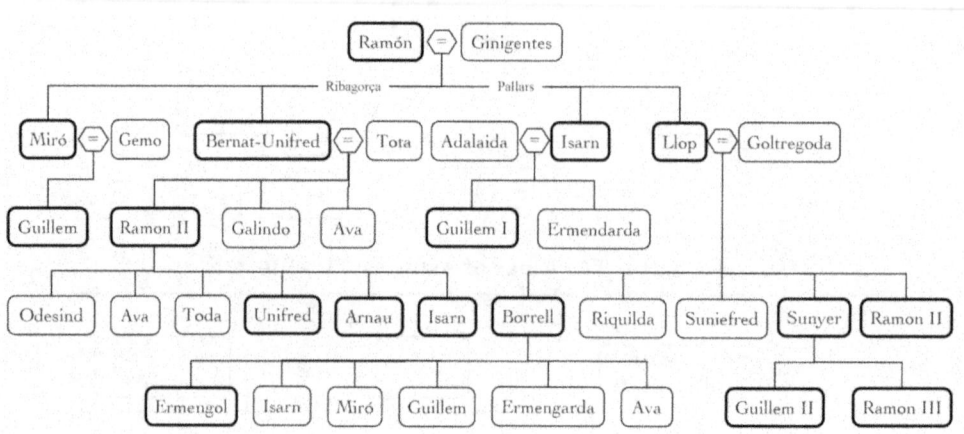

Chart 4: The Counts of Ribagorça-Pallars.

Appendix III: Genealogical Charts 213

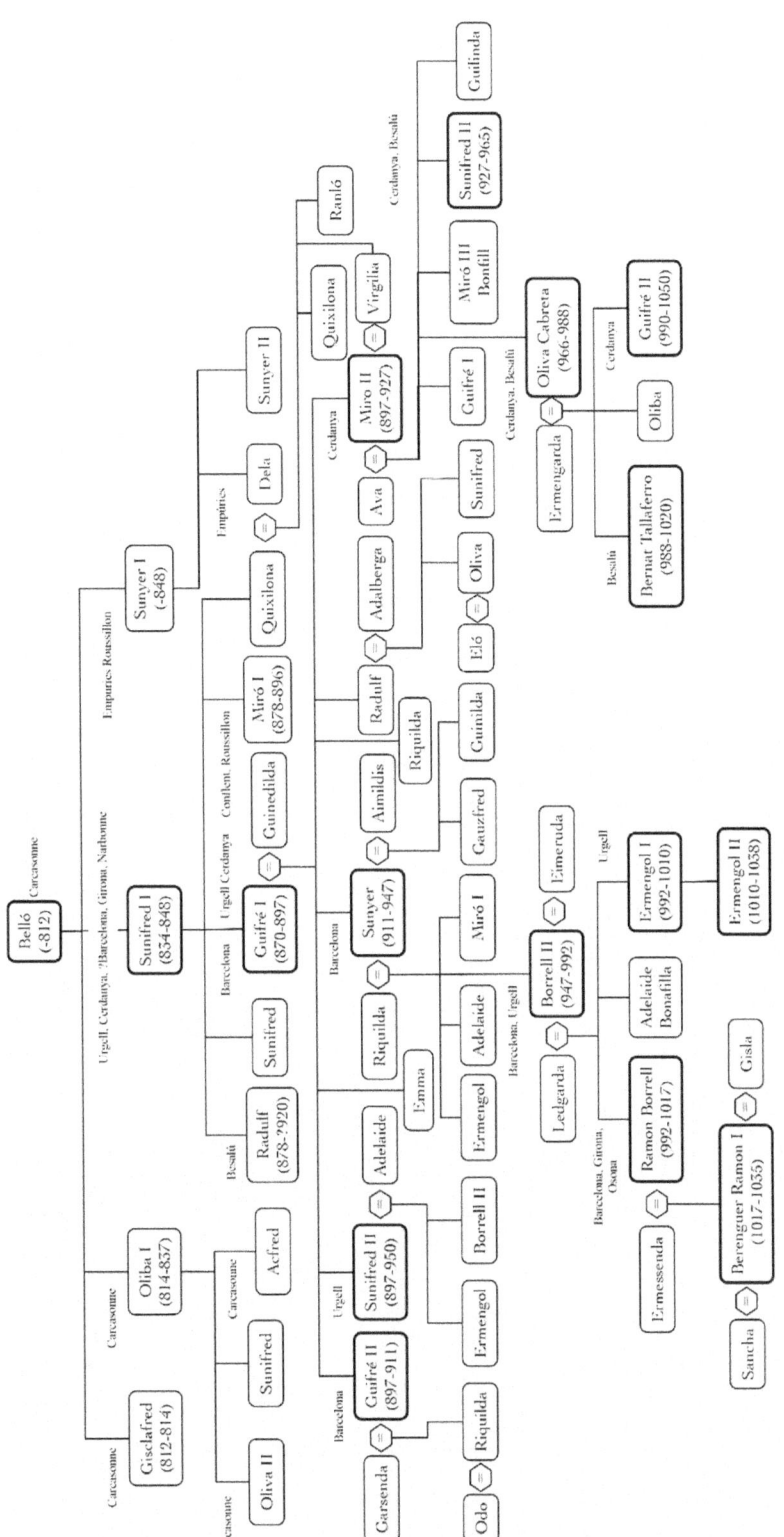

Chart 5: The Counts of the Eastern Pyrenees: 812–1038.

Appendix III: Genealogical Charts

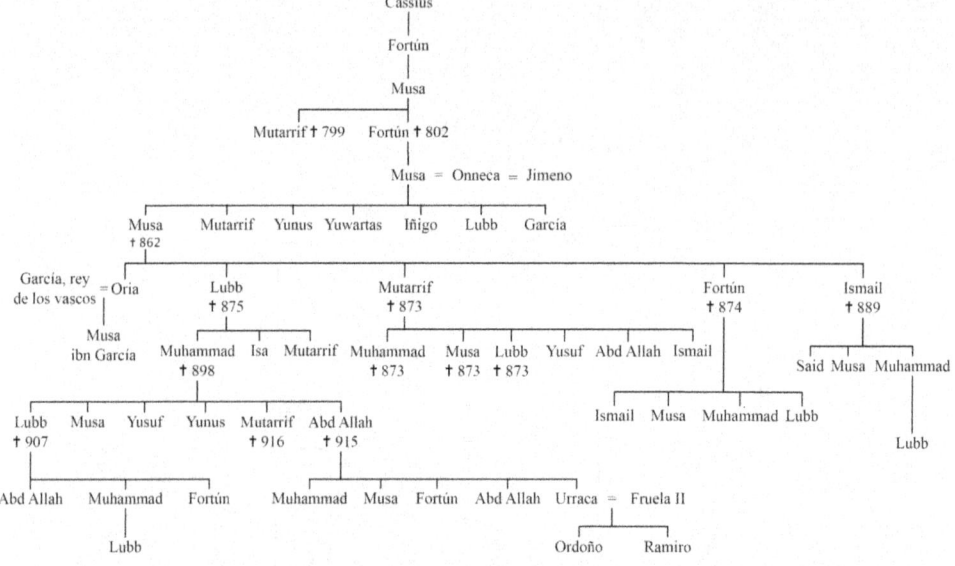

Chart 6: The Banu Qasi.

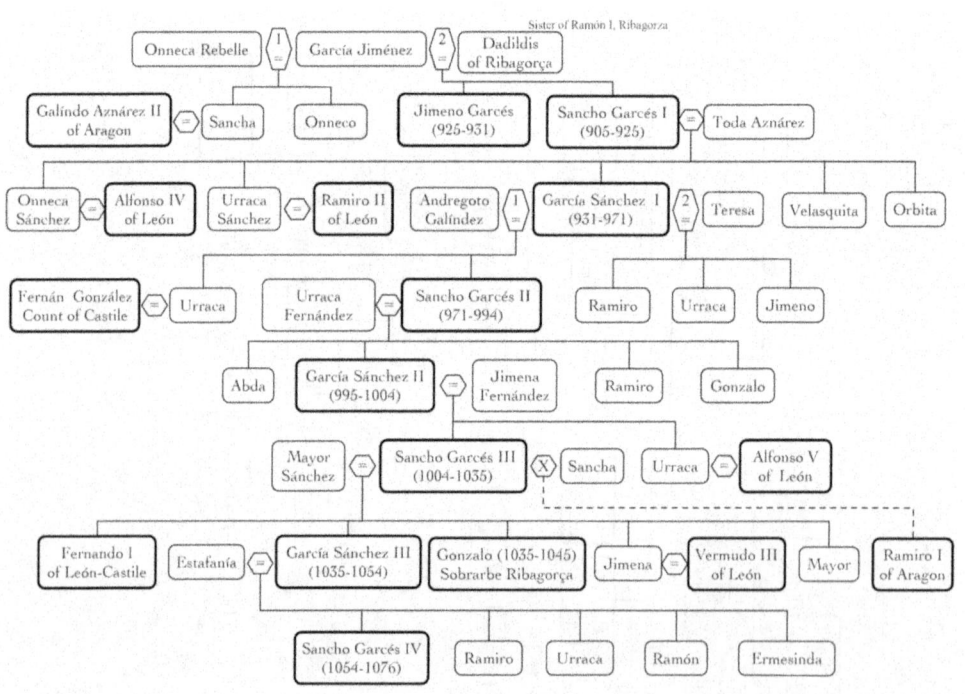

Chart 7: The Kings of Navarre: 905–1076.

Appendix III: Genealogical Charts

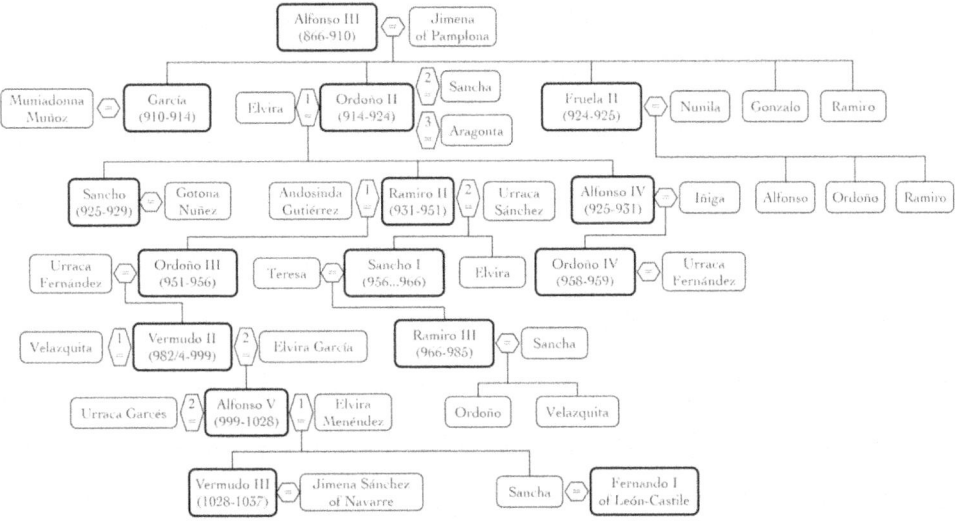

Chart 8: The Kings of León: 866–1037.

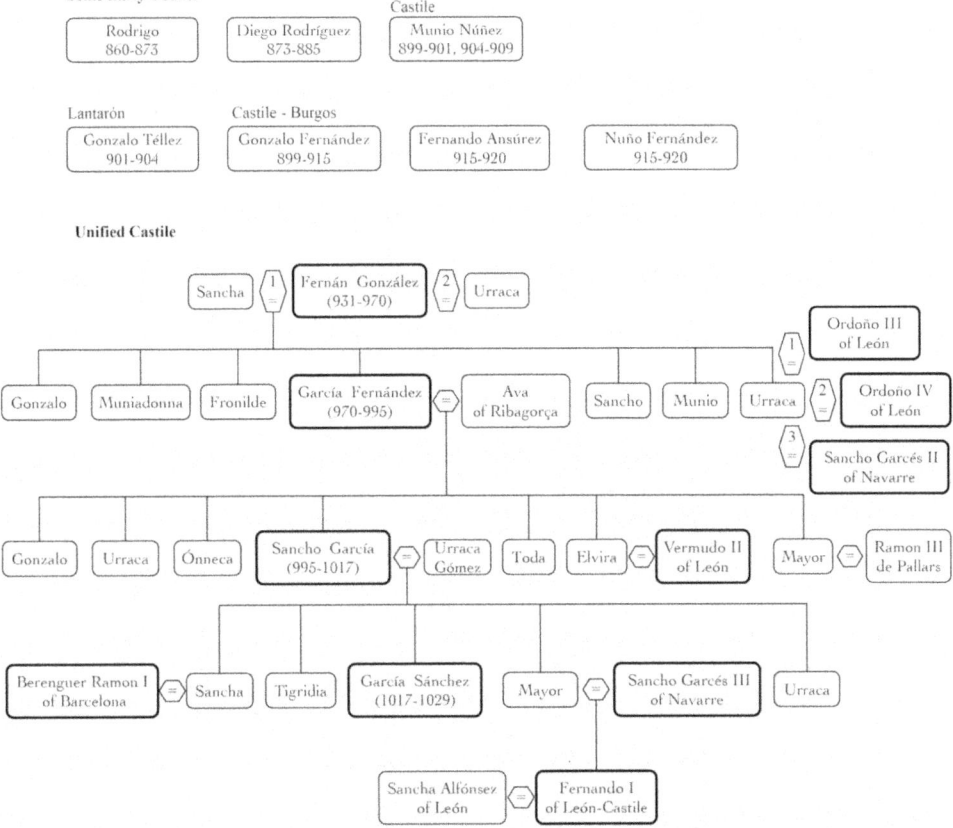

Chart 9: The Counts of Castile: 931–1037.

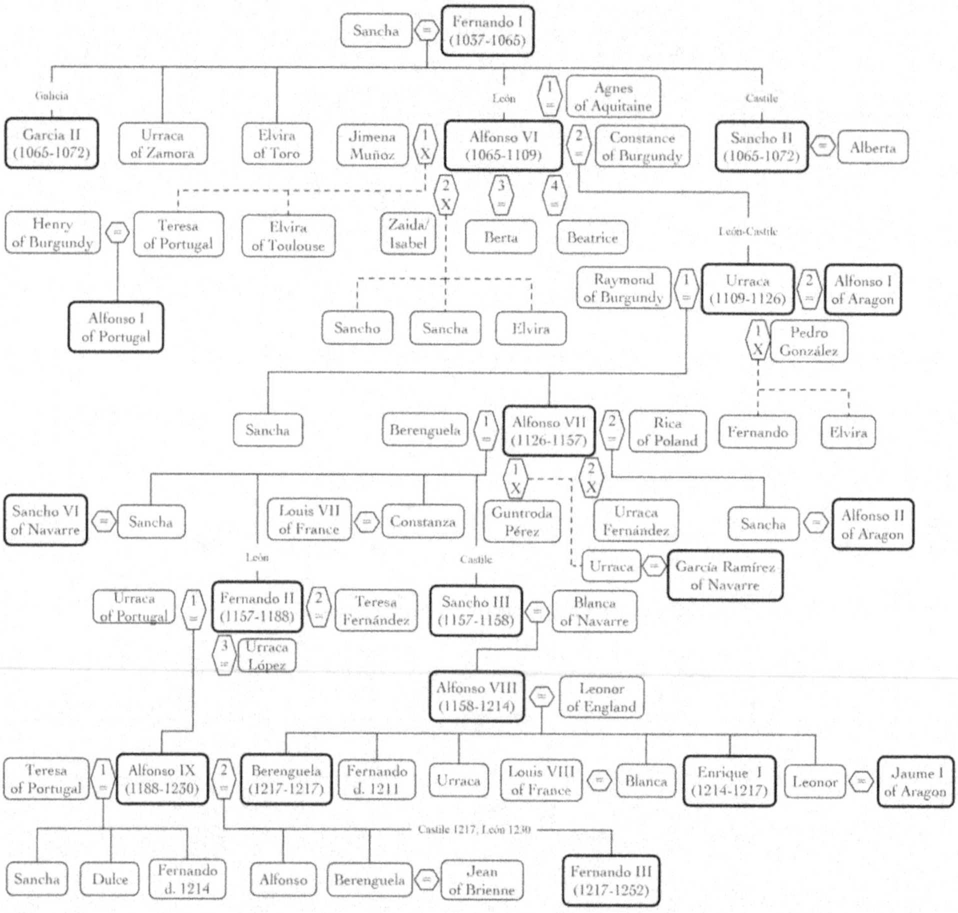

Appendix III: Genealogical Charts

Chart 10: The Kings of León-Castile: 1037–1252.

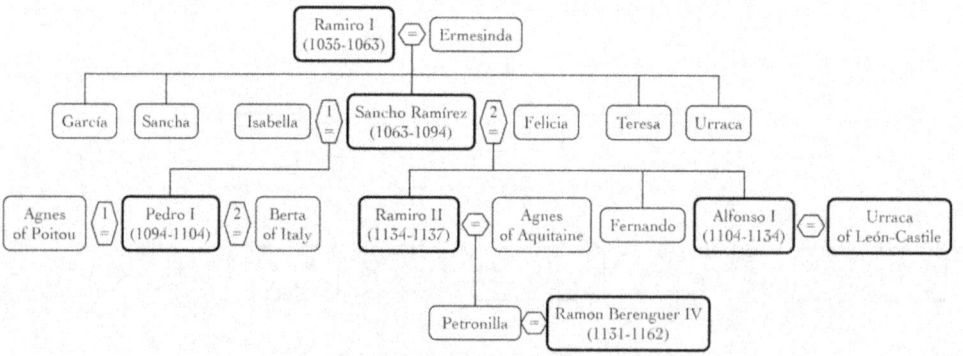

Chart 11: The Kings of Aragon: 1035–1162.

Appendix III: Genealogical Charts 217

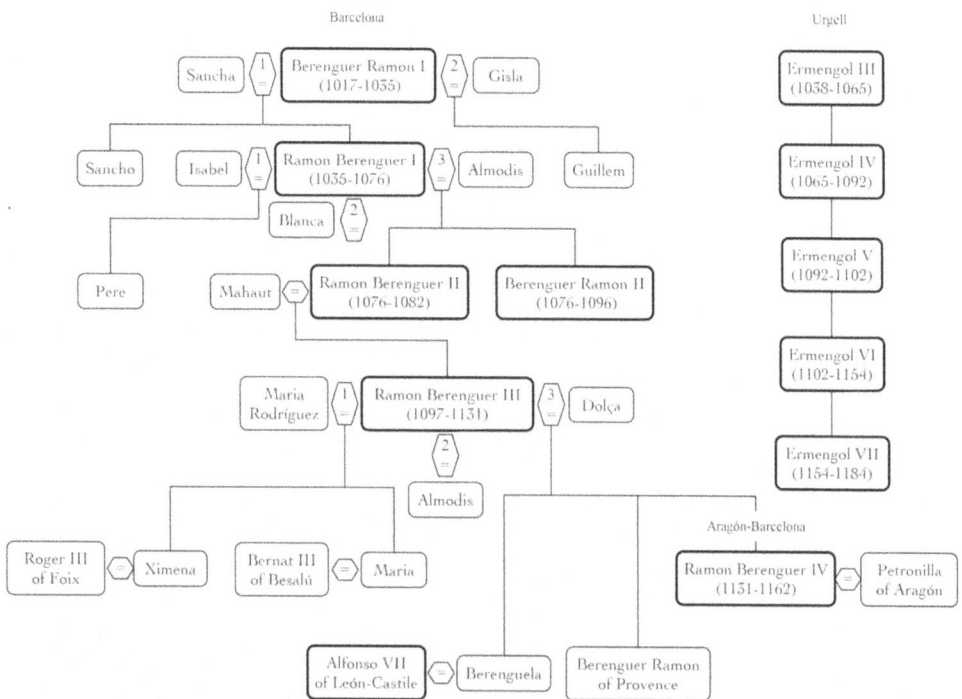

Chart 12: The Counts of the Eastern Pyrenees: 1035–1162.

Appendix III: Genealogical Charts

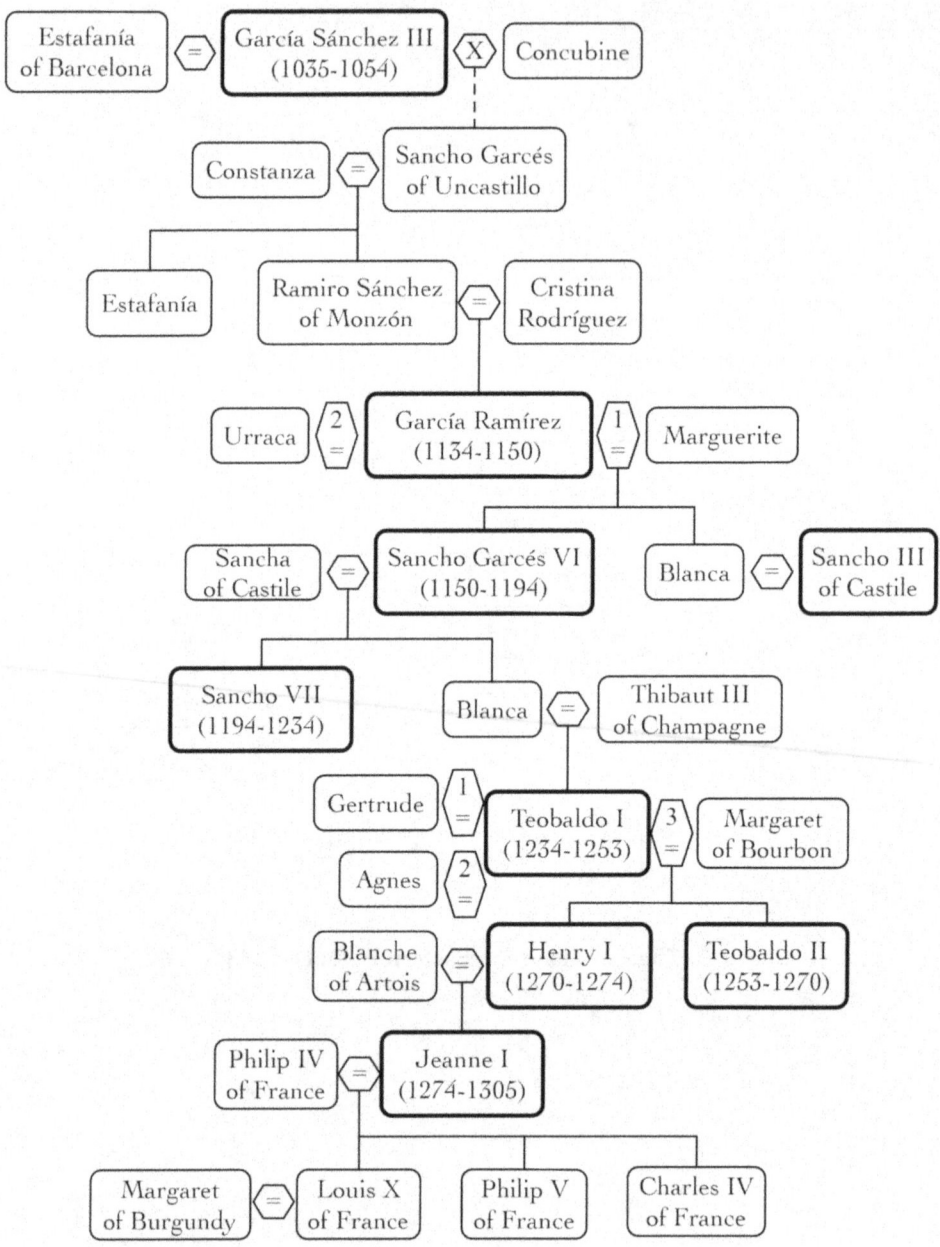

Chart 13: The Kings of Navarre Restored: 1134–1305.

Appendix III: Genealogical Charts

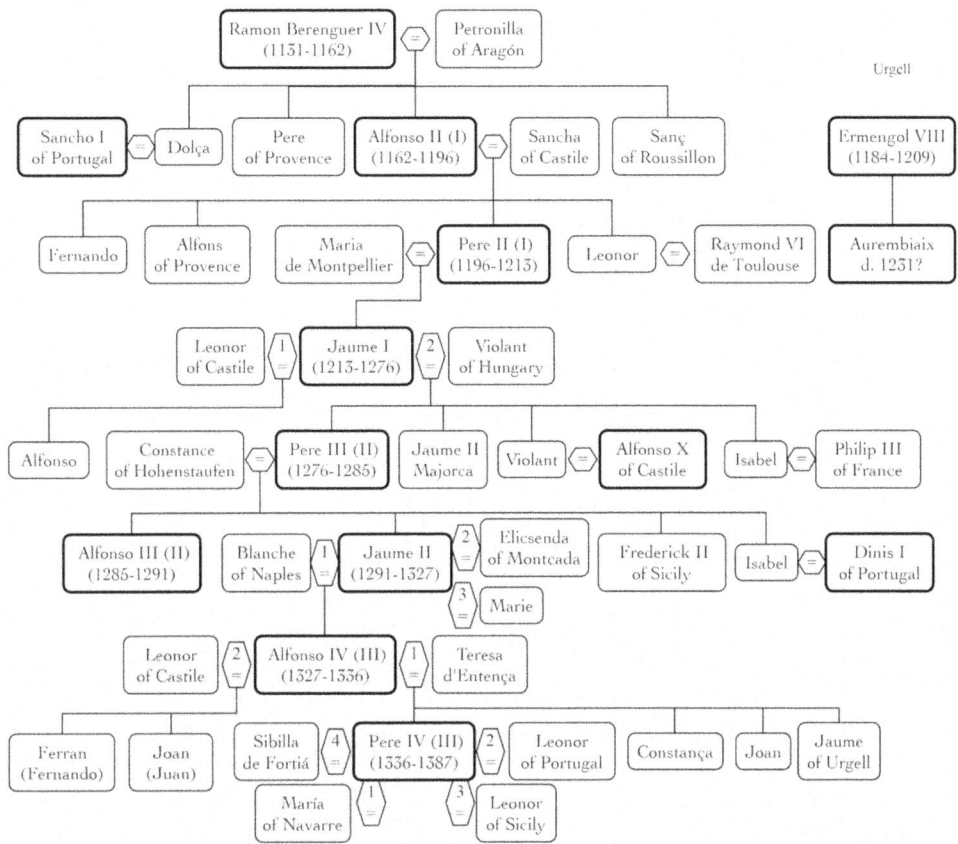

Chart 14: The Count-Kings of Aragon-Barcelona: 1131–1387.

220   APPENDIX III: GENEALOGICAL CHARTS

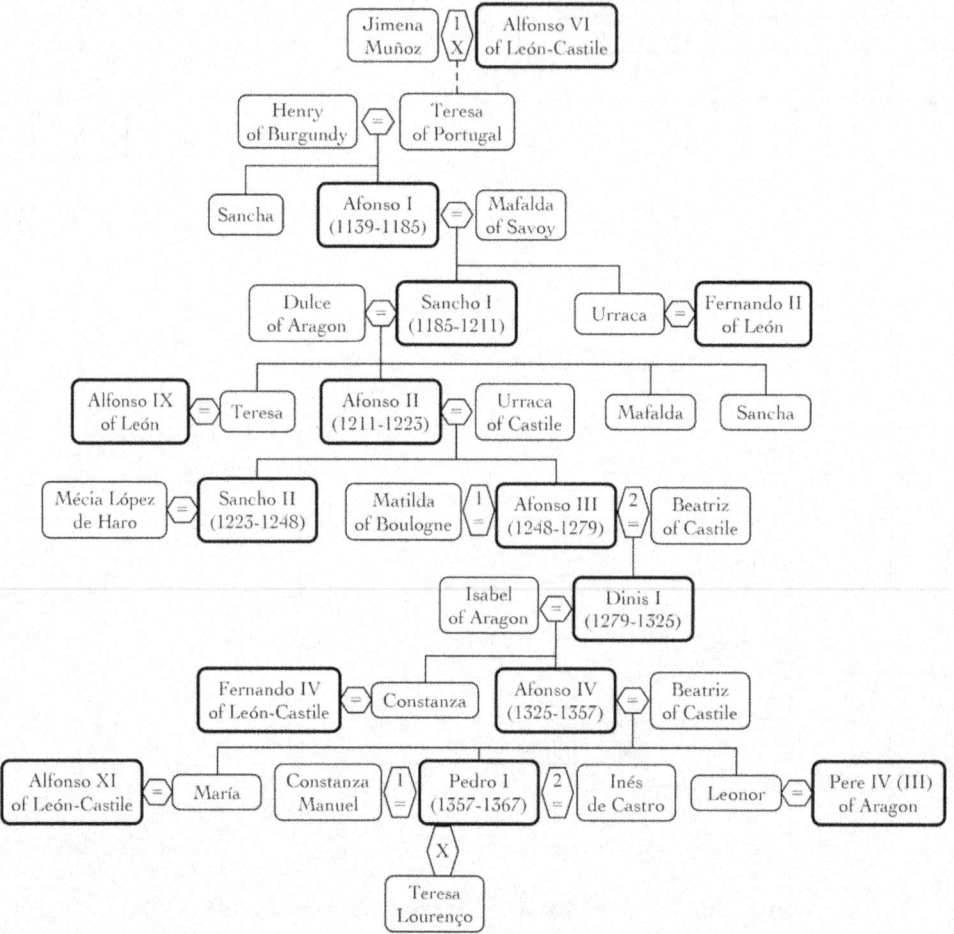

Chart 15: The Kings of Portugal: 1139–1367.

Appendix III: Genealogical Charts

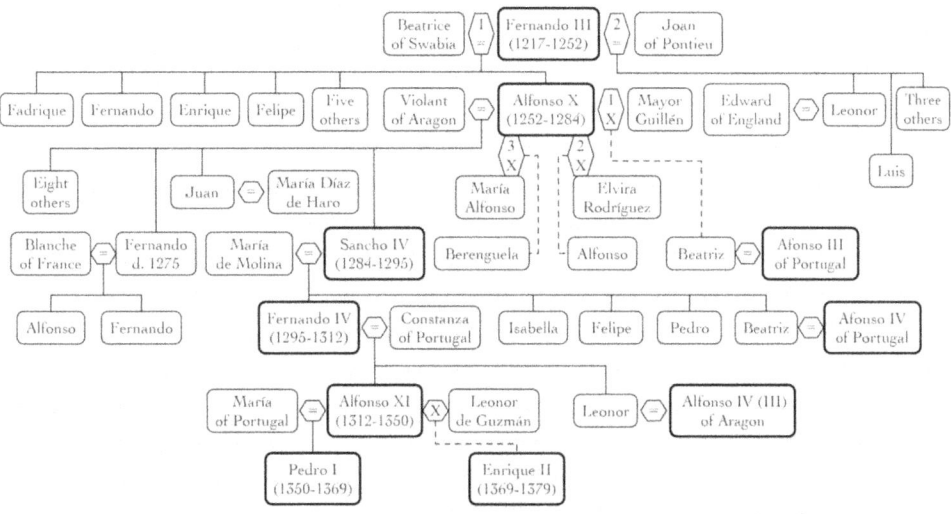

Chart 16: The Kings of León-Castile: 1252–1369.

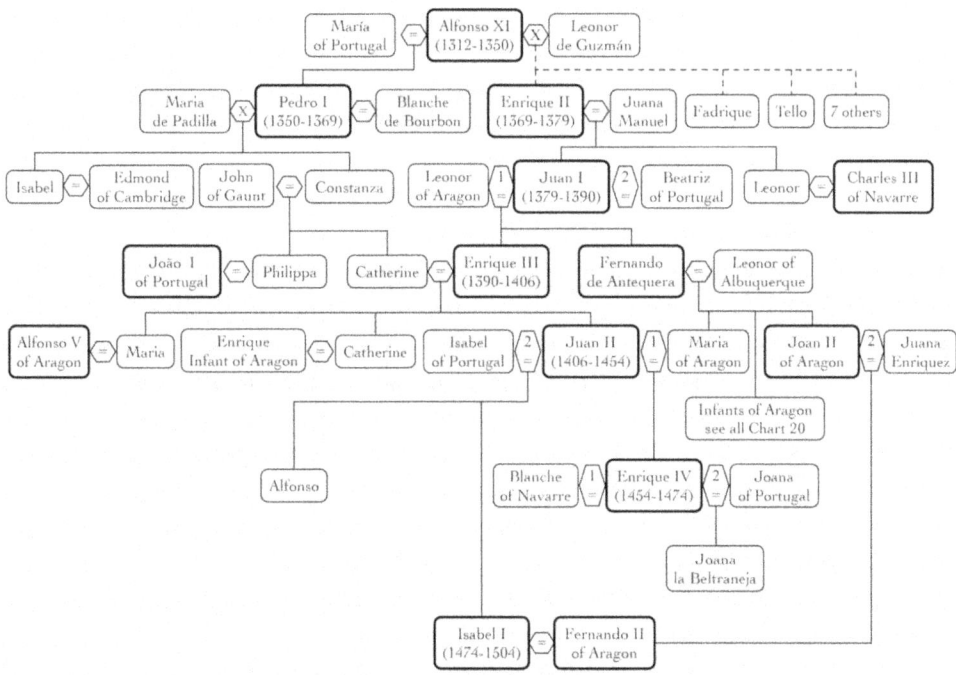

Chart 17: The Kings of León-Castile: 1350–1504.

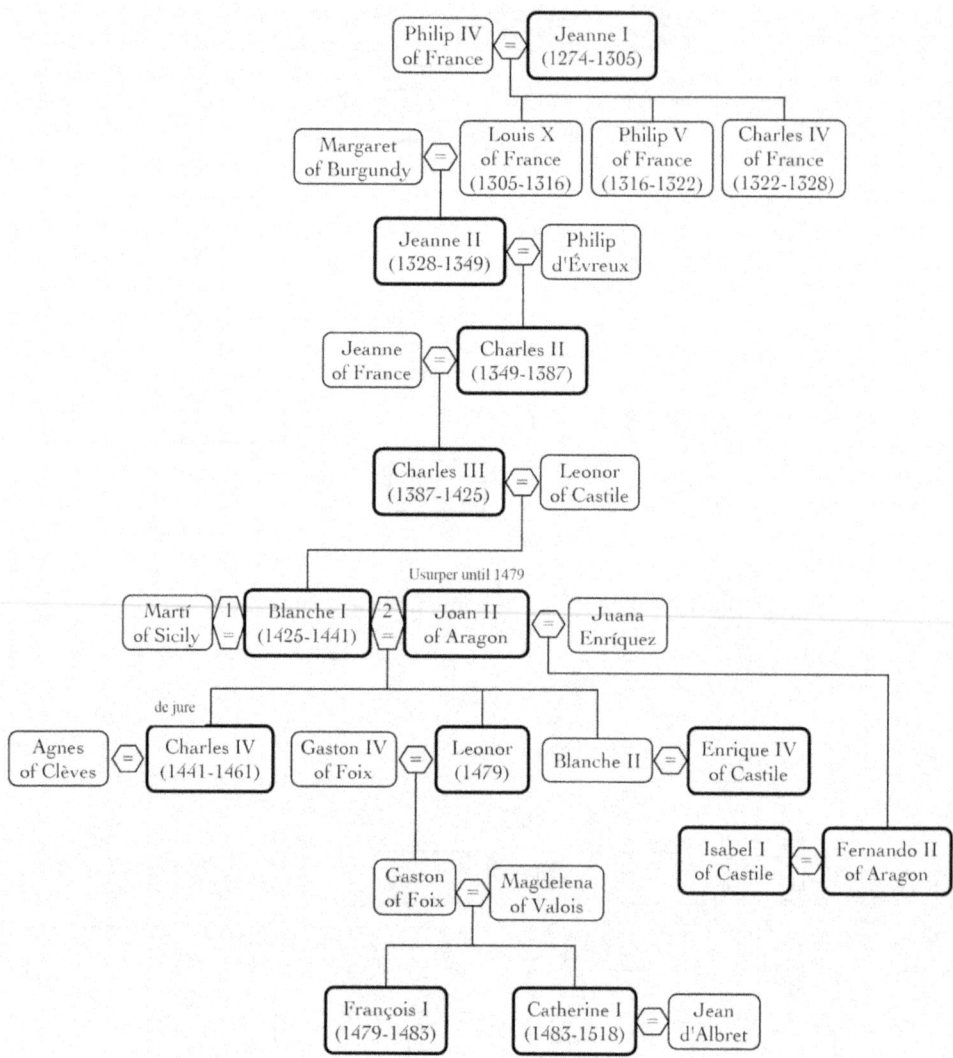

Chart 18: The French Rulers of Navarre: 1305–1518.

Appendix III: Genealogical Charts 223

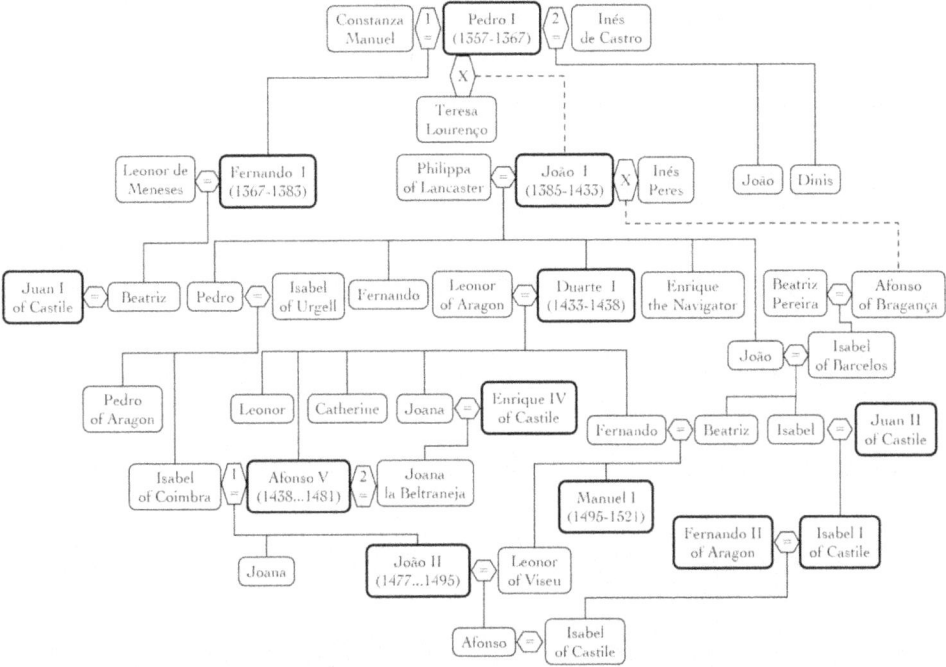

Chart 19: The Kings of Portugal: 1357–1495.

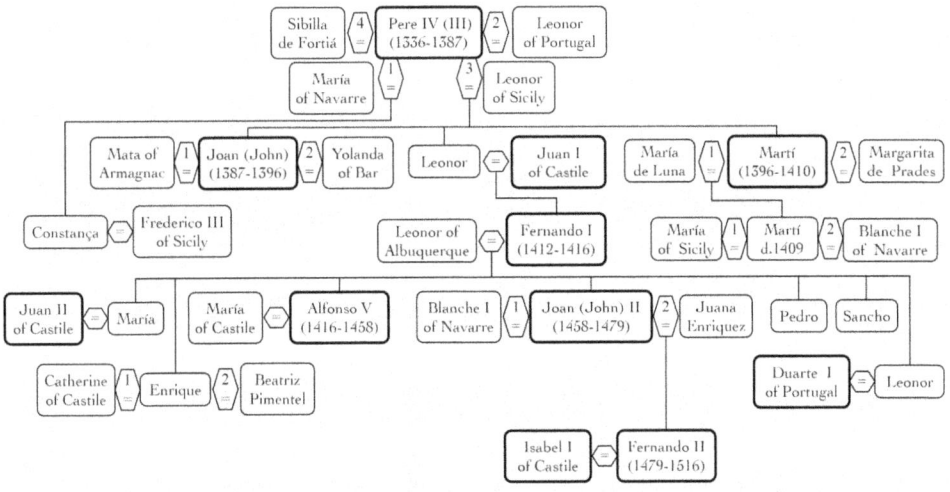

Chart 20: The Count-Kings of Aragon-Barcelona: 1387–1516.

Works Consulted

Abadal i de Vinyals, Ramón d'. *Els comtats de Pallars I Ribagorça*. Catalunya Carolíngia, volum III. Barcelona: edició facsímil, 2009.

———. *Els primers comtes catalans*. Barcelona: RBA Libros S.A., 2011.

Altamira y Crevea, Rafael. *A History of Spanish Civilization*. London: Constable & Co Ltd, 2nd corr. ed., 1977.

Álvarez Palenzuela, Vicente Ángel, coord. *Historia de España de la edad media*. Barcelona: Ariel, 2011.

Arbeloa, Joaquín. *Los orígenes del reino de Navarra (710–925)*. San Sebastian: Editorial Auñamendi, 3 volumes, 1969.

Badia I Margarit, Antoni M. *La Formació de la llengua catalana: Assaig d'interpretació històrica*. Barcelona: Abadia de Montserrat, 1981.

Baer, Yitzhak. *A History of the Jews in Christian Spain*. Philadelphia-Jerusalem: The Jewish Publication Society, 2 vols., 1992.

Baldinger, Kurt. *La formación de los dominios lingüísticos en la península ibérica*. Madrid: Gredos, 1963.

Ballesteros-Baretta, Antonio. *Alfonso X el Sabio*. Barcelona-Madrid: Salvat Editores, S. A., 1963.

Barton, Simon. *The Aristocracy in Twelfth-Century León and Castile*. Cambridge: The Cambridge University Press, Paperback, 2002.

———. *A History of Spain*. New York: Palgrave Macmillan, 2nd ed., 2009.

Bisson, T. N. *The Medieval Crown of Aragon: A Short History*. Oxford: The Oxford University Press, Paperback, 1991.

Blöcker-Walter, Monica. *Alfons I. Von Portugal: Studien zu Geschichte un Sage des Begründers der Portugiesichen Unabhängigkeit*. Zürich: Fretz und Wasmuth Verlag AG, 1966.

Bonnassie, Pierre. *La Catalogne du milieu du Xe à la fin du XIe siècle: croissance et mutations d'une société*. Toulouse: L'Université de Toulouse-Le Mirail, 1975.

Bourdon, Albert-Alain. *Histoire du Portugal*. Paris: Presses Universitaires de France, 1re édition, 1970.

Bramon, Dolors. *De quan érem o no Musulmans: Textos del 713 al 1010*. Institut d'Estudis Catalans. Barcelona: Eumo Editorial, 2000.

Calo Lourido, Francisco, et al. *Historia Xeral de Galicia*. Vigo: Edicións a Nosa Terra, N/A.

Cañada Juste, Alberto. "Los Banu Qasi (714–924)," *Príncipe de Viana* 41 (1980): 5–96.

———. "Doña Onneca, una princesa vascona en la corte de los emires cordobeses," *Príncipe de Viana* 74 (2013): 481–501.

Cañas Gálves, Francisco de Paula. *Intinerario de Alfonso XI de Castilla: Espacio, poder y corte (1325–1350)*. Madrid: Ediciones de La Ergástula, 2014.

Carr, Raymont. *Spain: A History*. Oxford and New York: Oxford University Press, Paperback edition, 2001.

Chalmeta, Pedro. *Invasión e islamización*. Madrid: Editorial MAPFRE, 1994.

Chaytor, Henry John. *A History of Aragon and Catalonia*. London: Methuan Publishing Ltd., 1933.

Collins, Roger. *The Arab Conquest of Spain: 710–797*. Oxford, UK and Cambridge USA: Reprinted, 1998.

———. *The Basques*. Oxford: Basil Blackwell, Ltd, 1986.

———. *Caliphs and Kings Spain, 796–1031*. Wiley-Blackwell, 2012.

———. *Early Medieval Spain: Unity in Diversity, 400–1000*. New York: St. Martin's Press, 1983.

———. *Visigothic Spain: 409–711*. Blackwell Publishing, 2004.

Constable, Olivia Remie, ed. *Medieval Iberia: Readings from Christian, Muslim, and Jewish Sources*. Philadelphia: University of Pennsylvania Press, 1997.

David, Pierre. "Le pacte successoral entre Raymond de Galice et Henri de Portugal," *Bulletin Hispanique*. 50: 3–4 (1948) 275–290.

Díaz Martín, Luis Vicente. *Pedro I el Cruel (1350–1369)*. 2a ed, Gijón: Ediciones Trea, 2007.

Edwards, John. *The Spain of the Catholic Monarchs*. Oxford, UK and Malden, MA, USA: Blackwell Publishers, 2000.

Esposito, John L, ed. *The Oxford History of Islam*. Oxford and New York: Oxford University Press, 1999.

Fletcher, Richard. *Moorish Spain*. Berkley and Los Angeles: University of California Press, Second Paperback Printing, 2006.

_____. *The Quest for El Cid*. New York: Oxford University Press, 1991.

Fromherz, Allen J. *The Almohads: The Rise of an Islamic Empire*. New York: I.B. Tauris, Paperback ed., 2013.

Gaibrois de Ballesteros, Mercedes. *Historia del reinado de Sancho IV de Castilla*. Madrid: 3 vols, 1922–1928.

García-Osuna y Rodríguez, José María. "El astur rey de León Fruela II Adefónsiz el Leproso," *Argutorio* 9:20 (2008): 25–8.

Gomez-Moreno, Manuel. *Introducción a la historia silense: con versión castellana de la misma y de la crónica de Sampiro*. Madrid: Tipográfico Sucessores de Rivadeneyra (S.A.), 1921.

González Jiménez, Manuel. *Alfonso X, El Sabio*. 1st ed. Barcelona: Ariel, 2004.

González Mínguez, César. *Fernando IV, 1295–1312*. Palencia: Editorial La Olmeda S.L., 1995.

Gordon, Stewart. *When Asia Was the World*. Philadelphia: Da Capo Press, 2008.

Green, Toby. *Inquisition: The Reign of Fear*. New York: Thomas Dunne Books, First U.S. Edition, 2009.

Grunebaum, Fustave E. von. *Medieval Islam: A Study in Cultural Orientation*. 2nd ed. New Delhi: Cosmo Publications., 2011.

Harvey, L. P. *Islamic Spain: 1250 to 1500*. Chicago and London: University of Chicago Press, 1990.

Heather, Peter. *The Goths*. Malden: Blackwell Publishers, 1998.

Holt, P. M., Lambton, Ann K. S., and Lewis, Bernard, eds. *The Cambridge History of Islam*. Volume I. Cambridge: Cambridge University Press, 1970.

Huici Miranda, Ambrosio. *Historia Política Del Imperio Almohade*. Granada: Editorial Universidad de Granada, 2000.

Iglesias Costa, Manuel. *Historia del condado de Ribagorza*. Huesca: Instituto de Estudios Altoaragoneses: Diputación de Huesca, 2001.

Jarrett, Jonathan. *Rulers and Ruled In Frontier Catalonia, 880–1010*. Suffolk, UK and Rochester, NY: The Boydell Press, 2010.

Jones, John Harris. *Ibn Abd el-Hakem's History of the Conquest of Spain (1858)*. Goettingen and London, Dietrich, Willians and Norgate, 1858. Kessinger Legacy Reprints.

Kennedy, Hugh. *The Great Arab Conquests: How the Spread of Islam Changed the World We Live In*. Philadelphia: Da Capo Press, 2007.

_____. *Muslim Spain and Portugal. A Political History of al-Andalus*. London and New York: Longman, 1996.

Lacarra, José Maria. *Alfonso El Batallador*. Zaragoza: Guara, 1978.

_____. *Historia del reino de Navarra en la edad media*. Caja de Ahorros de Navarra, 1975.

_____. "Textos navarros del Códice de Roda," *Estudios de Edad Media de la Corona de Aragón*, 1:194–283 (1945).

Lagardère, Vincent. *Les Almoravides. Le djiâd andalou (1106–1143)*. Paris: L'Harmattan, 1998.

Lapeña Paúl, Ana Isabel. *Ramiro II de Aragón, el rey monje (1134–1137)*. Gijón: Ediciones Trea, 2008.

Lévi-Provençal, Évariste. *Histoire de l'Espagne musulmane*. Paris: Éd. G.-P. Maisonneuve & Cie, 3 Volumes, 1950, 1965.

_____. "Du nouveau sur le royaume de Pampelune au IX siècle," *Bulletin Hispanique* 55.1 (1953): 5–22.

Lewis, Archibald R. *The Development of Southern French and Catalan Society, 718–1050*. Austin: The University of Texas Press, 1965.

Lewis, David Levering. *God's Crucible: Islam and the Making of Europe, 570 to 1215*. New York and London: W. W. Norton, 2008.

Linehan, Peter. *History and Historians of Medieval Spain*. Oxford: Clarendon Press, 1993.

_____. *Spain, 1157–1300: A Partible Inheritance*. Malden, MA, Oxford, UK, and Chichester, UK: Wiley-Blackwell, Paperback, 2011.

Lomax, Derek W. *The Reconquest of Spain*. New York and London: Longman 1978.

Manzano Moreno, Eduardo. *Conquistadores, emires y califas: los omeyas y la formación de al-Andalus*. Bacelona: Crítica, Premera edición en rústica, 2011.

Martín Duque, Angel J. "Del reino de Pamplona al reino de Navarra." *Príncipe de Viana* 63 (2002): 841–50.

Martínez Díez, Gonzalo. *Alfonso VIII, rey de Castilla y Toledo (1158–1214)*. Gijón: Ediciones Trea, 2007.

_____. *El condado de Castilla (711–1038). La historia frente la leyenda*. 2 vols. Junta de Castilla y León: Marcial Pons Historia, 2005.

_____. *Fernando III:1217–1252*. Palencia: Diputación Provincial de Palencia, 1993.

Menéndez Pidal, R. *La España del Cid*. Quinta ed. 2 vols. Madrid: Espasa-Calpe, S. A., 1956.

_____. *Orígenes del español: estado lingüístico de la península ibérica hasta el siglo XI*. Sexta ed. Madrid: Espasa-Calpe, S.A., 1968.

Messier, Ronald A. *The Almoravids and the Meanings of Jihad*. Santa Barbara: Praeger, 2010.

Monsalvo Antón, José María. *Atlas histórico de la España medieval*. Madrid: Editorial Síntesis, S.A., 2010.

Montes Romero-Camacho, Isabel. "La Polémica del Testamento de Juan I de Castilla y sus Implicaciones Sevillanas." *Historia. Instituciones. Documentos*. 25 (1999): 435–472.

Moxó, Salvador de. *Repoblación y sociedad en la España cristiana medieval*. Madrid: Ediciones Rialp, S.A., 1979.

Nieto Soria, José Manuel. *Sancho IV de Castilla (1284–1295)*. Gijón: Ediciones Trea, 2014.

O'Callaghan, Joseph F. *The Gibraltar Crusade: Castile and the Battle for the Strait*. Philadelphia: University of Pennsylvania Press, 2011.

_____. *A History of Medieval Spain*. Ithica and London: Cornell University Press, 1975.

_____. *The Learned King: The Reign of Alfonso X of Castile*. Philadelphia: University of Pennsylvania Press, 1993.

_____. *Reconquest and Crusade in Medieval Spain*. Philadelphia: University of Pennsylvania Press, 2003.

Oliveira Marques, A. H. de. *History of Portugal*. Vol 1. New York: Columbia University Press, 1972.

Olivera Serrano, César. *Beatriz de Portugal: La pugna dinástica Avís-Trastámara*. Betanzos (A Cpruña): Lugami A. G., 2005.

Orlandis, José. *Historia del reino visigodo español*. Madrid: Ediciones Rialp, S.A., 2011.

O'Shea, Stephen. *Sea of Faith: Islam and Christianity in the Medieval Mediterranean World*. New York: Walker & Company, 2006.

Palenzuela see Álvarez Palenzuela.

Pérez-Bustamante, Rogelio, and José Manuel Calderón Ortega. *Enrique IV de Castilla: 1454–1474*. Burgos: Editorial La Olmeda, S.L., 1998.

Phillips, William D., Jr. *Slavery in Medieval and Early Modern Iberia*. Philadelphia: University of Pennsylvania Press, 2014.

Phillips, William D., Jr., and Carla Rahn Phillips. *A Concise History of Spain*. Cambridge: Cambridge University Press, 2010.

Porras Arboledas, Pedro A. *Juan II: 1406–1454*. Palencia: Editorial La Olmeda, S.L., 1995.

Reilly, Bernard F. *The Contest of Christian and Muslim Spain: 1031–1157*. Cambridge, MA, USA and Oxford, UK: Blackwell Publishers, Paperback, 1995.

_____. *The Kingdom of León-Castilla under King Alfonso VI, 1065–1109*. Princeton: Princeton University Press, 1999. *The Library of Iberian Resources Online*. Web. 7 Aug. 2014.

_____. *The Kingdom of León-Castilla under King Alfonso VII, 1126–1157*. Philadelphia: University of Pennsylvania Press, 1998.

_____. *The Kingdom of León-Castilla under Queen Urraca, 1109–1126*. Princeton, N.J.: Princeton University Press, 1982.

_____. *The Medieval Spains*. Cambridge: Cambridge University Press, 1993.

Rodríguez Fernández, Justiniano. *Reyes de León: Garcia I, Ordoño II, Fruela II, Alfonso IV*. Burgos: Editorial La Olmeda, S.L., 1997.

Rogerson, Barnaby. *The Heirs of Muhammad: Islam's First Century and the Origins of the Sunni-Shia Split*. Woodstock and New York: The Overlook Press, 2007.

Ruiz, Teofilo F. *Spain's Centuries of Crisis: 1300–1474*. Malden, MA, Oxford, UK, and Chichester, UK: Wiley-Blackwell, Paperback, 2011.

Salas Merino, Vicente. *La Genealogía de los Reyes de España*. 5a ed. Madrid: Vision Libros, 2015.

Salazar y Acha, Jaime de. "Reflexiones sobre la posible historicidad de un episodio de la Crónica Najerense." *Príncipe de Viana* Annex 14: 537–564.

San Miguel Pérez, Enrique. *Isabel I de Castilla: 1474–1504*. Burgos: Editorial La Olmeda, S.A., 1998.

Sánchez Albornoz, Claudio. *De la Andalucía islámica a la de hoy*. 3rd ed. Madrid: Rialp, 2007.

_____. *España, un enigma histórico*. 2 vols. Barcelona: Edhasa, 2000.

_____. *Orígenes de la nación Española: El reino de Asturias*. Estudios críticos sobre la historia del reino de Asturias (Seleccion). Madrid: Sarpe, 1985.

Sánchez-Arcilla Bernal, José. *Alfonso XI (1312–1350)*. 2nd ed. Gijon: Ediciones Trea, 2008.

Sánchez Candeiry, Alfonso. *El Regnum-Imperium Leonés hasta 1037*. Madrid: Escuela de Estudios Medievales, 1951.

Santos Coco, Francisco, ed. *Historia Silense*. Madrid: Sucesores de Rivadeneyra, S.A., 1921.

Scales, Peter C. *The Fall of the Caliphate of Córdoba. Berbers and Andalusis in Conflict*. Leiden: E. J. Brill, 1994.

Serrano y Sanz, Manuel. *Noticias y documentos históricos del condado de Ribagorza hasta la muerte de Sancho Garcés III (año 1035)*. Madrid: 1912, presente edición Valladolid: Maxtor, 2007.

Sobrequés i Vidal. *Els grans comtes de Barcelona*. Barcelona: Vicens-Vives, 1961.

Suárez Bilbao, Fernando. *Enrique III, 1390–1406*. Palencia: Editorial La Olmeda S.L., 1994

Suárez Fernández, Luis. *Historia del reinado de Juan I de Castilla. Tomo I: Estudio*. Madrid: Universidad Autónoma, 1977.

_____. *Juan de Trastámara (1379–1390)*. Palencia: Editorial La Olmeda S.L., 1994.

_____. *Nobleza y monarquía: Puntos de vista sobre la historia política castellana del siglo XV*. Secunda ed. Valladolid: Andrés Martín, 1975.

Taha, Abdulwahid Dhanun. *The Muslim Conquest and Settlement of North Africa and Spain.* London & New York: Routledge, 1989.

Thompson, E. A. *The Goths in Spain.* Oxford: Oxford U Press, 1969.

_____. *The Visigoths in the Time of Ulfila.* London: Gerald Duckworth & Co. Ltd. 2nd ed., 2008.

Ubieto Arteta, Antonio. "Estudios en torno a la división del Reino por Sancho el Mayor de Navarra." *Príncipe de Viana* 78–79 (1960): 5–56; 80–81 (1960): 163–236.

_____. *Historia de Aragón: La formación territorial.* Zaragoza: Anubar Ediciones, 1981.

_____. "Los reyes pamploneses entre 905 y 970." *Príncipe de Viana* 24 (1963): 77–82.

_____. "El sitio de Huesca y la muerte de Sancho Ramírez." *Argensola: Revista de Ciencias Sociales del Instituto de Estudios Altoaragoneses* 13 (1953): 61–70; 14 (1953): 139–148.

_____. "Sobre Sancho Ramírez y su muerte." *Argensola: Revista de Ciencias Sociales del Instituto de Estudios Altoaragoneses* 20 (1954): 353–356.

Usunáriz Garoya, Jesús María. *Historia breve de Navarra.* Madrid: Sílex ediciones S.L., 2007.

Valdeón Baruque, Julio. *Alfonso El Sabio: La Forja de la España Moderna.* Madrid: Temas de Hoy, 2011.

_____. *Enrique II, 1369–1379.* Palencia: Editorial La Olmeda S.L., 1996.

_____. *Los Trastámaras: El triunfo de una dinastía bastarda.* Madrid: Temas de Hoy, 2010.

Viguera, María J. *Aragón musulmán.* Zaragoza: Mira Editores, S.A., 1988.

Villapalos Salas, Gustavo. *Fernando V de Castilla: 1474–1516.* Palencia: Editorial La Olmeda S.L., 1998.

Wallace-Hadrill. *The Fourth Book of the Chronicle of Fredegar with its Continuations.* Westport: Greenwood Press, 1981.

Wasserstein, David. *The Rise and Fall of the Party-Kings: Politics and Society in Islamic Spain 1002–1086.* Princeton, New Jersey: Princeton University Press, 1985.

Watkins, Calvert, rev. and ed. *The American Heritage Dictionary of Indo-European Roots,* 2nd ed. Boston: Houghton Mifflin Company, 2000.

Wolf, Kenneth Baxter. *Conquerors and Chroniclers of Early Medieval Spain.* Liverpool: Liverpool University Press, Second Edition, 1999.

Wolfram, Herwig. *History of the Goths.* Trans. Thomas J. Dunlap. Berkeley: University of California Press, 1988.

Wright, Roger. *Early Ibero-Romance. Twenty-one studies on language and texts from the Iberian Peninsula between the Roman Empire and the Thirteenth Century.* Newark: Juan de la Cuesta, 1994.

_____, ed. *Latin and the Romance Languages in the Early Middle Ages.* University Park: The Pennsylvania State University Press, 1996.

Index

Abbasids 23–5, 46, 129
Abd al-Aziz, governor of al-Andalus 15–6
Abd al-Malik al-Muzaffar, son of al-Mansur 60–63, 69
Abd al-Malik ibn Qatan al-Fihri, governor of al-Andalus 19–21
Abd al-Mumin, Almohad commander 105–6, 108, 111–2
Abd al-Rahman I, first Umayyad emir in Córdoba 23–5
Abd al-Rahman II of Córdoba 29
Abd al-Rahman III of Córdoba 38–40, 45–51
Abd al-Rahman IV ibn Muhammad ibn Abd al-Malik 67–8
Abd al-Rahman V ibn Hisham ibn Abd al-Jabbar 67
Abd al-Rahman ibn Abd Allah al-Ghafiqi, governor of al-Andalus 18–9
Abd al-Rahman ibn Abi Amir, "Sanchuelo" 56, 58, 61–3, 69, 73–4
Abd al-Rahman ibn Ibrahim 39
Abd Allah, son of al-Mansur 55
Abd Allah, *taifa* ruler of Granada 87–8
Abd Allah al-Adil, Almohad governor of Murcia and later emir 126–9
Abd Allah ibn Muhammad of Córdoba 34
Abu Abd Allah Muhammad XII 194–200
Abu Abd Allah Muhammad XIII 194–9
Abu Abd Allah Muhammad ibn Yusuf ibn Hud al Yudami *see* ibn Hud
Abu al-Abbas Abd Allah, Abbasid imam 23
Abu al-Ala Idris, the governor of Córdoba and later emir 126–9
Abu al-Hassan, Merinid emir 160–1
Abu al-Juyush Nasr, Nasrid of Granada 155
Abu al-Kattar, governor of al-Andalus 20–1
Abu al-Ula (Abu Dabbus) Idris II al-Wathiq, Almohad emir 143

Abu Amir Muhammad ibn Abi Amir al-Mafiri al-Mansur 53–63
Abu Bakr, first caliph 10
Abu Bakr ibn Ya'ish ibn Muhammad, *taifa* ruler of Toledo 73
Abu l-Hasan Ali 193–6
Abu Muhammad Abd al-Wahid I al-Makhlu, Almohad emir 126–7
Abu Muhammad Abu Abd Allah al-Bayyasi 126–8
Abu Muhammad Sir, Almoravid governor 106
Abu Nasr Sad, Nasrid of Granada 183–4
Abu Yaqub Yusuf, Almohad emir 111–5
Abu Yaqub Yusuf II al-Mustansir 122, 126
Abu Yusuf Hasday 50
Abu Yusuf Yaqub al-Mansur, Almohad emir 115–8
Abu Yusuf Yaqub ibn Abd al-Haqq, Merinid emir 141, 143, 145, 147
Abu Zakariya, Hafsid ruler of Tunis 131–2
Adrianople 3
Afonso, duke of Bragança 189
Afonso I of Portugal *see* Alfonso I of Portugal
Afonso II of Portugal 125–7
Afonso III of Portugal 136–7, 139, 141
Afonso IV of Portugal 154, 156–7, 159, 161, 163–4, 167
Afonso V of Portugal 188–93
Agde 25
Agila I 6
Ajarquía 133, 195
al-Ahmar *see* Muhammad ibn Yusuf ibn Nasr ibn al-Ahmar
al-Bayyasi *see* Abu Muhammad Abu Abd Allah al-Bayyasi
al-Hakam I, emir of Córdoba 26–9
al-Hakam II 51–3
al-Haythan ibn Ubayd al-Kilabi, governor of al-Andalus 19
al-Kasim, ruler of Córdoba 67
al-Kattar *see* Abu al-Kattar

al-Mamun *taifa* ruler of Toledo 79–80, 82, 84
al-Mansur *see* Abu Amir Muhammad ibn Abi Amir al-Mafiri
al-Mughira, brother of al-Hakam 54
al-Mundhir of Córdoba 32–34
al-Mundir I ibn Yahya al-Tujibi, ruler of Zaragoza 70, 73
al-Muqtadir, *taifa* ruler of Zaragoza 76–7, 81, 84
al-Murabitun see Almoravids
al-Mushafi 53
al-Mustain *see* Sulayman ibn Hud al-Mustain
al-Mutadid, *taifa* ruler of Seville 74, 77
al-Mutamid, *taifa* ruler of Seville 74, 80–1, 87–8
al-Mutawakkil, *taifa* ruler of Badajoz 81–2, 84
al-Muzaffar *see* Abd al-Malik al-Muzaffar
al-Qadir, *taifa* ruler 80–2, 84
al-Samh, governor of al-Andalus 17–9
al-Sumail, governor of Zaragoza 23
al-Tawil *see* Muhammad al-Tawil
al-Walid I, Caliph of Damascus 15
al-Zagal *see* Abu Abd Allah Muhammad XIII
al-Zahira palace 61, 62
al-Zahra, palace 46, 65
Alans 4
Alarcos 117–20
Alaric 4
Alaric II 5–6
Alatheus 3
Alava 31–3, 37, 42–45, 47, 71, 75–6, 80, 100, 102–3, 114, 119, 166
Alavivus 3
Albelda 30–1
Albigensian heresy 121
Alcácer do Sal 108, 111, 117, 126–7
Alcaçobas 191
Alcalá de Henares 63, 155, 172; Ordinance of 162

Alcañices, treaty of 154, 157
Alcántara 111, 113, 191
Alexander II, pope 115
Alfonso, brother of Enrique IV of León-Castile 185
Alfonso I of Aragón 91–5, 99–101
Alfonso I of Asturias 17, 21–2, 26
Alfonso I of Portugal 92–4, 99, 103–4, 106–9, 111–2, 115, 139
Alfonso II of Aragón 111–12, 115–7, 132
Alfonso II of Asturias 26
Alfonso III of Aragón 149
Alfonso III of Asturias 32–3, 37, 44
Alfonso IV of Aragón 154, 156–7, 159, 161, 163–4
Alfonso IV of Asturias 43, 47
Alfonso IX of León 115–20, 123–4, 127, 129–30, 135
Alfonso V of Aragón 178–82, 184, 187, 189
Alfonso V of León 71
Alfonso VI of León-Castile 78–82, 87–91, 98
Alfonso VII of León-Castile 90–6, 99–103, 106–9, 130
Alfonso VIII of Castile 110, 112–23, 125, 132, 140
Alfonso X of León-Castile 124, 130, 139–45
Alfonso XI of León-Castile 152, 155–62, 164, 166, 174
Alfonso de Molina, brother of Fernando III 137
Alfonso Enríquez *see* Alfonso I of Portugal
Alfonso Raimúndez *see* Alfonso VII
Algeciras 12–4, 20, 39, 64–5, 74, 82, 87–8, 106, 143, 147, 149, 155, 161–2, 167
Alhama 194
Alhambra 181, 184, 197, 199
Ali ibn Hammud, ruler of Córdoba 66
Ali ibn Yusuf, Almoravid emir 105–6
Alicante 15, 114, 153–4
Aljubarrota, battle of 172
Almanzor *see* Abu Amir Muhammad ibn Abi Amir al-Mafiri
Almería 68, 74, 87, 107–8, 134–5, 155, 183, 186, 196–9
Almizra, treaty of 135
Almodis, wife of Ramon Berenguer I 83–4, 97
Almohads 104–122, 128–9, 134, 137, 139–40
Almoravids 74, 84–94, 96–102, 104–108, 111, 132, 140
Alvar Fañez, Castilian commander 82, 94
Alvar Nuñez Osorio 159
Alvar Pérez de Castro, Christian knight 128, 130, 133

Alvaro de Luna, favorite of Juan II of Castile 179–83
Alvaro Herramélliz, count of Castile 45
Alvaro Nuñez de Lara 123
Amalaric 6
Amaya 14, 22, 45
Amrus, Berber commander 26
Anagni, treaty of 152
Anbassa, governor of al-Andalus 18
Ansemund, Gothic count 25
Antequera 45, 177
Antequera, el de see Fernando I of Aragón
aprisiones 27
Arévalo 81, 190
Astorga 5, 14, 22, 43, 57–9, 71, 94
Atapuerca, battle of 76
Athanagild 6
Athaulf 4
Atienza 54, 90, 96, 167
Aurelius, king of Asturias 26
Aureolus, early count of Aragón 28
Aurembiaix 125
Autillo 123–4
Ava of Ribagorça 69
Ávila 22, 81, 90, 111, 122, 146, 156, 185
Axaçaf 138
Ayamonte 136, 174, 176
Aznar Galindez of Aragón 28
Aznar Galindez II of Aragón 32

Badajoz 32–3, 46, 74, 76, 78, 81, 87–89, 111–2, 115, 129, 142, 146, 171
Baeza 35, 111, 121–2, 127–9, 176
Balj ibn Bishr al-Qushayri 20–1
Banu Abbad 73
Banu Abi al-Ula 158
Banu Ashqilula 141
Banu Hammud 74
Banu Hud 73
Banu Jahwar 73
Banu Marin *see* Merinids
Banu Qasi 15, 27–31, 36, 40–1, 99
Banu Sarraj 181, 183, 194
Banu Tujibi 73
Barcelona 5, 15, 28, 36, 44, 56, 60, 82–4, 188
the Battler *see* Alfonso I of Aragón
Bayonne 185
Beatrice, wife of Fernando III and daughter of Philip of Swabia 124, 131, 140
Beatriz de Bragança 191
Beaumont, Jean de and family 187–8
Belchite 100
Belló, count of Carcassonne 28, 36
Beltrán de la Cueva, favorite of Enrique IV of León-Castile 184–5, 190

Benedict XIII, pope 176, 178
Benimarines *see* Merinids
Bera, count of Barcelona 28, 36
Berenguela, daughter of Ramon Berenguer III 101
Berenguela, wife of Alfonso IX and sister of Enrique I 123–4, 137
Berenguer I of Barcelona 70, 82
Bernard, bishop of Toledo 94, 96
Bernard, count of Toulouse 35
Bernard Plantevelue 35
Bernat Guillem, count of Cerdanya 97
Bernat III, count of Besalú 97
Bernat-Unifred, count of Ribagorça 44
Bertram du Guesclin 166–7
Besalú 27, 8, 44, 83, 97
Béziers 25, 111, 121–2
Black Death 162, 173
Blanche I of Navarre 179–80, 182, 184, 186
Blanche of Bourbon, wife of Pedro I of Castile 163, 165
Blanche of Navarre, wife of Enrique IV of León-Castile 184
Boabdil *see* Abu Abd Allah Muhammad XII
Bocanegra, Ambrosio 168
Boniface VIII, pope 152, 154
Bordeaux 5, 27, 166, 169
Borrell 44
Borrell II 52, 56
Briones, treaty of 170
Burgos 45, 47, 51, 79, 94, 124, 137, 156, 161, 163, 185

Cáceres 111, 113, 115, 127, 129
Calahorra 29, 40–2, 47, 76, 80, 166
Calatayud 14, 41, 73, 76, 100, 165, 182
Calatrava 30, 62, 107, 117–20; order of 194
Calixtus, pope 95
Calixtus II, pope 183
campus stellarum 27
Candespino, battle of 94
Cangas de Onís 26
Cantigas de Santa María 145
Carcassonne 18, 27–8, 36, 121
Carmona 14, 24, 39, 73–4, 88, 111, 137, 167–8
Castronuño 182, 190
Catherine I of Navarre 193
Cazola, treaty of 132, 135
Cerdanya 27, 28, 36, 44, 83, 97
Ceuta 11–2, 20, 23, 63, 86–7, 138, 188–90
Charlemagne 25, 27, 144
Charles II of Navarre 165–6, 168–70
Charles III of Navarre 169, 173, 179–80, 186
Charles IV of France 158
Charles IV of Navarre 182, 184, 186–7

Charles Martel 19
Charles of Anjou 150–1
Charles of Valois 150, 152
Charles of Viana *see* Charles IV of Navarre
Charles the Bald, king of France 30
Chindasuinth 8
Chintila 8
el Cid see Rodrigo Díaz de Vivar
Ciudad Real 38, 143, 148, 152
Ciudad Rodrigo 111, 113, 115, 167
Clement VII, pope 170
Coimbra 15, 42, 57–8, 60, 76–7, 99, 125, 169, 171–2, 188–9, 191
Commission of Caspe 178
El Conde Lucanor 156
Constanza Manuel 157, 159, 164
conversos 173
Corbeil, treaty of 144
Córdoba 7, 13–4, 17, 19–21, 24–6, 28–39, 49–69, 73–4, 80–1, 88, 94, 96, 99, 104, 106–8, 115–20, 126–8, 130–5, 138, 143, 145, 153, 173, 177, 184, 194–8
Coria 59, 81, 87, 104, 146
A Coruña 30, 172
Covadonga 17
Cuéllar 56, 81
Cuenca 81, 113–4, 118–9, 128, 146, 148, 160, 178

Dadildis 36
Denia 7, 68, 74, 84, 88, 90, 107–8, 114, 128, 135
Diego García de Padilla 165
Diego López de Haro 120, 148, 153
Diego López Pacheco 190, 199
Diego Rodriguez, second count of Castile 45
Dinis I of Portugal 142, 145, 149, 151, 153–4, 156–7, 163, 167, 171
Dolça, wife of Ramon Berenguer III 97
Duarte, king of Portugal 179, 184, 189–9
Duke of Lancaster *see* John of Gaunt

Ecija 13, 35, 38, 111, 133, 143, 159, 173
Edmond, duke of Cambridge 168
Edward I of England 140
Edward II of England 169
Egica 9
Elche 153–4
Elvas 129, 171
Enneco *see* Iñigo
Enrique, brother of Alfonso X 153–4
Enrique, Henry the Navigator, duke of Viseu 188–90
Enrique, Infante of Aragón 179–182
Enrique I of León-Castile 122
Enrique II of León-Castile 163–70

Enrique III of León-Castile 172–4, 176, 178
Enrique IV of León-Castile 179–86
Enrique de Guzmán, duke of Medina-Sidonia 184
Ermengol I, count of Urgell 64, 70
Ermengol II, count of Urgell 70
Ermengol III 77
Ermengol IV 84
Ermengol VI 97, 107
Ermengol VII 125
Ermengol VIII 125
Ervig 8
Espéculo de las leyes 142–3, 145
Estella 40, 80, 185, 187–8
Estoria de Espanna 145
Estudo Geral em Lisboa 157
Eudes (Odo), duke of Aquitaine 18–9
Eugenius III, pope 107
Euric 5–6
Evora 15, 40, 111, 126

Fadrique de Trastámara 163–4
Fafila, second king of Asturia 17
farce of Avila 185
Faro 137
Fernán González, count of Castile and Alava 45, 47–52, 76, 80
Fernando, Infante son of Alfonso VIII of Castile 120
Fernando I of Aragón 171, 176–9, 191, 194
Fernando I of Leon-Castile 71, 75–78
Fernando I of Portugal 168–71, 176–9, 183, 194–5
Fernando II of Aragón 187
Fernando II of León 108–115, 139
Fernando III of León-Castile 119, 124, 127–39
Fernando IV of León-Castile 147, 149, 152–7, 162, 164
Fernando Ansúrez, count of Castile 45
Fernando de la Cerda 143–4
Fernando Martínez, archdeacon of Ecija 173
Fernando Pérez 95–6, 98
Ferran, son of Pere IV 158, 160, 164–5
Fortún, of the Banu Qasi 28
Fortún Garcés of Pamplona 36–7
Fraga 101, 107
Francisco Febo 192–3
Frederick II 150, 175
Fritigern 3
Fruela, king of Asturias 22, 26
Fruela II 39–42; sons of 42–3
Fuero Real 142

Galindo Aznárez 36, 44
Galindo Garcés of Aragon 28, 30

Galla Placidia 4–5
García, king of Asturias and Oviedo 39–40
García II of Galicia 78–80
García Fernández, count of Castile 52, 54–6
García Garcés, tutor of Alfonso VIII of Castile 110
García Iñiguez 29–30, 32, 36
García Jimenez 36
García Ramírez of Navarre 102–3, 107, 158
García Sánchez I 49–50
García Sánchez II of Navarre 56, 58
García Sánchez III of Navarre 74, 76, 158
García Sánchez of Castile 70–1, 5
García the Bad 28
Garcilaso de la Vega 159
Gelasius II, pope 95
Gelmírez, Diego, bishop of Santiago de Compostela 93–96
General Estoria 145
Geraldo Sem Pavor, Portuguese commander 111–2
Gerberga, heiress of Provence 97
Gesalic 6
Ghalib, Muslim general 51–56
Gibraltar, fortress 111, 141, 155, 160, 162, 184
Gijón 14, 16, 163, 167, 174
Girona 15, 26–8, 36, 44, 56, 60, 70, 82–3, 147, 151, 175, 187–8
Golpejera, battle of 79
Gómez García, abbot of Valladolid 147
Gómez González de Lara 93
Gonzalo Garcés of Sobrarbe and Ribagorça 75
Gonzalo Pérez Gudiel, archbishop of Toledo 146
Gonzalo Ruíz Girón 123–4
Gormaz 52–3, 81
Gramont, family 187
Granada 67, 74, 80–1, 87–8, 106–8, 128, 131, 134–7, 141–3, 158–61; conquest of 193–200
Gratian 3
Gregory X, pope 142–3
Gregory XI, pope 170
Greuthungi 3
Guadalajara 31, 47–9, 55, 118
Guadix 67, 108, 134, 141, 195–9
Guesclin, Bertram du *see* Bertram du Guesclin
Guifré *see* Guifred
Guifré II *see* Borrell
Guifred 36–7, 44, 84, 97, 176
Guillem de Montrodon 124–5
Guillem Ramon, seneschal of Alfonso II 112
Guillem Torroja, bishop of Barcelona 112
Guillermo Isárnez 69
Guimarães 99, 117
Guipúzcoa 76, 80, 102–3, 114, 119, 166, 187

Gundemar 7
Guntroda Pérez, paramour of Alfonso VII 104
Gutierre Fernández de Castro 110
Guy of Burgundy 95

Hafsids 131–2, 137, 139–40, 143, 181
Henry I of Navarre 144
Henry III of England 140
Henry of Burgundy 88–90, 93–4, 96, 98
hermandades 151, 155–6, 159, 191
Hisham I, emir of Córdoba 26
Hisham II of Córdoba 53, 56, 60–2, 64–5
Hisham III ibn Muhammad ibn Abd al-Malik 68
Hisham ibn Sulayman ibn Abd al-Rahman 63
Holy Roman Empire 124, 140, 142, 145
Honorius 4
Hospitallers 101, 107, 119
Las Huelgas 121, 123, 131, 166, 170, 173
Huesca 25, 32, 35, 37, 40, 42, 76, 89, 111, 198
Huete 110, 113, 115, 118
Hujefa, governor of al-Andalus 19

ibn Ganiya, Alvoravid governor 102, 104, 106–7
ibn Hafsun *see* Umar ibn Hafsun
ibn Hud, anti-Almohad rebel 129–31, 134
ibn Mahfuz 131, 134
ibn Mardanish, *el rey lobo* 107–8, 111–113
ibn Marwan al-Jilliqi 32–3, 46
ibn Saïd, Almohad commander 108
ibn Tashfin, Almoravid emir 86 86–8, 90, 104–6
ibn Tumart *see* Muhammad ibn Tumart
Ibrahim ibn Hajjaj of Seville 38
Inés de Castro 164–5, 170–1
Infantes de la Cerda, Alfonso and Fernando sons of Fernando 144–6, 148, 151, 153–4
Infantes of Aragón 179–84
Iñigo Arista 28–9
Iñigo Vela 71
Innocent III, pope 119, 122, 124–5
Innocent IV, pope 136
inquirições 126, 157
Isabel of León-Castile 183, 185–7, 189–3, 197–99
Isarn, count of Pallars 44
Isarn, count of Ribagorça 69
Ishaq, last Almoravid emir 105–6
Ismail I, Nasrid of Granada 156–7
Ismail II, Nasrid of Granada 165

Jaén 35, 38, 65, 88, 107–8, 111, 117, 119, 127–31, 134–8, 144, 153, 155, 173, 194, 198
Jaime I *see* Jaume I
Játiva 74, 114, 128, 135
Jaume, count of Urgell 177–8
Jaume I of Aragón 124–5, 127–32, 144, 149–50
Jaume II of Aragón 149–58
Jaume II of Majorca 151
Jeanne I of Navarre 144, 156, 158
Jeanne II of Navarre 156, 158
Jews 7, 9, 50, 173, 175, 196
Jimeno Garcés of Pamplona 43
Joan I of Aragón (John) 174–5, 180, 182
Joan II of Arageon and king of Navarre 179–80, 184–8, 192
Joan of Navarre *see* Joan II of Aragon and king of Navarre
João I of Portugal 171–2, 181, 188
João II of Portugal 193
John of Gaunt 168–72
Juan I of León-Castile 169–74, 176
Juan II of León-Castile 174, 176–83
Juan Alfonso de Albuquerque 148, 162–3, 167
Juan *el Tuerto* 156, 159
Juan García Manrique, archbishop of Santiago 173
Juan Manuel 155–61, 163–4
Juan Nuñez de Lara 153–4, 159–60
Juan Pacheco, favorite of Enrique IV 182, 184–6
Juana, *la Beltraneja*, wife of Enrique IV of León-Castile 185–6, 190–1
Juana Enríquez 182, 187
Juana Manuel 157, 163
Jufré Tenoria, Castilian admiral 161
Julian, Count, literary character 11
Juromenha 111, 129

Ledesma 22, 54, 56, 185
Leodegundia, daughter of Ordoño I 30
León 14, 16, 22, 39, 40, 42–3, 47–8, 57, 71, 77, 90, 154, 159
Leonor de Guzmán 157, 160, 162–3, 166
Leonor of Castile, sister of Alfonso XI 158–9
Leonor Teles de Meneses 168, 171
Leovigild 6
Lérida 14, 36, 60, 76–7, 84, 100–1, 106–7, 124
Libro del Repartimiento 139
Lisbon 27, 49, 52, 88, 99, 106–7, 110–1, 116–7, 126, 169–72, 181, 189
Liuva 6
Liuva II 7

Llantada, battle of 78
Llop, count of Pallars 44
Logroño 31, 114, 168, 169
Lope Díaz, brother-in-law of Alfonso IX 124
Lope Díaz III de Haro 147
Louis VII of France 108
Louis IX of France 144
Louis X of France 158
Louis the Pious, king of Aquitaine 25
Lubb ibn Muhammad, of the Banu Qasi 40
Lugo 22, 29, 57, 71
Lupicinus 3
Lupo, duke in Gascony 27
Lutos 26

Madrid 47, 111, 118, 120, 123, 145, 161, 174, 178, 180, 186, 190
Madrigal 186, 191; *Ordenamiento* 191
Mafalda of Portugal 123, 125
Magelonne 25
Majano, treaty of 181
Málaga 7, 15, 33, 39, 65, 67–8, 74, 88, 90, 106, 108, 134–5, 194–8
Manrique Pérez de Lara 110
Marca Hispanica 28
María de Molina, wife of Sancho IV 146–9, 152–7, 159
María de Padilla 163, 165, 168
María of Portugal, wife of Afonso IV 157
Martí of Aragón 174–7
Martí the Younger 176, 179
Martin IV, pope 146–7, 150–1
Martin V, pope 178
Martos 128–9, 133, 158
Marwan II, caliph in Damascus 23
Mauregatus 26
Mazdali, Almoravid governor of Córdoba 94
Medina de Rioseco 115, 182
Medina del Campo 81, 170
Medina-Sidonia 7, 13–4, 165, 184, 194
Medinaceli 41, 49, 52, 54, 56, 60–1, 63–4, 90, 96
Menendo González, tutor of Alfonso V 60–1
Merinids 129, 140–1, 143–5, 147, 149, 155, 157–63
Merovingians 6, 18
Mértola 74, 106, 136
Mir Geribert 83
Miró, count of Ribagorça 44
Miró II of Cerdanya 44
Monfragüe, Order of 119
Monteleón 38–9
Mourão 154
Mouro 154
Muawiya, Umayyad founder 10, 23
mudéjares 140–2, 196
Muhammad I of Córdoba 30–2, 36–7

Muhammad II, Nasrid of Granada 142, 149, 154
Muhammad II ibn Hisham ibn Abd al- Jabbar ibn Abd al-Rahman, caliph of Córdoba 62–5
Muhammad III, Nasrid of Granada 154, 5
Muhammad III ibn Abd al-Rahman ibn Ubaid Allah, caliph of Córdoba 68
Muhammad IV, Nasrid of Granada 156–9, 160
Muhammad V, Nasrid of Granada 164–5, 167, 174
Muhammad VI, Nasrid of Granada 165
Muhammad VII, Nasrid of Granada 174, 176–7
Muhammad VIII, Nasrid of Granada 181, 183
Muhammad IX, Nasrid of Granada 181, 183
Muhammad X, Nasrid of Granada 183
Muhammad XI, Nasrid of Granada 183–4
Muhammad XII, Nasrid of Granada *see* Abu Abd Allah Muhammad XII; *see also* Boabdil
Muhammad XIII, Nasrid of Granada *see* Abu Abd Allah Muhammad XIII; *see also* al-Zagal
Muhammad al-Nasir, Almohad emir 119, 122
Muhammad al-Tawil 37, 40, 42
Muhammad ibn Abd Allah al-Ashjai, governor of al-Andalus 19
Muhammad ibn Hashim al Tujibi 47–9
Muhammad ibn Ibrahim 39
Muhammad ibn Lubb, of the Banu Qasi 36–7
Muhammad ibn Tumart, founder of the Almohads 104–5
Muhammad ibn Yusuf ibn Hud, son of ibn Hud 134–5
Muhammad ibn Yusuf ibn Nasr ibn al-Ahmar, founder of the Nasrids of Granada 131, 134–7, 141–2
Muley Hacén *see* Abu l-Hasan
Murcia 15, 21, 74, 84, 88, 102, 106, 108, 111, 113–4, 126, 128–9, 134–6, 141, 145, 148, 151–6, 159, 164, 168
Musa ibn Fortún, of the Banu Qasi 28
Musa ibn Musa 28–31
Musa ibn Nusayr 11, 13–4, 27, 99
Mutarrif ibn Musa, of the Banu Qasi 27–8
muwallids 35

Nájera 37, 40–1, 55, 59, 76, 80, 89, 102, 165
Narbonne 5, 18–9, 25, 27, 111
Nasrids 142–3, 147, 149, 158, 160–3, 165 176–7, 181, 184–5, 193–5, 197–9
Navas de Tolosa 118–22, 125, 127
Nepotian of Asturias 29
Nicolas IV, pope 152
Niebla 14, 24, 74, 106, 110, 131, 134, 136, 139, 141
Nîmes 18, 25
Nuño González de Lara 143

Olmedo 81; battles of 179, 182, 185
Oporto 22, 59, 107, 171–2
Ordenamiento de Madrigal 191
Ordenamiento de las Cortes de Toledo 193
Ordenanzas Reales de Castilla 196
Ordinance of Alcalá de Henares 162
Ordoño I of Asturias 30–1, 44–5
Ordoño II 37, 39–42; sons of 42–3
Ordoño III 49
Ordoño IV 49–52
Orihuela 15, 74, 135, 154
Osma 22, 41, 55, 58, 65, 109
Oviedo 14, 26–7, 30, 39

Pacheco *see* Juan Pacheco; *see also* Diego López Pacheco
Palencia 92, 110, 123, 153, 155, 172, 190
Palenzuela 163
Pallars 27–8, 35, 37, 44, 59, 69–70, 77
Palma 130, 151
Pamplona 7, 15–6, 19, 25, 27–32, 36–7, 41–2, 49–50, 56–9, 61, 71, 75–6, 80, 102, 179
parias 69, 74, 78, 80, 82, 84, 87, 100–1, 107, 163, 167
Paschal II, pope 94
Pedro, duke of Coimbra 188
Pedro, Infante of Aragón 179, 181
Pedro I of Aragón 89
Pedro I of León-Castile 162–7
Pedro I of Portugal 161, 164, 170
Pedro II of Aragón 118–22, 124
Pedro de Luna *see* Benedict XIII
Pedro Froílaz 94–5
Pedro González of Castile 101
Pedro Tenorio, archbishop of Toledo 173
Pelagius *see* Pelayo
Pelayo, first king of Asturias 16–7, 21
Peñafiel 76, 94, 161, 181
Peñalen, el de 80–1, 102
el Peñón see Gibraltar, fortress
Pepin the Short 25
Pere I of Catalonia *see* Pedro II of Aragón
Pere II of Catalonia 144–5

Pere III of Catalonia 147, 150–1
Pere IV of Catalonia 158, 160, 164–6, 168–9, 174–8
petritas 167–8, 172
Petronilla of Aragon 102–3, 111
Philip II of Navarre 158
Philip III d'Evreux 158
Philip III of France 144, 146–7, 150–1
Philip IV of France 144, 147–8, 158
Plasencia 115, 118
Pravia 26
Prince of Viana *see* Charles IV of Navarre
Puig de Cebolla 132

quadrivium 145

Radagaisus 4
Radulf 44
Ramiro I of Aragón 75–7
Ramiro I of Asturias 29–30
Ramiro II of Aragón 101–3
Ramiro II of León 43–5, 47–9, 80
Ramiro III of León 52, 56–7
Ramon Berenguer I of Barcelona 82–4
Ramon Berenguer II of Barcelona 83–4
Ramon Berenguer III of Barcelona 84, 96–8
Ramon Berenguer IV 98, 103, 106–7, 109–111
Ramon Berenguer V of Provence 144
Ramón Bonifaz 137–8
Ramon Borrell, count of Barcelona 60, 64, 70
Ramón of Ribagorça *see* Raymond
Rampon, count of Barcelona 28
Ronda 33, 39, 64, 73–4, 176, 194, 196
Raymond, count of Ribagorça and Pallars 35–7, 44
Raymond VI of Toulouse 121–2
Raymond of Burgundy 88–9, 92, 96, 98
Reccarred 7
Reccarred II 8
Reccesuinth 8
Rechiarius 5
el Restaurador 103
el rey lobo see ibn Mardanish
Ribagorça 27
Roderic 9, 13
Rodrigo, first count of Castile 45
Rodrigo Díaz de Vivar, *el Cid* 77, 79, 81, 84, 89, 90, 97
Rodrigo González of Asturias 101
Rodrigo Jiménez de Rada, archbishop of Toledo 119, 130
Rodrigo Vela 71
Roger III of Foix 97
Roger Trencavel, viscount of Bésiers and Carcasonne 121
Roncesvalles 25

Sad *see* Abu Nasr Sad
Saint James 27
Salado, Río 161
Salamanca 22, 49, 52, 56–7, 81, 90, 111; university 145
Salvatierra 119–20
San Esteban 36, 39–41, 58, 65, 92, 180
San Millán de la Cogolla 55, 59–60
Sanç, count of Roussillon 124–5
Sancho I of León 49–51
Sancho I of Portugal 115–7, 125
Sancho II of Castile 78–80
Sancho II of Portugal 126, 129, 136
Sancho III of Castile 104, 108–10, 139
Sancho IV of León-Castile 143–153 164, 167
Sancho VI of Navarre 108–10
Sancho VII of Navarre 120, 127, 131
Sancho Alfónsez, son of Alfonso VI 89–90, 92
Sancho Garcés I of Navarre 36–7, 40–3, 54
Sancho Garcés II of Navarre 52, 56, 58
Sancho Garcés III of Navarre 61, 69–70, 74, 101–2
Sancho Garcés IV of Navarre 78, 81, 102
Sancho García, count of Castile 58, 60, 63–5, 69
Sancho Ramírez of Aragón 78, 89, 121
Sanchuelo *see* Abd al-Rahman ibn Abi Amir
Santarém 15, 79, 88, 99, 107, 115–6, 157, 169, 171–2
Santiago, Order of 119, 163–4, 185, 188–9
Santiago de Compostela 27, 59, 93, 95–6, 133, 172–3
Santo Domingo de la Calzada 169–70, 193
Saphrax 3
Saqaliba 74
Scipio, Asturian count 29
Segovia 22, 57, 81, 94, 110, 144, 190
Seguin, count of Bordeaux 27
Sepúlveda 22, 57, 81
Serpa 111, 154
Setenil 176, 195–6
Seville: under Christian control 143, 145–7, 149, 153, 159–62, 165–6, 172–3, 176–7, 191, 196, 199; under Muslim emirs and caliphs 39, 67; under Muslim governors 16, 24, 30, 34–5; under siege by Fernando III 137–8; under *taifa* rulers and foreign governors 73, 77, 79–81, 87–90, 106, 110, 112–3, 117–20, 127–31, 136–7; under the Visigoths 6–8, 14

Sicilian Vespers 150
Sicily 146–7, 149–52, 175–6, 191
Siete Partidas 142, 145, 155, 162
Sigeric 5
Sigüenza 14, 76, 90, 96, 181
Silo, king of Asturias 26
Silves 74, 106, 116–7
Simancas 22, 48–9, 57
Simon de Montfort 121–2, 124
Sintra 88, 191
Sisebut 7
Sobrarbe 44, 61, 69–70, 75, 77, 102
Sonna, Asturian count 29
Stilicho 4
Subh 53
Sueves 4–5
Suinthila 8
Sulayman ibn al-Hakam ibn Sulayman ibn Abd al-Rahman, caliph of Córdoba 63–6, 70, 74
Sulayman ibn Hud al-Mustain I 73, 76, 82, 89, 93, 99
Sulayman ibn Yaqzan, governor of Zaragoza 25
Sunifred I 36
Sunifred II 44
Sunyer 44
Sunyers, count of Pallars 69

taifa states 73–4, 76–82, 84, 86–89, 93, 99, 100, 106–8, 129, 134
Tamarón, battle of 75
Tangier 11, 20, 66, 85–6, 138, 189–90
Tarazona 32, 37, 114, 150, 164, 180
Tarifa 81, 88, 116–7, 141, 143, 147, 149, 154, 161
Tarik ibn Ziyad 11, 13–4
Tawaba ibn Yazid, governor of al-Andalus 15
Tello de Trastémara 162–4, 167
Templars 101, 107, 116
Teresa d'Entença 159
Teresa of Portugal 88–8, 92–6, 98–9, 103
Tervingi 3
Thalaba *see* Tawaba ibn Yazid
Thawaba ibn Salama *see* Tawaba ibn Yazid
Theodoric I 5
Theodoric II 5
Theodoric III 6
Theodosius 3
Theudis 6 *see* Theodoric III
Theudisclus 6
Thibault I of Champagne 132, 140
Thorismund 5
tierra de campos 110, 117–8, 124, 153
Toda, countess of Sobrarbe and Ribagorça 69
Toda of Navarre 47–8, 50
Toledo 14, 17, 20–1, 26, 30–1, 33, 46, 47–9, 80–2, 88, 90–4, 120–1, 140, 146, 182–3
Tordesillas 179
Toro 57–8, 76, 131, 159, 164, 174, 190, 193
Toros de Guisando 186
Torrellas, treaty of 154, 157
Torres Nova 116, 118
Torrevicente 54, 56
Toulouse 5–6, 18–9, 27, 35–6, 88, 110, 121–2
transductinis promonturiis 13
Trastámaras 157, 160, 162–73
Triana 138
trivium 145
Trujillo 111, 115, 118, 181, 191
Tudején, treaty of 108–9, 111, 114, 135
Tudela 14, 28–9, 31–2, 36–7, 40–2, 76, 93, 99, 102, 104
Tudelién *see* Tudején
Tulga 8

Uclés 68, 91–2, 118–9
Udhrah ibn Abd Allah al-Fihri, governor of al-Andalus 18
Ulfila 4
Umar, second caliph 10
Umar ibn Hafsun 33–35, 38–9; sons of 45–6
Uqba ibn al-Hajjaji al-Saluli, governor of al-Andalus 19–20
Urban VI, pope 170
Urgell 27–8, 35–6, 44, 56, 64, 70, 77, 84, 107, 125, 177
Urraca, daughter of Alfonso VI 88, 90–6, 98–104
Uthman, third caliph 10
Uthman ibn Abi Nasah, governor of al-Andalus 19

Valdejunquera 41
Valdevez 120, 125
Valencia 81–2, 84, 89–90, 106–8, 111, 113–4, 126, 128, 131–2, 134–5, 150–1, 164–5
Valens 3
Valladolid 118, 123–4, 135, 145, 153–4, 156, 159, 163, 186
Valtierra 36, 40–2, 93
Vandals 4–5
Vardulia 22, 29, 44
Vega, battle of 158
Velasco, of Pamplona 28
Vermudo, king of Asturias 26
Vermudo II of León 57–9
Vermudo III of León 71, 75
Viguera 35–7, 41
Viseu 56, 59, 71, 76–7, 169
Vitoria 168–9
Vouillé 6

Wadih, Muslim general 60, 63–5, 70–1
Waiofar, duke of Aquitaine 25
Wallia 5
Wamba 8
William of Toulouse 27

Witiza 9
Witteric 7

Ximena, daughter of Ramon Berenguer III 97

Yahya al-Mustasim, Almohad emir 129
Yahya al-Nayyar 198–9
Yahya ibn Ibrahim, Almohad founder 85
Yahya ibn Salama al-Qalbi, governor of al-Andalus 18
Yaqub of Salé 141
Yuçaf de Ecija 159

Yusuf I *see* Abu Yaqub Yusuf
Yusuf I, Nasrid of Granada 158, 160–3
Yusuf II, Nasrid of Granada 174
Yusuf III, Nasrid of Granada 174, 177–8, 181
Yusuf IV, Nasrid of Granada 181
Yusuf ibn Abd al-Rahman, governor of al-Andalus 21, 23

Zahara 176–7, 194–5
Zalaca, battle of 87–8
Zamora 22, 39, 43, 50, 56–8, 61, 76, 79, 110, 114, 133, 159, 167–8, 190–1
Zaragoza 14, 21, 24–5, 27, 29, 31–2, 36–7, 41, 46–8, 55, 61, 66, 70, 73, 76–7, 80–2, 84, 87, 89–90, 93, 96, 99–109, 129, 150–1, 175, 177–8
Zawi ibn Ziri, Berber general 67, 74
Zayd Abu Zayd, Almohad governor of Valencia 126, 128, 131–2
Zayyan, ruler of Valencia 131–2, 134

www.ingramcontent.com/pod-product-compliance
Lightning Source LLC
Chambersburg PA
CBHW080803300426
44114CB00020B/2813